M.
1975

Your Role in
Oral
Interpretation

SECOND EDITION

Your Role in
Oral
Interpretation

VIRGIL D. SESSIONS
   Orange Coast College

JACK B. HOLLAND
   Orange Coast College

Holbrook Press, Inc.   Boston

Cover design and cartoons by Marilyn Grastorf

Library of Congress Cataloging in Publication Data

Sessions, Virgil D
Your role in oral interpretation.

Bibliography: p.
1. Oral interpretation.   I.   Holland, Jack B.,
joint author.   II.   Title.
PN4145.S4   1975   808.5'45   74–13886

Acknowledgments

EDITIONS GALLIMARD   for "La République du Silence," from *Situations, III,* by Jean-Paul Sartre, Editions Gallimard, 1949.

CHARLES SCRIBNER'S SONS   for an excerpt from *Look Homeward, Angel.* Reprinted with permission of Charles Scribner's Sons from *Look Homeward, Angel,* pages 550–554, by Thomas Wolfe. Copyright 1929, Charles Scribner's Sons; renewal copyright © 1957 by Edward C. Aswell, Administrator, C.T.A. and/or Fred Wolfe.

PRENTICE-HALL, INC.   for *Go Ask Alice,* anonymous. Copyright © 1971 by Prentice Hall, Inc. Published by Prentice-Hall, Inc., Englewood Cliffs, New Jersey.

WALTER J. BLACK, INC.   for "The Sphinx" and "The Tell-Tale Heart," from *The Works of Poe* by Edgar Allan Poe. (Walter J. Black, Inc., Roslyn, New York, 1927).

ROD SERLING   for *Requiem for a Heavyweight.* Reprinted by permission of the author, who is the sole owner of all literary rights. Requests for any production of part or all of this play must be submitted to the author.

THE SOUTH DAKOTA REVIEW   for "Indian Love Letter" by Soge Track, and "Loneliness" by Loyal Shegonee. Reprinted from *The South Dakota Review,* Vol. 7, No. 2, with permission of John Milton, Editor.

GROVE PRESS, INC.   for an excerpt from the book *How It Is* by Samuel Beckett. Copyright © 1964 by Grove Press, Inc. Reprinted by permission of the publishers.

THE SOCIETY OF AUTHORS   on behalf of the Bernard Shaw estate, for permission to reprint excerpts from *Pygmalion* by George Bernard Shaw.

HOLT, RINEHART AND WINSTON, INC.   for an excerpt from *Cyrano de Bergerac* by Edmond Rostand (Translation by Brian Hooker). Copyright 1923 by Holt, Rinehart and Winston, Inc. Copyright 1951 by Doris C. Hooker. Reprinted by permission of Holt, Rinehart and Winston, Inc.

PAUL R. REYNOLDS, INC.   for an excerpt from *The Sea of Grass* by Conrad Richter. Copyright 1936 by The Curtis Publishing Company, Inc. Reprinted by permission of Paul R. Reynolds, Inc., 599 Fifth Avenue, New York, New York 10017.

COWARD-MCCANN, INC.   for excerpts from *Becket,* reprinted by permission of Coward-McCann, Inc. from *Becket* by Jean Anouilh, copyright © 1960 by Jean Anouilh; and for an excerpt from *Lord of the Flies,* reprinted by permission of Coward-McCann, Inc. from *Lord of the Flies* by William Golding, copyright © 1954, 1955 by William Golding, copyright © 1962 by Coward-McCann, Inc.

APPLETON-CENTURY-CROFTS   for an excerpt from *Antigone,* from *Sophocles' Oedipus The King and Antigone,* translated and edited by Peter D. Arnott. Copyright © 1960 by Appleton-Century-Crofts, Inc. Reprinted by permission of Appleton-Century-Crofts, Division of Meredith Publishing Company.

THE VIKING PRESS, INC.   for excerpts from *Sons and Lovers* by D. H. Lawrence. Copyright 1913 by Thomas B. Seltzer, Inc. All rights reserved. Reprinted by permission of The Viking Press, Inc.

YALE UNIVERSITY PRESS   for an excerpt form *More Stately Mansions,* reprinted by permission of Carlotta Monterey O'Neill and Yale University Press from *More Stately Mansions* by Eugene O'Neill. Copyright © 1964 by Carlotta Monterey O'Neill; and for an excerpt from *Long Day's Journey Into Night,* reprinted by permission of Carlotta Monterey O'Neill and Yale University Press from *Long Day's Journey Into Night* by Eugene O'Neill. Copyright © 1955 by Carlotta Monterey O'Neill.

HARCOURT BRACE JOVANOVICH, INC.   for excerpt from *Wind, Sand and Stars* by Antoine de Saint-Exupéry, translated by Lewis Galantiere, copyright 1939 by Antoine de Saint-Exupéry, renewed 1967 by Lewis Galantiere. Reprinted by permission of Harcourt Brace Jovanovich, Inc.; and for "Jazz Fantasia," from *Smoke and Steel* by Carl Sandburg, copyright 1920 by Harcourt, Brace, Jovanovich,

Inc., renewed 1948 by Carl Sandburg. Reprinted by permission of Harcourt Brace Jovanovich, Inc.

HARPER & ROW, PUBLISHERS, INC.   for an excerpt from *Life On The Mississippi* by Mark Twain, Harper & Row, Publishers, Inc. Printed by permission of the Trustees of the estate of Samuel L. Clemens (Mark Twain), deceased.

THE DEPARTMENIT OF STATE BULLETIN   for excerpts from a speech delivered by John F. Kennedy, President of the United States, January 1961–November 22, 1963, at the commencement exercises at The American University in Washington, D.C., on June 10, 1963. Reprinted with the permission of the publishers of The Department of State Bulletin, XLIX, No. 1253 (July 1, 1963) pp. 2–6.

DOUBLEDAY & COMPANY, INC.   for an excerpt from *I, Michelangelo, Sculptor* by Irving Stone and Jean Stone. Copyright © 1962 by Doubleday & Company, Inc. Reprinted by permission of the publisher.

THE ATLANTIC MONTHLY COMPANY   for "Three Days To See," by Helen Keller. Copyright © The Atlantic Monthly Company, Boston, Mass. 02116. Reprinted with permission.

ROBERT W. GOLDSBY   for *Let's Get A Divorce* by Sardou and Najac. Translated by Robert W. Goldsby. Reprinted by permission of the translator.

LITTLE, BROWN AND COMPANY   for an excerpt from "The Wild Duck" by Henrik Ibsen, translated by Otto Reinert, from *Classic Through Modern Drama: An Introductory Anthology,* Otto Reinert, ed., pp. 417–421, 431. Copyright © 1970 by Little, Brown and Company (Inc.). Reprinted by permission; and for "I'm Nobody! Who Are You?" "The Chariot," and "My Sabbath" from *The Complete Poems of Emily Dickinson,* edited by Thomas H. Johnson, reprinted by permission of Little, Brown and Company (Inc.); and for "The Tale of Custard the Dragon" from *Verses From 1929 On* by Ogden Nash. Copyright 1936, reprinted by permission of Little, Brown and Company (Inc.).

GEORGE SAVAGE AND GEORGE SAVAGE, JR.   for *The Garbage Hustlers.* Reprinted by permission of the authors. No performance of this play may be given without prior approval of the authors.

J. V. PICKERING AND DICKENSON PUBLISHING COMPANY, INC.   for "Elijah" from *Readers Theatre* by J. V. Pickering, copyright © 1975 by Dickenson Publishing Company, Inc., Encino, California. Reprinted by permission of the publisher. No performance of this play may be given without prior permission of the author and the publisher.

LUCILLE FLETCHER AND DRAMATISTS PLAY SERVICE, INC.   for "Sorry, Wrong Number," copyright 1952, 1948. Reprinted by permission of the Dramatists Play Service, Inc. and the author. CAUTION: "Sorry, Wrong Number," being duly copyrighted, is subject to a royalty. The amateur acting rights are controlled exclusively by the Dramatists Play Service, Inc., 440 Park Avenue South, New York, New York 10016. No amateur production of the play may be given without obtaining in advance the written permission of the Dramatists Play Service, Inc., and paying requisite fee.

ESTER LEE   for "Oh of Little Worth to Dream" and "Wake Me Each Morning." Reprinted by permission of the author.

NEW DIRECTIONS PUBLISHING CORPORATION   for "Constantly risking absurdity and death . . ." from Lawrence Ferlinghetti, *A Coney Island of the Mind.* Copyright © 1958 by Lawrence Ferlinghetti. Reprinted by permission of the New Directions Publishing Corporation.

INDIANA UNIVERSITY PRESS   for "Face of Poverty" by Lucy Smith, from *New Negro Poets: USA,* Langston Hughes, ed. Reprinted by permission of Lucy Smith and Indiana University Press.

THE BOBBS-MERRILL COMPANY, INC.   for "Where Is The Romantic Life" from *Black Magic Poetry 1961–1967,* copyright © 1969 by LeRoi Jones. Reprinted by permission of The Bobbs-Merrill Company, Inc.

ALFRED A. KNOPF, INC.   for "Harlem" by Langston Hughes, copyright 1948 by Alfred A. Knopf, Inc., reprinted from *The Panther and The Lash,* by Langston Hughes, by permission of the publisher; for "Freedom" from *The Panther and The Lash* by Langston Hughes, copyright © 1967 by Arna Bontemps and George Houston Bass, reprinted by permission of Alfred A. Knopf, Inc.; and for "Freedom's Plow" from *Selected Poems* by Langston Hughes, copyright 1942 by Langston Hughes. Reprinted by permission of Alfred A. Knopf, Inc.

E. P. DUTTON & COMPANY, INC.   for an excerpt from the book *Winnie-The-Pooh* by A. A. Milne. Copyright 1926 by E. P. Dutton & Company, Inc. Renewal, 1954 by A. A. Milne. Reprinted by permission of the publisher.

*To Jean and Jodi
who suffered the pangs of birth with us
as we have with them*

Contents

PART THREE   UNDERSTANDING LITERATURE   199

Preface

Before we began this revision, we made a detailed survey of the views and reactions of instructors who had been using the first edition of *Your Role in Oral Interpretation*. Based on the idea that our best critics are those professors and students who have used the text, we asked them for candid criticisms of what they thought should be retained and what they did not find useful.

As a result of their suggestions, we have added, omitted, and rearranged material. The chapter sequence has been rearranged to give the student a more definite idea of the steps of development in the art of oral interpretation. We hope that this reorganization will be of value without being restrictive.

This second edition is written to the students. It is our primary purpose to share with them our own appreciation of literature, and our commitment to the fact that oral interpretation is an art to be enjoyed.

Oral interpretation is a dynamic art, and this revision has given us an opportunity to update the literature and incorporate material that is currently significant. We have also done our best to insure that the selections in the text are set up in effective manuscript form. In this edition we have given consideration to the increased opportunities for oral interpretation in radio, television, and Readers Theatre. Scripts and practice selections have been included to help the student in adapting oral readings to these media.

For the most part, the style and philosophy of our first edition remain unchanged. We appreciate the acceptance that *Your Role in Oral Interpretation* has enjoyed, and hope that this revision will be a positive contribution to the study of oral interpretation.

Virgil D. Sessions
Jack B. Holland

The authors wish to thank the following for their assistance and advice: Dr. Earl Cain, California State University, Long Beach; Dr. Martin Andersen, Emeritus, California State University, Fullerton; Dr. Jerry Pickering, California State University, Fullerton; and of course, our thanks to the many authors whose works are used in this book.

Part One

INTRODUCTION

chapter one

Is this the way
to oral interpretation?

So you're taking a course in oral interpretation. What made you decide to do it? Academic requirements for future teaching? Extra credits to graduate? To fulfill a speech requirement at your college? Or did it sound easy?

Well, let's see what you have done to yourself. Here's what other students had to say about it.

"I took it because I didn't like to have to write my own speeches." ... "I had no idea we'd have to put some feeling into the literature we read." ... "I was afraid to get up in front of people."

And after completing the course:

"It made me aware, of how beautiful and exciting literature is." ... "I never used to like poetry, but now I can see its beauty." ... "Drama was always something vague to me. I'd never read any plays, but now I regard this as an exciting new field." ... "I feel as though I'll never be the same after taking this course because now I've been exposed to just enough new things in literature to have an appetite for more." ... "I'm no longer afraid of reading in front of other people."

What can this course do for *you*? One thing is certain—you will not leave this course without having gained something. For one thing, your reading vocabulary will be increased. In your search for material to read and from listening to the selections read by your classmates, you will have been exposed to all varieties of literature. And you will have read selections by many authors, both classic and modern— people like Carl Sandburg, Ernest Hemingway, F. Scott Fitzgerald, Jean-Paul Sartre, James Thurber, Robert Frost, William Shakespeare, Edgar Allan Poe, Eugene O'Neill, and many others.

And lastly, you will probably find that your own oral reading ability has greatly improved—an accomplishment which can be very helpful in your other classes.

FOUR-WAY EXPERIENCE

Oral interpretation is, first of all, a bringing together of the author, the reader, and the audience. Even more than that, it is a four-way experience. There is, first, *the author who writes the material and experiences the emotional impact of creativity;* then there is *the reader who searches for the proper selection to read and experiences various reactions, physiologically, to what he reads before making his final choice;* the third is *the experience of the reader as he performs before an audience, his reaction to his material and to his audience;* and the fourth experience is *the audience who, by its visible and audible response, lets the reader know how his reading is being received.* This response, in turn, adds to the reader's total presentation since it serves as a guide to the effectiveness of the reading.

Now let's look at these four ways in more detail.

What do we mean by experience? Let us say an author feels strongly about a social problem. To express his emotions and principles, he puts them down in a language and style uniquely his own, so that others may share his views and either accept them or debate them. He is expressing his own experiences. For example, Jean-Paul Sartre in his "Republic of Silence" discusses the full meaning of freedom as seen by the French during the Nazi Occupation. In this selection he shows that every thought, every word, every idea of the French was treasured because freedom of speech, as an action, was denied them.

From

The Republic of Silence

Jean-Paul Sartre

We were never more free than during the German occupation. We had lost all our rights, beginning with the right to talk.

Every day we were insulted to our faces and had to take it in silence. Under one pretext or another, as workers, Jews, or political prisoners, we were deported *en masse*. Everywhere, on billboards, in the newspapers, on the screen, we encountered the revolting and insipid picture of ourselves that our oppressors wanted us to accept. And, because of all this, we were free.

Because the Nazi venom seeped even into our thoughts, every accurate thought was a conquest. Because an all-powerful police tried to force us to hold our tongues, every word took on the value of a declaration of principles. Because we were hunted down, every one of our gestures had the weight of a solemn commitment. The circumstances, atrocious as they often were, finally made it possible for us to live, without pretense or false shame, the hectic and impossible existence that is known as the lot of man. Exile, captivity, and especially death (which we usually shrink from facing at all in happier times) became for us the habitual objects of our concern. We learned that they were neither inevitable accidents, nor even constant and exterior dangers, but that they must be considered as our lot itself, our destiny, the profound source of our reality as men. At every instant we lived up to the full sense of this commonplace little phrase: "Man is mortal!" And the choice that each of us made of his life and of his being was an authentic choice because it was made face to face with death, because it could always have been expressed in these terms: "Rather death than . . ." And here I am not speaking of the élite among us who were real Resistants, but of all Frenchmen who, at every hour of the night and day throughout four years, answered NO.

But the very cruelty of the enemy drove us to the extremities of this condition by forcing us to ask ourselves questions that one never considers in time of peace. All those among us —and what Frenchman was not at one time or another in this situation—who knew any details concerning the Resistance asked themselves anxiously, "If they torture me, shall I be able to keep silent?" Thus the basic question of liberty itself was posed, and we were brought to the verge of the deepest knowledge that man can have of himself. For the secret of a man is not his Oedipus complex or his inferiority complex: it is the limit of his own liberty, his capacity for resisting torture and death.

To those who were engaged in the underground activities, the conditions of their struggle afforded a new kind of experience. They did not fight openly like soldiers. In all circumstances they were alone. They were hunted down in solitude, arrested in solitude. It was completely forlorn and unbefriended that they held out against torture, alone and naked in the presence of torturers, clean-shaven, well-fed, and well-clothed, who laughed at their cringing flesh, and to whom an untroubled conscience and boundless sense of social strength gave every appearance of being in the right. Alone. Without a friendly hand or a word of encouragement.

Yet, in the depth of their solitude, it was the others that they were protecting, all the others, all their comrades in the Resistance. Total responsibility in total solitude—is this not the very definition of our liberty? This being stripped of all, this solitude, this tremendous danger, were the same for all. For the leaders and for their men, for those who conveyed messages without knowing what their content was, as for those who directed the entire Resistance, the punishment was the same—imprisonment, deportation, death. There is no army in the world where there is such equality of risk for the private and for the commander-in-chief. And this is why the Resistance was a true democracy: for the soldier as for the commander, the same danger, the same forsakenness, the same total responsibility, the same absolute liberty within discipline. Thus, in darkness and in blood, a Republic was established, the strongest of Republics. Each of its citizens knew that he owed himself to all and that he could count only on himself alone. Each of them, in complete isolation, fulfilled his responsibility and his role in history. Each of them, standing against the oppressors, undertook to be himself, freely and irrevocably. And by choosing for himself in liberty, he chose the liberty of all. This Republic without institutions, without any army, without police, was something that at each instant every Frenchman had to win and to affirm against Nazism. No one failed in this duty, and now we are on the threshold of another Republic. May this Republic about to be set up in broad daylight preserve the austere virtues of that other Republic of Silence and of Night.

Freedom became an experience and not just a word. Sartre's feelings are compellingly evident in this selection. One cannot help feeling, as he reads the essay, Sartre's surge of pride in his country, a sense of hope in a time of despair. He presents a theory that men are freer when freedom is denied them. It is an idea—but an idea fulfilled by the emotional experience of living it.

Now how about the author who writes a piece of fiction—or poetry? How does experience enter in here?

In *Native Son,* Richard Wright deals with a fictionalized plot, but the sentiments and the emotions underlying this story of a black man caught in a web of prejudice and bias are those of Wright himself— the feelings, the experiences he has had. The same is true of James Baldwin in his *Notes of a Native Son.*

Elizabeth Barrett Browning in her collection of poems, *Sonnets from the Portuguese,* expresses the love she felt for her husband, Robert Browning. The two segments which follow best express her innermost feelings.

From

Sonnets from the Portuguese

Elizabeth Barrett Browning

22

When our two souls stand up erect and strong,
Face to face, silent, drawing nigh and nigher,
Until the lengthening wings break into fire
At either curved point—what bitter wrong
Can the earth do to us, that we should not long
Be here contented? Think! In mounting higher,
The angels would press on us and aspire
To drop some golden orb of perfect song
Into our deep, dear silence. Let us stay
Rather on earth, Beloved—where the unfit,
Contrarious moods of men recoil away
And isolate pure spirits, and permit
A place to stand and love in for a day,
With darkness and the death-hour rounding it.

44

Beloved, thou hast brought me many flowers
Plucked in the garden, all the summer through
And winter, and it seemed as if they grew
In this close room, nor missed the sun and showers.
So, in the like name of that love of ours,
Take back these thoughts which here unfolded too,
And which on warm and cold days I withdrew
From my heart's ground. Indeed, those beds and bowers
Be overgrown with bitter weeds and rue,
And wait thy weeding; yet here's eglantine,
Here's ivy!—take them, as I used to do
Thy flowers, and keep them where they shall not pine.
Instruct thine eyes to keep their colors true,
And tell thy soul their roots are left in mine.

(See also "How Do I Love Thee," on page 157)

John Milton also writes about his personal experience in "On His Blindness."

On His Blindness

John Milton

When I consider how my light is spent
Ere half my days, in this dark world and wide,
And that one talent which is death to hide
Lodged with me useless, though my soul more bent
To serve therewith my Maker, and present
My true account, lest He returning chide;
"Doth God exact day labor, light denied?"
I fondly ask. But Patience, to prevent
That murmur, soon replies, "God doth not need

Either man's work or his own gifts. Who best
Bear his mild yoke, they serve him best. His state
Is kingly: thousands at his bidding speed,
And post o'er land and ocean without rest;
They also serve who only stand and wait."

But what about the books, the poems, the plays that are not directly related to a writer's experience? We cannot always presume to know the author's purpose in writing—nor should we be tempted to attach a purpose, or a meaning, to every piece of literature. The author is still experiencing an emotion that is familiar to him when he draws the word pictures of his characters and describes their emotions. He has undoubtedly felt love or hate or jealousy or revenge—or any of the basic moods—and he recreates them in his work.

The actual writing down of these feelings, these ideas, these principles is *an experience on the part of the author.*

Your experience as the reader begins with a visit to the library. You are looking for material to read. You pore over endless stories or articles. Suddenly one strikes you as exciting or moving or stimulating. It interests you—*it means something to you.* You have in this process taken the second step in communication. You have discarded some material as not suitable to you or not creating sufficient emotional response for you. You have selected literature that appeals to you, that recalls to you some similar emotion or event in your own life.

The third step is to convey, through technical skills, the response you had to the material so that your audience will gain the same appreciation of the author and his work that you have—so that it will share in your emotional reactions.

Now you come to the fourth step.

It is conceivable that not everyone will share your response. Audiences consist of different types of people with different interests. It is your responsibility as a reader to create as uniform a response as possible. How can you tell whether you are succeeding in this purpose? By audible and visible signs—by a smile, a laugh, by complete silence during a sorrowful or suspenseful moment in the reading, by restless movement in seats—these and many other responses will indicate whether or not you have communicated. When you have received such a response from your audience, you have achieved the fourth experience.

Such is the process of communication.

ORAL INTERPRETATION IS NOT ACTING

Oral interpretation has in many ways been like a wayward child. It has not been an unwanted child, for it has been adopted by both the speech and theatre departments of major universities and colleges. The theatre departments have laid claim to it because of its close relationship to the dramatic arts. The speech departments have zealously clung to it as an integral member of the speech arts.

So—what is all this to you? Basically, it poses the problem—do you "act" in oral interpretation or do you "interpret," and if you do the latter, what does that mean? What is the difference? Herein lies the conflict.

To avoid any confusion, let us make one thing clear: There is one significant difference between acting and interpretation—an interpreter reads a manuscript and does not "stage" his material while the actor's work is staged with scenery, lights, and an array of props. It is largely in the physical limitations that the difference exists.

To further understand the distinction, you have to know something of what the actor and the interpreter really do.

The actor is chosen, after an audition, by a director, to play a role. He learns his part—memorizes it—after carefully studying the character's personality, his relationship with other characters in the play, the type of dialogue he engages in, where his personality changes, grows, and is motivated. All such refinements of the characterization are based on a thorough study of the total plan, on the director's constant observation of the performance during rehearsals. The actor moves about the stage, he wears costumes, he attempts to hide his identity and to create another person. At all times he is concerned primarily with his own role, although he, of course, must react to, and interact with, the other characters in the play. The audience, in turn, is asked to believe that the actor is the character he is portraying. Members of the audience participate in what is called a "willing suspension of disbelief"; they voluntarily accept the role-playing as reality.

In contrast to the actor, the interpreter chooses the material he wishes to read, studies it in its entirety, and without the benefit of a director, without the use of props, scenery, and lights, he must create a vivid and meaningful interpretation of the material. He is his own director, the sole judge, aside from his audience, of the interpretation. He works on a stage or platform with a reading stand. His rehearsals are conducted alone. He is not responsible for reading only the dialogue sections, as is the actor, but he must also bring to life the narrative and expository sections—those sections in literature which help to build the scene. He doesn't move about as the actor does, but he does use gestures and body movement to help add meaning to the reading. In all cases, the interpreter remains himself. But what does this mean?

Let's suppose you are the interpreter—a male interpreter. You have chosen to read the section from *Gone With the Wind* in which Melanie is going through labor pains. Obviously, you cannot be taken for Melanie or for Scarlett who are both in the scene. No audience expects you to. You are yourself. Yet you have to present the material in a meaningful and moving way. You must, therefore, involve yourself in that material, but not to the same degree as the actor must involve himself in the play.

How much do you involve yourself? How far do you let your own emotions carry you? Do you submerge yourself into the mood, the feelings of the characters, into the dramatic content of the story?

Let's return to *Gone With the Wind*. You have to be concerned not only with Melanie's trial and agony and with her strength as a person, but you have to picture, through your own sensitive reading, the oppressive heat, the endless waiting, the "atmosphere" of the scene. You are dealing with all the elements in the scene, all the descriptions, all the character motivations and interactions. Each part is equally important. Melanie cannot become a full-bodied, understandable person if you treat her superficially or objectively. You can't make her suffering vivid without successfully handling the material describing the scene itself. Everything builds to the climax—the heat, Melanie's writhing on the bed, Scarlett's reaction to the scene.

If you read a play, however, you have to make your characters believable and lifelike. Suppose you are a girl and you choose the confrontation scene between the Grand Duchess and the girl posing as Anastasia in the play *Anastasia*. You must distinguish between the two women, make each of the personalities clear and vivid, and you must make certain you successfully indicate the changes in both character and plot development in the scene. Yet no one expects you to be other than yourself while reading both parts. You are to show only the Grand Duchess' initial distrust, disbelief, and dislike and the girl's anxiety for the Duchess to believe in her. You must show how the little bits of information the girl gives about her past and her life in court begin to shake the Duchess' conviction that this girl is not Anastasia. Then you must finally bring the scene to a climax when the Duchess is convinced— and show her tearful joy at the discovery.

Since you must do all these things, ask yourself: Can I do all of this without involving myself, without responding to the characters as they "feel"?

WHAT DOES INVOLVEMENT MEAN?

What does "involve" mean? Or "feel"? Both of these words mean that you physiologically react to the emotions in the story. You "enter into" the emotions of the characters in the story and become part of them. This kind of involvement is vitally necessary for the interpreter.

An audience can see a play—see people moving about, see the props and the setting, but when the interpreter reads they must rely on imagination. The audience must see the action in their minds, because there are no visual supports.

It has been said that the interpreter should merely "suggest," that he should remain apart and not become involved. He must depict only what the author had in mind—to the extent that he knows what the author had in mind. This theory indicates an objective, unfeeling, purely analytical approach. Although it is true that all elements of the material must be analyzed, this analysis should serve to heighten the emotional involvement of the interpreter. In other words, to communicate feeling, both interpreter and actor must "feel."

But, for the interpreter *total* involvement is impossible because of the many shifts of attention he must make. He must be one person, then another, then narrator or expositor. His success in these roles depends on his degree of involvement. Don't think for an instant that you can successfully move your audience by an indifferent, unfeeling reading.

Perhaps you plan to read James Baldwin's *Notes of a Native Son.* At some time in your life you may have been oppressed or hurt—or you know someone who has been. This experience lets you share in Baldwin's despair, his bitterness and anger, and his loneliness; and it enables you to give a more meaningful reading.

In interpreting *Death of a Salesman* you must feel the tragedy of Willy Loman's useless life, understand Biff's frustration, and Lydia's loyalty. If you have experienced defeat or failure, you can know Willy. Or if you have ever been unable to communicate with your parents, you can understand Biff's feelings. At any rate, you cannot read this play without involving yourself.

We have taken a look at involvement and the responsibilities of the interpreter. You will find and use emotions and feelings you didn't know you had, for you must transport yourself into the world of literature. In the final analysis, you are in the business of making literature come alive to excite an audience—you must give them an experience. This is your task, your responsibility, and it can also be your pleasure.

chapter two

It's been around for centuries

In these few pages we cannot hope to give a detailed picture of the history of oral interpretation, but it is important that beginning students have some knowledge of the background, growth, and development of the art.

Most records agree that Herodotus (484 B.C.) was the first professional storyteller. After Herodotus, poets from the early Greek period began to read their own poetry aloud. These poetic presentations were known as rhapsodies, and became the center of a controversy between the followers of Plato's ideology and the followers of men like Aristotle who believed poetry and the delivery of it was art. To Plato, poets could not consider their work art because they were not governed by rules and discipline. In Plato's mind they were guided by emotion and could not be called artistic. He also condemned them because their goal was not truth.

The Greek orators, on the other hand, felt that poets were wise and regarded them as teachers with the ability to impart knowledge. Aristotle distinguished between poets and artists by placing the oral reading of poetry in a separate category from the art of oral discourse, or rhetoric, as practised in the law courts. To him, poetry was the product of the imagination operating through the process of creative imitation. The ultimate aim of poetry was to evoke an aesthetic response, for which drama was best suited. The primary characteristic of poetry was emotion.

To Aristotle, the essential difference between rhetoric and the poetic lay in their different goals. The purpose of rhetoric is persuasion; while the goal of poetics is to create a work that can, when understood, awaken an aesthetic response. Just as art interprets, reading poetry aloud should be classified as interpretation.

The art of oral reading reached great heights in Rome during the Golden Age of Literature—76 B.C. to 14 A.D. Although men like Cicero and Quintilian were more interested in the matter of speaking, in the arranging of speeches and devising rules for the ideal orator, they did give some attention to oral reading. Like Aristotle, they stressed the need for training the voice. Cicero believed that rhetoric and interpretation by association belonged in the frame of a liberal arts education. He felt that the speaker or reader must possess talent and native ability, and that he must be moved by "a passionate inclination, an ardor like that of love."[1]

Oral interpretation—though it was not called that—fits best into two of Cicero's five canons: elocution or style in written composition, and *pronuntiado* or delivery. Cicero also felt that meaning influenced ideas and emotions and determined the nature of the delivery. "Nature herself has assigned to every emotion a particular look and tone of voice and bearing of its own."[2]

Quintilian was, in most respects, an echo of Cicero. He proposed what is the Golden Rule for interpreters: "he (the reader) must first understand what he reads." His concept of delivery was based largely on naturalness; he felt that simplicity and naturalness were standards of excellence in performance. Although he advised the reader to observe and *imitate* the technique of the actor, he cautioned the interpreter to avoid a delivery that is too obviously theatrical. Quintilian said, "that art is best which conceals its art." Or as Aristotle put it, "We should disguise the means we employ."

With the death of Cicero, around 43 B.C., the Augustan Age began. This was the beginning of new emphasis on interpretative reading. Virgil and other poets made a practice of reading their own poems and courts began to employ their own special readers. Virgil detested any abuse in reading and was known to read only to select audiences. Horace also disliked artificial performances which stressed the performance more than the literary merits of the material.

Both the Augustan Age, which lasted about 165 years, and the Silver Age (14 A.D. to 180 A.D.) were periods in which the art of oral reading flourished. But around 359 A.D. the Golden Ages in Greece and Rome came to an end, and oral reading as an integral part of cultural life ended, too.

While there was some reading of literature in the sixth century, there was no noticeable revival until around 1066 when there appeared a new type of reading accompanied by music. Other forms of reading with song took on significance in everyday life because of groups such as troubadours, jongleurs, the Dutch poetry guilds, and the Meistersingers in Germany. These balladeers, primarily in Italy, Spain, and France, went from town to town commenting on the political and moral issues of the day through their songs and stories. For instance, the Meistersingers traveled from one court to another giving performances on the theme of the deification of women. Their plots usually centered around knights and languishing ladies.

Eventually the oral reading of literature attracted the attention of such poets as Chaucer. He often read his own works and he wrote mainly for court members. To Chaucer, oral reading was the elocution of literature.

It was, however, Stephen Hawes, the author of *Pastime of Pleasure,* who in the fifteenth century presented the first theory of oral interpretation, emphasizing the importance of the delivery. Then during the Renaissance, it became very popular to read aloud and the art of oral reading was firmly established. Boccaccio, one of the most notable figures of this time, spent the last two years of his life reading and lecturing on Dante. And Castiglione felt that the practice of reading poetry aloud added grace and distinction to a person's life.

In 1644 John Bulwer wrote *Chirologia* and *Chironomia,* detailed studies of gesture and bodily action in which he stated that gestures were not perfect by nature and should be controlled. He taught by imitation and by adherence to systems used by the best "models." Because gestures are now considered an integral part of the communication process in oral reading, Bulwer's contribution is worth noting.

For many years following the Renaissance, emphasis centered on the style of the written word rather than on delivery. However, in eighteenth century England there was renewed interest in the spoken word and once again the delivery became most important. During the eighteenth century, two schools of thought regarding oral interpretation emerged. One group, loosely called the *Mechanical School,* was concerned with rules for using gestures and with controlling the voice to simulate different emotions. The other group was called the *Natural School* and they emphasized the importance of the meaning of literature. Rules, they felt, hampered any kind of natural expression and meaningful recreation of the author's purpose. Both schools believed that they were stressing the same thing— a meaningful interpretation of the literature.

This new movement came to be called the Elocutionary Movement, and it was born from a sudden interest in the English language and a new awareness of the influences of discourse in the persuasion of people to certain issues.

The physiological aspects of voice and speech became important and the tenets of science were applied to oral reading. Elocution was concerned with speech correction, the vocal physiology, and the physics of sound production. Gesture was also emphasized, and rules were devised for proper use of phrases, emphasis, pace, force, rhythm, and tone. In 1748 John Mason stressed his theories for pauses in *Essay on Elocution or Pronunciation.* He felt that a reader should pause one beat at a comma, two beats at a semicolon, three at a colon, and four at a period. James Burgh's *Art of Speaking* was a guideline on how to use certain emotions. He believed that if a reader followed this guide, he could find any emotion necessary by simply looking up the rule governing that emotion.

But the man who gave definition to the entire movement was Thomas Sheridan, an actor who became interested in the study of elocution and pronunciation. He emphasized the need for qualified teachers and he urged that elocution be added to school curriculums. Sheridan felt that the ideal delivery was characterized by grace, sincerity, and naturalness, and he introduced a new code for the use of emphases, duration of pauses, rapidity, and duration of long and short syllables.

There were other theorists who belonged to these schools. John Rice, for instance, believed you did not have to be affected by what you read. William Cockin believed that you had to feel what you read. But ultimately, both schools taught, to a greater or lesser degree, that the sense of what was read was the most important consideration.

The Elocutionary Movement also spread to America. The attention of this movement was centered on Dr. James Rush, author of *Philosophy of the Human Voice,* a complicated study of the physiological aspects of the voice. Rev. Ebenezer Porter was also active in America, stressing sense and emphasis as necessary elements for oral reading. He felt that.the faults of elocution were in lack of feeling and in errors in pronunciation. William Russell and James Murdock, both former actors, stressed early training in elocution to eliminate mechanical, unfeeling reading. Samuel Curry proposed the theory that the mind had to be trained first for there to be any creativity in thought and imagination. This he called the "think the thought" method. Many American schools began to use the theories of the French actor and singer, Delsarte. He had devised an elaborate system based on the Holy Trinity, with Man being divided into life, mind, and soul. According to Delsarte, the vocal sounds expressed life, words the mind, and movement the soul. The American teachers gave attention primarily to the theories regarding the physical movement of the body.

Toward the latter part of the century, schools began to teach diction and basic exercises for the voice, and they frowned on stereotyped delivery. It was believed that man must speak through all his being, and that the voice should be subservient to the idea being expressed. Among the schools that taught these theories were those run by Samuel Curry, J. W. Shoemaker, May Blood and Ida Reilly, and Leland Powers, one of the most prominent figures in the Elocutionary Movement. Powers was an actor and a recognized interpreter. To him, oral interpretation was the art of embodying the spirit and essence of literature. This could be conveyed only when the reader understood the material and his voice and body responded to it.

The American schools had almost identical aims: developing character, enriching personality, studying fine literature, freeing the voice from restricting habits and tensions, developing good articulation, and variation in pitch and tone. But as time went on, elocution acquired an unfavorable and unfortunate connotation. Today, the term "elocution" is often associated with the term "ham" as it is applied to the theatre. Today the emphasis is more on subtlety and suggestion, and the emotional aspects of the literature being read. Some poets have read their own works. Robert Frost and Dylan Thomas are good examples. Many actors and actresses have also become involved in oral interpretation through recordings. Julie Harris made an album on Emily Dickinson; Judith Anderson recorded Edna St. Vincent Millay; in *Ages of Man* Sir John Gielgud reads Shakespeare, and Paul Scofield recorded the poems of Dryden.

In recent years a new kind of oral interpretation has developed which more closely resembles acting. It is called Readers Theatre and a group of readers perform selections such as *Spoon River Anthology, John Brown's Body,* or a play such as *Don Juan in Hell.* Charles Laughton, director of one group, did more than any other single person to stimulate public interest in interpretative reading. His group traveled all over America, and through the reading of various types of literature, he helped to revitalize interpretation as we know it today.

The art of oral interpretation has developed over many centuries under the guidance of many great minds, and as you can see even from this brief survey, the history of oral interpretation as an art is rich and deeply rooted.

Part Two

THE PERFORMANCE

can also check the subject card catalog in the library for up-to-date books on the area of interest.

There are many authors who have contributed to expository prose. Among the most prominent are James Thurber, W. Somerset Maugham, Bruce Catton in his books on the Civil War, John Gunther, Jean-Paul Sartre, Mark Twain, and Richard Armour. A more detailed list of expository passages is given at the end of this chapter.

When it comes to narrative prose, the problem is more complex since there are an endless number of novels and short stories. Here you have to do more than simply find a piece of material. You must find a selection that can be taken from a whole novel or short story and still be complete within itself—or that can be cut and still represent with clarity the novel's intent. In many cases this will necessitate reading the entire selection thoroughly so as to know exactly what the story entails. You cannot read a segment of a novel and know the *total* story. However, since it is literally impossible for you to read four or five novels to find one selection for oral interpretation, you should try to remember those you have read in the past and liked. If you haven't done very much reading, the *Masterpieces of World Literature in Digest Form,* published by Harper's, can provide plot summaries. Then —once a book is chosen and a particular selection made, the book should be read in its entirety for a clear picture of the total work.

Another source of information is, of course, book reviews in magazines, particularly in the *New York Times Book Review* and in *Saturday Review of Literature.* Weekly news magazines and *Harper's* and *Atlantic* carry good review sections, as do some of the more reputable newspapers. By reading a review you can discover the type of novel a book is and the nature of its plot.

In addition, there are best seller lists to guide you. These can be found posted in the library, in bookstores, in newspapers. Bookstores can also provide an excellent source of possible material.

As for short stories, there are countless anthologies, many of which are listed at the end of this chapter. Stories by Flannery O'Connor, Eudora Welty, Katherine Anne Porter, Shirley Jackson, and others are reliable sources. Go to your favorite authors for possible selections.

When it comes to finding poetry, there is an equally difficult problem in that there are so many anthologies that you might be lost in a maze of titles. The *Poetry Index* is an excellent choice for locating appropriate material. It not only classifies poetry by type but it also is annotated so as to give you at least an idea of the basic theme of a poem. Many students select the writings of T. S. Eliot (not always a good choice because of the difficulty in understanding the symbolism in some of his writings), Dylan Thomas (who presents the same problem), Edgar Allan Poe (he did write other poems besides "The Raven"), Lawrence Ferlinghetti, W. H. Auden, Karl Shapiro, Matthew Arnold, Keats, Shelley, Browning, Carl Sandburg, Robert Frost, and Amy Lowell. A few suggestions have been made at the close of this chapter but again the *Poetry Index* is your best bet.

In the matter of drama, reviews of current plays on Broadway or of plays in your local community can offer good suggestions. There is also a *Play Index* in the libraries, a Burns Mantle edition of *Best Plays* of each year and other such "Best Play" collections. However, these editions must be used with care because mere summaries of plots are often inadequate in guiding a reader in the characterizations involved in plays. A sketchy summation of plot cannot go into sufficient detail on characterization, the essential concern of the interpreter.

In drama there are also the classics which are too often overlooked—plays by Molière, Shaw, Shakespeare, Voltaire, Corneille, Sheridan, Oliver Goldsmith, and many more. There are also any number of dramatic anthologies, such as the *Theatre Guild Anthology, Masters of Modern Drama* (published by Random House), *World Encyclopedia of Drama, Thirty Famous One Act Plays, Theater World,* and others.

The library is, of course, the most reliable place to find material. If you have an idea about an author you have liked, you can look up that author in the card catalog for references to his works. Or, if you know the title of a work but are not sure of the author, look in the card catalog under the title. In drama, also, a motion picture is often adapted from a play; so if you happen to have seen a film you liked, check the title to see if it is based on a play. That information is always given in the film titles at the beginning. Finally, if you do not find the information you want in the catalog, check with your librarian.

All readers should immediately become acquainted with *The Reader's Adviser and Bookman's Manual.* As it states on the cover, it is "A guide to the best in print in Literature, Biographies, Dictionaries, Encyclopedias, Bibles, Classics, Drama, Poetry, Fiction, Science, Philosophy, Travel, and History." It is an endless source of material with clear annotations of contents of all fields of literature. It also tells exactly what type of material is contained in the anthologies.

So much for suggestions about material, but what about information about the author? It is always helpful to know something about the author of a selection you are to read.

There are, of course, various encyclopedias that can be consulted. On the jackets of most modern novels and on many editions of plays, biographical data is given about the authors. *The Reader's*

Encyclopedia provides information on just about every author of importance. And there is the *Dictionary of National Biography* which gives detailed data on literary figures. Occasionally you may select the work of an obscure writer. If you do, there are definite possibilities that you will not find any information. In this case, you may want to reconsider your choice of material. Is it of the literary quality necessary for oral interpretation?

What is the test then for good literature? For one thing, the fact that it has withstood the test of time—that generations have continued to consider it worthy of study—is a good criterion. But this is not meant to imply that only the so-called classics are of significance. Often works from the past are better designed for silent reading than oral, just as some contemporary literature is best read silently. For example. Erich Fromm's *The Art of Loving* is profound, but it does not lend itself to very arresting or compelling oral reading.

If the selection is well-written and has a universal theme it should be suitable. The fact that the material is contemporary is not always a sufficient criterion for judgment. Many articles that have been written about drugs or Black Power are of superficial value to the interpreter. Irresponsible and uninformed columnists and, in some cases, magazine writers have indulged themselves with analyses of Viet Nam. The reader must make every effort to check into the writer's background to make certain that he is qualified to write about a subject.

While the suggestions above refer mainly to expository writings, the same judgment is necessary in choosing contemporary fiction writers and dramatists.

Much of contemporary literature is highly stylized, loosely structured, and consequently needs careful scrutiny. And with much of today's fiction devoted to sexual excursions, it is wise to find out whether such excursions are the stories' only claim to attention. It is not to be inferred that suggestive scenes, if done well, should be avoided, but it is advisable to decide just how well done they are. For instance, Henry Miller is considered by some literary authorities as an excellent writer, but there are others who think him somewhat overrated. Consequently, any reading of his material should undergo critical judgment. Laurence Durrell excels in dramatic imagery; his use of word color and descriptive effects is like words set to music. Much of his writing, therefore, would be acceptable.

Jean Genet, the noted French author, is critically accepted, and yet certain sections from, for instance, *The Balcony* would be questionable for a classroom situation. On the other hand, Edward Albee's *Who's Afraid of Virginia Woolf* is frequently read by students and is considered by most to be acceptable.

In deciding what is "correct" material to choose, the reader must act as his own censor, although we dislike the word. It is our contention that students in oral interpretation must be exposed to all types of literature. If we ban certain works because they may appear suggestive, then we must ban many of the classics, such as Boccaccio, Balzac, *Song of Solomon,* some of Shakespeare, and Wycherley's *The Country Wife.* We cannot limit the field of oral interpretation by assuming that "acceptable by the majority" is the only rule, because in this case the "majority" is poorly defined, as is "acceptable." Students have an obligation to deal with good literature in all its phases, and usually passages are offensive only when poorly read. For example, if *Who's Afraid of Virginia Woolf* is approached with emphasis on all the profanity, the meaning, the basic theme Albee had in mind would be obscure. In the same way, J. D. Salinger's *Catcher in the Rye* could be—and has been—distorted by reading with an attitude that all it contains is a teenager's profanity and sexual experiences. Both of these qualities take on new meaning when you consider the moral concepts behind this story.

Censoring is part of the process of choosing material. You must be careful not to approach a selection with the same attitude that existed in one Eastern college where an English instructor was discharged for teaching salacious literature. His assigned topic was *To His Coy Mistress* by Andrew Marvell, a recognized poet and poem of classical value.

Do not settle for insignificant material just because it seems safe. The shelves are full of pointless writings that are "safe" and not worthy of study—and certainly not worthy of reading aloud. Ask yourself: Does the selection say something? Does it mean something? Is it well written? Do the characters come to life? Does its message have clarity and significance? Does the plot deal with real people in a real life situation? Is there imagination in its treatment? Does it provoke the mind as well as the heart?

There is one last thought: some students ask to read material they—or their friends—have written. As a rule, this is not too advisable since few students have sufficient training to produce well-written selections. There are, of course, exceptions, and if the instructor decides the work is *worthy* of being read, he should be more than willing to give the student that opportunity—as an honest kind of encouragement. But you must remember that it is far more difficult to read poorly written material than it is to read good literature. Critically accepted works have better language, better organization, a better theme, and better characterizations, all of which add to the effectiveness of oral reading.

Naturally, in selecting material you must consider your own personality and interests. We have previously advised you to read what interests you, but in the same way it is unwise to attempt anything that is too difficult for you with your background and experience. For instance, if you are sensitive and emotional, the reading of a purely technical, unemotional article would not serve you well. Relate your choice to your own interests. Do not choose anything that does not "speak" to you.

Your audience, of course, must be considered too. While it is advisable to read something that has universal appeal to your audience, it is usually possible to captivate listeners with almost any reputable material that is *well read.* So the first obligation should be to prepare the reading carefully.

You cannot always judge what an audience's tastes are since you cannot really know each and every member of your audience. Humor is generally a safe bet because laughs from the audience provide an immediate response and everyone enjoys humor. Yet, no reader can successfully broaden himself by reading only one type of literature. Audiences' tastes should be considered, for example, in reading material that is morally offensive or unnecessarily gruesome. A selection which is juvenile or poorly written is also not a good choice because if you insult the intelligence of your audience, they will not be attentive.

The occasion for which a reading is given also influences choice of material. While we are concerned here primarily with the classroom situation, there are possibilities that students will engage in speech tournaments, in specially arranged concert performances, or in programs where the reading will be the principal entertainment of the evening.

Reading for the class gives you a chance to experiment with different types of literature. Your intention in class is to broaden your reading ability and to be exposed to various forms of writing. With this in mind your choice is highly diversified.

Occasionally students are engaged in concert performances before an invited audience, apart from the classroom. If the audience is sophisticated, as is often the case, more mature types of literature should be read. Reading which has variety and gives the reader a chance to exploit this versatility is desirable. By the time the reader is ready for such an occasion he will already have passed the embryonic stage as an interpreter and will be expected to read with a good deal of finesse.

For speech tournaments the choice is extremely important, for only the best in literature is accepted—and more than one form of material often must be used. Here the interpreter is judged for his selection of material as well as his delivery.

If a reading is the primary offering for an evening, if it is being given for a club or some organization, then the type of club will influence to a large extent the kind of material to be used. For instance, if you were to appear before a PTA group or a woman's club, you very likely would avoid anything suggestive or too frank in context.

Choosing material is your first job. Make it a meaningful experience.

SUMMARY

Finding material is one of your primary problems. It is one that should be met early in the course by a conscientious study of the sources available to you.

For readings of expository prose, the *Reader's Guide to Periodical Literature* is perhaps the best source for discovering significant periodical writings on all types of subjects. It is indexed by topic area. Other sources are *Saturday Review of Literature, Atlantic, Harper's, Time, Newsweek,* and *The Reporter.* Textbooks, particularly in English, American, and foreign literature courses, provide excellent examples of such prose.

Narrative prose differs from expository prose in that it tells a story, deals with characterization, dialogue, climax, and is emotional, while expository prose is more factual. It is found in journals, diaries, letters, descriptive studies. Novels and short stories make up narrative prose. For summaries of plots of novels, *Masterpieces of World Literature in Digest Form* is one of the best sources. Anthologies which include such short novels as James Hilton's *Lost Horizon* and John Steinbeck's *The Red Pony* are recommended. In addition, book reviews in newspapers and magazines, best seller lists, and book stores also provide good research material.

Short stories are contained in many anthologies, some of which are listed at the end of this chapter. Some reputable writers of short stories are Flannery O'Connor, Eudora Welty, Katherine Anne Porter, Shirley Jackson, and such classical examples as Edgar Allan Poe, O. Henry, and Guy de Maupassant.

Poetry is represented in all major literary anthologies, but the *Poetry Index* provides the most comprehensive source of material.

Some popular poets are T. S. Eliot, Dylan Thomas (both of whom present problems to the interpreter because of the complexity of their works), W. H. Auden, Karl Shapiro, Matthew Arnold, John Keats, Percy Shelley, Robert and Elizabeth Browning, Amy Lowell, Edna St. Vincent Millay, Robert Frost, Carl Sandburg, and Ogden Nash.

For ideas in drama, the *Play Index* is highly recommended. In addition, collections of best plays of the year, such as the Burns Mantle editions and *Theatre World,* are helpful. There are also many dramatic anthologies like *Elizabethan Plays,* Bertolt Brecht's *Seven Plays, Masters of Modern Drama, Seven Plays of the Modern Theatre, A Treasury of the Theatre,* plus many collections of one-act plays. It is advisable to exercise caution in using readings from any abridged versions of plays, like those found in Burns Mantle, because such condensations do not delve into characterization sufficiently. The entire play should be read before any one scene is taken from it for reading.

When involved in the reading of drama you should also consider the works of such classical authors as Shakespeare, Richard Sheridan, Oliver Goldsmith, Ferenc Molnar, Molière, Corneille, Racine, and others.

For further help in locating material, the *Reader's Adviser* and *Bookman's Manual* are excellent source books.

The choice of reading is, of course, largely up to you, and you must act as your own "censor." Oral interpretation involves a consideration of all types of literature, and care should be taken that certain works are not overlooked simply because they may be "suggestive" in some areas. Literature is often distorted by the wrong approach in the oral reading. You must learn to evaluate critically the worth of material, as well as its suitability to audiences' tastes. Always keep in mind that oral interpretation adds to your cultural background and that unwise censoring limits your exposure. A good rule is: If you are in doubt about the "rightness" of some material, check with your professor.

It is necessary, too, to select readings that relate to you, that fit your own interests, experience, and background. Consider your audience, their general tastes, and make certain that what you read will not prove offensive to a number of the listeners. It is not always possible to avoid offending one or two, and you cannot be too concerned about that, but you can take steps not to offend—or unnecessarily bore—the majority.

The following list is presented as a guide in the search of material for reading. It is not to be considered the only list of sources, but will serve as a starting point in your search.

APPROPRIATE SELECTIONS
FOR ORAL INTERPRETATION

Expository Prose

AGEE, JAMES   *On Film.* Reviews of films.

ARMOUR, RICHARD   *Twisted Tales from Shakespeare.* Satirical plots of Shakespeare's plays.

BENCHLEY, ROBERT   Countless articles of satirical note.

CAPOTE, TRUMAN   *In Cold Blood.* A non-fiction account of a murder that reads like a novel. (Has considerable suspense.)

CATTON, BRUCE   *A Stillness at Appomattox.* One of his many books on the Civil War.

CIARDI, JOHN   "A Way to a Poem." An essay on the structure of a poem. Would need careful reading to make it interesting for oral reading.

EMERSON, RALPH WALDO   *Selected Writings* (by Signet-Mentor). Includes 14 essays and 21 poems.

FAULKNER, WILLIAM   Nobel acceptance speech.

HEMINGWAY, ERNEST   "Big Two Hearted River." A descriptive account of a fishing trip.

HART, MOSS   *Act One.* The autobiography of one of America's greatest playwrights.

KERR, JEAN   *Please Don't Eat The Daisies.* Partly expository but offers a humorous observation of Mrs. Kerr's experiences as a wife and mother.

MANCHESTER, WILLIAM   *Death of a President.* A moving account of the death of John F. Kennedy.

MILLER, MERLE   *Plain Speaking.* Brisk sayings and recollections of President Harry S. Truman.

MAUGHAM, W. SOMERSET   *The Summing Up.* The writer's philosophy of life and writing. Excellent choice of material since it is divided into easily edited sections.

NABOKOV, VLADIMIR   *Speak, Memory.* The autobiography of the Russian writer.

SARTRE, JEAN-PAUL   *The Words.* A revealing autobiography. "Republic of Silence." An essay on the meaning of freedom to the French during the Nazi occupation.

SEVAREID, ERIC   "Dark of the Moon." An essay propounding some worthwhile thoughts for humanity to consider while it rushes to the moon.

SKINNER, CORNELIA OTIS *Madame Sarah.* A biography of Sarah Bernhardt that has many good sections.

STEINBECK, JOHN *Travels with Charley.* Accounts of his trips across the United States.

THOREAU, HENRY DAVID *Selected Journals, Walden.* Both deal with Thoreau's philosophy of living.

THURBER, JAMES "University Days." An amusing account of Thurber's difficulty with the microscope in biology. "The Last Flower." Ironic commentary on civilization.

TWAIN, MARK *The Innocents Abroad.* Twain's satirical views of Europe. His letters To and From the Earth are great satire.

TYNAN, KENNETH *Curtains.* Reviews of Broadway and London plays that offer good reading.

WHITE, THEODORE *The Making of the President, 1960. The Making of the President, 1964. The Making of the President, 1968.* All contain segments that lend themselves to oral reading. They also deal with material of current interest.

WOOLLCOTT, ALEXANDER Several fascinating character studies and short stories.

WHITMAN, WALT *Specimen Days.* Whitman's jottings over twenty years, including his Civil War experiences (Signet-Mentor).

YUTANG, LIN *The Importance of Living.* Some profound observations on life, culture, and habits.

NOTE: For others consult the Best Sellers List, Non-fiction, in newspapers.

Narrative Prose

Humorous

BEMELMANS, LUDWIG *I Love You—I Love You—I Love You.* Bemelmans is one of contemporary literature's most accomplished humorists.

HEGGENS, THOMAS *Mister Roberts.* A hilarious and often sentimental account of a group of men on a "wreck of a ship" during World War II.

HELLER, JOSEPH *Catch 22.* An excellent satire of the military life in World War II.

JACKSON, SHIRLEY *The Magic of Shirley Jackson,* edited by S. E. Hyman. An excellent collection of Jackson short stories. Includes "The Bird's Nest" and "Life Among the Savages."

LARDNER, RING   *The Best Short Stories of Ring Lardner, Haircut and other Stories.* These two volumes contain stories that run the gamut of Lardner's talent. There are other volumes that are equally good.

LEWIS, SINCLAIR   *Babbitt.* A preceptive novel of a middle-class man living in middle-class America.

PARKER, DOROTHY   *The Collected Stories of Dorothy Parker.* An excellent collection of her stories showing the depth and breadth of her talent.

PORTER, KATHERINE ANNE   *Collected Stories, Flowering Judas and Other Stories.* Excellent collections by this noted author. Deserves wide reading.

PORTER, WILLIAM SYDNEY (O. HENRY)   *The Gentle Grafter, O. Henry Stories.* There are several volumes of O. Henry stories. All contain excellent material; it's just a matter of choosing what you like.

SHULMAN, MAX   *Max Shulman's Guided Tour of Campus Humor, Potatoes are Cheaper.* There are other volumes by this author. His stories and articles are easily excerpted for oral interpretation.

THURBER, JAMES   "If Grant Had Been Drinking At Appomattox," "The Catbird Seat," *The Thurber Carnival.* One of our most versatile humorists. Wide range of subjects and interests.

TWAIN, MARK (SAMUEL LANGHORNE CLEMENS)   *The Complete Short Stories of Mark Twain, The Innocents Abroad, Letters from the Earth, Life on the Mississippi, Roughing It.* One of our best known and most loved American humorists with an abundance of material for nearly every interest.

Serious

BENÉT, STEPHEN VINCENT   *The Devil and Daniel Webster.* A classic account of Webster's defense against the Devil.

BIBLE   Any number of passages.

BUCK, PEARL   *The Good Earth.* The prize-winning novel of a humble Chinese farmer and his family.

DAHL, RAOLD   "The Wish." A horror short story, almost entirely descriptive in effect. The vision of terror drawn by a young boy as he crosses a carpet.

BALZAC   *Droll Stories.* Fables of suggestive interest.

FIELDING, HENRY   *Tom Jones.* The bawdy and amusing amorous experiences of Tom Jones. A recognized classic.

HEMINGWAY, ERNEST   *Old Man and the Sea.* A short novel that provides excellent opportunities for oral reading.

JACKSON, SHIRLEY   "The Lottery." A classic of a horror story.

MAUGHAM, W. SOMERSET   *Of Human Bondage.* The story of the near destruction of a sensitive man by an unprincipled streetwalker.

MELVILLE, HERMAN   *Moby Dick.* The memorable novel of a man's conflict with himself in the person of a whale.

MITCHELL, MARGARET   *Gone With the Wind.* The ever-popular novel of the Civil War. A modern-day classic.

O'CONNOR, FLANNERY   Reputable short stories.

POE, EDGAR ALLAN   "The Cask of Amontillado," "The Tell-Tale Heart." Both too well-known to need explaining. Both offer problems because of their over-use. As such, of course, they present a challenge to a reader.

PORTER, KATHERINE ANNE   *Ship of Fools.* A complex novel of the people aboard a ship before World War II.

SALINGER, J. D.   *Catcher in the Rye.* Salinger's probing, biting, and often amusing story of a teenager with no place to go.

STEINBECK, JOHN   *Grapes of Wrath.* Steinbeck's prize-winning novel about the depression and the lives it influenced.

THURBER, JAMES   "The Catbird Seat," "The Night the Bed Fell." Thurber's own satirical thrusts. "The Secret Life of Walter Mitty."

WELTY, EUDORA   Many famous short stories.

WOLFE, THOMAS   *Look Homeward, Angel, Of Time and the River.* One of the twentieth century's most renowned novelists with two of his most famous novels. Wolfe was a master of descriptive writing.

WRIGHT, RICHARD   *Native Son.* A violent novel of racial prejudice.

Anthologies

Points of View, Kenneth McElheny and James Moffett, eds. (Signet); *Great Modern Short Novels, Great Short Novels, This Is My Best* (Whit Burnett), *Bedside Book of Famous British Stories, The Woollcott Reader, East and West,* and *Mr. Maugham Himself,* edited by W. Somerset Maugham.

Drama

Humorous

FRIEL, BRYAN   *Philadelphia, Here I Come.* An amusing modern comedy by a new playwright.

GIBSON, WILLIAM   *Two for the Seesaw.* Comedy drama of the relationship between a good-hearted girl from Brooklyn and a man about to get a divorce. Two characters only.

GOLDSMITH, OLIVER   *She Stoops to Conquer.* A comedy of errors. Restoration period and very funny.

HEGGEN, THOMAS and JOSHUA LOGAN   *Mister Roberts.* Play version of the novel.

KANIN, GARSON   *Born Yesterday.* The long-time hit of a gangster and his seemingly dumb blonde girlfriend.

KERR, JEAN   *Mary, Mary.* A sophisticated comic romp about the complications of a couple getting a divorce.

MANHOFF, BILL   *The Owl and the Pussycat.* A comedy of a lady of easy virtue who moves in on a musician. Two characters only.

PATRICK, JOHN   *Teahouse of the August Moon.* A gentle and very funny play about the American occupation of Okinawa.

SCHISGALL, MURRAY   *Luv.* A bawdy, broad farce about two men and a woman and their antics in love. Three people only.

SHAKESPEARE, WILLIAM   *As You Like It, Midsummer Night's Dream.*

SHAW, GEORGE BERNARD   *Pygmalion.* Adapted for *My Fair Lady.*

SHERIDAN, RICHARD   *The School for Scandal.* Another Restoration play, hilarious even today.

SIMON, NEIL   *Barefoot in the Park, The Odd Couple, Plaza Suite.* Three modern comedies.

VAN DRUTEN, JOHN   *The Voice of the Turtle.* Comedy, drama of a man and two women, of love and commitment.

Serious

ANDERSON, MAXWELL   *Elizabeth the Queen.* In blank verse. Deals with the great queen and her love for Lord Essex. *Mary of Scotland.* The conflict between Mary of Scotland and Queen Elizabeth.

ANOUILH, JEAN   *Becket.* The personal conflict between two former friends, King Henry and Thomas Becket.

ALBEE, EDWARD   *Who's Afraid of Virginia Woolf.* A violent, scathing drama of married life. Two men, two women. Excellent scenes.

BECKETT, SAMUEL   *Waiting for Godot.* Allegorical and symbolical, heavily dependent on a strong sense of theater to bring it off. *Endgame.* Farcical action but an oppressive mood of futility and inescapable doom.

BOLT, ROBERT   *A Man for All Seasons.* The prize-winning play of Sir Thomas More's martyrdom. Fine scenes for men.

BRECHT, BERTOLT   *Three Penny Opera Mother Courage.* Considered two of Brecht's best plays.

CHAYEFSKY, PADDY   *Marty.* Basically a comedy but also contains some moving scenes of a humble Italian who finally, at middle age, falls in love.

CHEKHOV, ANTON   *The Cherry Orchard.* The famous Russian play. (His four major plays are contained in an edition by Signet-Mentor titled *The Major Plays.*)

DELANEY, SHELAGH   *A Taste of Honey.* A sensitive, moving play of a young girl who seems to belong to no one until she finds understanding with a homosexual and a colored seaman. Well-written.

FORESTER, C. S.   *Payment Deferred.* A suspenseful play of an Englishman who commits murder and his slow disintegration.

GIBSON, WILLIAM   *The Miracle Worker.* The story of Helen Keller as a child. Brilliant play with excellent scenes.

GILROY, FRANK   *The Subject was Roses.* A Pulitzer prize play. A son's return from the service forces a man and his wife to look at themselves—and for the son to re-evaluate his life. Excellent scenes.

HANSBERRY, LORRAINE   *A Raisin in the Sun.* A dramatic, moving play of a Negro family who desire to move into a white neighborhood.

HELLMAN, LILLIAN   *The Children's Hour.* Fine play for two women. Subject is accused homosexuality between two women teachers. Beautifully handled theme. *Toys in the Attic. The Little Foxes.* A story of greed and destructiveness of a southern family.

HERTZOG, JAN   *The Fourposter.* A play depicting the life of a couple from their wedding night to their old age. Fine choice.

IBSEN, HENRIK   *Ghosts, A Doll's House.*

IONESCO, EUGENE   *The Chairs.* A probing, complex study of two old people and the universe today. Difficult but rewarding. Also great, *Exit the King* and *The Lesson.*

MILLER, ARTHUR   *Death of a Salesman.* His classic play of a man's refusal to face himself and the world. *The Crucible.* A drama on the Salem witch trials.

O'NEILL, EUGENE   *Long Day's Journey Into Night.* The tragic play that is said to be an autobiography of the author. Two men and two women. *Mourning Becomes Electra.* O'Neill's version of the Greek trilogy. Contains powerful scenes for two people.

OSBORNE, JOHN   *Look Back in Anger.* An angry look at a fading marriage. *Inadmissible Evidence.* A courtroom drama with fine speeches for one reader.

PINTER, HAROLD   *The Caretakers.* An unusual study of a tramp who moves in on two brothers and almost wrecks their lives. Part of the avant-garde movement. *The Birthday Party.*

RICE, ELMER *The Adding Machine.* Good soliloquies. Amusing and yet bitter commentary on society.

ROSTAND, EDMOND *Cyrano de Bergerac.* Has several notable soliloquies of value, including the "nose" speech and the equally famous "no thank you."

SARTRE, JEAN-PAUL *No Exit.* A remarkable one act of people in hell who look back on life.

SCHARY, DORE *Sunrise at Campobello.* A dramatic account of Franklin Delano Roosevelt's fight against paralysis.

SCHNITZLER, ARTHUR *La Ronde.* A delicate treatment of love through several characters' eyes. Good choice.
Leibelei. A drama of a young girl who leaves the security of her father's love to find her own life.

SHAFER, PETER *Royal Hunt of the Sun.* Almost a poetic play in the confrontation between Pizarro and an Inca chief. Last act contains a superb scene for two men.

WEISS, PETER *Marat/Sade.* An unusual poetic commentary on the French Revolution. Avant-garde theatre.
The Investigation. More of a testimony than a play dealing with the Nazi war crimes. Good choice for one reader.

WHITING, JOHN *The Devils.* An intensely moving drama dealing with exorcism and the possession by Satan of the bodies of a group of nuns. Based on an historical incident of the 17th century.

WILLIAMS, TENNESSEE *A Streetcar Named Desire.* Already a classic. The fantasies and tragedy of a woman whose mind leads her into the past and into a distorted view of her life today.
The Night of the Iguana. A derelict priest faces life and influences many people.
The Glass Menagerie. The tender account of a woman who lives in the past and cannot face reality. (Williams has also written several one-act plays that lend themselves to expert reading.)

Anthologies

Theatre Guild Anthology; Elizabethan Plays; Masters of Modern Drama; Seven Plays of the Modern Theatre; 24 Favorite One Act Plays; 30 Famous One Act Plays; Complete Book of the American Musical Theatre; All the Plays of Molnar; World Encyclopedia of Drama; Consult a *Concise Encyclopedia of Modern Drama* for information.

Also, musical plays often contain good scenes. The following are worth considering: *South Pacific, Oklahoma, King and I, Carousel, Funny Girl, How To Succeed in Business Without Really Trying, Man of La Mancha, Auntie Mame, High Spirits, Hello Dolly, Fanny, Fiddler on the Roof, Promises, Promises.*

Poetry

ARNOLD, MATTHEW   "Dover Beach." Perhaps his most noted poem.

BALLADS   Basically lyrics to folk ballads. "Lord Randall" is one example.

BROWNING, ELIZABETH BARRETT   *Sonnets from the Portuguese.* Love sonnets to her husband, Robert Browning.

BROWNING, ROBERT   A major poet. "My Last Duchess" and "Porphyria's Lover" are two of his best known.

BYRON, GEORGE GORDON, LORD   A prolific poet. "She Walks in Beauty" is one of his better known.

DICKINSON, EMILY   A contemporary poet. Not all of her poetry is immediately understandable, but she is one of the most popular poets of today.

DONNE, JOHN   One of the greatest of poets. His themes are many and varied. Examples: "Song," "The Good Morrow," "The Funeral."

FERLINGHETTI, LAWRENCE   *A Coney Island of the Mind.* A modern poet. Includes some of his most popular poems.

FROST, ROBERT   A favorite with students. His best are "Mending Wall," "Road Not Taken," "Stopping By Woods on a Snowy Evening."

JOHNSON, JAMES WELDON   "The Creation." A poem of a Negro minister's concept of the·creation of the world.

KEATS, JOHN   "Ode on a Grecian Urn," "La Belle Dame Sans Merci," "When I Have Fears that I May Cease To Be" are only a few of his great poems.

LOWELL, AMY   A contemporary poet. "Patterns" is one of her more famous.

MARVELL, ANDREW   "To His Coy Mistress." A satirical poem of seduction.

MILLAY, EDNA ST. VINCENT   A contemporary poet of genuine merit.

NASH, OGDEN   A satirical poet of note. Responsible for most of America's modern light verse.

SANDBURG, CARL   A vigorous poet whose themes deal with contemporary problems and with pride in country. "Chicago" and "Prairie" are only two of the many, many poems he has written.

Anthologies

There are endless poetry anthologies, many listed according to the period, in addition to collections of complete works of such poets as Keats, Browning, Shelley, and Sandburg.

chapter four

Prepare! Prepare!

One of the most important aspects of oral interpretation is also one of the most frequently overlooked—preparation.

Preparation begins with the typing of a manuscript for these reasons: (1) The pages in a book are not printed with oral reading in mind; it is a simple matter for a silent reader to turn the page to find the next word in a sentence, but for an oral reader this will result in a break in the idea. (2) Margins in a book are not set with oral interpretation in mind; you will want to write marginal notes to guide your interpretation. (3) The print in the book is often too small to allow the interpreter to maintain eye contact with his audience and with the printed page at the same time. So—prepare a manuscript!

Here are some general rules to follow in preparing your manuscript for easy oral reading: (1) Choose paper of a quality heavy enough to prevent *rustling* and to stand up under use. (2) Each sentence which begins on a page should end on that page. (3) At least double space your manuscript (triple spacing is even better); this allows space for you to identify pauses and emphases. (4) Leave wide margins so that you can write notes to yourself concerning your interpretation. (5) Devise a set of signals such as virgules (/) which will indicate phrasing, word groupings, and changes of thought, mood, or idea.

/—signifies a momentary hesitation, a chance to breathe, to help give variety to the pace and a chance to add emphasis.

//—signifies a longer pause, a change in idea, an introduction of a new mood.

_____—under a word signifies a word to be emphasized or "colored."

Along with these markings, you can note in the margins of the manuscript what mood is involved in each particular section. Is it anger, love, hate, fear, passion, resentment? Write it out in one or two words. Then when the mood changes, draw a line to the margin, and write in "mood changes to . . . ," indicating what the new mood is.

The following selection illustrates the use of such symbols. Words in the left margin indicate changes in mood; those on the right indicate changes in pace (rate of reading). Read the selecton closely noting each change of pace and mood, emphasizing the words which are underlined and pausing as indicated by slant marks.

Look Homeward, Angel

Thomas Wolfe

As <u>darkness</u> came upon the <u>gray</u> <u>wet</u> day, / the family gathered in the parlor, / in the <u>last</u> <u>terrible</u> <u>congress</u> before death, / *silent* — *ominous* / silent, / waiting. / / Gant rocked <u>petu-lantly</u>, / spitting into the fire, / making a <u>weak</u> <u>whining</u> moan from time to time. / / <u>One</u> by <u>one</u>, / at intervals, / they left the <u>room</u>, / <u>mounting</u> the stairs <u>softly</u>, / and <u>listening</u> outside the door / of the sick-room. / And they heard <u>Ben</u>, / as, with <u>in-cessant</u> <u>humming</u> <u>repetition</u>, / like a <u>child</u>, / he <u>sang</u> his <u>song</u>, "There's a mother there at twilight / Who's glad to know—" / /

Eliza sat <u>stolidly</u>, / hands <u>folded</u>, / be-fore the parlor fire. / / Her <u>dead</u> <u>white</u> face had a <u>curious</u> <u>craven</u> look; / the <u>in-flexible</u> <u>solidity</u> / of <u>madness</u>. / /

"Well," / she said at length, slowly, / "you never know. / Perhaps this is the crisis. / Perhaps—" // her face hardened into granite again. // She said no more. //

retreat within herself

Coker came in and went at once, / without speaking, / to the sick-room. // Shortly before nine o'clock, / Bessie Gant came down. // "All right," / she said quietly. "You had all better come up now. / This is the end." //

quiet, resigned

Eliza got up and marched out of the room with a stolid face. / Helen followed her: / she was panting with hysteria, / and had begun to wring her big hands. /

frenzied

"Now, get hold of yourself, Helen," / said Bessie Gant warningly. / "This is no time to let yourself go." //

command

Eliza went steadily upstairs, / making no noise. / But as she neared the room, / she paused, / as if listening for sounds within. / Faintly, / in the silence, / they heard Ben's song. // And suddenly, / casting away all pretense, / Eliza staggered, and fell against the wall, / turning her face into her hand, / with a terrible wrenched cry:

apprehension

deep grief

"O God! If I had known! / If I had known!" /

Then, weeping with bitter unrestraint, / with the contorted and ugly grimace of sorrow, / mother and daughter embraced each other. // In a moment they composed themselves, / and quietly entered the room. //

composed

Eugene and Luke pulled Gant to his feet / and supported him up the stairs. // He sprawled upon them, / moaning in long quivering exhalations. /

self-pity

"Mer-ci-ful God! / That I should have to bear this in my old age. / That I should—"

annoyance

"Papa! / For God's sake!" / Eugene cried sharply. / "Pull yourself together! / It's Ben who's dying—not us! / Let's try to behave decently to him for once." //

This served to quiet Gant for a moment. / But as he entered the room, / and saw Ben lying in the semi-conscious coma that precedes death, / the fear of his own death overcame him, / and he began to moan again. // They seated him in a chair, at the foot of the bed, / and he rocked back and forth, weeping:

selfishness "O Jesus! / I can't bear it! / Why must you put this upon me? / I'm old and sick, / and I don't know where the money's to come from. // How are we ever going to face this fearful and croo-el winter? It'll cost a thousand dollars before we're through burying him, / and I don't know where the money's to come from." // He wept affectedly with sniffling sobs. /

self-pity

"Hush! hush!" cried Helen, / rushing at him. / In her furious anger, / she seized him and shook him. / "You damned old man you, / I could kill you! / How dare you talk like that when your son's dying? // I've wasted six years of my life nursing you, / and you'll be the last one to go!" // In her blazing anger, she turned accusingly on Eliza: /

anger

contempt

"You've done this to him. / You're the one that's responsible. / If you hadn't pinched every penny / he'd never have been like this. // Yes, / and Ben would be here, too!" // She panted for breath

for a moment. // Eliza made no answer.
/ She did not hear her. //

almost hysterical

"After this, I'm through! / I've been
looking for you to die—and Ben's the one
who has to go." // Her voice rose to a
scream of exasperation. / She shook Gant
again. / "Never again! / Do you hear that,
/ you selfish old man? / You've had everything— / Ben's had nothing. / And now
he's the one to go. / I hate you!" //

anger—hatred

"Helen! Helen!" said Bessie Gant
quietly. / "Remember where you are."//

"Yes, that means a lot to us," / Eugene
muttered bitterly. //

change to silence of death

Then, / over the ugly clamor of their
dissension, / over the rasp and snarl of
their nerves, / they heard the low mutter
of Ben's expiring breath. // The light had
been re-shaded: / he lay, / like his own
shadow, / in all his fierce gray lonely
beauty. // And as they looked and saw
his bright eyes already blurred with
death, / and saw the feeble beating flutter of his poor thin breast, / the strange
wonder, / the dark rich miracle of his life
surged over them its enormous loveliness.

awe

// They grew quiet and calm, // they plunged below all the splintered wreckage of their lives, / they drew together in a superb communion of love and valiance, / beyond horror and confusion, / beyond death. //

feeling of awe, inspirational

And Eugene's eyes grew blind with love and wonder: / an enormous organ-music sounded in his heart, // he possessed them for a moment, / he was a part of their loveliness, // his life soared magnificently out of the slough and pain and ugliness. // He thought:

revelation

"That was not all! / That really was not all! //

Helen turned quietly to Coker, / who was standing in shadow by the window, / chewing upon his long unlighted cigar. //

hopeful

"Is there nothing more you can do? / Have you tried everything? / I mean—*everything?*" //

Her voice was prayerful and low. // Coker turned toward her slowly, / taking the cigar between his big stained fingers. / Then, / gently, / with his weary yellow smile, / he answered: "Everything.

Not all the king's horses, / not all the doctors and nurses in the world, / can help him now." /

hopelessness

"How long have you known this?" she said. //

"For two days," he answered. / "From the beginning." // He was silent for a moment. / "For ten years!" he went on with growing energy. // "Since I first saw him, at three in the morning, in the Greasy Spoon, with a doughnut in one hand and *resignation* a cigarette in the other. // My dear, / dear girl," he said gently / as she tried to speak, / "We can't turn back the days that have gone, // We can't turn life back to the hours when our lungs were sound, / our blood hot, / our bodies young. / We *facing reality* are a flash of fire— / a brain, / a heart, / a spirit. // And we are three-cents-worth of lime and iron—which we cannot get back." //

regret

He picked up his greasy black slouch hat, / and jammed it carelessly upon his head. / Then he fumbled for a match and lit the chewed cigar. //

wanting to have hope "Has everything been done?" / she

said again. / "I want to <u>know!</u> / Is there <u>anything</u> left worth <u>trying?</u>" /

He made a <u>weary</u> <u>gesture</u> of his arms. / *cold, firm* "<u>My</u> dear <u>girl!</u>" he said. / "<u>He's</u> <u>drowning! Drowning!</u>" //

shock She <u>stood</u> <u>frozen</u> with the <u>horror</u> of his <u>pronouncement.</u> //

Coker looked for a moment at the <u>gray</u> <u>twisted</u> shadow on the bed. / Then, / *sad* <u>quietly,</u> / <u>sadly,</u> / with <u>tenderness</u> and <u>tired</u> wonder, / he said: "Old <u>Ben.</u> / <u>When</u> shall we see *his* <u>like</u> again?" //

Then he went <u>quietly</u> out, / the <u>long</u> <u>cigar</u> <u>clamped</u> <u>firmly</u> in his mouth. //

In a moment, / Bessie Gant, breaking <u>harshly</u> in upon their silence / with <u>ugly</u> and <u>triumphant</u> <u>matter-of-factness,</u> / *disgust* *contempt* said: "<u>Well,</u> / it will be a <u>relief</u> to get <u>this</u> over. / I'd rather be called into forty <u>outside</u> cases / <u>than one in which any of</u> <u>these damn</u> relations are <u>concerned.</u> / I'm *concern for self* dead for sleep." //

Helen turned <u>quietly</u> upon her. /

"<u>Leave</u> the <u>room!</u>" she said. / This is our affair now. / We have the <u>right</u> to be *angry* left alone." //

Surprised, / Bessie Gant stared at her for a moment with an angry, / resentful face. / Then she left the room. / /

silent

lifeless

The only sound in the room now / was the low rattling mutter of Ben's breath. / He no longer gasped; / he no longer gave signs of consciousness or struggle. / / His eyes were almost closed; / their gray flicker was dulled, / coated with the sheen of insensibility and death. / / He lay quietly upon his back, / very straight, / without sign of pain, / and with a curious up-turned thrust of his sharp thin face.

sense of unreality

/ / His mouth was firmly shut. / / Already, / save for the feeble mutter of his breath, / he seemed to be dead—/ he seemed detached, / no part of the ugly mechanism of that sound which came to remind them / of the terrible chemistry of flesh, / to mock at illusion, / at all belief in the strange passage and continuance of life. / /

finality emptiness

He was dead, / save for the slow running down of the worn-out machine, / save for that dreadful mutter within him of which he was no part. / / He was dead.

Some students find it difficult to read such a marked paper. The signs distract. In that case, use a carbon copy for marking in rehearsal and an unmarked copy for the classroom performance.

It is important to point out two things: (1) The mechanical markings of the selection are not meant to indicate that such an interpretation is the only right one—not at all; each reader will interpret in his own way. (2) The system is devised primarily to aid in analysis of selection, to help teach the value of pauses, of breathing, to discover the changes in ideas and mood, to help in understanding the emotional content, and to understand the value of word coloring and emphasis. Such markings can—and should—be dropped as soon as you are able to conduct such analysis without them. *The authors in no way recommend a purely mechanical delivery.* What truly matters is that the meaning of the material is conveyed, and each reader will have his own way of meeting that requirement. Yet, it is found that this system of marking can be of particular help to the beginning student who is inclined to read everything in a selection with the same pace and inflectional pattern and with little understanding of the material itself.

For a reading that lasts five minutes, it is safe to say that you should rehearse the selection carefully at least ten times. Some students may be more skilled in interpretation than others and can get by with less time, but the average reader will need at least that much practice for an effective reading.

It is recommended that you begin to rehearse about ten days before you are to give the reading.

Obviously, you should read the selection in its entirety first. If you are going to read from a play, you should read the entire play because a scene taken out of context can often be distorted. One student read the confrontation scene between the Captain and Mr. Roberts from *Mister Roberts.* In the student's reading the Captain emerged as a sophisticated intellectual. When asked where he got the idea for such an interpretation, he said he'd read a short condensation and this was the impression he had received of the personality of the Captain. It is even more amazing that such a characterization could have been formulated when one considers the type of language the Captain uses in this scene. Condensations of plays like those found in Burns Mantle's *Best Plays* are primarily designed to indicate the main line of action in the play, and are generally too brief to be of any value to the oral interpreter.

It may be difficult to read an entire novel in preparation for an oral reading; however, if you are going to read a cutting of fiction, it is better to select a scene from a novel you have already read and liked. If you have not read many novels—and you should get in the habit of reading good ones—then you should consult a *reliable* condensation of the plot. However, bear in mind that condensations are never detailed enough, particularly in reference to characterizations. Exercise caution when you use them.

Once you have made your choice of material and have read it to yourself, start again and read it aloud. All rehearsals should be oral. Silent reading will never produce the results that oral reading does. Too many students think they can get along by reading the selection aloud for the first time in class. Forget that.

On the first day, spend an hour or possibly more reading the selection aloud—getting the "feel" of it, checking any words you do not understand. It is important that you get in the habit of knowing what each word means. Do not rush over one that is vague to you because it can easily give a different meaning to that part of the selection.

The second day, you should start to work on the selection again —paying particular attention to your pacing. Note the following: Does it seem too fast to you? Is there sufficient emotional involvement in the material? Are you aware of the changes in mood and idea that are in the material? Does the selection really mean something to you? Work to correct any faults.

Before continuing rehearsal, you should begin thinking about the introduction to your reading. The introduction has a two-fold purpose: to give the audience any necessary background information about the material and the author, and to help set the mood for the reading so the audience will more readily respond. It does not interpret the selection—that is up to the reader himself—and it does not summarize the contents of that material. Nor is it a biography of the author. It prepares the audience for the interpretation you are to give.

For example, let's say you were going to read Edna St. Vincent Millay's poem, "Interim," the grief-stricken thoughts and emotions of someone whose lover has died. You might begin this way:

Death has many faces to each of us. Yet, to all of us it means searing pain, the ache of loneliness, the hollow emptiness inside. We try to recapture memories or to touch physical objects left behind by the one who has died so we can draw closer to that person in our grief. Edna St. Vincent Millay, one of our most prominent contemporary poets, graphically shows us the broken heart of the bereaved in her poem, "Interim."

Introductions should, of course, be in a mood comparable to that of the selection. An amusing satire would not be introduced in a laborious, serious manner—and vice versa.

On the third day, read the selection again. Analyze further all aspects of the material and your interpretation of it, with special emphasis on characterization, dialogue, and descriptive elements. By this time, you should be familiar enough with the selection to be very critical.

The fourth and fifth days can be spent in polishing. You should begin to "feel" the selection; it should come alive.

The sixth day, read it straight through with no stops. Again, put it on tape if you have a recorder. This session may not take more than half an hour.

It is quite possible that by now you are getting tired of the whole thing; it may begin to bore you. We can assume that you chose the selection in the first place because you liked it. If you start to lose that interest, you should put it aside at this point for a couple of days. You may not be rehearsing it orally, but you will be thinking about it.

The day before you are to give the reading, go back to it, and this time read it straight through with no stops at least two times. If you make a mistake in the reading, don't stop to correct it, but go on—act just as though you are in the classroom actually giving the performance. This is a technique similar to the final rehearsal of a play. Many directors have the cast run through the show just as if they were in performance. If mistakes are made, you will have to get over them as well as you can. After all, a mistake may be apparent to you, but the audience may not even notice, so don't draw attention to it by laboring over corrections. Move on.

Naturally, after you have given the reading twice in this way, it is wise to go back to check over any trouble spots and correct them.

The day of the reading, if possible, read it once more before you give it. By now you should be very well prepared. You should have confidence in your ability to do the reading, and you should feel secure—not frightened.

SUMMARY

Preparation is vital to effective oral interpretation. It begins with the typing of a manuscript for three good reasons:

1. The pages in a book are not printed with oral interpretation in mind, and therefore, sentences do not always end on the same page on which they begin.
2. Margins in a book are too narrow to allow guiding notes.
3. The print in a book is often too small for easy reading.

There are five general rules to follow in preparing a manuscript:

1. Choose heavy paper.
2. Make sure each sentence ends on the same page on which it begins.
3. Double or triple space the manuscript.
4. Leave wide margins.
5. Devise a set of signals and use them on the manuscript to guide you in conveying meaning and pausing.

Careful rehearsal or practice should begin about ten days before the reading is due and you should allow yourself at least ten practice sessions. All rehearsals should be oral.

chapter five

Let yourself go!

Achieving emotional involvement is not easily accomplished. Most people are taught that they should keep their emotions under control at all times. Now, you are being told to "let yourself go," to become involved in what you read. If you are saying to yourself at this point, "That's going to take some doing," you're right. But, to be a successful oral interpreter, you must achieve emotional involvement. To be able to show honest emotion is a significant objective of any course in oral interpretation. Sincerity will never be laughed at. Yet, it takes time to *learn* to display emotion. Think about a movie you've seen that really had you on the edge of your seat. If a movie doesn't come to mind, recall a book you've read that kept you entranced to the end, a book with real people in it who became your friends or enemies because you became so involved in their lives. Remember how you were caught up in them, living their problems or joys.

What you want to achieve in this course is to bring together the way you feel as you read silently and the way you feel (and guide your audience to feel) as you read orally. Yes, there's the problem: to become immersed in the material so that the audience comes to know the characters and "feel with" them as they move through the set of circumstances that you describe. During one semester a young man tried to read *Oedipus Rex*. It was obvious that he liked the play, that he felt it deeply, but he was not projecting any emotion. It was flat, lifeless. It was after this reading that he asked to talk with the instructor. During their conversation, the professor asked him if he were an American Indian.

"Yes, I am," he said.

"And have you been trained to believe that any show of emotion is a sign of weakness?"

After a pause, he replied, "Yes."

So the problem was not with his feeling but with an inherent tendency to draw away from any outward show of emotion.

THREE KEYS TO EMOTIONAL INVOLVEMENT

There are three keys to achieving emotional response: *empathy, experience,* and *finding the meaning.* Empathy is feeling *with* someone. If you feel sympathy for someone, you are sorry that he lost his job or that he failed a class. If you share in the loss, suffering as he suffers, what you feel is empathy. Choosing material of worth will help you become empathically involved; empathic involvement in what you read, and how you read it, is essential to effective oral interpretation. We might do well to look at the author, the reader, and the audience as a team in the understanding and appreciation of literature.

If the author has done his work well, you, the reader, can become involved and, in turn, through your understanding of the author's work and effective use of reading techniques, you can involve the audience in the literature. In other words, if you can identify with a piece of material, if you can feel an empathy with it, you will be able to respond emotionally to its demands more easily. The following poem, written by an anonymous student, is an example of literature that "speaks" to (and for) many young people.

Please Hear What I'm Not Saying

Anonymous

Don't be fooled by me.
Don't be fooled by the face I wear.
For I wear a mask; I wear a thousand masks,
masks that I'm afraid to take off,
and none of them are me.
Pretending is an art that's second nature with me,
but don't be fooled, for God's sake don't be fooled.
I give you the impression that I'm secure,
that all is sunny and unruffled with me,
within as well as without,
that confidence is my name and coolness my game,

that the water's calm and I'm in command,
and that I need no one.
But don't believe me.
Please.
My surface may seem smooth, but my surface is my mask,
my ever-varying and ever-concealing mask.
Beneath lies no smugness, no complacence.
Beneath dwells the real me in confusion, in fear, in loneliness.
But I hide this.
I don't want anybody to know it.
I panic at the thought of my weakness and fear being
    exposed.
That's why I frantically create a mask to hide behind,
a nonchalant, sophisticated façade to help me pretend,
to shield me from the glance that knows.
But such a glance is precisely my salvation. My only salvation.
And I know it.
That is if it's followed by acceptance, if it's followed by love.
It's the only thing that can liberate me from myself,
from the barriers that I so painstakingly erect.
It's the only thing that will assure me of what I can't assure
    myself,
that I'm really worth something.
But I don't tell you this. I don't dare. I'm afraid to.
I'm afraid your glance will not be followed by acceptance and
    love.
I'm afraid you'll think less of me, that you'll laugh,
and your laugh would kill me.
I'm afraid that deep-down I'm nothing, that I'm just no good,
and that you will see this and reject me.
So I play my game, my desperate pretending game,
with a façade of assurance without, and a trembling child
    within.
And so begins the parade of masks,
the glittering but empty parade of masks.
And my life becomes a front.
I idly chatter to you in the suave tones of surface talk.
I tell you everything that's really nothing,
and nothing of what's everything, of what's crying within me.

So when I'm going through my routine do not be fooled by what
I'm saying.
Please listen carefully and try to hear what I'm *not* saying,
what I'd like to be able to say, what for survival I need to say,
but what I can't say.
I dislike hiding. Honestly.
I dislike the superficial game I'm playing, the superficial, phony game.
I'd really like to be genuine and spontaneous, and me,
but you've got to help me.
You've got to hold out your hand
even when that's the last thing I seem to want, or need.
Only you can wipe away from my eyes the blank stare
of the breathing dead.
Only you can call me into aliveness.
Each time you're kind and gentle and encouraging,
each time you try to understand because you really care,
my heart begins to grow wings, very small wings, very feeble wings, but wings.
With your sensitivity and sympathy, and your power of understanding,
you can breathe life into me. I want you to know that.
I want you to know how important you are to me,
how you can be a creator of the person that is me if you choose to.
Please choose to.
You alone can break down the wall behind which I tremble,
You alone can remove my mask,
You alone can release me from my shadow-world of panic and uncertainty,
from my lonely prison.
So do not pass me by. Please do not pass me by.
It will not be easy for you.
A long conviction of worthlessness builds strong walls.
The nearer you approach to me, the blinder I may strike back,
It's irrational, but despite what the books say about man, I am irrational.
I fight against the very thing that I cry out for. But I am told that

love is stronger than strong walls, and in this lies my hope.
My only hope.
Please try to beat down those walls with firm hands, but with
gentle hands—
for a child is very sensitive.
Who am I, you may wonder? I am someone you know very
well.
For I am every man you meet and I am every woman you
meet.

Let's look further at ways of achieving empathy, the first key to emotional response with literature. Here we would do well to borrow a page from the actor's handbook. Because we were taught to play down our emotions, to control them in most of our activities as adult Americans, we must find a way, as the actor does, to synthesize emotion. He learns how to laugh or cry at the drop of a hat; the experienced actor can switch from a death scene to a rollicking comedy bit and back again with only a moment's pause. With experience, so can you! Practice doing so with the exercises at the end of this chapter, and after you've tried all of our suggestions think of some others yourself.

Experience is the second key to emotional involvement. There are basically two types of experience—primary, things we learn first-hand, and vicarious, what we learn from hearing about the experiences of others. These are examples of primary experience: if you ever lived in Alaska, you'd be able to answer questions about it much better than if you'd only heard of the place. If you'd been in an accident, you could describe what it was like better than if you'd only heard of someone's being in an accident or merely read about one in a newspaper. The alternative in each case would be a learned or vicarious experience.

The more often you read material orally, the more effective you will find you are in achieving emotional responses. In short, repeated readings will give you more primary experience, and will make you a better judge of your own involvement. The more you read, the easier it will be to let yourself go. The words used to describe experience primary or secondary—may not be understood by your listeners as you intend them to be understood. Words have *denotative* meaning, to be sure, but they also have *connotative* meanings. The denotations we can get by looking up the word in the dictionary; the connotations we get from past experience. Thus the word "pain" will mean a toothache to one, a broken arm to another, a strained muscle to still another. Each of us will immediately associate the word with his own experience. And this is true with all such abstract words. Words like freedom, loyalty, justice, happiness, and pleasure—the list is endless—all conjure up precise meanings in our thinking, colored by events in our lives. Therefore, when we prepare materials for oral interpretation we attempt to discover the author's meaning, denotative and connotative, and convey that meaning to our audience.

Finding the meaning is the third key to effective emotional response. In the following essay by Francis Bacon, there is very little emotion and its meaning might not be readily understood. It will take some study to comprehend fully the author's concepts.

Of Studies

Francis Bacon

Studies serve for delight, for ornament, and for ability. Their chief use for delight is in privateness and retiring; for ornament, is in discourse; and for ability, is in the judgment and disposition of business. For expert men can execute and perhaps judge of particulars, one by one; but the general counsels, and the plots and marshaling of affairs come best from those that are learned. To spend too much time in studies is sloth; to use them too much for ornament is affectation; to make judgment wholly by their rules is the humor of a scholar. They perfect nature, and are perfected by experience; for natural abilities are like natural plants, that need pruning by study; and studies themselves do give forth directions too much at large, except they be bounded in by experience. Crafty men contemn studies; simple men admire them; and wise men use them: for they teach not their own use; but that is a wisdom without them and above them, won by observation. Read not to contradict and confute, nor to believe and take for granted, nor to find talk and discourse, but to weigh and consider. Some books are to be tasted, others to be swallowed, and some few to be chewed and digested: that is, some books are to be read only in parts; others to be read but not curiously, and some few to be read wholly, and with diligence and attention. Some books also may be read by deputy, and extracts made of them by others; but that would be only in the less important arguments and the meaner sort of books; else distilled books are, like common distilled waters, flashy things. Reading maketh a full man; conference a ready man; and writing an exact man. And, therefore, if a man write little, he had need have a great memory; if he confer little, he had need have a present wit; and if he read little, he had need have much cunning, to seem to know that he doth not. Histories make men wise; poets, witty; the mathematics, subtile; natural philosophy, deep, moral, grave; logic and rhetoric, able to contend, "Abeunt studia in mores." Nay, there is no stand or impediment in the wit but may be wrought out by fit studies: like as diseases of the body may have appropriate exercises. Bowling is good for the stone and reins, shooting for the lungs and breast, gentle walking for the stomach, riding for the head and the like. So if a man's wit be wandering, let him study the mathematics; for in demonstrations, if his wit be called away never so little, he must begin again. If his wit be not apt to distinguish or find differences, let him study the schoolmen; for they are "cymini sectores." If he be not apt to beat over matters, and to call up one thing to prove and illustrate another, let him study the lawyers' cases; so every defect of the mind may have a special receipt.

Now that you have read the entire selection, look up the words that you didn't immediately recognize. For example, what is the meaning of *confute? meaner? contend? Abeunt studia in mores? stand? impediment? cymini sectores?*

Any good dictionary will help with all but the Latin terms. The first of the two, *Abeunt studia in mores,* means "studies develop into habits." *Cymini sectores* (Bacon's reference to schoolmen) are "hair-splitters." You could look up such terms in the *Dictionary of Foreign Phrases and Abbreviations.* But knowing the dictionary meaning won't help with other words Bacon used: *tasted, swallowed, chewed* and *digested.* In these instances the context helps with the connotations of the words.

After you have read the entire selection and have become sure of the word meanings, both denotative and connotative, you'll want to identify the mood of the selection. Doing so will help you to highlight the author's purpose in writing the piece. Is he merely reporting, or is he presenting a satirical view of the situation he describes? Bacon, for example, has often had his style referred to as "crisp." His mood is light, witty, often tongue-in-cheek, as he chides his reader into discovering his meaning. Read Bacon's essay again and relate it to your own idea of study. How does the philosophy impress you—sympathetically, indifferently, or antagonistically? Do his thoughts relate to your own reactions as a student?

Edgar Allan Poe has long been regarded as the father of the horror story. His mood is almost universally somber, seeking its effect through shock and vivid, bloodcurdling description. Notice how the words in the following story are woven together to produce a single pervading mood. In contrast to the intellectual and unemotional content of the Bacon essay, every word in this selection adds to the meaning and emotional intensity. Poe builds gradually to heighten the listener's responses to the final climax.

In reading "The Tell-Tale Heart" note the problems the story creates. It begins on an expository level—the main character (actually the only speaking character) simply but nervously relating the story. There is a clue to the lack of emotion in the second paragraph by Poe's use of the lines, "Object there was none. Passion there was none." It is vital that the character (voice and manner) be established from the beginning. You will notice that there is a climactic point when the old man cries out, "Who's there?" Then there's a lull in the emotion until it begins to build again, reaching a second climax with the line, "With a loud yell I threw open the lantern and leaped into the room." Following this climax there is another period of inner tension that builds gradually to the final climax of the story. By the time you reach that point in the story where the murderer shrieks, "Villains! dissemble no more! I admit the deed!" your reaction should be spontaneous. In fact, anything less than a muffled scream betrays your lack of involvement in the story. Don't read this story for an audience unless you can become sufficiently involved that you go progressively "mad" as you build to the final scream. Suggestions have been inserted directly into the story to guide your emotional involvement and understanding.

The Tell-Tale Heart

Edgar Allan Poe

True!—nervous—very, very dreadfully nervous I had been and am! but why *will* you say that I am mad? The disease had sharpened my senses—not destroyed—not dulled them. Above all was the sense of hearing acute. I heard all things in the heaven and in the earth. I heard many things in hell. How, then, am I mad? Hearken! and observe how healthily —how calmly I can tell you the whole story.

It is impossible to say how first the idea entered my brain; but once conceived, it haunted me day and night. Object there was none. Passion there was none. I loved the old man. He had never wronged me. He had never given me insult. For his gold I had no desire. I think it was his eye! yes, it was this! One of his eyes resembled that of a vulture—a pale blue eye, with a film over it. Whenever it fell upon me, my blood ran cold; and so by degrees—very gradually—I made up my mind to take the life of the old man, and thus rid myself of the eye for ever.

(In these first two paragraphs the mood is unemotional, candid. But there is a clue to the man's psychotic state in the line, "I think it was his eye! yes, it was this!" Your tone of voice (bring wonder into it) and rate of speech (slower) will telegraph the clue to the audience. Use of "eye" as a symbol of horror and exclamation point shows Poe means it to be emphasized.)

Now this is the point. You fancy me mad. Madmen know nothing. But you should have seen *me*. You should have seen how wisely I proceeded—with what caution—with what foresight—with what dissimulation I went to work!

I was never kinder to the old man than during the whole week before I killed him. And every night, about midnight, I turned the latch of his door and opened it—oh, so gently! And then, when I had made an opening sufficient for my head, I put in a dark lantern, all closed, closed, so that no light shone out, and then I thrust in my head. Oh, you would have laughed to see how cunningly I thrust it in! I moved it slowly—very, very slowly, so that I might not disturb the old man's sleep. It took me an hour to place my whole head within the opening so far that I could see him as he lay upon his bed. Ha!—would a madman have been so wise as this?

(The lines up to this point have been expository again. Your tone and rate should reflect this mood and add his conceit with himself and his plan. A straight reading of the lines up to this point will convey his conceit and his matter-of-fact attitude to the audience.)

And then, when my head was well in the room, I undid the lantern cautiously—oh so cautiously—cautiously (for the hinges creaked)—I undid it just so much that a single thin ray fell upon the vulture eye. And this I did for seven long nights—every night just at midnight—but I found the eye always closed; and so it was impossible to do the work; for it was not the old man who vexed me, but his Evil Eye.

(Again, the clue to the man's psychotic state. Reflect his madness by emphasizing the words, "but his Evil Eye.")

And, every morning, when the day broke, I went boldly into the chamber, and spoke courageously to him, calling him by name in a hearty tone, and inquiring how he had passed the night. So you see he would have been a very profound old man, indeed, to suspect that every night, just at twelve, I looked in upon him while he slept.

(Notice that the author supplies periods, such as the above lines, of momentary relief—a slackening of the emotion. This pattern of builds followed by relief continues as the story develops with gradually diminishing moments of relief. Feel them as you read.)

Upon the eighth night I was more than usually cautious in opening the door. A watch's minute hand moves more quickly than did mine. Never before that night had I *felt* the extent of my own powers—of my sagacity. I could scarcely contain my feelings of triumph. To think that there I was, opening the door, little by little, and he not even to dream of my secret deeds or thoughts. I fairly chuckled at the idea; and perhaps he heard me; for he moved on the bed suddenly, as if startled. Now you may think that I drew back—but no. His room was as black as pitch with the thick darkness, (for the shutters were close fastened, through fear of robbers,) and so I knew that he could not see the opening of the door, and I kept pushing it on steadily, steadily.

I had my head in, and was about to open the lantern, when my thumb slipped upon the tin fastening, and the old man sprang up in the bed, crying out—"Who's there?"

(The suspense begins quietly; then it is intensified as the lantern is opened; it rises gradually to a climax with the cry, "Who's there?" Relief again follows in the coming lines.)

I kept still and said nothing. For a whole hour I did not move a muscle, and in the meantime I did not hear him lie down. He was still sitting up in the bed listening;—just as I have done, night after night, hearkening to the death watches in the wall.

(Relief is indeed momentary this time; the emotion begins to build again right here. Build it slowly and subtly because it is some time before another respite comes.)

Presently I heard a slight groan, and I knew it was the groan of mortal terror. It was not a groan of pain or of grief— oh no!—it was the low stifled sound that arises from the bottom of the soul when overcharged with awe. I knew the sound well. Many a night, just at midnight, when all the world slept, it has welled up from my own bosom, deepening, with its dreadful echo, the terrors that distracted me. I say I knew it well. I knew what the old man felt, and pitied him, although I chuckled at heart. I knew that he had been lying awake ever since the first slight noise, when he had turned in the bed. His fears had been ever since growing upon him. He had been trying to fancy them causeless, but could not. He had been saying to himself—"It is nothing but the wind in the chimney—it is only a mouse crossing the floor," or "it is merely a cricket which has made a single chirp." Yes, he had been trying to comfort himself with these suppositions; but he had found all in vain. *All in vain;* because Death, in approaching him, had stalked with his black shadow before him, and enveloped the victim. And it was the mournful influence of the unperceived shadow that caused him to feel —although he neither saw nor heard—to *feel* the presence of my head within the room.

When I had waited a long time, very patiently, without hearing him lie down, I resolved to open a little—a very, very little crevice in the lantern. So I opened it—you cannot imagine how stealthily, stealthily—until, at length, a single dim ray, like the thread of a spider, shot out from the crevice and full upon the vulture eye.

It was open—wide, wide open—and I grew furious as I gazed upon it. I saw it with perfect distinctness—all a dull blue, with a hideous veil over it that chilled the very marrow in my bones; but I could see nothing else of the old man's face or person: for I had directed the ray as if by instinct, precisely upon the damned spot.

(The voice rate quickens and the pitch increases gradually as his madness again takes over. Feel the growing tension and panic. The paragraph that follows is only slightly relieving. Maintain the pace and let the pitch drop a notch to show it.)

And now have I not told you that what you mistake for madness is but over-acuteness of the senses?—now, I say, there came to my ears a low, dull, quick sound, such as a watch makes when enveloped in cotton. I knew *that* sound well too. It was the beating of the old man's heart. It increased my fury, as the beating of a drum stimulates the soldier into courage.

But even yet I refrained and kept still. I scarcely breathed. I held the lantern motionless. I tried how steadily I could maintain the ray upon the eye. Meantime the hellish tattoo of the heart increased. It grew quicker and quicker, and louder and louder every instant. The old man's terror *must* have been extreme! It grew louder, I say, louder every moment!—do you mark me well? I have told you that I am nervous: so I am. And now at the dead hour of the night, amid the dreadful silence of the old house, so strange a noise as this excited me to uncontrollable terror. Yet, for some minutes longer I refrained and stood still. But the beating grew louder, louder! I thought the heart must burst. And now a new anxiety seized me—the sound would be heard by a neighbor! The old man's hour had come! With a loud yell, I threw open the lantern and leaped into the room. He shrieked once—once only. In an instance I dragged him to the floor, and pulled the heavy bed over him. I then smiled gaily,

(This paragraph continues the emotion—the madness— as the man relives the murder. Rate and pitch—feeling —climax again with the line, "I then smiled gaily, to find the deed so far done." Following this line the rate slows and pitch drops. The mood is one of self-satisfaction again in the following paragraph with the line, "Yes, he was stone, stone dead.")

to find the deed so far done. But, for many minutes, the heart beat on with a muffled sound. This, however, did not vex me; it would not be heard through the wall. At length it ceased. The old man was dead. I removed the bed and examined the corpse. Yes, he was stone, stone dead. I placed my hand upon the heart and held it there many minutes. There was no pulsation. He was stone dead. His eye would trouble me no more.

If still you think me mad, you will think so no longer when

I describe the wise precautions I took for the concealment of the body. The night waned, and I worked hastily, but in silence. First of all I dismembered the corpse. I cut off the head and the arms and the legs.

I then took up three planks from the flooring of the chamber, and deposited all between the scantlings. I then replaced the boards so cleverly, so cunningly, that no human eye—not even *his*—could have detected anything wrong. There was nothing to wash out—no stain of any kind—no blood-spot whatever, I had been too wary for that. A tub had caught all —ha! ha!

(Notice how subtly the author builds toward the sardonic laugh in this paragraph. He conveys the feeling that no human eye—not even the old man's—could detect anything wrong.)

When I had made an end of these labors, it was four o'clock —still dark as midnight. As the bell sounded the hour, there came a knocking at the street door. I went down to open it with a light heart—for what had I *now* to fear? There entered three men, who introduced themselves, with perfect suavity, as officers of the police. A shriek had been heard by a neighbor during the night: suspicion of foul play had been aroused; information had been lodged at the police office, and they (the officers) had been deputed to search the premises. I smiled,—for what had I to fear? I bade the gentlemen welcome. The shriek, I said, was my own in a dream. The old man, I mentioned, was absent in the country. I took my visitors all over the house. I bade them search—search *well*. I led them, at length, to *his* chamber. I showed them his treasures, secure, undisturbed. In the enthusiasm of my confidence, I brought chairs into the room, and desired them here to rest from their fatigues, while I myself, in the wild audacity of my perfect triumph, placed my own seat upon the very spot beneath which reposed the corpse of the victim.

(The above paragraphs are reflective of the complete conceit of the man. They should be read with abandon.

*The sentences which follow gradually move from aban-
don to concern as again the man relives his deed. Final
climax of the story begins building with the line, "But,
ere long, I felt myself getting pale and wished them
gone." Rate and tone grow faster and higher until in the
final lines your own muffled shriek is natural and spontaneous.)*

The officers were satisfied. My *manner* had convinced
them. I was singularly at ease. They sat, and while I answered cheerily, they chatted of familiar things. But, ere long,
I felt myself getting pale and wished them gone. My head
ached, and I fancied a ringing in my ears: but still they sat
and still chatted. The ringing became more distinct—it continued and became more distinct: I talked more freely to
get rid of the feeling: but it continued and gained definitive-
ness—until, at length, I found that the noise was *not* within
my ears.

No doubt I now grew very pale;—but I talked more
fluently, and with a heightened voice. Yet the sound increased
—and what could I do? It was a *low, dull, quick sound—
much such a sound as a watch makes when enveloped in cotton.* I gasped for breath—and yet the officers heard it not. I
talked more quickly—more vehemently; but the noise
steadily increased. I arose and argued about trifles, in a high
key and with violent gesticulations, but the noise steadily increased. Why would they not be gone? I paced the floor, to
and fro with heavy strides, as if excited to fury by the observation of the men—but the noise steadily increased. Oh God!
what *could* I do? I foamed—I raved—I swore. I swung the
chair upon which I had been sitting, and grated it upon the
boards, but the noise arose over all and continually increased.
It grew louder—louder—*louder*! And still the men chatted
pleasantly, and smiled. Was it possible they heard not? Al-
mighty God!—no, no! They heard!—they suspected!—they
knew!—they were making a *mockery* of my horror!—this I
thought, and this I think. But anything was better than this
agony! Anything was more tolerable than this derision! I
could bear those hypocritical smiles no longer! I felt that I

must scream or die!—and now—again!—hark! louder! louder! *louder!*—

"Villains!" I shrieked, "dissemble no more! I admit the deed!—tear up the planks!—here, here!—it is the beating of his hideous heart!"

Drama demands that the student of interpretation involve himself in the emotions of the characters he presents. In the following scene from Rod Serling's, *Requiem For A Heavyweight,* the emotional content is subdued in contrast to the explosive intensity of the Poe story. This scene begins quietly and grows stronger as it reaches a climax. Here are two people who are entirely different in interests and background and culture, and yet who see in each other something that fulfills their individual needs. The emotional peak is reached in the sudden realization that they are in love.

From

Requiem for a Heavyweight

Rod Serling

MCCLINTOCK: Miss Carrie, what're you doin' here?

GRACE: Well, I . . .

(*She is suddenly conscious of the rest of the men looking at her, and McClintock sees this, too. He takes her arm.*)

MCCLINTOCK: Let's go over here and sit down. (*He takes her across to a booth, and they sit down. The men move away chuckling with an occasional glance at them.*)

GRACE: A friend of mine and I had dinner over at McCleary's. It isn't very far from here. She got a headache and went on home, and I—

MCCLINTOCK: Yeah?

GRACE: And I remembered your giving me your hotel and—

MCCLINTOCK: It was real nice of you to look me up. (*She looks around the room and smiles a little embarrassedly.*)

GRACE: You know—I've never been around here before.

MCCLINTOCK (*Nods*):   No change. If you're here once, you've seen it all.

GRACE: (*Smiles*)   Atmosphere.

MCCLINTOCK: Yeah, you might call it atmosphere. (*She looks over his shoulder at the men in the back of the room. One fighter is going through the motions of battle. Grace looks questioningly at him and then at McClintock.*)

MCCLINTOCK: That? That goes on all the time around here. Maish says this part of the room is a graveyard. And those guys spend their time dying in here. Fighting their lives away inside their heads. That's what Maish says.

GRACE: That's . . . that's kind of sad.

MCCLINTOCK: I suppose it is.

GRACE: (*With a smile leans toward him.*) I've got a confession to make. I didn't eat at McCleary's, I ate at home. I came on purpose. I asked for you at your hotel. I've been thinking about you a lot, Mr. McClintock. (*There is a long pause.*) I was just wondering—

MCCLINTOCK: Yeah? Go ahead.

GRACE: I was just wondering if you ever thought of working with children. (*There's a long pause.*)

MCCLINTOCK: What?

GRACE: Work with children. Like a summer camp. You know, in athletics.

MCCLINTOCK: I—I never give it much thought.

GRACE: Do you like children?

MCCLINTOCK: Children? Well, I haven't had much to do with kids, but I've always liked them. (*Then thoughtfully, going over it in his mind.*) Yeah I like kids a lot. You were thinking of a summer camp or something—

GRACE: That's right. That sort of thing. In a month or so, there'll be a lot of openings. I was thinking . . . well, perhaps you ought to give that some thought.

MCCLINTOCK: (*His hand goes to his face*)   But they'd see me and listen to me talk and—

GRACE: Why not? You've got to begin someplace. You've got to give it a try.

MCCLINTOCK: Sure, I'm going to have to. (*Then he stares at her intently.*) Why did you come here tonight?

GRACE: (*Looks away*)   I've been thinking about you. I

want to help—if I can. (*Then as if to dispel the seriousness of the mood, she cocks her head, grins very girl-like.*) How about it, Mr. McClintock—could I have a beer?

MCCLINTOCK: A beer? You mean here?

GRACE: I kind of like it here.

MCCLINTOCK: (*Grins at her.*) Why sure. (*He stands up and calls to the Bartender, who is passing.*) Hey, Charlie! Two beers, huh? (*The Bartender acknowledges with a wave, goes back toward the bar. McClintock sits down again and looks across the table at her.*)

GRACE: (*Points to the jukebox.*) How about music?

MCCLINTOCK: What?

GRACE: Don't you like to listen to music when you drink beer?

MCCLINTOCK: Music? Why . . . I never even gave it much thought. Sure. Sure, we can play music. (*He rises, fishes in his pocket, takes out a coin, puts it in the jukebox.*)

(*Cut to: A tight close-up of FIGHTER #2 across the room, a toothless, terribly ugly little man.*)

FIGHTER #2:   (*Smiles.*) Hey Mountain—play "My Heart Tells Me."

(*There's laughter at this. McClintock quickly turns his face away, shoves a coin in the slot, indiscriminately punches a few buttons, then returns to the booth. Bartender brings over two bottles of beer, slops them down in front of them.*)

MCCLINTOCK: How about a glass, Charlie, for the lady?

BARTENDER: (*Over his shoulder as he heads back to the bar.*) Fancy-schmancey. (*There's another moment's pause.*)

GRACE: Pretty.

MCCLINTOCK: (*Listens for a moment.*) Yeah. Yeah, it is kind of pretty. Them are violins.

GRACE: (*Smiles.*) Beautiful.

MCCLINTOCK: I never paid much attention to music before. I never had much time.

GRACE: What's that?

MCCLINTOCK: Music. Just plain old music. (*He looks away thoughtfully for a moment.*) The only music I know by heart really is the National Anthem because they play it before every fight. The National Anthem. (*Grace smiles at this.*) Oh, yeah—there was Smiley Collins, too.

GRACE: Who's Smiley Collins?

MCCLINTOCK: He was a fighter. He used to play a violin. (*A pause.*) That's funny, ain't it? He was a fighter, but he used to play a violin. (*As McClintock talks, we can see him losing himself in the conversation and in the sheer delight of having a girl across from him.*)

GRACE: He used to play the violin? Seriously?

MCCLINTOCK: Real serious. Oh, I don't know nothin' about his violin playing—but, oh man, did that boy have a right hand. Like dynamite. He could knock down a wall with it.

GRACE: What about his violin—

MCCLINTOCK: (*Interrupts her, not even hearing her.*) I remember his last fight. He fought a guy by the name of Willie Floyd. Floyd had twenty pounds on him. (*At this moment the Bartender brings a glass, puts it down in front of Grace, then walks away. McClintock picks up her bottle and pours the beer for her.*)

GRACE: (*Smiles.*) Thanks.

MCCLINTOCK: They don't have many ladies here—that's the reason he forgets to put glasses out. (*He holds up his bottle to her glass.*) Drink hearty. That's what Maish always says. Drink hearty.

GRACE: (*Smiles.*) Drink hearty. Drink hearty, Mr. McClintock. (*The two of them drink. His eyes never leave her face. She notices this and smiles again.*) You think a lot of Maish, don't you?

MCCLINTOCK: He's number one. They don't come like him.

GRACE: He was your manager.

MCCLINTOCK: (*Nods.*) Yeah, for fourteen years. He's been a real great friend, not just a manager. In the old days . . . in the old days when I was just getting started—Maish would stake me to everything from clothes to chow. He's a real great guy. (*Then he stops abruptly and stares at her.*) Why ain't you married?

GRACE: (*Laughs.*) Should I be?

MCCLINTOCK: (*Nods.*) You're pretty. Not just pretty— you're beautiful.

GRACE: Thank you.

MCCLINTOCK: Pretty as a young colt. That's what my old man used to say.

GRACE: Your father?

MCCLINTOCK: (*Nods.*)   Yeah. A girl's as pretty as a young colt, so he used to tell me.

GRACE: (*Very interested*)   Go ahead, Mountain—

MCCLINTOCK: About my father? Big guy. Nice old guy. I remember once—I fought a guy named Jazzo. Elmer Jazzo. And looked just like my old man. Spittin' image. And in the first round I didn't even want to hit him. Then in round two I shut my eyes and I—

GRACE: (*Interrupts.*)   Mountain.

MCCLINTOCK: (*Looks at her.*)   Yeah?

GRACE: There isn't much else, is there—besides fighting?

MCCLINTOCK: (*Very thoughtfully looks away.*)   No. No, there isn't, I guess. I'm . . . I'm sorry . . .

GRACE: Don't be. It's just that there is so much more for you that you'll be able to find now.

(*They look at each other and both smile. The music is playing, and they are both aware of it suddenly.*)

GRACE: Hey, Mountain—

MCCLINTOCK: Yeah?

GRACE: Them are violins.

(*They both laugh. The camera pulls away from them as they start to talk, lost in an awareness of each other and in the pleasantness of being together. We continue a slow dolly away from them, and then a slow fade-out to black.*)

(*Fade on: With a shot of the alley outside the arena. Grace and McClintock walk slowly away from the door toward the street. They walk slowly, looking around.*)

MCCLINTOCK: (*Kicks a can out of the way.*)   A garden, ain't it?

GRACE: Where are the flowers?

MCCLINTOCK: (*Flicks his ear.*)   Right here. (*Grace smiles a little forcedly.*)

GRACE: It's late, Mountain. I've got to go home.

MCCLINTOCK: I'll get you a cab. (*She starts to walk off.*)

MCCLINTOCK: Grace—(*She turns to him.*) I . . . I've had a good time.

GRACE: I have, too.

MCCLINTOCK: You know, when we came out of the bar I heard Charlie say that I had a pretty date.

GRACE: (*Smiles.*) Thank Charlie for me.

MCCLINTOCK: It wasn't just that he thought you were pretty, he said that I had a date. It's like with the music. I don't even think I ever had a real date in all this time. A real one. Not somebody I liked. Somebody I wanted to be with.

GRACE: I think that's a compliment.

MCCLINTOCK: One time . . . one time Army had a girl friend living in St. Louis. She had a friend. Army fixed me up. We were supposed to meet after the fight. These two girls were waitin' for us outside. This girl that I was supposed to go with—she takes one look at me and she . . . she—

GRACE: She what, Mountain?

MCCLINTOCK: She turned around and she ran away. She looked at my face and she turned around and ran away. (*Grace instinctively touches his arm and holds it tightly.*) They should have been used to it. I know what I sound like, too. But it . . . it did hurt. I didn't want it to happen again so I never let it happen.

(*Cut to: A tight close-up of Grace as she stares at him and wonderingly shakes her head, feeling that acme of tenderness a woman can feel for a man.*)

GRACE: (*Softly.*) The cab, Mountain. It's late.

MCCLINTOCK: Sure.

(*The two start walking again toward the opening of the alley.*)

GRACE: Remember to think about what I told you. I think you'd like working with children.

MCCLINTOCK: I'll think about it. I'll think about it a lot. Don't build me up none, Miss Carrie. Don't say I'm anything special. (*Pause.*) Tell 'em . . . tell 'em I fought a hundred and eleven fights. Tell 'em I never took a dive. I'm proud of that.

(Grace looks at him intently for a moment, and there's a continuing softness on her face.)

GRACE: *(Whispers.)* Sure, you are, Mountain. You must be very proud.

(She quickly kisses him on the side of his face, studies him for a moment and hurriedly walks away from him. He stands there touching his face, looking after her.)

There are other aspects of getting the meaning, such as literary structure and imagery. It will suffice here to say that you will want to examine your material for theme as a part of getting the meaning, Too, you will find it helpful, and often necessary, to do some research on the author if the mood, and thus the meaning, of your selection is not readily clear to you on first or second reading. Learning about the author—his life and times—will help you to appreciate more fully his point of view. Don't assume, however, that reading about the author will always give you insight into the purpose of a particular piece of his writing. Failure to understand the selection will most certainly result in a faulty interpretation of the author's meaning. This is especially true of satire. Read the following cutting of this essay as though the author, Jonathan Swift, meant every word of it. In reality, Swift used biting satire to make the point that the English were brutally tyrannizing the Irish. At the same time he pointed up faults in many aspects of the life and thinking of the period. Analysis provided by the authors will help to point up Swift's satire.

A Modest Proposal

Jonathan Swift

It is a melancholy object to those who walk through this great town or travel in the country, when they see the streets, the roads and cabin doors crowded with beggars of the female sex, followed by three, four, or six children, all in rags, and importuning every passenger for an alms. These mothers, instead of being able to work for their honest livelihood, are forced to employ all their time in strolling, to beg sustenance for their helpless infants, who as they grow up, either turn thieves for want of work, or leave their dear native country to fight for the Pretender in Spain, or sell themselves to the Barbadoes.

I think it is agreed by all parties that this prodigious number of children, in the arms, or on the backs, or at the heels of their mothers, and frequently their fathers, is in the present deplorable state of the kingdom a very great additional grievance; and therefore whoever could find out a fair, cheap, and easy method of making these children sound, useful members of the commonwealth, would deserve so well of the public as to have his statue set up for a preserver of the nation.

(In these first two paragraphs Swift appeals to the reader for compassion in the matter to be discussed and introduces the first point of satire, that anyone solving the problem of the Irish poor would deserve such recognition as to have his statue set up—a hollow payment for service. This material must be handled in a straightforward, matter-of-fact reading to be effective. The emotion lies as much in what is not said as in what is presented.)

But my intention is very far from being confined to provide only for the children of professed beggars; it is of a much greater extent, and shall take in the whole number of infants at a certain age, who are born of parents in effect as little able to support them as those who demand our charity in the streets.

As to my own part, having weighted the several schemes of other projectors, I have always found them grossly mistaken in their computation. It is true, a child, just dropped from its dam, may be supported by her milk for a solar year with little other nourishment, at most not above the value of two shillings, which the mother may certainly get, or the value in scraps, by her lawful occupation of begging and it is exactly at one year old that I propose to provide for them in such a manner as instead of being a charge upon their parents or the parish, or wanting food and raiment for the rest of their lives, they shall, on the contrary, contribute to the feeding and partly to the clothing of many thousands.

(Satire in the two paragraphs above includes the reference to the mother as a "dam," reducing the Irish mother and child to an animal state. The plan is more plausible when one thinks in terms of animals rather than humans. Heighten the satire by emphasizing "dam." Reference to "two shillings" is also satirical since it is such a small sum to use in reference to the worth of human life.)

The number of souls in this kingdom being usually reckoned one million and a half, of these I calculate there may be about two hundred thousand couples whose wives are breeders; from which number I subtract thirty thousand couples who are able to maintain their own children . . . there will remain an hundred and seventy thousand breeders. I again subtract fifty thousand for these women who miscarry, or whose children die by accident or disease within the year. There only remain an hundred and twenty thousand children of poor parents annually born. The question therefore is, how this number shall be reared and provided for . . .

I shall now therefore humbly propose my own thoughts, which I hope will not be liable to the least objection.

(These calculations should be handled lightly. They set the stage in numbers for the details of Swift's "plan.")

I have been assured by a very knowing American of my acquaintance in London, that a young healthy child well nursed is at a year old a most delicious, nourishing, and wholesome food, whether stewed, roasted, baked, or boiled, and I make no doubt that it will equally serve in a fricassee or a ragout.

*(The obvious reference in this paragraph was to the bar-
baric American. It was popular at the time to regard the
American as little better than the savages with whom he
lived in America.)*

I do therefore humbly offer it to public consideration that
of the hundred and twenty thousand children already computed, twenty thousand may be reserved for breed . . . (and)
that the remaining hundred thousand may at a year old be
offered in sale to the persons of quality and fortune through
the kingdom, always advising the mother to let them suck
plentifully in the last month, so as to render them plump and
fat for a good table. A child will make two dishes at an entertainment for friends, and when the family dines alone, the
fore or hind quarter will make a reasonable dish, and seasoned with a little pepper or salt will be very good boiled on
the fourth day, especially in winter.

*(The plan is detailed. Satire dominates this paragraph.
Reference is again made to Irish animals with the use of
the word "breed." Persons of quality and fortune, it will
later develop, are landlords, again a satirical play on
words. Final satirical reference is made to how far one
"suckling" (a term which refers to pigs) will go in feeding "persons of quality." The subtle points of satire
should be brought out in your reading by emphasizing
those key words or by tossing off the others in the sentence.)*

I grant this food will be somewhat dear, and therefore very
proper for landlords, who, as they have already devoured
most of the parents, seem to have the best title to the children.

I have already computed the charge of nursing a beggar's
child (in which list I reckon all cottagers, labourers, and four-
fifths of the farmers) to be about two shillings per annum,
rags included, and I believe no gentleman would repine to
give ten shillings for the carcass of a good fat child, which,
as I have said, will make four dishes of excellent nutritive

meat, when he has only some particular friend or his own family to dine with him. Thus the squire will learn to be a good landlord, and grow popular among his tenants, the mother will have eight shillings net profit, and be fit for work till she produces another child.

Those who are more thrifty (as I must confess the times require) may flay the carcass; the skin of which, artificially dressed, will make admirable gloves for ladies, and summer boots for fine gentlemen.

Secondly, the poor tenants will have something valuable of their own, which by law may be made liable to distress, and help to pay their landlord's rent, their corn and cattle being already seized, and money a thing unknown.

(These lines bring in a direct sarcastic note with references to the products to be made from the skin and the fine folks who will wear them, and ending again on the abject poverty of the peasants.)

Thirdly, whereas the maintenance of a hundred thousand children, from two years old and upward, cannot be computed at less than ten shillings apiece per annum, the nation's stock will be thereby increased fifty thousand pounds per annum, besides the profit of a new dish, introduced to the tables of all gentlemen of fortune in the kingdom who have any refinement in taste, and the money will circulate among ourselves, the goods being entirely of our own growth and manufacture.

Fourthly, the constant breeders, besides the gain of eight shillings sterling per annum, by the sale of their children, will be rid of the charge of maintaining them after the first year . . . This would be a great inducement to marriage, which all wise nations have either encouraged by rewards, or enforced by laws and penalties. It would increase the care and tenderness of mothers toward their children, when they were sure of a settlement for life, to the poor babes, provided in some sort by the public, to their annual profit instead of expense. We should see an honest emulation among the married women, which of them could bring the fattest child to the market. Men would become as fond of their wives, during the time of their pregnancy, as they are now of their mares in foal, their cows in calf, their sows when they are ready to farrow, nor offer to beat or kick them (as is too frequent a practice) for fear of a miscarriage . . .

(*The satire branches out in the above paragraph to include the areas of promiscuity, mother love, father love, and the treatment of wives by their husbands.*)

I can think of no one objection, that will possibly be raised against this proposal, unless it should be urged that the number of people will be thereby much lessened in the kingdom. This I freely own, and it was indeed one principal design in offering it to the world. I desire the reader will observe, that I calculate my remedy for this one individual kingdom of Ireland, and for no other that ever was, is, or, I think, ever can be upon earth. Therefore let no man talk to me of other expedients: Of taxing our absentees at five shillings a pound: Of using neither clothes, nor household furniture, except what is of our own growth and manufacture: Of utterly rejecting the materials and instruments that promote foreign luxury: Of curing the expensiveness of pride, vanity, idleness, and gaming in our women: Of introducing a vein of parsimony, prudence and temperance: Of learning to love our Country, wherein we differ even from Laplanders, and the inhabitants of Topinamboo: Of quitting our animosities and factions: . . . Of being a little cautious not to sell our country and conscience for nothing: Of teaching landlords to have at least one degree of mercy toward their tenants. Lastly of putting a spirit of honesty, industry, and skill into our shopkeepers, who, if a resolution could now be taken to buy only our native goods, would immediately unite to cheat and exact upon us in the price, the measure, and the goodness, nor could ever yet be brought to make one fair proposal of just dealing, though often and earnestly invited to it.

Therefore I repeat, let no man talk to me of these and the like expedients till he hath at least some glimpse of hope that there will ever be some hearty and sincere attempt to put them in practice.

(Notice in the above lines, the range of grievances that Swift identifies. Nearly every aspect of life comes under his indictment.)

But as to myself, having been wearied out for many years with offering vain, idle, visionary thoughts, and at length utterly despairing of success, I fortunately fell upon this proposal. . . . I am not so violently bent upon my own opinion as to reject any offer, proposed by wise men, which shall be found equally innocent, cheap, easy and effectual. But before something of that kind shall be advanced in contradiction to my scheme . . . I desire those politicians, who dislike my overture, and may perhaps be so bold as to attempt an answer, that they will first ask the parents of these mortals, whether they would not at this day think it a great happiness to have been sold for food at a year old, in the manner I prescribe, and thereby have avoided such a perpetual scene of misfortunes as they have since gone through by the oppression of landlords, the impossibility of paying rent without money or trade, the want of common sustenance, with neither house nor clothes to cover them from the inclemencies of the weather, and the most inevitable prospect of entailing the like or greater miseries upon their breed forever.

I profess, in the sincerity of my heart, that I have not the least personal interest in endeavouring to promote this necessary work, having no other motive than the public good of my country, by advancing our trade, providing for infants, relieving the poor, and giving some pleasure to the rich. I have no children by which I can propose to get a single penny; the youngest being nine years old, and my wife past child-bearing.

The next selection centers around the diary of a young girl, a teenager. The events described could have happened yesterday; they may happen again to someone else tomorrow. *Go Ask Alice* is the story of a young person who gets caught up in the activities of the drug sub-culture, innocently at first, but then willingly, recklessly. Notice, as you read the several diary entries, how her language, her attitudes toward life, people, and herself change as she slips deeper into a dependency on drugs. You will want to read the whole book after you get involved with her in these excerpts and, when you do, you will find yourself hoping she will "make it," and gain control over her life again. She almost does.

From

Go Ask Alice

Anonymous

December 10
    When I bought you, Diary, I was going to write religiously in you every day, but some days nothing worth writing happens and other days I'm too busy or too bored or too angry or too annoyed, or just too me to do anything I don't have to do. I guess I'm a pretty lousy friend—even to you. Anyway I feel closer to you than I do to even Debby and Marie and Sharon who are my very best friends. Even with them I'm not really me. I'm partly somebody else trying to fit in and say the right things and do the right thing and be in the right place and wear what everybody else is wearing. Sometimes I think we're all trying to be shadows of each other, trying to buy the same records and everything even if we don't like them. Kids are like robots, off an assembly line, and I don't want to be a robot!

    (The entire story covers a little over a year of the girl's life. She is in high school; her father is a college dean. The book begins with the above entry. The next one, a month and a half later, shows her already a member of the drug culture; notice the changes in language and attitude.)

January 24

Oh damn, damn, damn, it's happened again. I don't know whether to scream with glory or cover myself with ashes and sackcloth, whatever that means. Anyone who says pot and acid are not addicting is a damn, stupid, raving idiot, unenlightened fool! I've been on them since July 10, and when I've been off I've been scared to death to even think of anything that even looks or seems like dope. All the time pretending to myself that I could take it or leave it!

All the dumb, idiot kids who think they are only chipping are in reality just existing from one experience to the other. After you've had it, there isn't even life without drugs. It's a prodding, colorless, dissonant bare existence. It stinks. And I'm glad I'm back. Glad! Glad! Glad! I've never had it better than I had it last night. Each new time is the best time and Chris feels the same way. Last night when she called and asked me to come over, I knew something terrible had happened. She sounded like she didn't know what to do. But when I got there and smelled that incredible smell I just sat down on the floor of her room with her and cried and smoked. It was beautiful and wonderful and we'd been without it for so long. I'll never be able to express how really great it is.

Later I called Mother and told her I was spending the night with Chris because she felt a little depressed. Depressed, no one in the world but a doper could know the true opposite of depressed.

(The girl—we never know her name—was given LSD at a party without her knowledge. She tried it again and then moved on to marijuana and stronger drugs. She just wanted to "try it." The next entry occurs some months later—after she has run away from home and is at a low point in her life. Notice her language now and her attitudes toward herself and others.)

(?)

I don't know what the hell hour or day or even year it is, or even what town. I guess I've had a blackout or they've been passing some bad pills. The girl on the grass beside me is white-faced and Mona Lisa like and she's preggers. I asked her what she was going to do with the baby and she just said. "It will belong to everybody. We'll all share her."

I wanted to go and find someone who's holding, but the baby thing really bugged me. So I asked her for an upper and she just shook her head like a stupid, blank, and I realized that she's completely burned out. Behind that beautiful stoned face is a big dried-up bunch of ashes and she's lying there like a stupid dumb shit who can't do anything.

Well, at least I'm not burned out and I'm not preg. Or maybe I am. I couldn't take the goddamn pill even if I had it. No doper can take the pill because they don't know what the hell day it is. So maybe I am pregnant. So what. There's a pre-med drop out wandering around somewhere who will take care of it. Or maybe some goddamn prick would stomp on me during a freak out and I'd lose it anyway. Or maybe the son-of-a-bitch bomb will go off tomorrow. Who knows?

When I look around here at all the ass draggers, I really think that we are a bunch of gutless wonders. We get pissed off when someone tells us what to do, but we don't know what to do unless some fat bastard tells us. Let somebody else think for us and do for us and act for us. Let them build the roads and the cars and the houses, run the lights and the gas and the water and the sewers. We'll just sit here on our blistered tails with our minds exploding and our hands out. God, I sound like a goddamn Establishmentarian, and I haven't even got a pill to take the taste out of my mouth or drive the bullshit thoughts away.

(*This next writing occurs after a decision to return home and after a period of "drying out."*

Later

I have just read the stuff I wrote in the last few weeks and I am being drowned in my own tears, suffocated, submerged, inundated, overpowered. They are a lie! A bitter, evil cursed lie! I could never have written things like that! It was another

person, someone else! It must have been! It had to be! Someone evil and foul and degenerate wrote in my book, took over
my life. Yes, they did, they did! But even as I write I know I
am telling even a bigger lie! Or am I? Has my mind been
damaged? Was it really just a nightmare and it seems real?
I think I've mixed up things which are true and things which
are not. All of it couldn't be true. I must be insane.

I have lamented until I am dehydrated, but calling myself
a wretched fool, a beggarly, worthless, miserable, paltry,
mean, pitiful, unfortunate, woebegone, tormented, afflicted,
shabby, disreputable, deplorable human being isn't going to
help me either. I have two choices: I must either commit
suicide or try to rectify my life by helping others. That is the
path I must take, for I cannot bring further disgrace and suffering upon my family. There is nothing more to say, dear
Diary, except I love you, and I love life and I love God. Oh
I do. I really do.

*(Did you notice the language in the above entry? What
attitudinal changes were evident? The entry came after
a period of "drying out." The next several entries occur
after a flash-back that sends her to a hospital. Note that
she hallucinates that her body is being eaten by worms,
a reflection over her grandfather's death.*

(?)

My dear precious friend,

I am so grateful that they would let Mom bring you to me
in your padlocked little case. I was terribly embarrassed when
the nurse made me use the combination and dump both of
you out and my extra pencils and pens. But I guess they
were just being careful and checking to see that you weren't
filled with drugs of one sort or another. I don't even feel real.
I must be somebody else. I still can't believe that this has
actually happened to me. The window is filled with heavy
wires, I guess that is better than bars but I still know that I
am in some kind of hospital jail.

I have tried to piece the whole thing together but I can't.

The nurses and doctors keep telling me I will feel better, but I still can't get straight. I can't close my eyes because the worms are still crawling on me. They are eating me. They are crawling through my nose and gnawing in my mouth and oh God . . . I must get off my bleeding writhing hands into your pages. I will lock you in. You will be safe.

(?)

I am feeling better today. They took the bandages off my hands and changed them and it is no wonder they hurt so much. The whole ends of my fingers have been torn off and two nails have been pulled out completely and the others are torn down almost in half. It hurts to write, but I shall lose my mind if I do not. I wish I could write to Joel, but what could I ever tell him and besides no one could ever read this scrawling since both hands are bandaged like boxing gloves. I am still crawling with worms, but I am beginning to be able to live with them, or am I actually dead and they are just experimenting with my soul?

(?)

The worms are eating away my female parts first. They have almost entirely eaten away my vagina and my breasts and now they are working on my mouth and throat. I wish the doctors and nurses would let my soul die, but they are still experimenting with trying to reunite the body and the spirit.

(?)

Today I woke up feeling rational and sound. I guess the bummer is over. The nurse says I have been here ten days, and when I read back what I have written I really must have been out of it.

The bummer was over and soon her father was able to take her home. She was on the way to recovery but some-

thing happened. No one knows whether it was an over-dose or what, but her parents came home and found her unconscious; she died within a few hours.

Go Ask Alice is a simple story told in a straightforward manner; it would be difficult not to become emotionally involved in her life as you read it. Some literature is so complex and abstract that the meaning is very difficult to find. The following excerpt from Samuel Beckett's, How It Is, is a graphic example. Devoid of any punctuation, involved in its structure and its imagery, it will seem on first reading to have no meaning at all. However, careful analysis and attention to changes in thoughts and mood will reveal a theme. Then you can phrase the thoughts to form a focus and convey the meaning you see in the selection. To each of several readers, the meaning may be somewhat different. This is a case where creativity of analysis will be necessary in order to express the creativity of an author's complex work.

From

How It Is

Samuel Beckett

I learn it natural order more or less before Pim with Pim vast tracts of time how it was my vanished life then after then now after Pim how it is my life bits and scraps

I say it my life as it comes natural order my lips move I can feel them it comes out in the mud my life what remains ill-said ill-recaptured when the panting stops ill-murmured to the mud in the present all that things so ancient natural order the journey the couple the abandon all that in the present barely audible bits and scraps

I have journeyed found Pim lost Pim it's over that life those periods of that life first second now third pant pant the panting stops and I hear barely audible how I journey with my sack my tins in the dark the mud crawl in an amble towards

Pim unwitting bits and scraps in the present things so ancient hear them murmur them as they come barely audible to the mud

part one before Pim the journey it can't last it lasts I'm calm calmer you think you're calm and you're not in the lowest depths and you're on the edge I say it as I hear it and that death death if it ever comes that's all it dies

it dies and I see a crocus in a pot in an area in a basement a saffron the sun creeps up the wall a hand keeps it in the sun this yellow flower with a string I see the hand long image hours long the sun goes the pot goes down lights on the ground the hand goes the wall goes

rags of life in the light I hear and don't deny don't believe don't say any more who is speaking that's not said any more it must have ceased to be of interest but words like now before Pim no no that's not said only mine my words mine alone one or two soundless brief movements all the lower no sound when I can that's the difference great confusion

I see all sizes life included if that's mine the light goes on in the mud the prayer the head on the table the crocus the old man in tears the tears behind the hands skies all sorts different sorts on land and sea blue of a sudden gold and green of the earth of a sudden in the mud

but words like now words not mine before Pim no no that's not said that's the difference I hear it between then and now one of the differences among the similarities

the words of Pim his extorted voice he stops I step in all the needful he starts again I could listen to him for ever but mine have done with mine natural order before Pim the little I say no sound the little I see of a life I don't deny don't believe but what believe the sack perhaps the dark the mud death perhaps to wind up with after so much life there are moments

Study the following poems. Use the three keys to emotional involvement in each case. Discuss their meaning in class or with friends. Your own understanding and appreciation will increase as you do.

My Last Duchess

Ferrara

Robert Browning

That's my last Duchess painted on the wall,
Looking as if she were alive. I call
That piece a wonder, now: Fra Pandolf's hands
Worked busily a day, and there she stands.
Will't please you sit and look at her? I said
"Frà Pandolf" by design, for never read
Strangers like you that pictured countenance,
The depth and passion of its earnest glance,
But to myself they turned (since none puts by
The curtain I have drawn for you, but I)
And seemed as they would ask me, if they durst,
How such a glance came there; so, not the first
Are you to turn and ask thus. Sir, 'twas not
Her husband's presence only, called that spot
Of joy into the Duchess' cheek; perhaps
Frà Pandolf chanced to say, "Her mantle laps
Over my lady's wrist too much," or "Paint
Must never hope to reproduce the faint
Half-flush that dies along her throat." Such stuff
Was courtesy, she thought, and cause enough
For calling up that spot of joy. She had
A heart—how shall I say?—too soon made glad,
Too easily impressed; she liked whate'er
She looked on, and her looks went everywhere.
Sir, 'twas all one! My favor at her breast,
The dropping of the daylight in the West,
The bough of cherries some officious fool
Broke in the orchard for her, the white mule
She rode with round the terrace—all and each
Would draw from her alike the approving speech,
Or blush, at least. She thanked men,—good! but thanked
Somehow—I know not how—as if she ranked
My gift of a nine-hundred-years-old name
With anybody's gift. Who'd stoop to blame

This sort of trifling? Even had you skill
In speech   (Which I have not)—to make your will
Quite clear to such an one, and say, "Just this
Or that in you disgusts me; here you miss,
Or there exceed the mark"—and if she let
Herself be lessoned so, nor plainly set
Her wits to yours, forsooth, and made excuse,
—E'en then would be some stooping: and I choose
Never to stoop. Oh, sir, she smiled, no doubt,
Whene'er I passed her; but who passed without
Much the same smile? This grew; I gave commands;
Then all smiles stopped together. There she stands
As if alive. Will't please you rise? We'll meet
The company below then. I repeat,
The Count your master's known munificence
Is ample warrant that no just pretense
Of mine for dowry will be disallowed;
Though his fair daughter's self, as I avowed
At starting, is my object. Nay, we'll go
Together down, sir. Notice Neptune, though,
Taming a sea-horse, thought a rarity,
Which Claus of Innsbruck cast in bronze for me!

Indian Love Letter

Soge Track

Lady of the crescent moon
tonight I look at the sky
You are not there
You are not mad at me, are you?
"You are angry at the people,
Yes, I know."
                they are changing
                be not too hard
If you were taken to
the mission school,

not because you wanted,
but someone thought it best for you
you too would change.

They came out of nowhere
telling us how to eat our food
how to build our homes
how to plant our crops.
Need I say more of what they did?
All is new—the old ways are nothing.
                they are changing
                be not too hard

I talk to them
they turn their heads.
Do not be hurt—you have me
I live by the old ways
I will not change.

Tonight—my prayer plumes in hand
with the white shell things—
to the silent place I will go
(It is for you I go, please be there.)
Oh! Lady of the crescent moon
with the corn-silk hair—I love you
      they are changing
      be not too hard.

Dover Beach

Matthew Arnold

The sea is calm tonight.
The tide is full, the moon lies fair
Upon the straits;—on the French coast the light
Gleams and is gone; the cliffs of England stand,
Glimmering and vast, out in the tranquil bay.
Come to the window, sweet is the night air!
Only, from the long line of spray
Where the sea meets the moon-blanch'd land,

Listen! you hear the grating roar
Of pebbles which the waves draw back, and fling,
At their return, up the high strand,
Begin, and cease, and then again begin,
With tremulous cadence slow, and bring
The eternal note of sadness in.
Sophocles long ago
Heard it on the Aegean, and it brought
Into his mind the turbid ebb and flow
Of human misery; we
Find also in the sound a thought,
Hearing it by this distant northern sea.

The Sea of Faith
Was once, too, at the full, and round earth's shore
Lay like the folds of a bright girdle furl'd.
But now I only hear
Its melancholy, long, withdrawing roar,
Retreating, to the breath
Of the night-wind, down the vast edges drear
And naked shingles of the world.

Ah, love, let us be true
To one another! for the world, which seems
To lie before us like a land of dreams,
So various, so beautiful, so new,
Hath really neither joy, nor love, nor light,
Nor certitude, nor peace, nor help for pain;
And we are here as on a darkling plain
Swept with confused alarms of struggle and flight,
Where ignorant armies clash by night.

Come Up From the Fields, Father

Walt Whitman

Come up from the fields, father, here's a letter from our Pete,
And come to the front door, mother—here's a letter from thy
    dear son.

Lo, 'tis autumn;
Lo, where the trees, deeper green, yellower and redder,
Cool and sweeten Ohio's villages, with leaves fluttering in the
    moderate wind;
Where apples ripe in the orchards hang, and grapes on the
    trellised vines;
(Smell you the smell of the grapes on the vines?
Smell you the buckwheat, where the bees were lately
    buzzing?)
Above all, lo, the sky, so calm, so transparent after the rain,
    and with wondrous clouds;
Below, too, all calm, all vital and beautiful—and the farm
    prospers well.

Down in the fields all prospers well;
But now from the fields come, father—come at the daughter's
    call;
And come to the entry, mother—to the front door come right
    away.
Fast as she can she hurries—something ominous—her steps
    trembling;
She does not tarry to smooth her hair, nor adjust her cap.
Open the envelope quickly;
O this is not our son's writing, yet his name is signed;
O a strange hand writes for our dear son—O stricken mother's
    soul!
All swims before her eyes—flashes with black—
    she catches the main words only;
Sentences broken—*gun-shot wound in the breast,*
    cavalry skirmish, taken to hospital,
At present low, but will soon be better.

Ah, now the single figure to me,
Amid all teeming and wealthy Ohio, with all its cities and
    farms,
Sickly white in the face, and dull in the head, very faint,
By the jamb of a door leans.
Grieve not so, dear mother, (the just-grown daughter speaks
    through her sobs;
The little sisters huddle around, speechless and dismay'd;)
See, dearest mother, the letter says Pete will soon be better.

Alas, poor boy, he will never be better (nor maybe needs to
  be better, that bravo and simple soul,)
While they stand at home at the door, he is dead already;
The only son is dead.
But the mother needs to be better;
She, with thin form, presently drest in black;
By day her meals untouch'd—then at night fitfully sleeping,
  often waking,
In the midnight waking, weeping, longing with one deep
  longing,
O that she might withdraw unnoticed—silent from life,
  escape and withdraw,
To follow, to seek, to be with her dear dead son.

The Parting

Michael Drayton

Since there's no help, come let us kiss and part—
Nay, I have done, you get no more of me;
And I am glad, yea, glad with all my heart,
That thus so clearly I myself can free.
Shake hands for ever, cancel all our vows,
And when we meet at any time again,
Be it not seen in either of our brows
That we one jot of former love retain.
Now at the last gasp of Love's latest breath,
When, his pulse failing, Passion speechless lies,
When Faith is kneeling by his bed of death,
And Innocence is closing up his eyes,
    —Now if thou wouldst, when all have given him over,
    From death to life thou might'st him yet recover.

SUMMARY

At the very center of oral interpretation is emotional involvement
in the material you are going to read. There are three keys to letting
yourself go —becoming involved:

The first key is *empathy*—feeling with the author and the characters in the selection.

The second key is *experience,* primary and vicarious. Call upon your past experience for help in becoming involved.

The third key is *finding the meaning.* Define unfamiliar words both connotatively and denotatively. Read the entire selection. Discover the author's purpose in writing the piece. Identify the mood. Learn what you can of the life of the author and his times.

EXERCISES

If you have trouble letting yourself go, role-playing is a device that will help you get involved. Try the exercises below.

The important thing with such exercises is not to feel silly doing them. Also, remember the physiological changes within your body with each emotion. The faster heartbeat, the short breaths, for fear; the exhilarating singing of your nerves, the lightness, when you feel happy; the tenseness, the blood rushing to your face, the feeling of everything inside building to a peak, when you feel anger; the sense of peace and relaxation, the confidence, when you are experiencing a quiet moment of real contentment.

1. Create a feeling of personal injustice. Your professor has just failed you in a course that you felt you had honestly passed. You feel he is putting into play his prejudices against you and you march into his office to protest.

2. A feeling of happiness is also part of our life. Suppose you are going to the airport to meet someone whom you have wanted to see for a long, long time. Perhaps you are in love with this person. He—or she—walks into the airport smiling and rushes to you. What is your feeling?

3. You have probably felt frustrated. Try this situation: it is vitally important that you complete an important assignment before nine o'clock that night. Suddenly, some people drop by your house and you don't wish to be rude by asking them to leave. So you stick it out —and they stay and stay. By 8:30 you know you're not going to make it. How do you feel?

4. Picture anger in your mind. Say the words "I hate it!" over and over until you really experience the feeling. Then try saying "I love you" until you get the right feeling. Or think of a funny story you

heard recently and keep thinking of it until it again becomes funny to you. Then start laughing.

5. Now recall a very sad moment in your life. Relive it. Feel the lump coming in your throat, the tears into your eyes. Hold the feeling and soon you'll feel like crying. Let go and cry.

chapter six

Let me out of here!

Stage fright is a traumatic experience known to almost every individual. Even seasoned performers have experienced it—feverish brow, rapidly pulsating heart, cold, sweaty hands, dry mouth and throat, shaking hands and knees.

Some students are affected by it more than others. Some break into visible drops of perspiration; others have said they felt as though they were going to faint. Another remarked, "So this is what it's like to be a teacher." Still another commented, "My doctor suggested I drop the class to cure my nerves." On the other hand, there are individuals who seem to "breeze" through the situation without much more than a slight case of butterflies, a sensation that lasts only about a minute or two.

Many studies have been made on stage fright. Attention has been focused on the problem in psychological journals as well as in texts on acting and speech. And yet the problem remains—with no sure cure ever offered. Unfortunately, it is not possible to take a shot to prevent it.

Stage fright, to reiterate an old saying, is good up to a point. The extra shot of adrenalin and the nervousness often provide a spurt of energy that gives a reading more interest. This is no new theory. But it is a theory few students will believe.

They are more concerned with such things as: How do I get over the dry mouth? How do I stop shaking? Can't it ever be cured? Consequently, they live with it and find their reading effectiveness cut in half by the results—a fast pace in reading, a colorless and unfeeling presentation, a lack of variety, and a noticeable drop in projection and vitality.

From a survey conducted by the authors among 150 students of beginning speech in a first semester oral interpretation course, it was learned that the biggest reason for stage fright in a classroom situation is fear of not doing a good job. No one wants to embarrass himself in front of his peers. The second and third reasons, according to this survey, were the attitudes of the class and the instructor. The emphasis put on making a mistake ties in with the fear of class reaction. As for the attitude of the instructor, it was found that an instructor who is very formal, reserved, and highly critical creates a tense atmosphere that causes an increase of stage fright. It is for this reason that many professors purposely work for less formality as one key to better results from their students.

To enable the class to become a cohesive group is important. Consequently, it is wise for students to make it a point of getting to know each other as soon as possible in the semester. Association with fellow class members provides a feeling of "belonging" and significantly reduces tension.

CONTROLLING STAGE FRIGHT

There are differences of opinion on how to handle stage fright. Some teachers refuse to discuss it at all in their classes, believing that any discussion only magnifies the problem. Others feel that frank and open acknowledgment of it helps by showing the students that everyone is in the "same boat," that the class is anxious to compliment rather than criticize, and that concentration on fear makes it impossible to concentrate on the task before them—giving the reading—so that increased fear is all that results. The first criterion, then, in overcoming stage fright is to concentrate on the material rather than on yourself. This is the surest way to control nervousness.

You have a choice; you can devote your time, energies and emotions to "Oh, I'm so frightened," and end up a petrified specimen, or you can put your mind and energies into the process of bringing a reading to life. This latter theory adds considerable support to the premise that a student can "talk himself" into believing he will do a good job.

In classes where free choice of material is the rule, students should choose only selections in which they are vitally interested: doing so has proven to be a most effective control of stage fright because it enables the reader to involve himself more in his material than in his nerves.

One student walked to the stand each time for a reading practically frozen with fear. It was a physically exhausting effort for him to finish. One day, in a drama-reading assignment, he chose Edward Albee's *The Zoo Story*. Suddenly, he became "unfrozen." He brought the incisive irony and bitterness of the play into focus for the class. His body relaxed. His response to his material was complete, meaningful. He was a different person. When he was asked why he was able to handle this assignment so well, he simply said, "Because I liked the selection, I guess."

Another student who spoke softly and without any feeling found a different situation in the reading of James Thurber's "University Days." He liked the selection, and when he got his first laugh from his audience, a smile came over his face. One could see the tension drop away, and he went on to give a most accomplished reading—just because he had liked the material and had received that greatest cure of all for stage fright, a favorable visible and audible response from the audience.

The next criterion in overcoming stage fright is solid preparation. No one can feel secure interpreting a selection he has hurriedly prepared. Only when you have prepared thoroughly can you feel confident in your reading. When students were asked, in the survey mentioned earlier, what helped them to overcome stage fright, they overwhelmingly said preparation was the big factor.

Oral interpretation offers problems to a student which are not always found in other courses of speech. In a speech fundamentals course, for instance, the focus is on making arguments clear and in presenting material in an organized manner. True, there is emotional content, as in speeches of persuasion, but not to the extent found in oral interpretation. Discussion courses deal with group efforts, so there is far less concentration on any one individual. Oral interpretation not only focuses direct attention on the reader, but it also calls for him to project emotion. He must deal with comedy, drama, tragedy, farce, all the significant moods and emotions of literature. Some students may not find it difficult to deliver a speech, but many exhibit great reluctance to show any feeling. Let's face it—many people are taught not to show emotion. Because these students cannot express feeling, fear is increased. However, it is generally true that the student who is at ease in oral interpretation is at ease in all speech courses.

Stage fright is magnified in the minds of some students who are certain everyone can see how frightened they are. One student asked, "Didn't you see my face turning red?" When he was told that his face was not red, he could hardly believe it. Another convinced the entire class throughout his reading that he was completely at ease, but all he could say at the end was, "But I was scared stiff! I thought everyone noticed." So it does not pay to assume that your audience knows you are nervous; the chances are others see you as being in control. Generally, only you know how frightened you are. Don't prejudge yourself. In the same way, do not assume that everyone is thinking of your reading in a negative way. There is the distinct possibility that the audience will find your reading effective. In short, you cannot be critic and reader at the same time. If you split yourself in half in this way, the reading is bound to suffer. Be a critic during your rehearsals.

There are other criteria for controlling stage fright. One good way is to get in the habit of breathing properly. Try this experiment. Firmly grasp the stand or the side of your chair. Make your body rigid. Then take a deep breath from the diaphragm, loosen your hold, swing your arms back and forth and feel the release of tension, the tingling of the spine, the feeling of ease and peace settling over you. This is the way proper breathing helps. It is especially important to remember this when nerves are forcing you to race through a reading. Pause appropriately, breathe deeply, and then go on.

It is also important to take time to look at your audience; give them a chance to settle down before starting the reading. This extra pause will give you a chance to calm down, too. There are some students who feel they become more nervous when they look at an audience, but it has been our experience that those who remain glued to the manuscript only become more rigid with fear. Often a visible response from an audience will give a reader more confidence. By ignoring the audience, you miss this support; fear builds up inside of you. By looking at them, you share an experience with them, and in sharing you cease to be a figure standing alone while a crowd stares at you. Of course, there are some selections which make it difficult to use this direct contact. For instance, in an intimate poem, such as "How Do I Love Thee?", it would not be particularly apt to address the reading directly to individuals in the audience.

It has been the experience of the authors, based on the findings of the survey, that with the right atmosphere in a class, with *conscientious preparation,* over 75 percent of stage fright should be lessened by the end of four to six weeks. We have found that over 90 percent of our students are afflicted with stage fright at the beginning of a semester, but only 10 percent have not effectively learned to control it within six to nine weeks. The reason is more experience and the chance to read before a class often enough to gain some self-confidence. The type of material read also enters into this picture. Many students find that drama readings make them less nervous because they become more involved due to the conversational quality of the dialogue. Others find poetry moves them into another world of involvement.

Whatever techniques are used, it is important that students help themselves in the most significant way—preparation. Read your material to your family, to friends, to anyone who will listen so that you become used to reading orally. It is also a good idea to read aloud other class assignments, newspapers, even the comics, for experience. If you are prepared, you will feel more confident.

One last suggestion is to seek out the help offered by the instructor. Most instructors are only too glad to assist students with their problems, and it is the shortsighted person who prefers to try to exist with his problem rather than to get the assistance which can make him feel more secure.

It may seem blunt to say it, but you actually have two choices: to continue to build up stage fright and to make the reading process torture or to convince yourself that concentration on nervousness will bring only undesired results. Emphasis on "I can do it" and on the material itself will insure self-satisfaction, pride in accomplishment, and a relaxed feeling which will make reading a pleasure. Then you will begin to believe in yourself.

Stage fright is up to you. What are you afraid of? Class censure? Classmates are your biggest supporters. Making a mistake? You are in class to make mistakes and to learn how to correct them. Attitude of the instructor? It is a rare case indeed when a teacher enjoys seeing a student do a bad job. Fear of doing a poor reading? Prepare—so you won't. You're probably a lot better than you think you are.

One thing is certain—oral Interpretation will bring changes in you that will remain with you all of your life. Don't minimize the experience by concentrating on your nerves.

SUMMARY

There are methods to help you gain control over stage fright:

1. Concentrate on the material and not on your nerves.
2. Believe in yourself.
3. Don't try to be critic and reader at the same time. What you may think to be a bad reading may be considered your best.
4. Breathe properly to relieve tension.
5. Look at your audience—they are your biggest support.
6. Read only material *you like.*
7. Prepare—long and often.
8. Read to anyone who will listen to you.
9. Remember the class is in "the same boat."

10. Get to know your classmates *early.*
11. Get help from your instructor.
12. Ask yourself: "What will I gain by thinking of fright so much?"
13. Don't be afraid of making a mistake.
14. Don't assume everyone thinks you look nervous.

You *can* control stage fright.

chapter seven

What do I do
with my voice?

You have a voice that is unique to yourself; it is part of the basic equipment that comes with your particular model when you are born. No one has an opportunity to order the deluxe model with ideal resonance and superior quality.

There's no trade-in value either, so a good attitude with which to begin a study of voice is shown in the question, "This is my voice; what can I do to improve it?"

Think of the person—man or woman—who has an ideal voice. What is it about this person's voice that makes you say it is ideal? Is it the pitch, quality, volume, resonance, articulation, or rate that you enjoy? Or is it all of these working in combination?

There is no single *ideal* voice! Be thankful that there is not. But the person you think of as having an *ideal* voice probably has worked to make his voice as effective as possible through manipulation of those variables listed above.

It is not necessary that you learn all of the anatomy of voice in order to improve your voice or to use it well, but you should learn, generally, how sound is produced.

Before you can make sound, even noise, a supply of air is necessary, so voice actually begins with breathing. Air from the lungs is forced upward through the vocal cords and out through the mouth and nose. Thus the lungs and diaphragm, working together to supply the air, become the motor of voice. How to breathe correctly is treated fully in Chapter Eight so it will suffice for now to say that correct breathing is a necessary first step in making effective use of your voice.

However, you should be aware that no part of the vocal anatomy has the production of voice (or sound) as its primary function. The primary function of breathing, for example, is to supply air for the oxygenation of the cells of the body; the fact is that man has devised a way of using the same supply of air for the production of sound.

What happens to the supply of air, stored in the lungs and controlled in its exhalation by the diaphragm, as it makes its way through the throat and out the mouth and nose determines whether the "voice" that is produced is a whisper or a shout and whether its pitch is high or low, and again what its quality will be. What happens with resonators and articulators determines whether the "speech" produced is deep or shallow, clear or cloudy. But first we must consider how sound is produced from this flow of air. The voice box, or *larynx,* is located in the throat at the point of the Adam's apple. You can locate it by placing your thumb on one side of the Adam's apple and forefinger on the other in a loose "pinching" manner. If you hum, you can feel the vibration.

Here again, the primary function of the larynx is to act as a valve, to keep food particles and other foreign objects out of the bronchial tubes and lungs. You know what happens when you swallow something and it "goes down the wrong way"—you cough. And you cough until the object is expelled. The system man devised of vibrating the cords with a flow of air is called *phonation.*

The opening between the two cords is greater when normal breathing is going on, and the cords are stretched tightly when phonation is in process. When you whisper, the cords tighten somewhat but not so tightly as in phonation. The cords do not vibrate during a whisper any more than they do during normal breathing or any more than they do during a sigh; thus the whisper depends on the articulators (lips, teeth, tongue, etc.) rather than on phonation for communication. The tighter the cords are stretched, the higher the note that is produced.

The sound that is produced by the vibration of the vocal cords will differ from person to person according to the length and thickness of the cords. While you should not think of the vocal cords as strings (they are more like lips), they can be compared with the strings of a guitar, in regard to length and thickness, vibrating to produce sound. The thin strings on a guitar produce the higher notes. They have less density and can be stretched more. The strings that produce the lower notes are thicker and have greater density. The order of the strings, in terms of length, also parallels that of the vocal cords. If you place your finger on a string high up on the neck of the instrument and slide it downward toward the body while sound is being produced there will be a rise in the pitch of the sound the string makes. The notes produced will become higher as the string being vibrated becomes shorter. Thus vocal cords that are thicker and longer will produce lower notes; vocal cords that are thinner and shorter will produce higher notes and, therefore, a higher voice. It might be said, then, that a man generally has thicker and longer vocal cords than a woman.

As the sound waves produced by the vibrating vocal folds travel upward through the throat and out the mouth and nose, they are *amplified* by the resonators. Amplified means that the sound waves act on the walls of the throat, mouth, and nose and on the cavities of the throat and head in such a way that there are additional vibrations in each of them and the sound produced is intensified or enlarged. In a sense, the sound is made larger rather than louder.

The final process affecting the sound is articulation. As the enlarged waves enter the mouth and nose and as they leave them, they are acted upon by the tongue, teeth, hard and soft palates, and lips, which divide them into words and shape them into appropriate utterances.

The resultant sound has a unique and distinctive *quality* which is identifiable with the person who originates it. It is this uniqueness that we call vocal quality. Your vocal quality is determined by the modifications that your amplification system works upon the sound wave produced by your vocal cords. One person can affect an approximation of another person's voice by concentrating on his quality. A good mimic can give an approximation of any number of famous people. President Kennedy was one who was imitated widely because his vocal quality was so interesting. James Cagney, Edward G. Robinson, George Raft, and Humphrey Bogart are other oft-imitated, easily identifiable personalities.

In several instances, criminals have been convicted of a crime largely on the basis of their *voice print* taken from a recording of their voices—particularly their vocal quality.

You can't substitute the quality of your voice for another, nor can you alter the quality of your voice tremendously, but you can work to improve it through more effective manipulation of the variables treated in this chapter. You are now ready to analyze and evaluate your voice in terms of some of the common problems or faulty uses of voice.

PROBLEMS IN THE USE OF VOLUME

The most easily identifiable problem of voice in interpretation centers around volume, the force of the air flow over the vocal cords. Beginning students oftentimes use too little force, which results in too little volume. Or they will use too constant a flow of air, thus creating a monotonous volume. In some instances the force of air is consistently too great; the result is a voice that is too loud, that *blasts* the audience.

Problems of volume are as easily solved as they are identified, however. Most often a person who uses too little volume has been told that he has inherited a weak voice, or he has grown up in a family in which any amount of loudness is considered rude. It is usually easy to point out to the first person that his voice is not weak but that he is making weak use of it. For the other person mentioned, it is typically sufficient treatment to point out that when one converses with three or four people at a time volume is not a problem, but when one faces an audience of larger numbers, volume must be increased to meet the demand. Those who cannot hear the presentation certainly can have no appreciation of it.

A good rule of thumb to follow in determining the amount of volume to use in a given situation is to try out your voice in the room before the time of your performance. Test the room for its ability to carry your voice. If possible, have a friend sit in the back of the room and signal to you when your volume is in the right range. Then when you are performing, watch the faces of various members of the audience to see that they are not having to strain to hear.

PROBLEMS IN THE USE OF PITCH

We have discussed how phonation takes place. Pitch is determined by the frequency of vibration of the vocal cords. Just as there are habits of dress, there are habits that we fall into regarding pitch. The pitch or tone of voice that you most commonly use is said to be your *habitual pitch*. The highest and lowest note you can reach mark the boundaries of your *pitch range*. The mid-point between the two notes identifies what is known as your most desirable or *optimum pitch*. In order to find your optimum level, try this exercise. Using the "ah" sound in a sharp, staccato manner, say "ah" in a low register and gradually, with slight pauses between notes, go up the scale. The note which seems the most comfortable to you is your optimum pitch; it is usually a note and a half below your habitual pitch. If your optimum pitch is the most suitable or desirable pitch for your voice, then practice should make it possible for you to make your habitual pitch and your optimum pitch the same.

You might notice that your voice is lower when you practice reading a selection than it is when you read in front of a group. We can look at the performance situation for the answer. In practice you are relaxed and alone; your throat and neck are also relaxed. When you are in performance, your throat and neck tighten with the rest of your body, if you experience stage fright, and your voice rises in pitch. Many beginning students have a problem with letting their pitch get too high. It takes practice and experience to keep the throat relaxed and open so that the desired pitch is achieved.

To determine whether or not you have a tight throat, use a tape recorder in several practice sessions and tape your voice again when you are in performance before an audience. Compare the several practice sessions with the performance and see if you or your friends can detect a rise in pitch. If you have a marked problem your instructor will undoubtedly point it out to you. A tape recorder is indispensable in overcoming pitch faults.

A second fault in the use of pitch and even more common than high pitch is a monotonous, unvaried pitch—a monotone. No aspect of voice will rob your reading of vitality and life more quickly than a monotonous repetition of the same pitch. Again, lack of emotional involvement, preparation, and stage fright are the culprits.

Try the following lines by Helen Keller in each of these two ways: First, read them in a monotone; work consciously to give the ideas meaning but keep the pitch constant. You will quickly see that without variety of pitch for emphasis, meaning is lost or at least badly distorted.

Now and then I have tested my seeing friends to discover what they see. Recently I was visited by a very good friend who had just returned from a long walk in the woods, and I asked her what she had observed. "Nothing in particular," she replied. . . . How was it possible, I asked myself, to walk for an hour through the woods and see nothing worthy of note? I who cannot see find hundreds of things to interest me through mere touch. I feel the delicate symmetry of a leaf. I pass my hands lovingly about the smooth skin of a silver birch or the rough shaggy bark of a pine.

Read the lines again and experiment with pitch. Another name for pitch is melody, so this time vary the melody—let it identify Miss Keller's enthusiasm and zest for living. Let your use of pitch reflect a positive, happy attitude toward life and vision. The essay these lines were taken from appears in its entirety in Chapter 10. Read the entire essay for a full appreciation of her ideas on the importance of *seeing* what we see.

A third fault in the use of pitch needs attention. It is identified in the voice that sends sentence after sentence running down hill like this:

<pre>
I asked   I feel
     her   the delicate
         what   symmetry of
             she had   a leaf.
                 observed.
</pre>

Again, a tape recorder will help in overcoming this reading fault. Interpreters who read in a pitch pattern are typically not aware of their problem. A tape recording of the voice quickly identifies the habit, and conscientious practice will eliminate it. Practice should include reading in a variety of new patterns, always in relationship to the meaning of the material itself, until the old pattern has been brought under control. Before long the old habit will disappear, and a voice with more vitality will take its place.

FAULTY USE OF RESONANCE

The only common fault that centers around resonance is too little use of the resonators. The fault is often called a tight throat or pinched throat and results in a voice that is thin and weak. The throat and mouth are the primary resonating cavities of the voice with the nasal cavity influencing primarily the *m, n,* and *ng* sounds. If the throat and lower jaw are tense and the mouth is dry, the resonating cavities are reduced in size and effectiveness; the voice produced doesn't get proper amplification. The point was made earlier in the chapter that it isn't the voice that is weak; rather, it is that poor use is being made of the resonators. Practice some isometrics for opening these cavities so that they can work more effectively in their amplifying function. Isometrics is a system of exercises that put strain on particular muscles and then follow the period of strain or tension with a period of relaxation. To work for more control in relaxation of the throat and neck and mouth try this: While standing in a comfortable, but erect, position with your weight balanced on the balls of both feet, let your lower jaw drop down as far as it will without force; now yawn and you will feel the throat and mouth enlarge. While still in this position sigh quietly several times.

Next, close your mouth, grit your teeth, and tighten the neck muscles —even hunching your shoulders if necessary to put tension on the throat and mouth. Make the cavities of throat and mouth as small as you can. Hold the tension for a few seconds, then relax and repeat the yawn and sigh. The purpose of this exercise is to gain sufficient control over the muscles that tense the throat and mouth that you can relax them at will, particularly when you feel them tensing up during a reading.

You will notice that you can't repeat the above exercise more than a couple of times in succession without feeling real tiredness in the throat and lower jaw. This is ready evidence of the need for relaxation of these muscles when you are in a performance situation. The full use of the resonating chambers with consequent amplification of the vocal tone serves many purposes in reading, among which is the establishment of character. For example, the voice of the ghost of Hamlet's father is often augmented on stage with mechanical amplification, such as the "echo-chamber" technique, but the same effect can be achieved with the full use of the resonators. Practice the following scene, paying close attention to the vividly descriptive words and images in the dialogue and the necessarily wide range of voice. Keep in mind the necessity of achieving a ghostly, unearthly, eerie vocal impression of this extra-worldly character.

Hamlet

William Shakespeare

GHOST

Ay, that incestuous, that adulterate beast,
With witchcraft of his wit, with traitorous gifts,—
O wicked wit and gifts, that have the power
So to seduce!—won to his shameful lust
The will of my most seeming-virtuous queen:
O Hamlet, what a falling-off was there!
From me, whose love was of that dignity
That it went hand in hand even with the vow
I made to her in marriage; and to decline
Upon a wretch, whose natural gifts were poor
To those of mine!
But virtue, as it never will be moved,

Though lewdness court it in a shape of heaven,
So lust, though to a radiant angel link'd,
Will sate itself in a celestial bed
And prey on garbage.
But, soft! methinks I scent the morning air;
Brief let me be. Sleeping within my orchard,
My custom always of the afternoon,
Upon my secure hour thy uncle stole,
With juice of cursed hebenon in a vial,
And in the porches of my ears did pour
The leperous distilment; whose effect
Holds such an enmity with blood of man
That swift as quicksilver it courses through
The natural gates and alleys of the body;
And with a sudden vigour it doth posset
And curd, like eager droppings into milk,
The thin and wholesome blood: so did it mine;
And a most instant tetter bark'd about,
Most lazar-like, with vile and loathsome crust,
All my smooth body.
Thus was I, sleeping, by a brother's hand
Of life, of crown, of queen, at once dispatch'd:
Cut off even in the blossoms of my sin,
Unhousel'd, disappointed, unaneled;
No reckoning made, but sent to my account
With all my imperfections on my head:
O, horrible! O, horrible! most horrible!
If thou hast nature in thee, bear it not;
Let not the royal bed of Denmark be
A couch for luxury and damned incest.
But, howsoever thou pursuest this act,
Taint not thy mind, nor let thy soul contrive
Against thy mother aught: leave her to heaven,
And to those thorns that in her bosom lodge,
To prick and sting her. Fare thee well at once!
The glow-worm shows the matin to be near,
And 'gins to pale his uneffectual fire:
Adieu, adieu, adieu! remember me.
[Exit]

FAULTY USE OF ARTICULATORS

The faults spoken of thus far have centered in one way or another around voice. When we examine the faulty use of the articulators, the lips, teeth, tongue, and soft palate, we are not concerned with voice but with speech. The articulators are used to divide the voice stream into speech sounds and into words—language. Faulty use of these articulators, then, must center around clarity. Any speech sound which draws attention to itself and, therefore, away from the ideas being expressed is faulty in that situation or location. Diction fault, or faulty pronunciation, arises from the regional nature of our American English. It isn't a problem that is limited to America by any means; a Southern Frenchman has difficulty communicating with a Parisian, and a cockney has difficulty with people of other regions of England. But this problem can't be helped without sufficient time to "localize" pronunciation, and other problems—faulty articulation—can be improved immediately with practice and concentration. Of course, the fault referred to here is casual or slovenly pronunciation of words. *Doin', thinkin', nuttin', sompin', fergit,* are examples. It is advisable to choose as a standard for effective pronunciation people in your community who are experienced in the use of language—ministers, educators, business leaders—and pattern your pronunciation after theirs.

Occasionally (rarely) a student will need to work for a less precise pattern of pronunciation than he is used to in order not to have attention drawn to his speech. An affected or too precise diction is distracting to an audience if it is inappropriate to the literature being read.

The tape recorder is of immense value in solving articulation problems.

FAULTY TYPES OF VOCAL QUALITY

It is possible that the problems discussed in this section are due to physical difficulties. If it is said that your voice is hoarse, harsh, nasal, or breathy, you would do well to have a physical check-up before starting any comprehensive program of improvement. For the larger number of students, though, problems of vocal quality are a result of improper vocal habits. Or at least the student can improve his vocal quality by first learning what the problems are and then working to reduce or eliminate them.

Hoarseness

The most common cause of hoarseness is overuse of the voice or unusual strain on it. A cold or sore throat might also be the cause. A neglected throat infection may well lead to permanently damaged vocal folds and thus a husky or hoarse vocal quality. Whatever the cause of the hoarseness, the vocal lips become swollen and irritated from rubbing together, and, therefore, vibrate less rapidly in phonation; hoarseness results in a raspy, unpleasant quality. If illness or throat infection is apparent, medical treatment is in order. In many instances, of course, hoarseness may be a valuable asset to the establishing of characters. In some works of literature, characters appear who by their very nature have and need a harsh, husky, brusque voice. Yank, in Eugene O'Neill's, *The Hairy Ape,* is one example. The following scene from Shakespeare's *King Henry IV —Part I,* is typical of this voice quality. Falstaff is a robust character who lives life heartily, who loves a fight and whose vitality is seemingly limitless. His imposing physical size also accentuates the character of the man.

From

King Henry IV—Part I

William Shakespeare

FALSTAFF

If I be not ashamed of my soldiers, I am a soused gurnet. I have misused the king's press damnably. I have got, in exchange of a hundred and fifty soldiers, three hundred and odd pounds. I press me none but good householders, yeomen's sons; inquire me out contracted bachelors, such as had been asked twice on the banns; such a commodity of warm slaves, as had as lieve hear the devil as a drum; such as fear the report of a caliver worse than a struck fowl or a hurt wild-duck. I pressed me none but such toasts-and-butter, with hearts in their bellies no bigger than pins'-heads, and they have bought out their services; and now my whole charge consists of ancients, corporals, lieutenants, gentlemen of companies, slaves as ragged as Lazarus in the painted cloth, where the glutton's dogs licked his sores; and such as indeed were never soldiers, but discarded unjust serving-men, younger sons to younger brothers, revolted tapsters, and ostlers trade-fallen; the cankers of a calm world and a long peace, ten times more dishonourable ragged than an old faced ancient: and such have I, to fill up the rooms of them that have bought out their services, that you would think that I had a hundred and fifty tattered prodigals lately come from swine-keeping, from eating draff and husks. A mad fellow met me on the way and told me I had unloaded all the gibbets and pressed the dead bodies. No eye hath seen such scarecrows. I'll not march through Coventry with them, that's flat: nay, and the villains march wide betwixt the legs, as if they had gyves on; for indeed I had the most of them out of prison. There's but a shirt and a half in all my company; and the half shirt is two napkins tacked together and thrown over the shoulders like a herald's coat without sleeves; and the shirt, to say the truth, stolen from my host at Saint Alban's, or the red-nose inn-keeper of Daventry. But that's all one; they'll find linen enough on every hedge.

Harshness-Stridency

Voices with a metallic or shrill quality are said to be strident or harsh. The problem in this case is strain on the vocal cords themselves. They are stretched too tightly during phonation and the result is a tone or quality that isn't fully developed. This voice is characteristic of the highly nervous individual who is easily irritated and quick to let everyone know it. He is a whiner as a male, a nag as a female. A good example of stridency in a woman is found in the character of Liza in *Pygmalion* by George Bernard Shaw. Liza's voice, like the screech of an angry alleycat, accentuates her background, her job as a hawker of flowers, and the people with whom she associates. In this excerpt from *Pygmalion,* note the manner in which Shaw's dialogue accentuates this vocal quality.

From

Pygmalion

George Bernard Shaw

HIGGINS: Come back to business. How much do you propose to pay me for the lessons?

LIZA. Oh, I know whats right. A lady friend of mine gets French lessons for eighteenpence an hour from a real French gentleman. Well, you wouldnt have the face to ask me the same for teaching me my own language as you would for French; so I wont give more than a shilling. Take it or leave it.

HIGGINS: [*Walking up and down the room, rattling his keys and his cash in his pockets*] You know, Pickering, if you consider a shilling, not as a simple shilling, but as a percentage of this girl's income, it works out as fully equivalent to sixty or seventy guineas from a millionaire.

PICKERING.   How so?

HIGGINS: Figure it out. A millionaire has about £150 a day. She earns about half-a-crown.

LIZA: [*haughtily*] Who told you I only—

HIGGINS: [*continuing*] She offers me\two-fifths of her day's income for a lesson. Two-fifths of a millionaire's income for a day would be somewhere about £60. It's handsome. By George, it's enormous! it's the biggest offer I ever had.

LIZA: [*rising, terrifi*ed] Sixty pounds! What are you talking about? I never offered you sixty pounds. Where would I get—

HIGGINS: Hold your tongue.

LIZA: [*weeping*] But I aint got sixty pounds. Oh—

MRS PEARCE: Dont cry, you silly girl. Sit down. Nobody is going to touch your money.

HIGGINS: Somebody is going to touch you, with a broom-
stick, if you dont stop snivelling. Sit down.

LIZA: [obeying slowly] Ah-ah-ah-ow-oo-o! One would think
you was my father.

HIGGINS: If I decide to teach you, I'll be worse than two
fathers to you. Here [he offers her his silk handkerchief]!

LIZA: What's this for?

HIGGINS: To wipe your eyes. To wipe any part of your face
that feels moist. Remember: thats your handkerchief; and
thats your sleeve. Dont mistake the one for the other if
you wish to become a lady in a shop.
Liza, utterly bewildered, stares helplessly at him.

MRS PEARCE: It's no use talking to her like that, Mr Higgins:
she doesnt understand you. Besides, youre quite wrong: she
doesnt do it that way at all [she takes the handkerchief]

LIZA: [snatching it] Here! You give me that handkerchief.
He give it to me, not to you.

PICKERING: [laughing] He did. I think it must be regarded
as her property, Mrs Pearce.

MRS PEARCE: [resigning herself] Serve you right, Mr Higgins.

PICKERING: Higgins: I'm interested. What about the ambassador's garden party? I'll say youre the greatest teacher
alive if you make that good. I'll bet you all the expenses of
the experiment you cant do it. And I'll pay for the lessons.

LIZA.   Oh, you are real good. Thank you, Captain.

HIGGINS: [tempted, looking at her] It's almost irresistible.
She's so deliciously low—so horribly dirty—

LIZA: [protesting extremely] Ah-ah-ah-ah-ow-ow-oo-oo!!! I
aint dirty: I washed my face and hands afore I come, I did.

The type of voice fault that Liza illustrates can be corrected with
conscientious effort. *Pygmalion* makes this point in the transforma-
tion in Liza from the above scene to the example below which occurs
near the end of the play. Liza, after much training, speaks with a new
refinement and with a beautifully modulated voice.

LIZA: [much troubled] I want a little kindness. I know I'm a
common ignorant girl, and you a book-learned gentleman;

but I'm not dirt under your feet. What I done [*correcting herself*] what I did was not for the dresses and the taxis: I did it because we were pleasant together and I come— came—to care for you; not to want you to make love to me, and not forgetting the difference between us, but more friendly like.

HIGGINS: Well, of course. That's just how I feel. And how Pickering feels. Eliza: youre a fool.

LIZA: That's not a proper answer to give me [*she sinks on the chair at the writing-table in tears*].

HIGGINS: It's all youll get until you stop being a common idiot. If youre going to be a lady, youll have to give up feeling neglected if the men you know dont spend half their time snivelling over you and the other half giving you black eyes. If you cant stand the coldness of my sort of life, and the strain of it, go back to the gutter. Work til you are more a brute than a human being; and then cuddle and squabble and drink til you fall asleep. Oh, it's a fine life, the life of the gutter. It's real: it's warm: it's violent: you can feel it through the thickest skin: you can taste it and smell it without any training or any work. Not like Science and Literature and Classical Music and Philosophy and Art. You find me cold, unfeeling, selfish, dont you? Very well: be off with you to the sort of people you like. Marry some sentimental hog or other with lots of money, and a thick pair of lips to kiss you with and a thick pair of boots to kick you with. If you cant appreciate what youve got, youd better get what you can appreciate.

LIZA: [*desperate*] Oh, you are a cruel tyrant. I cant talk to you: you turn everything against me: I'm always in the wrong. But you know very well all the time that youre nothing but a bully. You know I cant go back to the gutter, as you call it, and that I have no real friends in the world but you and the Colonel. You know well I couldn't bear to live with a low common man after you two; and it's wicked and cruel of you to insult me by pretending I could. You think I must go back to Wimpole Street because I have nowhere else to go but father's. But dont you be too sure that you have me under your feet to be trampled on and talked down. I'll marry Freddy, I will, as soon as he's able to support me.

HIGGINS: [*sitting down beside her*] Rubbish! you shall marry an ambassador. You shall marry the Governor-General of India or the Lord-Lieutenant of Ireland, or somebody who wants a deputy-queen. I'm not going to have my masterpiece thrown away on Freddy.

LIZA: You think I like you to say that. But I havnt forgot what you said a minute ago; and I wont be coaxed round as if I was a baby or a puppy. If I cant have kindness, I'll have independence.

HIGGINS: Independence? Thats middle class blasphemy. We are all dependent on one another, every soul of us on earth.

LIZA: [*rising determinedly*] I'll let you see whether I'm dependent on you. If you can preach, I can teach. I'll go and be a teacher.

HIGGINS: Whatll you teach, in heaven's name?

LIZA: What you taught me. I'll teach phonetics.

HIGGINS: Ha! ha! ha!

LIZA: I'll offer myself as an assistant to Professor Nepean.

HIGGINS: [*rising in a fury*] What! That impostor! that humbug! that toadying ignoramus! Teach him my methods! my discoveries! You take one step in his direction and I'll wring your neck. [*He lays hands on her*]. Do you hear?

LIZA: [*defiantly non-resistant*] Wring away. What do I care? I knew youd strike me some day. [*He lets her go, stamping with rage at having forgotten himself, and recoils so hastily that he stumbles back into his seat on the ottoman*]. Aha! Now I know how to deal with you. What a fool I was not to think of it before! You cant take away the knowledge you gave me. You said I had a finer ear than you. And I can be civil and kind to people, which is more than you can. Aha! Thats done you, Henry Higgins, it has. Now I dont care that [*snapping her fingers*] for your bullying and your big talk. I'll advertize it in the papers that your duchess is only a flower girl that you taught, and that she'll teach anybody to be a duchess just the same in six months for a thousand guineas. Oh, when I think of myself crawling under your feet and being trampled on and called names, when all the time I had only to lift up my finger to be as good as you, I could just kick myself.

HIGGINS: [*wondering at her*] You damned impudent slut,

you! But it's better than snivelling; better than fetching
slippers and finding spectacles, isn't it? [*Rising*] By George,
Eliza, I said I'd make a woman of you; and I have. I like
you like this.

LIZA: Yes: you turn round and make up to me now that I'm
not afraid of you, and can do without you.

HIGGINS: Of course I do, you little fool. Five minutes ago
you were like a millstone round my neck. Now youre a
tower of strength: a consort battleship. You and I and
Pickering will be three old bachelors together instead of
only two men and a silly girl.
Mrs Higgins returns, dressed for the wedding. Eliza in-
stantly becomes cool and elegant.

MRS HIGGINS: The carriage is waiting, Eliza. Are you ready?

LIZA: Quite. Is the Professor coming?

MRS HIGGINS: Certainly not. He cant behave himself in
church. He makes remarks out loud all the time on the
clergyman's pronunciation.

LIZA: Then I shall not see you again, Professor. Goodbye.
[*She goes to the door*].

MRS HIGGINS: [*coming to Higgins*] Goodbye, dear.

HIGGINS: Goodbye, mother. [*He is about to kiss her, when
he recollects something*]. Oh, by the way, Eliza, order a
ham and a Stilton cheese, will you? And buy me a pair of
reindeer gloves, number eights, and a tie to match that new
suit of mine, at Eale & Binman's. You can choose the color.
[*His cheerful, careless, vigorous voice shows that he is
incorrigible*].

LIZA: [*disdainfully*] Buy them yourself. [*She sweeps out*].

MRS HIGGINS: I'm afraid youve spoiled that girl, Henry. But
never mind, dear: I'll buy you the tie and gloves.

HIGGINS: [*sunnily*] Oh, dont bother. She'll buy em all right
enough. Goodbye.

Breathiness

If excess air escapes during phonation a breathy quality is the
result. It may well be that this is an organic fault which will require

professional help, but many cases of breathiness are improved by awareness of the problem and consistent practice. Breathiness is characteristic of the seductive female and the confidence man. It is evident in various readings when a vocal whisper is necessary. Marilyn Monroe was noted for the breathy quality in her speech.

Nasality

A "nasal twang" or *nasality* is caused from an excess of air escaping through the nose or an excessive nasal resonation. If there are no physical defects, it means simply that you use the nose for resonating other sounds than *m, n,* or *ng.* You can hear the difference between a nasal pronunciation and a normal pronunciation of *ah* by pronouncing it first while keeping open the mouth and the back of the throat (behind the soft palate or *velum*) so that a good portion of the sound goes through the nose. Try it several times that way and then pronounce it again with the mouth open but allow the soft palate and *velum* to close off the nose. You will notice that the second way produces a clearer *ah* and a de-nasalized one.

Nasality is, however, at times a desirable character trait. It is quite possible for an actor or actress to portray a role so successfully that all later interpretations are modeled after that performer's creation. Such was the case in Judy Holliday's performance as Billie in *Born Yesterday.* She adopted a high pitched, nasal voice that accentuated the "dumb blonde" concept of the role. It also served as an emphasis on Billie's complete lack of culture and heightened the comedy aspects of the character. Nasality is not, though, superimposed on Billie. It is a part of her.

Brock can be another example of the husky, coarse person illustrated earlier in the discussion of hoarseness. His vocal quality gives further stress to his authoritative, gruff, domineering character.

Effective Quality

The key to your most effective vocal quality is relaxation. In order for the various parts of the body that work together to produce voice to operate efficiently, you must be relaxed. Unnecessary strain in the use of the breathing, phonating, resonating, and articulating mechanisms will result in a distortion of your most effective quality.

Another important point must be made about vocal quality. The problems identified give useful insight to the interpreter of literature, especially when it becomes necessary or advantageous to character-ize people in performance of drama and narrative prose. You can learn to approximate the various qualities discussed in this chapter and by doing so you will create more believable characters in the plays and stories you read. Experiment with quality as you do with rate, volume, resonance, and pitch.

SUMMARY

There is no single ideal voice, but the student can learn to make the most effective use of the voice he has.

Sound is produced by allowing a column of air from the lungs to pass over the vocal folds causing them to vibrate. The sound thus produced is amplified by the resonating chambers of the throat, mouth, and nose and formed into speech sounds by the articulators —the tongue, teeth, and lips.

Problems with voice arise from the faulty use of resonance, volume, pitch, quality, and rate. Some faulty use may be due to physical malfunction or handicap which should have medical attention before the student attempts to eliminate these problems.

The key to making most effective use of the voice is relaxation of the parts of the body that produce voice. A consistent program of practice will insure improvement.

EFFECTIVE VOCAL EXERCISES

For Projection:

1. Place your hand on your abdomen and say "ah" as you might for a throat examination. Then take a moderately deep but comfortable breath and again, say "ah." This time apply pressure with your hands suddenly. You should note appreciable loudness. Repeat, producing three loud "ahs" without straining. Breathe in if necessary after each "ah."

2. Say the following commands, each on a single breath, with-out strain and without an increase in pitch level toward the end:

All aboard!
He's out!
Come here!
Away with you!
I'll go when ready!
I mean what I say!
There you go again!

3. Start an "ah" in a tone which is barely audible, gradually increase the volume to the count of ten, then gradually decrease the volume from the count of ten to twenty. Count from one to twenty` slowly. This is to be done in one breath.

4. Say the following, first in a conversational tone, then as if you were trying to reach the back row, and then as if you were talking to someone about a half a block away:

I'll go in a few minutes.
The time is now.
I'll say this for the last time.
Listen if you wish to understand.

5. To improve articulation and diction, practice this speech from *Hamlet*. The sentence structure and the language provide specific problems for the reader. You will note that it also contains some significant suggestions for gestures. While Hamlet is directing his comments primarily to actors, bodily communication is also part of the interpreter's art.

Scene II. *A hall in the castle*

HAMLET

Speak the speech, I pray you, as I pronounced it to you, trippingly on the tongue: but if you mouth it, as many of your players do, I had as lief the town-crier spoke my lines. Nor do not saw the air too much with your hand, thus; but use all gently: for in the very torrent, tempest, and, as I may say, whirlwind of your passion, you must acquire and beget a temperance that may give it smoothness. O, it offends me to the soul to hear a robustious periwigpated fellow tear a passion to tatters, to very rags, to split the ears of the groundlings, who, for the most part, are capable of nothing but inexplicable dumb-shows and noise: I would have such a fellow whipped for o'erdoing Termagant; it out-herods Herod: pray you, avoid it.

chapter eight

What do I do
with my body?

A persistent question with students as they start a course of oral interpretation is: What do I do with my hands? Too often they answer the question with the customary system of tightly clenching their hands behind them, folding them in front, or casually dipping them into their slacks or coat pockets.

The inability to use gestures—and this is what we are talking about when we refer to hands—is a typical problem. Yet, oral interpretation does not depend just on gestures as such. It depends on the total use of the body—on proper breathing, on posture, on non-verbal communications such as facial expressions. This chapter, then, concerns itself with the various aspects of the body in communication.

USE OF THE BODY

It is therefore important to learn early the importance of the body in the process of communication, for communication is not just a matter of the voice and the ear—the entire body is an expressive medium. The face conveys emotion through a smile, a frown, a look of consternation. The shoulders can "speak"—a shrug of the shoulders can indicate indifference, uncertainty. The posture of the body can show confidence or despair. The posture you use as you walk to the stand for your reading tells how you are feeling inside. A slouching attitude, with the shoulders drooped, the spine curved, the chest pulled in, indicates a lack of energy, laziness, or indifference and conveys to the audience that same feeling. In contrast, a brisk walk to the stand, the body erect but not strained, the chest out, indicates confidence, assurance, a positive quality. The posture of the body is of vast importance in creating the right audience response. Carelessly leaning on the reading stand, crossing the legs in an awkward position which puts the weight all on one part of the body are habits that should be changed as soon as possible.

The body is the machine, our physical self. Its muscles, its nervous system regulate our actions. When you are tense or angry, the muscles are taut. Think of yourself as violently angry. Feel what is happening to you. Or hang on to an object tightly, purposely straining every muscle as suggested on page 104.

For still another example, imagine yourself riding in a car. It is going very fast down a mountain road. You hear the tires whining. Suddenly, a sharp curve looms ahead. The driver attempts to slow down but—can he make it? The sensation you feel at this time is fear. The heart beats faster. There is a shortness of breath. Every nerve seems to be screaming inside. Panic, terror, all these feelings come over you. Muscles grow tighter. The car makes the curve— just barely. The driver sighs heavily; he slows down. You breathe more deeply. The muscles begin to relax. The heart beats more slowly. You feel an aftereffect almost like fainting. The blood seems to drain out of your head. Gradually, the nerves begin to quiet down. You can breathe more normally. A sense of security, of safety comes over you. You return to a more natural state. These are examples of functions of the body—emotions you can call on for your reading.

BREATHING

Let's consider one of the body's primary functions—one of the essential functions to the reader—breathing.

It is a common habit among beginning students to raise the chest when told to "breathe." It is only through experience that you learn that clavicular breathing, or breathing from the chest only, adds no force and does not improve breath control. The mechanism involved in breathing is a complicated one, but we shall simplify it here for purposes of clarity.

The motor controls the breath when sounds are produced and regulates the force and volume of the vocal tone. To use the motor properly, there must be a constant supply of fuel—air. Remember— breath is the fuel used in the production of speech sounds. But at no time should the chest be lowered while sound is being produced. The motor is composed largely of respiratory muscles in the general region of the diaphragm. It provides the power necessary for expulsion, regulation, and control of the air in the production of voice and speech.

One point should be stressed. The average reader breathes only about one-half as often as he should for ease in reading and total effect.

Insufficient and improper breathing robs a selection of all emotional content because there is no time for an expression of feeling. Improper breathing makes reading more difficult. For instance, new students of interpretation are often more concerned with getting to the first punctuation mark before their breath runs out than with communicating the meaning of the literature they are reading. Also, faulty breathing adds to tension. Taking a proper breath with sufficient frequency relieves tension and makes it possible for you to phrase more effectively and easily.

For example, read St. Paul's first Epistle to the Corinthians, Chapter 13. Try it breathing at each place marked by (B). This is the usual reading of a new reader:

Though I speak with the tongues of men and of angels, and have not charity, I am become as sounding brass, or a tinkling cymbal (B) And though I have the gift of prophecy, and understand all mysteries and all knowledge (B) and though I have all faith, so that I could remove mountains, and have not charity, I am nothing. (B)

Now try the selection a second way, taking a breath at the end of each line; the lines are arranged in breath groups to illustrate proper breathing.

Though I speak with the tongues
Of men and of angels
And have not charity
I am become as sounding brass
Or a tinkling cymbal.
And though I have the gift of prophecy
And understand all mysteries
And all knowledge
And though I have all faith
So that I could remove mountains
And have not charity
I am nothing.

This second example could produce choppiness in delivery unless breathing is handled properly. Sharp, sudden intakes of breath or overly prolonged pauses do not create a smooth flow, but natural, gentle inhalations of breath add immeasurably to the reader's ease and the beauty of the selection.

Proper breathing is not governed solely by punctuation marks. In the selection above you will note that pauses are made and breath taken often within a phrase which is not set off by punctuation marks. The sense and mood of the material and your emotional relationship to it, are the determining factors. The way you breathe and how often you breathe depend largely on how you feel about a selection. And yet, conversely, the proper breathing increases the emotional response to the material being read. Punctuation marks, therefore, are not designed simply to identify breathing places. Their purpose in writing is primarily grammatical.

Breathing properly can also help students who find certain combinations of words difficult to pronounce. Often the reader will rush through a passage with complex alliterative or consonant sounds for fear that he will stumble over them. Such a "block" is caused by pressure, often by fear of garbling a line. If a breath is taken before that particular line, usually the pressure is relieved, the muscles relax, and the reader can go through it with no difficulty. Often a breath can be taken before a troublesome word within a phrase to relieve the tension and make the reading easier.

One student had a long-standing problem in which he became "terrified" of certain lines in a speech or a reading. It was only when he learned to use sufficient breath, to take in enough fuel, that he found the way to get rid of this fear and to regard words as valuable tools instead of terrifying monsters.

Do not think that a breath must be taken only before or after a phrase. It can be taken for only one word, such as "Ah" or "So!" or "What!"

GESTURES

In addition to the matter of breathing, one is also faced with the use of the hands—and the body itself.

Gestures are of two kinds—autistic, those which are a part of our automatic physical mannerisms such as a tic, wink, or grimace— and those that are partly planned and yet come as the result of an inner response.

There is nothing worse than the mechanical, thoroughly planned gesture. In the eighteenth and nineteenth centuries, students were taught how to gesture, how to use the arms and the hands to express an emotion. The result was an effect of windmills, of gestures that had too little relation to the emotion being expressed.

It is safe to say that gestures must be felt—they cannot really be taught. It is possible to show when one is being badly used; it is possible to define a certain set of typical movements, but a reader will find that gestures will come only when he is so deeply responsive to his material that his body physiologically responds to the reactions of his nervous system. If he is immersed in a selection dealing with deep sorrow, he may find it natural to put his hands over his face as if to wipe away tears—or if he is angry he may feel like clenching his fist. But gestures are an intimate part of each person's physical makeup and few people react with the same kind of physical movement to express an emotion.

It is important, though, to realize that gestures add much to a reading. For example, Mister Roberts: suppose you were reading the scene in the play where Pulver returns, his uniform in tatters and covered with soap suds, after blowing up the laundry. This scene demands physical action since it is a physically hilarious scene. You could not read it effectively without gestures, without some bodily movement. In another way, James Weldon Johnson's "The Creation" calls for gestures to help make the images come alive. On the other hand, introspective material such as "When I Have Fears That I May Cease To Be" would not call for gestures to add either clarity or beauty. It is a selection that is too "within" the person. Bodily movement would detract.

In some cases bodily movement is so important that interpretative reading is not the proper medium. Let us take Eugene Ionesco's The Chairs. This avant-garde play depends a great deal on illusion. While the old man and the old woman talk throughout the play to imaginary people, the physical action of bringing on the chairs is an integral part of the play itself. To stand at a rostrum and merely read this play would destroy much of the necessary illusion.

There are some suggestions to be made for gestures and a few examples are given at the end of this chapter, but remember that they are only suggestions. The gestures would be mechanical unless accompanied by the proper emotional inner response.

For example, consider a feeling of anger: a direct verbal assault on the object of that anger would ordinarily require a sharp, forceful straight-armed gesture. A feeling of resignation, of indifference, might be identified with a shrug of the shoulders, or a listless moving of the hands ending with the palms upward; a desire to avoid something repugnant would require a gesture of sharpness, the hand and arm perhaps moving up from the face and down across the body to the side; a feeling of disbelief or amazement might be accentuated by raising hands and arms upward past the sides of the head.

But—any gesture which looks right, which does not draw attention to itself and which adds clarity to the material, is a good gesture. Any gesture that draws attention away from the material or to itself is a bad one. The body must move for complete communication.

PHYSICAL EXPRESSION IN INTERPRETATION

Let us now consider the total involvement of the body. Suppose you are going to read a selection which involves an older man or woman. You must make a distinction between that person and a younger character. Here the body serves the interpreter. A slight slouching of the body, bent spine, and limpness of the body can give the illusion of age. In contrast, a character of strength and vigor would be pictured with a straight, erect posture, shoulders back, head high.

If a man were reading a woman's part, his movements would be lighter, not as strong. Or if he were reading the part of an old man, his arms and hands might shake visibly, his movements would be slower, more halting. The posture of the body would reflect such characters.

Keep in mind that in using the term "movement," reference is made to gestures and actions that are within the realm of the interpreter only—not those more expansive movements demanded by the stage.

There is also the matter of facial expressions, in the use of the body, for the face, more than any other part of the body, does much to insure total communication. Too many students read with no change of expression. A smile adds richness to a humorous selection. If the selection calls for anger, a tightness of the facial muscles, a contraction of the eyes, a menacing frown helps. If slyness and subtlety are indicated, a lifting of the eyebrows works. The important thing to remember is that the face can add much to the effect of what you are reading. The face is a reflection of how you feel inside, a part of your emotional response. Let it reveal your feelings.

Gestures and bodily movement will never develop as long as you hang onto a rostrum as you read. Let your body become free and it will begin to support your voice, to talk for you. Once you learn to involve your body in what you read, tension will diminish and you will find yourself more at ease in the reading situation.

SUMMARY

The body is an essential part of communication, for the interpreter speaks with his hands, face, shoulders, his entire body—not just his voice.

The manner in which you walk to the stand and the posture you use at the stand are indicators of how you feel inside. If you are nervous and insecure, bodily posture indicates this. If you are prepared, secure, a confident erectness of the body conveys this feeling of security to your audience.

Breathing properly is of first importance in the use of the body. One of the most common faults in oral reading is not breathing often enough and not taking in sufficient fuel. Improper intake of air causes dull, flat, monotonous reading. It also results in increased tension within the reader. To breathe correctly, it is necessary to breathe from the diaphragm. The common practice of raising the shoulders and breathing from the chest is one to be eliminated as quickly as possible.

Learning to use the diaphragm in breathing will also do much to relieve diction "blocks" that occur in some cases.

Gestures are a vital part of the reading process. No one can teach you when to use a gesture. Gestures are best when they come from a physiological reaction within you. They must be a part of the response you have to the literature you read. Nothing is worse than a mechanical display of waving hands. Such excesses draw attention to the reader rather than to the material.

The body can also aid the interpreter in suggesting characters. Stooped shoulders, a bent spine, and frail movements add to the impression of old age. Vigorous, firm, positive movements of the body help to identify a strong character, a dynamic personality.

Facial expressions, too, are of vital importance. When an interpreter reveals, through his facial expressions, how he is reacting "inside" to his material, the material itself takes on new and more meaningful dimensions.

The body is the frame around you; learn to make it a supportive and useful frame.

EXERCISES

The following exercises are helpful in learning to use the body effectively in oral interpretation.

For Proper Breathing

1. To insure proper breathing lie flat on your back and note the movement of the middle portion of your body as you breathe. Or—place three or four heavy books on this section of the body, breathe, and note the movement of the books.
2. To further increase the desired activity in the diaphragm, place your hands across the stomach, breathe in and out without raising the shoulders and feel the expansion in front and sides.
3. Read the following selection in one breath, not hurrying the reading and making certain you are articulating properly:

> Ring out, wild bells, to the wild sky,
> The flying cloud, the frosty light;
> The year is dying in the night;
> Ring out, wild bells, and let him die.

For Breath Control

1. Inhale normally. Now release the breath while producing the sound "s." Sustain the sound for ten seconds. Repeat with the sound "sh" and then "th" as in "think" and "f" as in "fall."
2. Inhale deeply. Repeat above exercises; see how much longer you can sustain "m" or "ah."
3. Try saying each of the following in a single breath. If you don't make it the first time, try a deeper inhalation later. Do not intentionally whisper.

   a. Harry had heroic inclinations and made energetic accomplishments.
   b. Fido, his friendly dog, shared Harry's inclinations.
   c. Heaven helps those who help themselves and the devil take the hindmost.
   d. What is truth for most of us is not truth for all of us.
   e. The crisp and crackly leaves fell from the tree.

   f.   The rushing stream washed the shrubbery along with it.
   g.   Double, double, toil and trouble;
        Fire burn and cauldron bubble.
   h.   Was this the face that launch'd a thousand ships,
        And burnt the topless towers of Illium?

4. *Important.* Never raise shoulders or chest in breathing. Stand
   before a mirror as you inhale and exhale and see if this is a fault
   you are committing. Also, stand up, lean forward, grasp an object
   firmly, and breathe. You'll see it is hard to raise your shoulders then.

For Effective Gestures

   The following can be used to help get you into the habit of using
gestures. It is important to keep in mind that these are *only* suggestions. You cannot operate as a robot. You must respond to literature
with your whole being before any physical reactions can be called
forth.

1. Since gestures involve the body, try swinging your arms back and
   forth loosely by your sides. Then let your arms draw circles at the
   side. The important thing is to keep them loose, free.
2. Picture yourself in a violent rage. Perhaps you have just found that
   someone you trusted has lied about you. Your anger rises higher
   and higher. Try slowly moving your hands into clenched fists. Be
   tense. As your anger increases, you make short, staccato movements with your fists. Suddenly, your hands spring open and you
   reach out with them to grab the person's throat. The hands touch
   the throat and tighten their grip around it. And you press hard,
   harder, harder. The anger subsides at last. Slowly you release the
   pressure. The hands come away and then   drop limply by your
   sides.
3. Imagine you are starving and you are begging for something to eat.
   You hold your hands in front of you in a cupped shape, reaching
   out only a short distance. You feel shame inside, despair. The
   hands are held in a curved manner, palms up. Now—no one comes
   near. Suddenly you see someone about twenty feet away walking
   towards you. Reach out your hands towards him. Stretch your arms
   as far as they will go. The hands are now not so cupped but the
   palms are still up. The person comes nearer and nearer. You reach
   out more anxiously, more pleadingly. He starts to move away. You
   stretch your arms and your hands after him, now more urgently.
   There is a slight strain in the arm. But the figure leaves. You draw

back the arms slowly, the hands return to their cupped position for a moment, and then you drop them limply at your side.

4. Take the scene in *Mister Roberts* after Pulver has blown up the laundry. By using gestures, describe how Pulver would act physically in telling of his experience with the fulminate of mercury, how he would react to the entire incident, particularly in describing the explosion itself.

5. Read the following poem by Percy Bysshe Shelley:

Ode to the West Wind

Percy Bysshe Shelley

1

O wild West Wind, thou breath of Autumn's being,
Thou, from whose unseen presence the leaves dead
Are driven, like ghosts from an enchanter fleeing,

Yellow, and black, and pale, and hectic red,
Pestilence–stricken multitudes: O thou,
Who chariotest to their dark wintry bed

The winged seeds, where they lie cold and low,
Each like a corpse within its grave, until
Thine azure sister of the Spring shall blow

Her clarion o'er the dreaming earth, and fill
(Driving sweet buds like flocks to feed in air)
With living hues and odours plain and hill:

Wild Spirit, which art moving everywhere;
Destroyer and preserver; hear, oh, hear!

2

Thou on whose stream, 'mid the steep sky's commotion,
Loose clouds like earth's decaying leaves are shed,
Shook from the tangled boughs of Heaven and Ocean,

Angels of rain and lightning: there are spread
On the blue surface of thine aëry surge,
Like the bright hair uplifted from the head

Of some fierce Maenad, even from the dim verge
Of the horizon to the zenith's height,
The locks of the approaching storm. Thou dirge

Of the dying year, to which this closing night
Will be the dome of a vast sepulchre,
Vaulted with all thy congregated might

Of vapours, from whose solid atmosphere
Black rain, and fire, and hail will burst: oh, hear!

3

Thou who didst waken from his summer dreams
The blue Mediterranean, where he lay,
Lulled by the coil of his crystalline streams,

Beside a pumice isle in Baiae's bay,
And saw in sleep old palaces and towers
Quivering within the wave's intenser day,

All overgrown with azure moss and flowers
So sweet, the sense faints picturing them! Thou
For whose path the Atlantic's level powers

Cleave themselves into chasms, while far below
The sea-blooms and the oozy woods which wear
The sapless foliage of the ocean, know

Thy voice, and suddenly grow gray with fear,
And tremble and despoil themselves: oh, hear!

4

If I were a dead leaf thou mightest bear;
If I were a swift cloud to fly with thee;
A wave to pant beneath thy power, and share

The impulse of thy strength, only less free
Than thou, O uncontrollable! If even
I were as in my boyhood, and could be

The comrade of thy wanderings over Heaven,
As then, when to outstrip thy skiey speed
Scarce seemed a vision; I would ne'er have striven

As thus with thee in prayer in my sore need.
Oh, lift me as a wave, a leaf, a cloud!
I fall upon the thorns of life! I bleed!

A heavy weight of hours has chained and bowed
One too like thee: tameless, and swift, and proud.

5

Make me thy lyre, even as the forest is:
What if my leaves are falling like its own!
The tumult of thy mighty harmonies

Will take from both a deep autumnal tone,
Sweet though in sadness. Be thou, Spirit fierce,
My spirit! Be thou me, impetuous one!

Drive my dead thoughts over the universe
Like withered leaves to quicken a new birth!
And, by the incantation of this verse,

Scatter, as from an unextinguished hearth
Ashes and sparks, my words among mankind!
Be through my lips to unawakened earth

The trumpet of a prophecy! O, Wind,
If Winter comes, can Spring be far behind?

Can you feel the exaltation in the poem, the surge of emotion, the contrast in the images? What do you feel when he says, "O wild West Wind?" What bodily involvement seems natural here? Do you get a feeling of utter freedom and elation or perhaps a feeling of supplication? With the line "the leaves dead are driven, like ghosts from an enchanter fleeing," feel the lifelessness, the dryness of the dead leaves, and then their floating like ghosts.

Read again the lines, "Angels of rain and lightning: there are spread/On the blue surface of thine aëry surge."

Angels are usually associated with something light, airy, delicate, not with such vigorous actions as rain and lightning. So your bodily responses here should be based on whether you feel that these angels were harbingers of nature's violent actions or whether they were to be used in the accustomed interpretation of the word. Certainly if you take the former interpretation, you will probably want to use a firm, decisive gesture, made sharply and vigorously.

Another possible section for gestures is found in the lines:

> If I were a dead leaf thou mightest bear;
> If I were a swift cloud to fly with thee,
> A wave to pant beneath thy power and share
> The impulse of thy strength . . .

Feel the emptiness of the dead leaf, and notice how your reaction changes in reference to the swift cloud. The cloud would call for fast, light reading—any gesture would be a relaxed one. But in dealing with the wave, which gives a feeling of bigness, of vast energy, of sweeping power, any gesture must be firm and vigorous.

The same feeling of urgency, of supplication would again occur in "Oh, lift me as a wave, a leaf, a cloud! I fall upon the thorns of life! I bleed!"

Let your body react quickly as the references move from "lift me," which has the feeling of giving of one's entire body to the weight of the wave, to the lightness and fragility of the leaf and the cloud. But then the change is abrupt and swift as you feel the heaviness of the body, the draining of exaltation and the drop to despair on "I fall upon the thorns of life! I bleed!" The line ends with a surrender of oneself—a lessening of all tension.

In analyzing this section, read it over quietly and when you feel like making a movement with the arms or hands or head or shoulders, do so. Pantomime it, then go back and read it aloud—and let your body support your voice.

Keep in mind, however, that there is much in poetry that defies the use of gestures. Poetry relates an intimate, personal, deeply emotional experience that would be unjustly invaded by gestures.

6. Let us turn to *Cyrano de Bergerac* by Edmond Rostand, a great romantic play combining comedy and tragedy with equal distinction. It has lived through time because of the beauty of its language and the magnificence of its portrait of Cyrano—a swashbuckler, a fighter, a sensitive man, in love but one who fears to express his love for a woman. Physically, he is noted for a rather prominent nose, and in this famous speech he replies to a man who has been taunting him about its size. Read his speech to yourself and visualize his feelings; then read it aloud and see how many of the movements you first felt you are able to incorporate in the oral reading:

From

Cyrano de Bergerac

Edmond Rostand

ACT 1

... Ah ... your nose ... hem! ...
Your nose is ... rather large!
CYRANO: (*gravely*) Rather.
VALVERT: (*simpering*) Oh well—
CYRANO: (*coolly*) Is that all?
VALERT: (*turns away, with a shrug*) Well, of course—
CYRANO: Ah, no, your sir!
You are too simple. Why, you might have said—
Oh, a great many things! Mon dieu, why waste
Your opportunity? For example, thus:
AGGRESSIVE: I, sir, if that nose were mine,
I'd have it amputated—on the spot!
FRIENDLY: How do you drink with such a nose?
You ought to have a cup made specially.
DESCRIPTIVE: 'Tis a rock—a crag—a cape—
A cape? say rather, a peninsula!
INQUISITIVE: What is that receptacle—
A razor-case or a portfolio?
KINDLY: Ah, do you love the little birds
So much that when they come and sing to you,
You give them this to perch on? *INSOLENT:*
Sir, when you smoke, the neighbors must suppose
Your chimney is on fire. *CAUTIOUS:* Take care—
A weight like that might make you topheavy.
THOUGHTFUL: Somebody fetch my parasol—
Those delicate colors fade so in the sun!
PEDANTIC: Does not Aristophanes
Mention a mythologic monster called
Hippocampelephantocamelos?
Surely we have here the original!
FAMILIAR: Well, old torchlight! Hang your hat
Over that chandelier—it hurts my eyes.

ELOQUENT: When it blows, the typhoon howls,
And the clouds darken. *DRAMATIC:* When it bleeds—
The Red Sea! *ENTERPRISING:* What a sign
For some perfumer! *LYRIC:* Hark—the horn
Of Roland calls to summon Charlemagne!—
SIMPLE: When do they unveil the monument?
RESPECTFUL: Sir, I recognize in you
A man of parts, a man of prominence—
RUSTIC: Hey? What? Call that a nose? Na, na—
I be no fool like what you think I be—
That there's a blue cucumber! *MILITARY:*
Point against cavalry! *PRACTICAL:* Why not
A lottery with this for the grand prize?
Or—parodying Faustus in the play—
"Was this the nose that launched a thousand ships
And burned the topless towers of Ilium?"
These, my dear sir, are things you might have said
Had you some tinge of letters, or of wit
To color your discourse. But wit,—not so.
You never had an atom—and of letters,
You need but three to write you down—an Ass.
Moreover,—if you had the invention, here
Before these folk to make a jest of me—
Be sure you would not then articulate
The twentieth part of half a syllable
Of the beginning! For I say these things
Lightly enough myself, about myself,
But I allow none else to utter them.

First of all, keep in mind the type of man Cyrano was. He was a swashbuckler, a fighter, an expert swordsman, a romanticist, a man who used his body freely and energetically. This speech cannot be read effectively without bodily involvement. Doing so would rob the scene of much of Rostand's meaning. Before going on with this scene it might be wise to review the differences between acting and oral interpretation as treated fully in Chapter One.

In analyzing the speech, one clue to physical support is the number of adjectives Cyrano uses to describe the distinctive aspects of his nose, such as *aggressive, friendly, respectful, eloquent*, etc.

Each calls for a different physical reaction. *Aggressive* requires a tightening of the muscles, a more rigid attitude, a firmness. *Friendly* shows the body more at ease, more relaxed, a lighter and happier attitude. And *Kindly* calls for a smoothness in bodily movement, an ease, a gentleness, a relaxation of the muscles.

The line, ". . . if that nose were mine," would very likely call for a gesture to the nose. "A rock—a crag—a cape!" might bring forth an expansive movement, a sweep of the arm to indicate the bigness. In the comment "when you smoke," a sweeping gesture from the nose up might be fitting; and a gesture with the arm sweeping down on "when it bleeds." On the *Rustic* section, "That there's a blue cucumber!" could be read with staccato-like pointings with the index finger. When Cyrano says "military," the body should be erect, tense, rigid, and on "Point against cavalry!" the gesture could be a firm outreaching of the arm in the order of a military command. When Cyrano again returns his comments to the man directly, there is a change in bodily reaction. Now he leaves the dramatic buffoonery and speaks directly to his adversary. He is sarcastic and also threatening.

Again, it is important to bear in mind that the suggestions made above are not to be considered as the only possible gestures or movements. You, as the reader, must respond in your own way. But before you can use your body, you must experience some physiological reaction to the character speaking, to what he is saying, to the changes in his views and emotions. Your reactions should follow naturally and add to the total effect of the reading.

Learn to use the body—but never become a stereotyped robot. The gestures must be part of you—not apart from you.

chapter nine

How fast do I read?

In Chapter Six a diacritical marking of *Look Homeward, Angel* was given to teach you how to analyze according to moods and emotions. It also indicated the use of virgules for proper phrasing and changes of thought. That model will serve as a good guide for the contents of this chapter.

No reading can be effective without the use of the three keys to oral interpretation: pacing, pausing, and emphasis. They can make or destroy interpretative reading.

RATE OR PACING

Certainly a typical problem for beginning interpreters is fast or choppy rate. Rate is the speed of utterance, the speed of reading. Faulty use of rate is almost always due to a combination of stage fright and too little preparation. The student who is frightened or ill-prepared will read at as fast a rate as he can in order to escape his situation. The result is obvious—instead of sharing conversation and ideas or mirroring characterization, he merely mouths words; in effect he'd have been better off not to read at all. In an earlier chapter the point was made that emotional involvement in the material you read is the core of effective interpretation, and it is emotional involvement that is the clue to controlling rate. Concentrate in practice sessions on letting the words work their magic. The rate of reading should be determined by the material being read. A good general rule to follow regarding rate is to read the material as you would speak it yourself in a real-life situation. The rate should be natural. A look at the following paragraph, taken from Thoreau's "The Battle of the Ants," will illustrate the point. Read it aloud as though the observations are your own and you are reporting them as they occur to you.

One day when I went out to my wood-pile, or rather my pile of stumps, I observed two large ants, the one red, the other nearly half an inch long, and black, fiercely contending with one another. Having once got hold they never let go, but struggled and wrestled and rolled on the chips incessantly. Looking farther, I was surprised to find that the chips were covered with such combatants, that it was a war between two races of ants, the red always pitted against the black, and frequently two red ones to one black.

Now read it again, as fast as you can pronounce the words. You will notice that when a descriptive passage such as this is read too fast, much of the detail—the color of description—is lost and the listener is left with a few bare facts if he is able to get even that much of the meaning.

One further example should convince you. Read the following letter in each of these two ways: First, read it as fast as you can. You will notice that in doing so, you rob it of its sincerity, its gratitude, its meaning. And, as important, you rob the listener of understanding and appreciation of both Mr. Lincoln and yourself.

Executive Mansion

Washington, November 21, 1864

Mrs. Bixby, Boston, Massachusetts.

Dear Madam:

I have been shown in the files of the War Department a statement of the Adjutant-General of Massachusetts that you are the mother of five sons who have died gloriously on the field of battle. I feel how weak and fruitless must be any words of mine which should attempt to beguile you from the grief of a loss so overwhelming. But I cannot refrain from tendering to you the consolation that may be found in the thanks of the republic they died to save. I pray that our Heavenly

Father may assuage to the anguish of your bereavement, and leave you only the cherished memory of the loved and lost, and the solemn pride that must be yours to have laid so costly a sacrifice upon the altar of freedom.

Yours very sincerely and respectfully,

Abraham Lincoln

Read it again now, after taking a moment to become involved in its message. Feel what Lincoln must have felt when the loss was brought to his attention.

Reading rate is dictated by the mood of the writing, by the weight of the ideas, and by the style of the author. Don't let stage fright or too little preparation force you into reading too rapidly.

Too ponderous a rate is a third fault. However, it is much less common in beginning readers of literature and the problem is usually solved once the person involved has a chance to hear himself on tape. Typically the person who reads too slowly does so for two reasons: he is anxious to avoid reading at a fast rate or he lacks the motivation and energy to read. One of the most common of all faults in the reading of literature is a sameness in rate of reading, or pacing, and the tendency to read in one breath, pausing only for punctuation marks. The beginning reader will read a sentence to a comma, pause momentarily (if at all) and then race quickly on to the period. In the process of this rapid and monotonous pacing, thought and meaning are lost.

Learn quickly that the elements that govern your reading are thought and content. You have to decide what the author is trying to say, what ideas he is bringing forth, how he builds to a climax, what are the characters he creates really like. When such matters are analyzed, you will find that pausing and pacing fall almost into a natural pattern.

Some sections need a slower, more precise pacing; for instance, in the reading of descriptive passages, a slower pace is usually necessary in order to bring out effectively the images used by the author. If he is trying to create a setting of sublimity, of peace and contentment, the pace should be relaxed, languid, slower, to stress the general effect of beauty. If the author is describing a scene of vivid action or vigorous movement, the pacing is more rapid. In Poe's "The Tell-Tale Heart," (see Chapter Four), the panic the man feels at the end as he believes he is being discovered requires a faster pace in order to heighten the excitement. In contrast, the irony of Swift's "A Modest Proposal" demands a slower, more emphatic kind of pacing in order to highlight the primary concepts. A relaxed love scene between two people should be read more slowly to convey the proper mood.

Of course, pacing must be varied. No selection has all the same mood throughout. The analysis of the moods and emotions is vitally important. A rate of speed that varies by degrees of rapidity adds variety and color to a reading. Pacing problems in poetry, prose, and drama are almost identical and all are based on a thorough understanding of the moods.

Poetry probably presents the most complex study of pacing. It is the general tendency of readers to read all poems with the same rate, and yet, incorporated within the poetic structure are images of differing emotions, concepts of different complexities, stories with suspense and action and romance, personal expressions of deep feeling which by their very nature demand a slower pacing and a more total involvement. Pacing in poetry also demands an awareness of the rhythm without a concentration on the rhythmic pattern, a "dum-de-dum" effect to the end of each line. Make the thought, the emotion, the experience in the poem your first concern and convey these to your audience. Then the amount of rhythm that should be present in your reading will be there.

Let us look at two poems to indicate the contrast.

Alfred Noyes' poem, "The Highwayman," is an example in which contrasting rates are used. The first part is read at a slower rate to help create the illusion of something ghostly and mysterious. Then in the description of the highwayman, to convey his cavalier attitude, a faster pace is used. Rate again becomes slower in the description of Tom, the caretaker, and in the references to Bess's appearance. Pacing in this segment is important to make the introduction of Bess more meaningful—and to give the sensual illusion of her long black hair falling over the highwayman's chest. The pace quickens with the entrance of the redcoats and in Bess's struggle to free herself, in her panic to try to warn her lover. The same faster pace for purposes of suspense continues until the highwayman's death and then it slows down noticeably after that, particularly with the last two stanzas of the poem where once more the ghostly and eerie setting returns and unreality becomes a part of the poem itself.

The Highwayman

Alfred Noyes

PART ONE

The wind was a torrent of darkness among the gusty trees,
The moon was a ghostly galleon tossed upon cloudy seas,
The road was a ribbon of moonlight over the purple moor,
And the highwayman came riding—
   Riding—riding—
The highwayman came riding, up to the old inn-door.

He'd a French cocked-hat on his forehead, a bunch of lace at
 his chin.
A coat of the claret velvet, and breeches of brown doe-skin.
They fitted with never a wrinkle: his boots were up to the
 thigh!
And he rode with a jewelled twinkle,
   His pistol butts a-twinkle,
His rapier hilt a-twinkle, under the jewelled sky.

Over the cobbles he clattered and clashed in the dark inn-
 yard,
And he tapped with his whip on the shutters, but all was
 locked and barred;
He whistled a tune to the window, and who should be waiting
 there
But the landlord's black-eyed daughter,
   Bess, the landlord's daughter,
Plaiting a dark red love-knot into her long black hair.

And dark in the dark old inn-yard a stable-wicket creaked
Where Tim the ostler listened; his face was white and peaked;
His eyes were hollows of madness, his hair like mouldy hay,
But he loved the landlord's daughter,
   The landlord's red-lipped daughter,
Dumb as a dog he listened, and he heard the robber say—

"One kiss, my bonny sweetheart, I'm after a prize to-night,
But I shall be back with the yellow gold before the morning
    light;
Yet, if they press me sharply, and harry me through the day,
Then look for me by moonlight,
        Watch for me by moonlight,
I'll come to thee by moonlight, though hell should bar the
    way."

He rose upright in the stirrups; he scarce could reach her
    hand,
But she loosened her hair i' the casement! His face burnt like
    a brand
As the black cascade of perfume came tumbling over his
    breast;
And he kissed its waves in the moonlight,
        (Oh, sweet black waves in the moonlight!)
Then he tugged at his rein in the moonlight, and galloped
    away to the West.

Part Two

He did not come in the dawning; he did not come at noon;
And out o' the tawny sunset, before the rise o' the moon,
When the road was a gipsy's ribbon, looping the purple moor,
A red-coat troop came marching—
        Marching—marching—
King George's men came marching, up to the old inn-door.

They said no word to the landlord, they drank his ale in-
    stead,
But they gagged his daughter and bound her to the foot of her
    narrow bed;
Two of them knelt at her casement, with muskets at their side!
There was death at every window;
        And hell at one dark window;
For Bess could see, through her casement, the road that *he*
    would ride.

They had tied her up to attention, with many a sniggering
  jest,
They had bound a musket beside her, with the barrel beneath
  her breast!
"Now keep good watch!" and they kissed her
        She heard the dead man say—
Look for me by moonlight;
        Watch for me by moonlight;
I'll come to thee by moonlight, though hell should bar the way!

She twisted her hands behind her; but all the knots held
  good!
She writhed her hands till her fingers were wet with sweat
  or blood!
They stretched and strained in the darkness, and the hours
  crawled by like years,
Till, now, on the stroke of midnight,
        Cold, on the stroke of midnight,
The tip of one finger touched it! The trigger at least was hers!

The tip of one finger touched it; she strove no more for the
  rest!
Up, she stood up to attention, with the barrel beneath her
  breast,
She would not risk their hearing; she would not strive again;
For the road lay bare in the moonlight;
        Blank and bare in the moonlight;
And the blood of her veins in the moonlight throbbed to her
  love's refrain.

Tlot-tlot; tlot-tlot! Had they heard it? The horse-hoofs ringing
  clear;
Tlot-tlot, tlot-tlot, in the distance? Were they deaf that they
  did not hear?
Down the ribbon of moonlight, over the brow of the hill,
The highwayman came riding,
        Riding, riding!
The red-coats looked to their priming! She stood up, straight
  and still!

Tlot-tlot, in the frosty silence! *Tlot-tlot,* in the echoing night!
Nearer he came and nearer! Her face was like a light!
Her eyes grew wide for a moment; she drew one last deep
breath,
Then her finger moved in the moonlight;
Her musket shattered the moonlight,
Shattered her breast in the moonlight and warned him—with
her death.

He turned; he spurred to the West; he did not know who
stood
Bowed, with her head o'er the musket, drenched with her
own red blood!
Not till the dawn he heard it, his face grew grey to hear
How Bess, the landlord's daughter,
The landlord's black-eyed daughter,
Had watched for her love in the moonlight, and died in the
darkness there.

Back, he spurred like a madman, shrieking a curse to the sky,
With the white road smoking behind him and his rapier bran-
dished high!
Blood-red were his spurs i' the golden noon; wine-red was his
velvet coat,
When they shot him down on the highway,
Down like a dog on the highway,
And he lay in his blood on the highway, with the bunch of
lace at his throat.

*And still of a winter's night, they say, when the wind is in the
trees,*
When the moon is a ghostly galleon tossed upon cloudy seas,
When the road is a ribbon of moonlight over the purple moor,
A highwayman comes riding—
Riding—riding—
A highwayman comes riding, up to the old inn-door.

Over the cobbles he clatters and clangs in the dark inn-yard;
*He taps with his whip on the shutters, but all is locked and
barred;*

He whistles a tune to the window, and who should be waiting
*   there*
But the landlord's black-eyed daughter,
*   Bess, the landlord's daughter,*
Plaiting a dark red love-knot into her long black hair.

Now let's look at "How Do I Love Thee?" by Elizabeth Barrett Browning. This is a lyric poem, reflective, and extremely personal. It deals with her deep love for Robert Browning and, therefore, is highly sensitive in nature. There is nothing in the poem to indicate a need for faster pacing. She is not thinking in excited terms, but in reflective ones. She is not dealing in suspense, but in her inner feeling. So the pace would be slower, more relaxed.

How Do I Love Thee?

Elizabeth Barrett Browning

How do I love thee? Let me count the ways.
I love thee to the depth and breadth and height
My soul can reach, when feeling out of sight
For the ends of Being and ideal Grace.
I love thee to the level of every day's
Most quiet need, by sun and candlelight.
I love thee freely, as men strive for Right;
I love thee purely, as they turn from Praise.
I love thee with the passion put to use
In my old griefs, and with my childhood's faith.
I love thee with a love I seemed to lose
With my lost saints—I love thee with the breath,
Smiles, tears, of all my life!—and, if God choose,
I shall but love thee better after death.

Pacing in the reading of expository prose adds to clarity of the author's ideas. Proper pacing of vivid descriptions adds to the fullness of appreciation of what is being described. Pacing is important in the reading of narrative prose to build suspense, to highlight action, and to prepare the audience for the climax. The attitudes of the characters as they are expressed in dialogue form are often different from the attitude of the author in expository writing. The general tendency in the reading of narrative is for a reader to come to life with feeling and proper pacing in the reading of dialogue and then fall back into a routinely consistent pacing in the other sections of the story. And yet, pacing is also vitally important in the reading of the narrative and expository sections that give a reason for the dialogue.

A good example of typical pacing needed for descriptive writing is found in *The Sea of Grass* by Conrad Richter.

From

The Sea of Grass

Conrad Richter

That lusty pioneer blood is tamed now, broken and gelded like the wild horse and the frontier settlement. And I think that I shall never see it flowing through human veins again as it did in my Uncle Jim Brewton riding a lathered horse across his shaggy range or standing in his massive ranch house, bare of furniture as a garret, and holding together his empire of grass and cattle by the fire in his eyes. His rude empire is dead and quartered today like a steer on the meat-block, but I still lie in bed at night and see it tossing, pitching, leaping in the golden sunlight of more than fifty years ago, sweeping up to his very door, stretching a hundred and twenty miles north and south along the river, and rolling as far into the sunset as stock could roam—a ranch larger than Massachusetts with Connecticut thrown in, his fabulous herds of Texas cattle sprinkled like grains of cinnamon across the horizons, his name a legend even then, his brand familiar as the ABC's in every packing-house, and his word the law, not dead sentences in a book, but a moving finger writing on a cottonwood tree where all who rode could very plainly read.

I can see his bedroom, just a bunk in the corner, with a

fancy horsehair bridle and ropes on the wall, and a brown buckskin partly cut away in strips for whang leather. And I can see his huge parlor, without rugs or furniture, piled to the pine rafters with white sacks of flour and burlapped hills of sugar and green coffee, and wooden buttes of boxed tobacco, dried fruits, and canned tomatoes, just the provisions for his hundred hands and everyone else who passed that way, rancher or cowboy, settler or prospector, Mexican, Indian, or outlaw, all welcome at his table.

But what moves across my eye unforgettably is his spring roundup when six or seven wagons working back from the Arizona line reached the headquarters range with a vast, almost mythical herd the like of which will never be seen in this country again.

Farther than the eye could strain through the dust, the grass was colored with milling cattle, while bulls rode and fought, and cows and calves bawled, and countless horns clacked, and sixty or seventy of us kept saddling fresh mounts and galloping here and there in a stirring, daylong excitement.

The free wild life we lived on that shaggy prairie was to me the life of the gods. And that there should be anyone who would not love it as we did, who should even hate it passionately and secretly, and yet the memory of whose delicate presence in that violent land still stirs me with emotion after fifty years, had not occurred to me then. But I was only a boy whose face had never known a razor, in a pair of California britches turned up to let my boots into the stirrups, that early fall day I rode with rebellious young back to Salt Fork to be shipped off to Missouri to school before my uncle would fetch back to the ranch the scarcest article in the territory, a woman, the one we had never seen, who was coming all the way from St. Louis to marry him.

The first paragraph should be read in a slower pace to make clear the author's theme and purpose. The second paragraph conveys a feeling of lifelessness and needs a still slower pacing until the line, "see it tossing, pitching, leaping in the golden sunlight." The adjectives used here demand a somewhat faster pace but it should change to a slower pace again for emphasis on "sweeping up to his very door, stretching a hundred and twenty miles north and south . . ."

The paragraph beginning with "I can see his bedroom" is reflective in nature and should be handled with a slower pace. Then the mood changes in the next paragraph which deals with the action of the herd and the pacing quickens. There is a change again with the line "The free wild life we lived . . ."

Now let's look at an example of the pacing for narrative prose.

From

Lord of the Flies

William Golding

The hunters were looking uneasily at the sky, flinching from the stroke of the drops. A wave of restlessness set the boys swaying and moving aimlessly. The flickering light became brighter and the blows of the thunder were only just bearable. The littluns began to run about, screaming.

Jack leapt on to the sand.

"Do our dance! Come on! Dance!"

He ran stumbling through the thick sand to the open space of rock beyond the fire. Between the flashes of lightning the air was dark and terrible; and the boys followed him, clamorously. Roger became the pig, grunting and charging at Jack, who side-stepped. The hunters took their spears, the cooks took spits, and the rest clubs of firewood. A circling movement developed and a chant. While Roger mimed the terror of the pig, the littluns ran and jumped on the outside of the circle. Piggy and Ralph, under the threat of the sky, found themselves eager to take a place in this demented but partly secure society. They were glad to touch the brown backs of the fence that hemmed in the terror and made it governable.

"Kill the beast! Cut his throat! Spill his blood!"

The movement became regular while the chant lost its first superficial excitement and began to beat like a steady pulse.

Roger ceased to be a pig and became a hunter, so that the centre of the ring yawned emptily. Some of the littluns started a ring on their own; and the complementary circles went round and round as though repetition would achieve safety of itself. There was the throb and stamp of a single organism.

The dark sky was shattered by a blue-white scar. An instant later the noise was on them like the blow of a gigantic whip. The chant rose a tone in agony.

"*Kill the beast! Cut his throat! Spill his blood!*"

Now out of the terror rose another desire, thick, urgent, blind.

"*Kill the beast! Cut his throat! Spill his blood!*"

Again the blue-white scar jagged above them and the sulphurous explosion beat down. The littluns screamed and blundered about, fleeing from the edge of the forest, and one of them broke the ring of biguns in his terror.

"Him! Him!"

The circle became a horseshoe. A thing was crawling out of the forest. It came darkly, uncertainly. The shrill screaming that rose before the beast was like a pain. The beast stumbled into the horseshoe.

"*Kill the beast! Cut his throat! Spill his blood!*"

The blue-white scar was constant, the noise unendurable. Simon was crying out something about a dead man on a hill.

"*Kill the beast! Cut his throat! Spill his blood! Do him in!*"

The sticks fell and the mouth of the new circle crunched and screamed. The beast was on its knees in the centre, its arms folded over its face. It was crying out against the abominable noise something about a body on the hill. The beast struggled forward, broke the ring and fell over the steep edge of the rock to the sand by the water. At once the crowd surged after it, poured down the rock, leapt on to the beast, screamed, struck, bit, tore. There were no words, and no movements but the tearing of teeth and claws.

Then the clouds opened and let down the rain like a waterfall. The water bounded from the mountain-top, tore leaves and branches from the trees, poured like a cold shower over the struggling heap on the sand. Presently the heap broke up and figures staggered away. Only the beast lay still, a few yards from the sea. Even in the rain they could see how small a beast it was; and already its blood was staining the sand.

Now a great wind blew the rain sideways, cascading the water from the forest trees. On the mountain-top the parachute filled and moved; the figure slid, rose to its feet, spun, swayed down through a vastness of wet air and trod with ungainly feet the tops of the high trees; falling, still falling, it sank toward the beach and the boys rushed screaming into the darkness. The parachute took the figure forward, furrowed the lagoon, and bumped it over the reef out to sea.

Toward midnight the rain ceased and the clouds drifted away, so that the sky was scattered once more with the incredible lamps of stars. Then the breeze died too and there was no noise save the drip and trickle of water that ran out of clefts and spilled down, leaf by leaf, to the brown earth of the island. The air was cool, moist, and clear; and presently even the sound of the water was still. The beast lay huddled on the pale beach and the stains spread, inch by inch. . . .

The line of his cheek silvered and the turn of his shoulder became sculptured marble. The strange attendant creatures, with their fiery eyes and trailing vapors, busied themselves round his head. The body lifted a fraction of an inch from the sand and a bubble of air escaped from the mouth with a wet plop. Then it turned gently in the water.

Somewhere over the darkened curve of the world the sun and moon were pulling, and the film of water on the earth planet was held, bulging slightly on one side while the solid core turned. The great wave of the tide moved farther along the island and the water lifted. Softly, surrounded by a fringe of inquisitive bright creatures, itself a silver shape beneath the steadfast constellations, Simon's dead body moved out toward the open sea.

The first paragraph requires a slower pacing to set the stage and to identify suspense. But then on "The littluns began to run about screaming," the pace quickens. The following paragraph should be read at a faster rate and with an increase in intensity. There is a change to a slower pace on "The dark sky was shattered by a blue-white scar," and then an increase in speed with "Kill the beast! Cut his throat! Spill his blood!" Rate gets even faster up to the point of "The sticks fell and the mouth of the new circle crunched and screamed." At "Then the clouds opened and let down the rain like a waterfall" the mood is more relaxed. The action has hit its peak. The author is again concerned with description. A faster pace is needed momentarily on "Now a great wind blew the rain sideways . . ." But the mood changes again to a slower rate on "It sank toward the beach." The slower rate continues with an even more relaxed feeling, an even slower pace on the last paragraph.

In drama, pacing is used to build scenes to their climaxes. If there is a scene of great suspense, the pacing gradually becomes faster until it hits the peak moment. Then there is usually a slowing down, an abrupt change of pace for the aftermath and the climax. A scene which features sophisticated chatter, as in Noel Coward's *Private Lives,* is usually read with fast pacing. A scene in which a man confesses some weaknesses or one in which he expresses some great conflict, as in Hamlet's famous speech "To be or not to be," requires a slower pace, a more introspective mood. After all, no one thinks aloud to himself in a meditative mood with a fast rate of speech.

As a further example of pacing in drama, let us look at the death scene from *King Lear.* Intermittent dialogue from other characters in the scene has been omitted.

From

King Lear

William Shakespeare

LEAR: Howl, howl, howl, howl! O, you are men of stones:
        Had I your tongues and eyes, I'ld use them so
        That heaven's vault should crack. She's gone for ever!
        I know when one is dead, and when one lives;
        She's dead as earth. Lend me a looking-glass;
        If that her breath will mist or stain the stone,
        Why then she lives. . . .

LEAR: This feather stirs; she lives! if it be so,
        It is a chance which does redeem all sorrows
        That ever I have felt. . . .

LEAR: A plague upon you, murderers, traitors all!
I might have sav'd her; now she's gone for ever!
Cordelia, Cordelia! stay a little. Ha!
What is't thou say'st? Her voice was ever soft,
Gentle, and low, an excellent thing in woman.
I kill'd the slave that was a-hanging thee. . . .

LEAR: And my poor fool is hang'd! No, no, no life!
Why should a dog, a horse, a rat, have life,
And thou no breath at all? Thou 'lt come no more,
Never, never, never, never, never!
Pray you, undo this button: thank you, sir.
Do you see this? Look on her, look, her lips,
Look there, look there!
(*He dies*)

The opening with "Howl, howl, howl, howl!" needs a slower, even ponderous pace with prolonged emphasis on the words. Then the pace changes with "She's gone forever" to denote the tragedy of death. It quickens somewhat with "Lend me a looking glass. If that her breath will mist or stain the stone, Why, then she lives." These lines are read at a faster pace to indicate Lear's excitement and his hope that his daughter is alive.

This note of hope and expectancy continues until "A plague upon you murderers, traitors all." Here Lear speaks with more anger and the pace quickens, but immediately it slows again to convey his sorrow as he says, "I might have saved her . . ." The conversation that follows moves rather fast with no need for any profound changes in pace. The many interrupted speeches indicate a fluidity of conversation. As Lear becomes more frantic and his failing mind more apparent with "And my poor fool is hang'd," the pace speeds up and increases on "Never, never . . ." But it changes abruptly to a slower pace on "Pray you undo this button," and again on "Thank you, sir." At this point rate quickens to denote his excitement as he says, "Do you see this?" And it gets even faster on "Look there, look there." After that there is a slowing of pace to give emphasis to the tragedy that has taken place.

In Sophocles' *Antigone,* Haemon comes to beg his father's mercy for Antigone, whom he loves and who has been condemned to death for going against Creon's edict. In the beginning of the scene, there is a slower pace as the two men spar and discuss their relationship.

Then with "So, my son, do not be led by passing fancy . . ." the pace becomes even slower—for emphasis. Emphasis is the key in those lines and remains so until the end of Creon's speech with "Let no-one call us woman's underlings." Haemon remains calm and tries to reason with his father, so the pace is slower, but it becomes slightly faster on "But I can hear these murmurs in the dark." As he continues to try to reason with his father, the pace remains slower. But as the two men begin to argue, it picks up with "And is a man of my age to be taught . . ." It builds to an even faster peak as they argue and condemn each other to "No, she will never perish at my side." Here Haemon has made his decision; he is firm, definite; his pace slows to his exit.

From

Antigone

Sophocles

CREON: . . . My son, have you heard that sentence has been
      passed
   On your betrothed? Are you here to storm at me?
   Or have I your good will, whatever I do?
HAEMON: Father, I am in your hands. You in your wisdom
   Lay down for me the paths I am to follow.
   There is no marriage in the world
   That I would put before my good advisor.
CREON: Yes, keep this always in your heart, my son:
   Accept your father's word as law in all things.
   For that is why men pray to have
   Dutiful children growing up at home,
   To repay their father's enemies in kind
   And honor those he loves no less than he does.
   But a man is sowing troubles for himself
   And enemies' delight—what else?—when he
   Sires sons who bring no profit to their father.
   So, my son, do not be led by passing fancy
   To lose your head for a woman's sake. You know,
   The warmth goes out of such embraces, when
   An evil woman shares your home and bed.

False friends are deadlier than a festered wound.
So turn from her with loathing; let her find
A husband for herself among the dead.
For now that I have caught her, the only one
Of all the city to disobey me openly,
My people shall not see me break my word.
I shall kill her. Let her plead the sacred ties
Of kinship! If I bring up my own family
To flout me, there will be no holding others.
A man who sees his family obey him
Will have authority in public matters.
But if anyone offends, or violates the laws,
No word of praise shall he ever have from me.
Whoever the state appoints must be obeyed,
In little things or great things, right or wrong.
I should have confidence that such a man
Would be as good a ruler as a subject
And in a hail of spears would stand his ground
Where he was put, a comrade you could trust.
But disobedience is the worst of evils;
It is this that ruins cities, it is this
That makes homes desolate, turns brothers in arms
To headlong rout. But those who are preserved
Owe their lives, the greater part of them to discipline.
And so we must stand up for law and order,
Not let ourselves be worsted by a woman.
If yield we must, then let us yield to a man.
Let no-one call us woman's underlings.

CHORUS: Unless the years have robbed me of my wits
You seem to have sound sense in what you say.

HAEMON: Father, the gods endow mankind with reason,
The highest quality that we possess.
It is not for me to criticize your words.
I could not do it, and would hate to try.
And yet, two heads are sometimes better than one;
At least, it is my place to watch, on your behalf,
All that men do and say and criticize.
Fear of your frown prevents the common man
From saying anything that would displease you,

But I can hear these murmurs in the dark,
The feeling in the city for this girl.
"No woman" they say "has ever deserved death less,
Or died so shamefully in a noble cause.
When her brother fell in the slaughter, she would not
Leave him unburied, to provide a meal
For carrion dogs or passing birds of prey.
Is she not, then, deserving golden honors?"
This is what men are whispering to each other.
Father, there is nothing dearer to my heart
Than your continuing prosperity.
What finer ornament could children have
Than a father's proud success   or he, than theirs?
So wear an open mind; do not suppose
That you are right, and everyone else is wrong.
A man who thinks he has monopoly
Of wisdom, no rival in speech or intellect,
Will turn out hollow when you look inside him.
However wise he is, it is no disgrace
To learn, and give way gracefully.
You see how trees that bend to winter floods
Preserve themselves, save every twig unbroken,
But those that stand rigid perish root and branch,
And also how the man who keeps his sails
Stretched taut, and never slackens them, overturns
And finishes his voyage upside down
Let your anger rest; allow us to persuade you.
If a young man may be permitted his opinion
I should say it would be best for everyone
To be born omniscient; but otherwise—
And things have a habit of falling out differently—
It is good to learn from good advice.

CHORUS: My lord, if he speaks to the point you ought to
   listen.
And Haemon, you to him. There is sense on both sides.

CREON: And is a man of my age to be taught
   What I should think by one so young as this?

HAEMON: Nothing that is not right; young though I may be,
   You should judge by my behavior, not my age.

CREON: What sort of behavior is it to honor rebels?

HAEMON: I would never suggest that the guilty should be honored.

CREON: And is she not infected with this disease?

HAEMON: The people of Thebes unanimously deny it.

CREON: Will the city tell me how I am to rule?

HAEMON: Listen to that! Who is being childish now?

CREON: Is the state to listen to any voice but mine?

HAEMON: There is no state, when one man is its master.

CREON: Is not the state supposed to be the ruler's?

HAEMON: You would do well as the monarch of a desert.

CREON: It seems the woman has a champion here.

HAEMON: Then you are the woman! It is you I care about!

CREON: Insolent cub! Will you argue with your father?

HAEMON: I will, when I see you falling into error.

CREON: Am I wrong to respect my own prerogatives?

HAEMON: It is no respect, when you offend the gods.

CREON: How contemptible, to give way to a woman!

HAEMON: At least I do not give way to temptation.

CREON: But every word you say is a plea for her.

HAEMON: And for you, and for me, and for the gods below.

CREON: You will never marry her this side of the grave.

HAEMON: Then she will die—and take somebody with her.

CREON: So! Do you dare to go so far? Are you threatening me?

HAEMON: Is it threatening, to protest a wrong decision?

CREON: You shall pay for this. A fine one to teach wisdom!

HAEMON: If you were not my father, I should call you a fool.

CREON: You woman's slave; do not try to wheedle me!

HAEMON: Would you stop everyone from speaking but your-self?

CREON: Indeed! I tell you, by the gods above us,
You shall pay for using such language to your father.
(*to the Attendants*)
Bring this abomination out, and let her die
Here, in his presence, at her bridegroom's side.

HAEMON: No, she will never perish at my side,
So do not think it. From this moment on
Your eyes will never see my face again.
So rave away, to those who have more patience!

Variety in pacing is needed not only for clear meaning and more exact emotional expression but to give you, the reader, moments of relaxation. You could never maintain an unvarying, fast pace or a consistently slow pace without finding the reading difficult and monotonous.

PAUSING

To many readers, there is one time to pause and that is when a period or a comma is reached. But, as in pacing, pausing is not regulated entirely by punctuation marks—but rather by thought group, thought content. Without pauses, reading becomes mechanical. There is no variety, no clarity, no use of emphasis, no meaning. It is like listening to a record that repeats itself over and over.

Pauses serve four purposes: (1) They clearly define changes in ideas and emotions. (2) They serve to emphasize key words and key thoughts. (3) They provide a basis for an emotional outlet in the reader. (4) They give the reader the necessary opportunity to breathe, to take in the fuel that is his ammunition.

Pauses give life, beauty, intensity to readings. If used properly, they are your best tool. If omitted or used incorrectly, they can disrupt continuity of thought and intention. To use too few pauses insures monotony. To use too many makes for a choppy reading that will be vague and confusing.

The duration of a pause is a vital matter. A pause for the purpose of taking a breath or for emphasizing a word or phrase is usually of short duration. The voice tone flows from the last sound of the previous word to the beginning sound of the next word. For example, "He knew her secret, / her desperate / secret." If there is a complete change of idea or mood, the pause is more abrupt and of longer duration. "He had had it. // His mind went back to the day he first met her, / a grey day. / But he tossed aside such reminiscences at once. // The hurt was too much." At the double slash lines, the pause is definite, of long duration, to heighten change in thought and idea. Pauses at the points identified in the following segment would introduce choppiness: "He went home // He walked down the street // slowly // He was in a hurry." // Notice that there is no sense of movement in the lines, only a feeling of choppiness.

Pauses are essential in poetry in order to convey mood and

meaning through the imagery the lines contain. Read the following poem without any pauses except at the end of each line.

Tears, Idle Tears

Alfred, Lord Tennyson

Tears, idle tears, I know not what they mean,
Tears from the depth of some divine despair
Rise in the heart, and gather in the eyes
In looking on the happy autumn-fields,
And thinking of the days that are no more.

Fresh as the first beam glittering on a sail,
That brings forth our friends up from the underworld,
Sad as the last which reddens over one
That sinks with all we love below the verge;
So sad, so fresh, the days that are no more.

Ah, sad and strange as in dark summer dawns
The earliest pipe of half-awakened birds
To dying ears, when unto dying eyes
The casement slowly grows a glimmering square;
So sad, so strange, the days that are no more.

Dear as remembered kisses after death,
And sweet as those by hopeless fancy feigned
On lips that are for others, deep as love.
Deep as first love, and wild with all regret;
O Death in Life, the days that are no more.

Now read the poem again with the following markings, pausing slightly and taking a breath when you come to a single virgule; make a more definite pause when you come to double virgules. Notice how the meaning is heightened.

Tears / idle tears / I know not what they mean //
Tears from the depth / of some divine despair

Rise in the heart / and gather in the eyes /
In looking on the happy / autumn fields /
And thinking of the days / that are no more / /

Fresh as the first beam / glittering on a sail
That brings forth our friends up from the underworld/ /
Sad as the last / which reddens over one
That sinks with all we love / below the verge / /
So sad / so fresh / the days that are no more / /

Ah / sad and strange / as in dark summer dawns
The earliest pipe / of half-awakened birds
To dying ears / when unto dying eyes /
The casement slowly grows / a glimmering square / /
So sad / so strange / the days that are no more / /

Dear as remembered kisses after death /
And sweet as those / by hopeless fancy feigned
On lips / that are for others / deep as love / /
Deep as first love / and wild with all regret / /
O Death in Life / the days / that are no more / /

John Keats' "Ode to a Nightingale" is an excellent example of
how pauses add to the beauty of the imagery and to the meaning.
Read it, noting the effect of the pauses.

Ode to a Nightingale

John Keats

My heart aches, / and a drowsy numbness pains
My sense, / as though of hemlock I had drunk, / /
Or emptied some dull opiate to the drains
One minute past, / / and Lethe-wards had sunk: / /
'Tis not through envy of thy happy lot, /
But being too happy in thine happiness,— /
That thou, light-wingèd Dryad of the trees, /

In some melodious plot
Of beechen green, / and shadows numberless, /
Singest of summer / in full-throated ease. / /

O, for a draught of vintage! / that hath been
Cooled a long age / in the deep-delvèd earth, / /
Tasting of Flora / and the country green, /
Dance, / and Provençal song, / and sunburnt mirth! / /
O for a beaker full of the warm South, /
Full of the true, / the blushful Hippocrene, /
With beaded bubbles winking at the brim, /
And purple-stainèd mouth; /
That I might drink, / and leave the world unseen, /
And with thee / fade away / into the forest dim: /

Fade far away, / dissolve, / and quite forget
What thou among the leaves hast never known, /
The weariness, / the fever, and the fret
Here, / where men sit and hear each other groan; / /
Where palsy shakes a few, / sad, / last grey hairs, / /
Where youth grows pale, / and specter-thin, / and dies; / /
Where but to think is to be full of sorrow
And leaden-eyed despairs, / /
Where Beauty cannot keep her lustrous eyes, /
Or new Love pine at them / beyond to-morrow. / /

Knowing when to pause as you read prose is equally important and there are differences in the reading of expository and narrative prose. John Donne's *Quis Homo* is a selection worthy of study since it deals in concepts and not in plot or characterization.

We are all conceived in close prison; in our Mothers' wombs, we are close prisoners all; when we are born, we are born but to the liberty of the house; prisoners still, though within larger walls; and then all our life is but a going out to the place of execution, to death. Now was there ever any man seen to sleep in the cart, between Newgate and Tyburn? Between the prison, and the place of execution, does any man sleep? And we sleep all the way; from the womb to the grave we are never thoroughly awake; but pass on with such dreams, and imaginations as these, I may live as well as another, and why should I die, rather than another? But awake, and tell me, says this text, *Quis Homo?* Who is that other that thou talkest of? *What man is he that liveth, and shall not see death?*

Donne's theory is that we are never entirely free, that we are in a kind of prison all our lives. We are imprisoned from the womb to the grave. Death is inevitable for us all and we tend to sleep through life rather than live life wide-awake. Now re-read this selection, noting the markings. See if the meaning is not clearer.

We are all conceived / in close prison / in our Mothers' wombs / we are close prisoners all / / when we are born / we are born but to the liberty / of the house / / prisoners still / though / within larger walls / / and then all our life / is but a going out to the place of execution / to death / / Now was there ever any man / seen to sleep in the cart / between Newgate and Tyburn? / / Between the prison and the place of execution / does any man sleep? / / And we sleep all the way / / from the womb to the grave / we are never thoroughly awake / but pass on with such dreams / and imaginations as these / / I may live as well as another / / and why should I die / rather than another? / / But awake / and tell me / says this text / *Quis homo?* / / Who is that other that thou talkest of? / / *What man is he that liveth* / *and shall not* / *see death?*

In line one, the pause before "in close prison" is given not only for smoother phrasing but to emphasize the key concept—prison. The pause before "when we are born . . ." stresses the idea that we enter life and live life as prisoners. The change of idea on "and then all our life . . ." requires a longer pause to emphasize life vs. death theory. There is another change in idea on "Now was there ever any man . . ." which brings in a new concept of prison—the actuality of the prison of Newgate where prisoners were taken in carts to Tyburn, the place of execution. This is a further extension of the idea of prison to death. The change before "And we sleep all the way" is to stress Donne's theory of our living only a half life. The personal reference comes in "I may live as well as another . . ." There is a further distinction and new concept in the reference to the title, which means "Who is the man?" The pause after "that liveth" and before "and shall not see death?" is to serve as emphasis on the contrast between life and death.

Keep in mind that this is part of a sermon that Donne gave, and since it was meant to be delivered, the use of pauses becomes even more significant.

Narrative prose, dealing as it does in characterization, mood, and dialogue makes special demands on the reader in regard to pauses. In the following selection from *Sons and Lovers* by D. H. Lawrence, we can see what the correct use of pauses does to make this section come alive.

From

Sons and Lovers

D. H. Lawrence

"You were late," she said.   *pause here to indicate the silence and need for next line*
"Was I?" he answered.
There was silence for a while.
another pause here to indicate "Was it rough riding?" she asked.
difficulty in keeping conversation going "I didn't notice it."
She continued quickly to lay the table. When she had finished—
"Tea won't be for a few minutes. Will you come and look at the daffodils?" she said.
He rose without answering. They went out into the back garden under the bud- *pause — Focus of attention changes here to the garden.* ding damson-trees. The hills and the sky were clean and cold. Everything *pause — focus changes again* looked washed, rather hard. Miriam *Pause emphasizes change*

glanced at Paul. He was pale and impassive. It seemed cruel to her that his eyes and brows, which she loved, could look so hurting.

"Has the wind made you tired?" she asked. She detected an underneath feeling of weariness about him.

pause to heighten her concern

"No, I think not," he answered.

"It must be rough on the road—the wood moans so."

"You can see by the clouds it's a southwest wind; that helps me here."

"You see, I don't cycle, so I don't understand," she murmured.

"Is there need to cycle to know that!" he said.

She thought his sarcasms were unnecessary. They went forward in silence . . . Miriam went on her knees before one cluster, took a wild looking daffodil between her hands, turned up its face of gold to her, and bowed down, caressing it with her mouth and cheeks and brow. He stood aside, with his hands in his pockets, watching her . . .

pause to show the strain between the two

"Why must you always be fondling things?" he said irritably.

"But I love to touch them," she replied, hurt.

"Can you never like things without clutching them as if you wanted to pull the heart out of them? Why don't you have a bit more restraint, or reserve, or something?"

pause to show her hurt

She looked up at him full of pain, then continued slowly to stroke her lips against a ruffled flower. Their scent, as she smelled it, was so much kinder than he; it almost made her cry.

"You wheedle the soul out of things," he said. "I would never wheedle—at any rate, I'd go straight."

He scarcely knew what he was saying. These things came from him mechanically. She looked at him. His body seemed one weapon, firm and hard against her.

pause to emphasize relation between them

"You're always begging things to love you," he said, "as if you were a beggar for love. Even the flowers, you have to fawn on them . . .

"You don't want to love—your eternal and abnormal craving is to be loved. You aren't positive, you're negative. You absorb, absorb, as if you must fill yourself up with love, because you've got a shortage somewhere."

pause to heighten the shock she feels

She was stunned by his cruelty, and did not hear. He had not the faintest notion of what he was saying. It was as if his fretted, tortured soul, run hot by thwarted passion, jetted off these sayings like sparks from electricity. She did not grasp anything he said. She only sat crouched beneath his cruelty and his hatred of her. She never realized in a flash. Over everything she brooded and brooded.

pause to show change of focus

After tea he played with Edgar and the brothers, taking no notice of Miriam. She, extremely unhappy on this looked-for holiday, waited for him. And at last he yielded and came to her. She was determined to track this mood of his to its origin. She counted it not much more than a mood.

slightly longer pause as a new thought and new characters are introduced

pause to show new attention on his past

"Shall we go through the wood a little way?" she asked him, knowing he never refused a direct request . . .

pause here to show Paul's unhappiness

*pause.—
mood
changes here*

"We will go back to the house," he
said, "I don't want to talk out."

They went past the lilac-tree, whose
bronze leaf-buds were coming un-
fastened. Just a fragment remained of the
haystack, a monument squared and
brown, like a pillar of stone. There was
a little bed of hay from the last cutting.

"Let us sit here a minute," said Miriam. . . .

At that moment a big bull-terrier came
rushing up, open-mouthed, pranced his
two paws on the youth's shoulders, lick-
ing his face. Paul drew back laughing.
Bill was a great relief to him. He pushed
the dog aside, but it came leaping
back.

"Get out," said the lad, "or I'll dot thee
one."

But the dog was not to be pushed
away. So Paul had a little battle with the
creature, pitching poor Bill away from
him, who, however, only floundered tu-
multuously back again, wild with joy.
The two fought together, the man laughing grudgingly, the dog grinning all over.
Miriam watched them. There was something pathetic about the man. He wanted
so badly to love, to be tender. The rough
way he bowled the dog over was really
loving. Bill got up, panting with happiness, his brown eyes rolling in his white
face, and lumbered back again. He
adored Paul. The lad frowned.

*pause —
abrupt
change of
mood*

"Bill, I've had enough o' thee," he said.

But the dog only stood with two heavy
paws, that quivered with love, upon his
thigh, and flickered a red tongue at him.
He drew back.

"No," he said—"no—I've had enough."

And in a minute the dog trotted off happily, to vary the fun.

pause —
mood changes

He remained staring miserably across at the hills, whose still beauty he begrudged. He wanted to go and cycle with Edgar. Yet he had not the courage to leave Miriam.

"Why are you sad?" she asked humbly.

"I'm not sad; why should I be," he answered. "I'm only normal."

She wondered why he always claimed to be normal when he was disagreeable.

"But what is the matter?" she pleaded, coaxing him soothingly.

"Nothing!"

pause to
emphasize
his lack
of composure

"Nay!" she murmured.

He picked up a stick and began to stab the earth with it.

"You'd far better not talk," he said.

"But I wish to know—" she replied.

He laughed resentfully.

"You always do," he said.

"It's not fair to me," she murmured.

He thrust, thrust, thrust at the ground with the pointed stick, digging up little clods of earth as if he were in a fever of irritation. She gently and firmly laid her hand on his wrist.

"Don't!" she said. "Put it away."

He flung the stick into the currant-bushes, and leaned back. Now he was bottled up.

"What is it?" she pleaded softly.

pause to
sharpen the
effect of what
he has to
say

He lay perfectly still, only his eyes alive, and they full of torment.

pause to
show how
hard it is
for him

"You know," he said at length, rather wearily—

"you know—we'd better break off."

It was what she dreaded. Swiftly

everything seemed to darken before her eyes.

"Why!" she murmured. "What has happened?"

"Nothing has happened. We only real- *pause to heighten the fact he can't find the words*
ize where we are. It's no good—"

She waited in silence, sadly, patiently. It was no good being impatient with him. At any rate, he would tell her now what ailed him.

"We agreed on friendship," he went on in a dull, monotonous voice. "How often have we agreed for friendship! And *pause to sharpen the silence* yet—it neither stops there, nor gets anywhere else."

He was silent again. She brooded. What did he mean? He was so wearying. There was something he would not yield. *slight pause to show difficulty in expressing himself.* Yet she must be patient with him.

"I can only give friendship—it's all I'm capable of—it's a flaw in my makeup. The thing overbalances to one side —I hate a toppling balance. Let us have done."

There was warmth of fury in his last phrases. He meant she loved him more *pause to heighten the reflection* than he her. Perhaps he could not love her. Perhaps she had not in herself that which he wanted. It was the deepest motive of her soul, this self-mistrust. It was *pause to show her reflection* so deep that she dared neither realize nor acknowledge it. Perhaps she was deficient. Like an infinitely subtle shame, it kept her always back. If it were so, she would do without him. She would never let herself want him. She would merely see.

"But what has happened?" she asked.

"Nothing—it's all in myself—it only

comes out just now. We're always like this towards Easter-time."

He grovelled so helplessly. She pitied him. At least she never floundered in such a pitiable way. After all, it was he who was chiefly humiliated. ——— *pause to add emphasis to next line*

pause — difficulty in expressing self

"What do you want?" she asked him.

"Why——I mustn't come often——that's all. Why should I monopolize you when I'm not——You see, I'm deficient in something with regard to you——" ——— *pause — the words seem to stop*

He was telling her he did not love her, and so ought to leave her a chance with another man. How foolish and blind and shamefully clumsy he was! . . .

pause — change of thought

"But I don't understand," she said huskily. "Yesterday——" ——— *pause — words come to an end*

The night was turning jangled and hateful to him as the twilight faded. And she bowed under her suffering.

"I know," he cried, "you never will! You'll never believe that I can't——can't physically, any more than I can fly up like a skylark——"

"What?" she murmured. Now she dreaded.

"Love you."

Note that the mood switches back and forth from the idyllic appreciation of nature to the obvious reluctance of Paul to tell Miriam the news that is so painful to him—and of her naive unawareness of the problem. It is essential for the reader to use pauses effectively to create the atmosphere, the tension, the confusion. Without pauses, their reactions would be blurred, indefinite. Without them Paul's final pronouncement would be lost. Note the references made on the marked copy and the reasons for the longer pauses for changes in mood and thought.

It is necessary to remember that these are not the only possible markings. You may feel a different emotional reaction. You may want to pause in places other than those identified. To do so is perfectly all right. Pause where it is best for you but be sure that continuity is smooth.

You will note that the author has used dashes often to indicate the need for an abrupt pause—or a prolonged one.

O'Neill uses the same technique in *More Stately Mansions.* The following excerpt from the play highlights the technique.

From

More Stately Mansions

Eugene O'Neill

SIMON: (*He pauses, then goes on. Gradually his eyes drop from Joel to his desk, and more and more it seems he is talking to himself.*)

I concentrate all my mind and energy to get a thing done. /

I live with it, / think of nothing else, / eat with it, / take it to bed with me, / sleep with it, / dream of it /—and then suddenly / one day / it is accomplished / —finished, / dead! // —and I become empty, // but at the same time restless and aimless, / as if I had lost my meaning to myself. // A vacation would be in order at such times, // But where? / How? / A voyage to France, / say— with Sara— / a second honeymoon. // But Sara would not leave the children, / and to take the children along would mean it would be their vacation with their mother, / not mine with my wife. // Perhaps Sara would even insist on taking Mother with us! / They have grown to be such loving friends, / drawn to each other by their devotion to the children! // I assure you, / I am left entirely out of it now. // That is Mother's doing, of course. // She imagines she has been very subtle, that I have not seen. / But I have promised myself that as soon as I had time, / I would put a stop to her greedy scheming, / and now the railroad deal is completed— //
(*He smiles strangely*)

That may be the change in activity I need. / /
(*He pauses*)
If you ever fall in love, Joel, / take my advice and do not
marry // Keep your love to your mistress / with no right of
ownership except what she earns day by day, / What she
can make you pay for possession. // Love should be a
deal forever incomplete / never finally settled, / with each
party continually raising the bids, / but neither one con-
cluding a final role. / /
(*He laughs mockingly at Joel's cold disapproval*)
Yes, / my advice to you would be to shun marriage / and
keep a whore instead!

JOEL: I cannot see why you wish to discuss such matters
with me.

SIMON: No, neither can I— / except that I can trust you to
listen without hearing much. / /
(*With a conciliating manner*)
Why is it you never come to visit Mother?

JOEL: You know she has as little desire to see me as I have
to see her.

SIMON: You would be astounded at the way she has transformed herself. // It is as though she had slowly taken
possession of Sara / in order to make of my wife a second
self through which she could live again. // Or, in another
aspect, / trick Sara into being an accessory in the murder
of that old self, / which was once my mother. // And so
leave me motherless. / But at the same time / by becoming
Sara, / leave me wifeless, / for naturally I could not
regard—//
(*He stops abruptly—then goes on with an increasing
brooding strangeness*)
Sometimes the two have appeared to lose their / separate
identities / in my mind's eye— / have seemed, / through
the subtle power of Mother's fantastic will, / to merge /
and become one woman— / a spirit of Woman made flesh
/ and flesh of her made spirit, / mother and wife in one—
/ to whom I was never anything more / than a necessary
adjunct of a means to motherhood— / a son in one case, /
a husband in the other— / but now no longer needed
since the mother / by becoming the wife / has my four

sons to substitute for me, / and the wife having them, / no longer needs a husband to use in begetting— // And so I am left alone, / an unwanted son, / a discarded lover, / an outcast without meaning or function / in my own home / but pleasantly tolerated in memory of old service / and as a domestic slave whose greed can be used to bring in money to support Woman! //

(*With vindictive calculation*)

Yes / that is what Mother flatters herself she has accomplished. / But she doesn't realize there are fundamental weaknesses in her plan, / that the past is never dead / as long as we live / because all we are is the past. // She is going to discover, / beginning today, / and Sara, too, / that whenever I wish, / I take back what belongs to me, / no matter— //

(*He checks himself with a sudden wary glance at Joel*)

But all these fanciful speculations are nonsense. //

JOEL: (*Gets up from his chair*)

If you have done, may I go back to my work?

SIMON: Yes. Take your idiotic conscience to hell out of here! //

(*Joel turns and goes into the bookkeeper's office at right, closing the door behind him*)

Even that dull fool realized / I was really addressing myself / —because I have no one but myself. // Yes, Mother has left me with no life but this one / which she always despised / —the ambition to be a Napoleon among traders! // I, who once dreamed—! // Rubbish! The possession of power is the only freedom, / and your pretended disgust with it is a lie. // You must allow for your present state of mind— / the reaction of emptiness / after success / —you've always felt it— / but never so strongly before— // There is a finality in this / —as if some long patient tension had snapped— // as if I no longer had the power / to discipline my will to keep myself united // —another self rebels / — secedes / —as if at last I must become two selves from now on— / division and confusion / —war / —a duel / to the death— //

(*With revengeful bitterness*)

Well, let those who are responsible for the challenge

beware, / for I will make it their duel, too! / / Yes, Mother and Sara, / henceforth I must demand that each of you / takes upon herself her full responsibility / for what I have become. / / Bah! What rubbishy fantasies!— / / As if I really desired two damned possessive women / prying and interfering in my private business! / / All I know is that on an impulse / I asked Sara to come here— / some confused feeling that if I get her alone away from Mother's influence, / I would desire her again, / / Hadn't I better think out more exactly how I shall attack?—/ /
No, wait until you feel her out / and see how much of old greedy Sara still lies behind her present self— / the ambitious Sara / who used to long to own an Irish-castle-in-Spain, / gentleman's estate!— / who was willing to use any means— / even her beautiful body / —to get what she wanted. / / I should have swindled her into giving herself by promising marriage / —and then having had all I wanted of her, / deserted her / —it would have served her right to be beaten / at her own game / / —I would have forgotten her and returned to Mother, / waiting for me in her garden— / /
But she wasn't waiting / —She was just as ruthless and unscrupulous about discarding you / as Sara was in taking you. / / Mother took pains to point it out to me / by implication / that day she deliberately made up the fairy tale about the exiled Prince and the magic door— / /

The scene is basically a long monologue by Simon with Joel making only brief responses. In these speeches, O'Neill uses the dashes heavily for sudden changes of thought, for interrupted thoughts. Simon is thinking aloud of the two women in his life and what both have done to him; the pauses heighten the changes of mood and emphasis as Simon considers first his mother and her influence on him and his marriage, and then the closeness both women share while he feels left out. His deep bitterness towards them both is prominently stressed. Note how often Simon switches his thought. Study the double slash marks for the introduction of new emotions and new thoughts even before the preceding one has been finished. Try reading these speeches without regarding all the double slashes, as merely slight pauses for breath, and you'll see that Simon's lines make no sense, have no real meaning While these marks add contrast and variety to the dialogue, the single slash marks serve to emphasize certain words or phrases and to provide momentary stops for the reader to accentuate key concepts.

This excerpt from O'Neill's play provides an excellent example of how often thoughts can change in a single speech—how different moods are heightened by such pauses. Without such pauses, the monologues would be masses of confusion.

To analyze a selection that is more familiar, look at Hamlet's "O, that this too too solid flesh would melt . . ."

HAMLET: O, that this too too solid flesh would melt,
Thaw, and resolve itself into a dew!
Or that the Everlasting had not fix'd
His canon 'gainst self-slaughter! O God! God!
How weary, stale, flat, and unprofitable,
Seem to me all the uses of this world!
Fie on't! oh fie, fie! 'Tis an unweeded garden,
That grows to seed; things rank and gross in nature
Possess it merely. That it should come to this!
But two months dead! Nay, not so much, not two.
So excellent a king; that was, to this,
Hyperion to a satyr; so loving to my mother
That he might not beteem the winds of heaven
Visit her face too roughly. Heaven and earth!
Must I remember? Why, she would hang on him
As if increase of appetite had grown
By what it fed on; and yet, within a month,—
Let me not think on't—Frailty, thy name is woman!—
A little month, or e'er those shoes were old
With which she followed my poor father's body,
Like Niobe, all tears,—why she, even she,—
O God! a beast, that wants discourse of reason,
Would have mourn'd longer—married with mine uncle,
My father's brother, but no more like my father
Than I to Hercules; within a month,
Ere yet the salt of most unrighteous tears
Had left the flushing of her galled eyes,

She married. O, most wicked speed, to post
With such dexterity to incestuous sheets!
It is not, nor it cannot come to good.—
But break, my heart, for I must hold my tongue.

Here we have an example of reflection, of a man's debating with himself his own reason for being, his own purpose. When one is in turmoil with himself, he does not think rapidly or freely. There is conflict, concern, uncertainty, and pauses are the chief means of identifying these for an audience.

STRESS

Pausing and pacing are only two of the tools necessary for the oral interpreter of literature. Emphasis, stress on words and on thoughts, is also vitally necessary. You can read a scene slowly or rapidly, you can pause in the right places, but if the thoughts and words that give meaning to the selection are not properly stressed, there is insufficient emotional involvement.

In poetry, images are heavily stressed. Impressions are compressed into a few words. Adjectives, verbs, nouns, and adverbs get the most stress. Least emphasis is given to the articles, "a" and "the." Rarely is the "a" pronounced with a long sound (ā).

Note how stress on the underlined words in the following selection from John Keats' "Eve of St. Agnes" adds to the richness and color of the imagery—and how, with appropriate pauses and phrasing, the atmosphere, the setting come alive.

The Eve of St. Agnes

John Keats

St. Agnes' Eve—Ah, bitter chill it was!
The owl, for all his feathers, was a-cold;
The hare limped trembling through the frozen grass,

And silent was the flock in wooly fold;
Numb were the Beadsman's fingers, while he told
His rosary, and while his frosted breath,
Like pious incense from a censer old,
Seemed taking flight for heaven, without a death,
    Past the sweet Virgin's picture, while his prayer he
      saith.
His prayer he saith, this patient, holy man;
Then takes his lamp, and riseth from his knees,
And back returneth, meagre, barefoot, wan,
Along the chapel aisle by slow degrees:
The sculptured dead, on each side, seem to freeze,
Emprisoned in black, purgatorial rails:
Knights, ladies, praying in dumb orat'ries,
He passeth by; and his weak spirit fails
    To think how they may ache in icy hoods and mails.
Northward he turneth through a little door,
And scarce three steps, ere Music's golden tongue
Flattered to tears this aged man and poor;
But no—already had his deathbell rung;
The joys of all his life were said and sung:
His was harsh penance on St. Agnes' Eve:
Another way he went, and soon among
Rough ashes sat he for his soul's reprieve,
    And all night kept awake, for sinners' sake to grieve.
That ancient Beadsman heard the prelude soft;
And so it chanced, for many a door was wide,
From hurry to and fro. Soon, up aloft,
The silver, snarling trumpets 'gan to chide:
The level chambers, ready with their pride,
Were glowing to receive a thousand guests:
The carvèd angels, ever eager-eyed,
Stared, where upon their heads the cornice rests,
    With hair blown back and wings put crosswise on
      their breasts.
At length burst in the urgent revelry,
With plume, tiara, and all rich array,
Numerous as shadows, haunting fairily
The brain, new stuffed, in youth, with triumphs gay
Of old romance. These let us wish away,

And turn, sole-thoughted, to one Lady there,
Whose heart had brooded, all that wintry day,
On love, and winged St. Agnes' saintly care,
   As she had heard old dames full many times declare.
They told her how, upon St. Agnes' Eve,
Young virgins might have visions of delight,
And soft adorings from their loves receive,
Upon the honeyed middle of the night,
If ceremonies due they did aright;
As supperless to bed they must retire,
And couch supine their beauties, lily white;
Nor look behind, nor sideways, but require
   Of Heaven with upward eyes for all that they desire.

For an even more graphic illustration, let us take "The Cry of the Children" by Elizabeth Barrett Browning. Note how the underlined words add richness to the specific meaning.

The Cry of the Children

Elizabeth Barrett Browning

Do ye hear the children weeping, O my brothers
Ere the sorrow comes with years?
They are leaning their young heads against their mothers,
And that cannot stop their tears.
The young lambs are bleating in the meadows,
The young birds are chirping in the nest,
The young fawns are playing with the shadows,
The young flowers are blowing toward the west—
But the young, young children, O my brothers,
They are weeping bitterly!
They are weeping in the playtime of the others,
In the country of the free.
Do you question the young children in the sorrow,

Why their tears are falling so?
The old man may weep for his to morrow
Which is lost in Long Ago;
The old tree is leafless in the forest,
The old year is ending in the frost,
The old wound, if stricken, is the sorest,
The old hope is hardest to be lost.
But the young, young children, O my brothers,
Do you ask them why they stand
Weeping sore before the bosoms of their mothers,
In our happy Fatherland?
They look with their pale and sunken faces,
And their looks are sad to see,
For the man's hoary anguish draws and presses
Down the cheeks of infancy.
"Your old earth," they say, "is very dreary;
"Our young feet," they say, "are very weak!
Few paces have we taken, yet are weary—
Our grave-rest is very far to seek.
Ask the aged why they weep, and not the children,
For the outside earth is cold;
And we young ones stand without, in our bewildering,
And the graves are for the old."
"True," say the children, "it may happen
That we die before our time;
Little Alice died last year—her grave is shapen
Like a snowball, in the rime.
We looked into the pit prepared to take her:
Was no room for any work in the close clay!
From the sleep wherein she lieth none will wake her,
Crying, 'Get up, little Alice! it is day.'
If you listen by that grave, in sun and shower,
With your ear down, little Alice never cries;
Could we see her face, be sure we should not know her,
For the smile has time for growing in her eyes:
And merry go her moments, lulled and stilled in
The shroud by the kirk-chime!
It is good when it happens," say the children,
"That we die before our time."

Without the necessary stress on these words, the effect the author is trying to create would be lost. It would be a jumble of words—with no emotion. For example, when you tell of a violent storm, you don't discuss it the same way you do a sunny day. If you describe a fat woman, you don't describe her as you would a slender, beautifully proportioned woman. When you say a thing is ugly, you don't treat it in terms you would use if you were talking of something beautiful and fragile. Remember—words are your tools, your equipment as an interpreter. Use them wisely.

For a simple exercise, see how stress changes the meanings in the following sentence: "I am going to see my uncle." "*I* am going to see my uncle"; this means "I" am and no one else. "I *am* going to see my uncle," a positive assertion. "I am *going* to see my uncle"; emphasis on "going" indicates definiteness of action. "I am going *to* see my uncle"; the stress here is on the direction the action is taking. "I am going to *see* my uncle"; now the emphasis is on the act of seeing. "I am going to see *my* uncle—" "my" uncle and nobody else's. "I am going to see my *uncle*—" not "my" aunt or brother but my uncle.

Proper use of stress also adds clarity of thought and meaning, and both are vital in the reading of expository prose.

This selection has been set up in a structural form to indicate, at the same time, where pauses and stress should occur. As you read the following excerpt, pause at the end of each line for breath or emphasis.

From

Les Miserables

Victor Hugo

At Jourdain's
The <u>common</u> room was <u>full</u> of customers,
as the <u>great</u> yard was full of <u>vehicles</u> of every sort—
<u>carts</u>,
<u>cabriolets</u>,
<u>chars-a-bancs</u>,
<u>tilburys</u>,
<u>unnamable carriages</u>,

shapeless,
patched,
with their shafts reaching heavenward like arms,
or with their noses in the ground
and their tails in the air.

The vast fireplace,
full of clear flame,
cast an intense heat against the backs of the row
on the right of the table.
Three spits were revolving,
laden with chickens,
pigeons, and legs of mutton;
and a delectable odor of roast meat,
and of gravy dripping from the browned skin,
came forth from the hearth,
stirred the guests to merriment
and made their mouths water.

All the aristocracy of the plough ate there,
at Mast' Jourdain's,
the innkeeper and horse trader—
a shrewd rascal who had money.

The dishes passed
and were soon emptied,
like the jugs of yellow cider.
Everyone told of his affairs,
his sales and his purchases.
They inquired about the crops.
The weather was good for green stuffs,
But a little wet for wheat.

The excerpt from Hugo is highly descriptive, with images demanding proper emphasis and coloring. In the second section, such
images as "cast an intense heat," "delectable odor of roast meat,"
"gravy dripping from the browned skin" need to be stressed because
the author is trying to create an atmosphere of a feast and the use of
stress on adjectives helps convey this.

In drama, stress plays a big part. Often one word will receive primary emphasis for effect, as in "You are nothing but—but—a murderer!" Or as in Yank's final speech in Eugene O'Neill's *The Hairy Ape,* where he says, "So you're what she seen when she looked at me—de white faced tart." Or in Hamlet's "To be or not to be," when Hamlet says, "To die, to sleep—no more." In each case the final words in the lines are stressed for emphasis of thought and for dramatic impact.

But emphasis is not used merely for dramatic effect. It can be used to heighten comedy lines. For example, two men are discussing a lady of questionable virtue. The line: "You mean she's a—a—lady?". The emphasis on the last word should convey the double meaning to the word.

In the following selection from Oliver Goldsmith's *She Stoops to Conquer,* stress is used effectively to heighten the comedy.

From

She Stoops to Conquer

Oliver Goldsmith

Scene: A Chamber in an old-fashioned House.
Enter Mrs. Hardcastle and Mr. Hardcastle.

MRS. HARDCASTLE: I vow, Mr. Hardcastle, you're very particular. Is there a creature in the whole country, but ourselves, that does not take a trip to town now and then, to rub off the rust a little? There's the two Miss Hoggs, and our neighbour, Mrs. Grigsby, go to take a month's polishing every winter.

HARDCASTLE: Ay, and bring back vanity and affectation to last them the whole year. I wonder why London cannot keep its own fools at home. In my time, the follies of the town crept slowly among us, but now they travel faster than a stage-coach. Its fopperies come down, not only as inside passengers, but in the very basket.

MRS. HARDCASTLE: Ay, your times were fine times, indeed; you have been telling us of them for many a long year. Here we live in an old rumbling mansion, that looks for all the world like an inn, but that we <u>never</u> see company. Our best visitors are old Mrs. Oddfish, the curate's wife, and little <u>Cripplegate</u>, the lame dancing-master; and all our <u>entertainment</u> your <u>old</u> stories of <u>Prince</u> <u>Eugene</u> and the <u>Duke</u> of Marlborough. I <u>hate</u> such <u>old-fashioned</u> <u>trumpery</u>.

HARDCASTLE: And I <u>love</u> it. I love everything that's <u>old</u>: <u>old</u> <u>friends</u>, <u>old</u> <u>times</u>, <u>old</u> <u>manners</u>, <u>old</u> <u>books</u>, <u>old</u> <u>wine</u>; and, I believe, <u>Dorothy</u>, (*taking her hand*) you'll own I have been <u>pretty</u> fond of an <u>old</u> wife.

MRS. HARDCASTLE: <u>Lord</u>, Mr. Hardcastle, you're for <u>ever</u> at your <u>Dorothy's</u> and your old <u>wife's</u>. You may be a <u>Darby</u>, but I'll be no <u>Joan</u>, I promise you. I'm not so <u>old</u> as you'd make me, by more than <u>one</u> <u>good</u> year. Add <u>twenty</u> to <u>twenty</u>, and make money of that.

HARDCASTLE: Let me see; <u>twenty</u> added to <u>twenty</u>, makes just <u>fifty</u> and <u>seven</u>.

MRS. HARDCASTLE: It's <u>false</u>, Mr. Hardcastle: I was but <u>twenty</u> when I was brought to bed of Tony, that I had by Mr. <u>Lumpkin</u>, my <u>first</u> husband; and he's not <u>come</u> <u>to</u> years of <u>discretion</u> yet.

HARDCASTLE: Nor ever <u>will</u>, I <u>dare</u> answer for him. Ay, you have <u>taught</u> <u>him</u> finely!

MRS. HARDCASTLE: No <u>matter</u>. Tony Lumpkin has a <u>good</u> fortune. My son is <u>not</u> to live by his <u>learning</u>. I don't think a boy wants much <u>learning</u> to spend <u>fifteen</u> <u>hundred</u> a year.

HARDCASTLE: By <u>learning</u>, <u>quotha</u>! A <u>mere</u> composition of <u>tricks</u> and <u>mischief</u>.

MRS. HARDCASTLE: <u>Humour</u>, my dear: nothing but <u>humour</u>. Come, Mr. Hardcastle, you must <u>allow</u> the boy a <u>little</u> humour.

HARDCASTLE: I'd sooner <u>allow</u> him an <u>horse-pond</u>! If burning the <u>footmen's</u> shoes, <u>frighting</u> the maids, and <u>worrying</u> the kittens, be <u>humour</u>, he has it. It was but <u>yesterday</u> he <u>fastened</u> my wig to the <u>back</u> of my chair, and when I went to make a <u>bow</u>, I <u>popt</u> my <u>bald</u> <u>head</u> in Mrs. <u>Frizzle's</u> face.

MRS. HARDCASTLE: And am <u>I</u> to blame? The <u>poor</u> <u>boy</u> was always too <u>sickly</u> to do any good. A <u>school</u> would be his death. When <u>he</u> <u>comes</u> to be a little stronger, <u>who</u> knows what a <u>year</u> or <u>two's</u> Latin may do for him?

HARDCASTLE: <u>Latin</u> for him! A <u>cat</u> <u>and</u> <u>fiddle</u>. No, no, the <u>alehouse</u> and the <u>stable</u> are the only schools he'll ever go to.

MRS. HARDCASTLE: Well, we <u>must</u> <u>not</u> <u>snub</u> the poor <u>boy</u>, now, for I believe we shan't have him long among us. Any body that <u>looks</u> in his face may see he's <u>consumptive</u>.

HARDCASTLE: Ay, if growing <u>too</u> <u>fat</u> be one of the <u>symptoms</u>.

MRS. HARDCASTLE: He <u>coughs</u> sometimes.

HARDCASTLE: Yes, when his <u>liquor</u> goes the <u>wrong</u> way.

MRS. HARDCASTLE: I'm <u>actually</u> afraid of his <u>lungs</u>.

HARDCASTLE: And <u>truly</u>, <u>so</u> <u>am</u> <u>I</u>; for he sometimes <u>whoops</u> <u>like</u> a <u>speaking</u> trumpet—(*Tony hallooing behind the scenes.*)—O, there he goes—A <u>very</u> consumptive figure, truly!

(*Enter Tony, crossing the stage*)

MRS. HARDCASTLE: Tony, where are you going, my <u>charmer</u>? Won't you give Papa and I a <u>little</u> of your company, <u>lovee</u>?

TONY: I'm in <u>haste</u>, Mother, I <u>cannot</u> stay.

MRS. HARDCASTLE: You shan't <u>venture</u> out this <u>raw</u> evening, my dear. You look most <u>shockingly</u>.

TONY: I can't stay, I tell you. The <u>Three</u> <u>Pigeons</u> expect me down <u>every</u> moment. There's some <u>fun</u> going forward.

HARDCASTLE: Ay; the <u>ale-house</u>, the <u>old</u> <u>place</u>: I thought so.

MRS. HARDCASTLE: A <u>low</u>, <u>paltry</u> set of <u>fellows</u>.

TONY: Not so low <u>neither</u>. There's <u>Dick</u> <u>Muggins</u> the excise-man, <u>Jack</u> <u>Slang</u> the horse doctor, <u>Little</u> <u>Aminadab</u> that <u>grinds</u> the music box, and Tom <u>Twist</u> that <u>spins</u> the pewter <u>platter</u>.

MRS. HARDCASTLE: Pray, my dear, <u>disappoint</u> them for one night at least.

TONY: As for <u>disappointing</u> them, I should <u>not</u> <u>so</u> much mind; but I can't <u>abide</u> to <u>disappoint</u> myself.

MRS. HARDCASTLE: (*detaining him*) You shan't go.

TONY: I <u>will</u>, I tell you.

MRS. HARDCASTLE: I say you <u>shan't</u>.

TONY: We'll see which is <u>strongest</u>, you or I.

(*Exits, hauling her out*)

HARDCASTLE: Ay, there <u>goes</u> a <u>pair</u> that only <u>spoil</u> each other. But is not the <u>whole</u> age in combination to drive <u>sense</u> and <u>discretion</u> out of doors? There's my <u>pretty</u> darling, <u>Kate</u>. The <u>fashions</u> of the times have almost <u>infected</u> her too.

By living a year or two in town, she is as fond of <u>gauze</u>, and <u>French</u> <u>frippery</u>, as the best of them.

This particular play is a light-hearted farce of the eighteenth century in England. It depends for its effect on a lighter treatment, a generally faster pace. The scene is mainly idle chit-chat but it serves also to introduce the two main characters. Stress, in this instance, is not used for heavily dramatic purposes, but for comedy. And, as such, there are fewer instances of stress than would be found in a more serious play.

SUMMARY

Pacing, pausing, and stress or emphasis are vital elements of interpretative reading. No one speaks at the same rate of speed, day in and day out, and no one speaks without use of pauses. Few speak without any regard for emphasis on certain words for effect. Yet, the average beginning reader in oral interpretation makes the mistake of using one rate, few pauses, and too little emphasis. Thought and content govern the use of pacing, pausing, and emphasis. All these problems are corrected if there is sufficient involvement on the part of the reader.

More exciting sections need a faster pace. More relaxed, more languid moments take slower pacing. Poetry presents special problems in pacing because of the tendency readers have to read all material at one pace to the end of each line, without regard for the thought or mood involved. The essential consideration in pacing is variety.

The use of pauses is a vital consideration in reading. Pauses add clarity, meaning, dramatic effect, emphasis, emotional values, and also give a reader the necessary chance to breathe and to present the contrasting moods in selections. Without pauses, with the system of reading only from one punctuation mark to the next, there is monotony and disruption of thought. Pauses heighten the dramatic effects in drama and clarify concepts in prose. If pauses are used incorrectly, or if they last too long, or if they are too abrupt, the reading will be choppy. If pauses are not used often enough, a fast pace and monotony will result.

Stress and emphasis bring richness and meaning to words. They emphasize primary thoughts or emotions. They help make ideas in prose explicit; through the use of descriptive words, they add atmosphere and color and excitement to narrative; and they are the key to a reading of drama in that they supply importance to the emotions being expressed.

EXERCISES

1. Read "How Do I Love Thee?" as given in this chapter at a fast pace. Notice how difficult it is to read. Then go back and read it again at a slower pace, with more pauses, reflecting a better understanding of the meaning. You should see that when you read slower you are able to present the full meaning of the poem.
2. Say "Peter Piper picked a peck of pickled peppers." Read it fast. Then go back and do it slower and see the difference in reading.
3. Read the following in a faster manner than you would ordinarily: "The day was warm, lazy, the kind you stretch out in, the kind the birds liked and the dogs found right for curling up under the shade of a tree." Now read the line to convey the laziness of the setting—at a slower pace.
4. Read this in a slow pace:

The tension mounted in him; his nerves were taut as steel; he was sure he'd have to scream out in anguish. And yet the thing kept coming closer and closer to him, its long arms reaching out for him, reaching for his throat. His heart beat loudly, he looked round for an escape. There was none. He had to get out! He had to get out!

You probably found a slower pace too difficult. Now read it faster and see the result.
5. Take an article in your newspaper or magazine. Mark it for pauses to indicate momentary hesitation and complete changes of thought. Read it first without the markings and then read it with the markings. Note the difference.

6. Read the following: "I hate you, you contemptible cad." Read it with no pause. Now read it with a pause before "you contemptible cad."
7. Read the following passage with no particular emphasis and then go back and mark the words that seem to need emphasis. Note the difference.

> "To be or not to be, that is the question.
> Whether 'tis nobler in the mind to suffer
> The slings and arrows of outrageous fortune,
> Or to take arms against a sea of troubles
> And by opposing end them."

8. Repeat the "I am going to see my uncle" exercise in this chapter and then rephrase it to say anything else you wish, such as "I love the lady you saw."

Part Three

chapter ten

How do I read prose?

More of our literature lies in the realm of prose than in either poetry or drama. Prose is the term we apply to any literature which is not poetry or drama. Even that statement is not entirely clear, however, because we have prose which is poetic and poems which, except for name, could be considered prose. The Gettysburg Address has been called "poetic" in its beauty. Some poetry of Whitman and Corso and others lacks much of the structure that we call *poetry* but retains enough of poetry's characteristics that we still call the works *poems*— in effect, they are prose poems.

Prose is generally divided into two categories, fiction and non-fiction. Several editors of collections of literature separate prose into three divisions—expository, narrative, and descriptive. However it is divided, there is much pleasure to be gained from reading it aloud. But let's look at each of these ways of categorizing prose and see what can be learned that will be beneficial to us as interpreters.

Nonfiction as a general category of prose concerns itself primarily with explanation and persuasion. It finds its outlet through essays, editorials, diaries, histories, and letters. Any prose which seeks to inform the reader or persuade him to behave in a certain fashion, treating the ideas directly, is nonfiction.

Biography and autobiography often fall somewhere between nonfiction and fiction. They are nonfiction to the extent that they are true representations of the lives they describe. But occasionally, the facts are misinterpreted—to the detriment of the person about whom the material was written. George Washington and the cherry tree is a classic example of such a fabrication. The idea struck the fancy of an author and he used it. Unfortunately, it *became* a well-known anecdote about George Washington's life.

Moving into fiction, we first run into the historical novel which is part truth, part fiction. *Johnny Tremain, Anne Boleyn,* and *Mutiny on the Bounty* are all examples of the historical novel. This form of prose centers on a historical event or character with a mixture of real and fictional characters moving about together through real and imaginary events. *Johnny Tremain* is a story about a young boy in Boston in pre-Revolutionary War times. Some of the other characters in the novel were Paul Revere, the Sons of Liberty, and many *real* political figures of the time. The hero participated in the Boston Tea Party and was present in Boston when the Revolutionary War started. Through this young man, the author, Esther Forbes, not only tells a fascinating story but gives the reader some additional insight into the influences of that period of history and into the personalities of some of our important historical figures.

That type of prose called fiction, then, finds its outlet in short stories, novels, fables, and tales. Fiction writing, whether it be short story or novel or one of the other forms listed, relieves the author of a need to stay within particular boundaries of truth in order to make his point. He creates the story and all its trappings and may manipulate characters and action according to his desire. He is not encumbered by what has happened in history; he may extend himself to make things happen in his story as he envisions them happening.

In dividing prose another way—as descriptive, expository, persuasive, or narrative—we can draw some further distinctions. Let's begin with descriptive prose because it is often part of the other two divisions.

DESCRIPTIVE PROSE

The chief characteristic of descriptive prose is its reliance on imagery. The author of descriptive prose works in the same way as an artist. The difference is in the medium he uses. While the artist might choose among pastels, water colors, oils, or charcoal, the creator of descriptive prose paints with words. In so doing he hopes to give his reader an empathic experience. Such imagery appeals directly to the reader's sense of smell, touch, taste, hearing, and sight. As you read the following sentences, concentrate on the appeal to your senses and watch for your own empathic reactions. Real concentration will make your own senses react in the way each sentence suggests.

1. Jack's mouth watered as he watched the boy squeeze and suck the lemon. The lad sat for fully ten minutes, squeezing and sucking and puckering, his face reflecting the sourness. (What does your mouth feel like?)
2. Jim had never seen the sky so red before; he felt as though he were dropping headlong into Dante's *Inferno*. The reds and or-

anges wcrc so intense he had to wing over and head the plane north in order to avoid the searing pain the colors brought to his eyes. (Do *your* eyes burn?)

3. He touched her gently and immediately drew back in terror; he was certain now that she was dead. She was cold and clammy and, well, sort of mushy—like a piece of fat that has been soaked in water overnight. (Do you feel a revulsion?)

4. What was that smell? Dan searched his memory for a moment. He knew he had smelled it before; it was a dry, acrid, musty smell—like books left too long in the attic. (Can you smell them?)

5. Oh, what torture! He sat there in front of me and burped; it was a long, low, deep-throated belch that rattled lazily and resonantly out of his mouth and nose. (Can you hear it?)

Imagery—appeal to the senses. These are the clues to effective description. Edgar Allan Poe's "The Sphinx" is an excellent example. Read this excerpt from the story and notice how deftly he uses words to describe. To test his effectiveness try your hand at drawing the sphinx after you have read the story, or close your eyes and see if you can picture the sphinx.

The Sphinx

Edgar Allan Poe

During the dread reign of cholera in New York, I had accepted the invitation of a relative to spend a fortnight with him in the retirement of his cottage Ornee on the banks of the Hudson. We had here around us all the ordinary means of summer amusement; and what with rambling in the woods, sketching, boating, fishing, bathing, music, and books, we should have passed the time pleasantly enough, but for the fearful intelligence which reached us every morning from the populous city. Not a day elapsed which did not bring us news of the decease of some acquaintance. Then, as the fatality increased, we learned to expect daily the loss of some friend. At length we trembled at the approach of every messenger. The very air from the South seemed to us redolent with death. That palsying thought, indeed, took entire possession of my soul. I could neither speak, think, nor dream of anything else. My host was of a less excitable temperament,

and, although greatly depressed in spirits, exerted himself to
sustain my own. . . .

His endeavors to arouse me from the condition of abnormal
gloom into which I had fallen, were frustrated, in great measure, by certain volumes which I had found in his library.
These were of a character to force into germination whatever
seeds of hereditary superstition lay latent in my bosom. I had
been reading these books without his knowledge, and thus
he was often at a loss to account for the forcible impressions
which had been made upon my fancy. . . .

The fact is, that soon after my arrival at the cottage there
had occurred to myself an incident so entirely inexplicable,
and which had in it so much of the portentous character, that
I might well have been excused for regarding it as an omen.
It appalled, and at the same time so confounded and bewildered me, that many days elapsed before I could make up
my mind to communicate the circumstances to my friend.

Near the close of an exceedingly warm day, I was sitting,
book in hand, at an open window, commanding, through a
long vista of the river banks, a view of a distant hill, the face
of which nearest my position had been denuded by what is
termed a landslide, of the principal portion of its trees. My
thoughts had been long wandering from the volume before
me to the gloom and desolation of the neighboring city. Up-
lifting my eyes from the page, they fell upon the naked face
of the hill, and upon an object—upon some living monster of
hideous conformation, which very rapidly made its way from
the summit to the bottom, disappearing finally in the dense
forest below. As this creature first came in sight, I doubted my
own sanity—or at least the evidence of my own eyes; and
many minutes passed before I succeeded in convincing myself that I was neither mad nor in a dream. Yet when I described the monster (which I distinctly saw, and calmly surveyed through the whole period of its progress), my readers,
I fear, will feel more difficulty in being convinced of these
points than even I did myself.

Estimating the size of the creature by comparison with
the diameter of the large trees near which it passed—the few
giants of the forest which had escaped the fury of the landslide—I concluded it to be far larger than any ship of the

line in existence. I say ship of the line, because the shape of the monster suggested the idea—the hull of one of our seventy-four might convey a very tolerable conception of the general outline. The mouth of the animal was situated at the extremity of a proboscis some sixty or seventy feet in length, and about as thick as the body of an ordinary elephant. Near the root of this trunk was an immense quantity of black shaggy hair—more than could have been supplied by the coats of a score of buffaloes; and projecting from this hair downwardly and laterally, sprang two gleaming tusks not unlike those of the wild boar but of infinitely greater dimensions. Extending forward, parallel with the proboscis, and on each side of it was a gigantic staff, thirty or forty feet in length, formed seemingly of pure crystal, and in shape a perfect prism,—it reflected in the most gorgeous manner the rays of the declining sun. The trunk was fashioned like a wedge with the apex to the earth. From it there were outspread two pairs of wings—each wing nearly one hundred yards in length—one pair being placed above the other, and all covered with metal scales; each scale apparently some ten or twelve feet in diameter. I observed the upper and lower tiers of wings were connected by a strong chain. But the chief peculiarity of this horrible thing was the representation of a *Death's Head*, which covered nearly the whole surface of its breast, and which was as accurately traced in glaring white, upon the dark ground of the body, as if it had been there carefully designed by an artist. While I regarded the terrific animal, and more especially the appearance on its breast, with a feeling of horror and awe—with a sentiment of forthcoming evil, which I found it impossible to quell by any effort of the reason, I perceived the huge jaws at the extremity of the proboscis suddenly expand themselves, and from them there proceeded a sound so loud and so expressive of woe, that it struck upon my nerves like a knell, and as the monster disappeared at the foot of the hill, I fell at once, fainting, to the floor.

Upon recovering, my first impulse, of course, was to inform my friend of what I had seen and heard—and I can scarcely explain what feeling of repugnance it was which, in the end, operated to prevent me.

At length, one evening, some three or four days after the occurrence, we were sitting together in the room in which I had seen the apparition—I occupying the same seat at the same window, and he lounging on a sofa near at hand. The association of the place and time impelled me to give him an account of the phenomenon. He heard me to the end—at first laughed heartily—and then lapsed into an excessively grave demeanor, as if my insanity was a thing beyond suspicion. At this instant I again had a distinct view of the monster—to which, with a shout of absolute terror, I now directed his attention. He looked eagerly—but maintained that he saw nothing—although I designated minutely the course of the creature, as it made its way down the naked face of the hill.

I was now immeasurably alarmed, for I considered the vision either as an omen of my death, or, worse, as the forerunner of an attack of mania. I threw myself passionately back in my chair, and for some moments buried my face in my hands. When I uncovered my eyes, the apparition was no longer visible.

You probably noted that about fifty percent of the story is a description of the sphinx and the other fifty percent, a narrative (the story of the retreat from New York and cholera). Without the vivid, detailed, artistic description, however, there would have been no story.

A further example of description is in order. This time the artist is Antoine de Saint-Exupéry, known around the world for his ability to share his experiences through vivid description. The two excerpts included here are from his book *Wind, Sand and Stars*.

From

Wind, Sand and Stars

Antoine de Saint-Exupéry

One thing that I had loved in Paraguay was the ironic grass that showed the tip of its nose between the pavements of the capital, that slipped in on behalf of the invisible but ever-present virgin forest to see if man still held the town, if the hour had not come to send all these stones tumbling.

I liked the particular kind of dilapidation which in Paraguay was the expression of an excess of wealth. But here, in Concordia, I was filled with wonder. Here everything was in a state of decay, but adorably so, like an old oak covered with moss and split in places with age, like a wooden bench on which generations of lovers had come to sit and which had grown sacred. The wainscoating was worn, the hinges rusted, the chairs rickety. And yet, though nothing had ever been repaired, everything had been scoured with zeal. Everything was clean, waxed, gleaming.

The drawing-room had about it something extraordinarily intense, like the face of a wrinkled old lady. The walls were cracked, the ceiling stripped; and most bewildering of all in this bewildering house was the floor: it had simply caved in. Waxed, varnished and polished though it was, it swayed like a ship's gangway. A strange house, evoking no neglect, no slackness, but rather an extraordinary respect. Each passing year had added something to its charm, to the complexity of its visage and its friendly atmosphere, . . .

It is fascinating that with so few lines of description, the author can give the reader such a full appreciation and clear vision of the state of "bewildering" but "adorable" decay.

In the second segment Exupéry describes one of several nights he and his mechanic spent in the Libyan desert after their plane crashed on a flight from Paris to Saigon. The excerpt included here took place a few nights before they were rescued.

Prisoner of the Sand

Antoine de Saint-Exupéry

In this air devoid of moisture the soil is swift to give off its temperature. It was already very cold. I stood up and stamped about. But soon a violent fit of trembling came over me. My dehydrated blood was moving sluggishly and I was pierced by a freezing chill which was not merely the chill of night. My teeth were chattering and my whole body had begun to twitch. My hand shook so that I could not hold an electric torch. I who had never been sensitive to cold was about to die of cold. What a strange effect thirst can have!

Somewhere, tired of carrying it in the sun, I had let my waterproof drop. Now the wind was growing bitter and I was learning that in the desert there is no place of refuge. The desert is as smooth as marble. By day it throws no shadow; by night it hands you over naked to the wind. Not a tree, not a hedge, not a rock behind which I could seek shelter. The wind was charging me like a troop of cavalry across open country. I turned and twisted to escape it: I lay down, stood up, lay down again, and still I was exposed to its freezing lash. I had no strength to run from the assassin and under the sabre-stroke I tumbled to my knees, my head between my hands.

A little later, I pieced these bits together and remembered that I had struggled to my feet and had started to walk on, shivering as I went. I had started forward wondering where I was and then I had heard Prévot. His shouting had jolted me into consciousness.

I went back towards him, still trembling from head to foot —quivering with the attack of hiccups that was convulsing my whole body. To myself I said: "It isn't the cold. It's something else. It's the end." The simple fact was that I hadn't enough water in me. I had tramped too far yesterday and the day before when I was off by myself, and I was dehydrated.

The thought of dying of the cold hurt me. I preferred the phantoms of my mind, the cross, the trees, the lamps. At least they would have killed me by enchantment. But to be whipped to death like a slave! . . .

Confound it! Down on my knees again! We had with us a little store of medicines—a hundred grammes of ninety per cent alcohol, the same of pure ether, and a small bottle of iodine. I tried to swallow a little of the ether: it was like swallowing a knife. Then I tried the alcohol: it contracted my gullet. I dug a pit in the sand, lay down in it, and flung handfuls of sand over me until all but my face was buried in it.

Prévot was able to collect a few twigs, and he lit a fire which soon burnt itself out. He wouldn't bury himself in the sand, but preferred to stamp round and round in a circle. That was foolish.

My throat stayed shut, and though I knew that was a bad sign, I felt better. I felt calm. I felt a peace that was beyond all hope. Once more, despite myself, I was journeying, trussed up on the deck of my slave-ship under the stars. It seemed to me that I was perhaps not in such a bad pass after all.

So long as I lay absolutely motionless, I no longer felt the cold. This allowed me to forget my body buried in the sand. I said to myself that I would not budge an inch, and would therefore never suffer again. As a matter of fact, we really suffer very little. Back of all these torments there is the orchestration of fatigue or of delirium, and we live on in a kind of picture-book, a slightly cruel fairy-tale.

A little while ago the wind had been after me with whip and spur, and I was running in circles like a frightened fox. After that came a time when I couldn't breathe. A great knee was crushing in my chest. A knee. I was writhing in vain to free myself from the weight of the angel who had overthrown me. There had not been a moment when I was alone in this desert. But now I have ceased to believe in my surroundings; I have withdrawn into myself, have shut my eyes, have not so much as batted an eyelid. I have the feeling that this torrent of visions is sweeping me away to a tranquil dream: so rivers cease their turbulence in the embrace of the sea.

Farewell, eyes that I loved! Do not blame me if the human body cannot go three days without water. I should never have believed that man was so truly the prisoner of the springs and freshets. I had no notion that our self-sufficiency was so circumscribed. We take it for granted that a man is able to stride straight out into the world. We believe that man is free. We never see the cord that binds him to wells and fountains, that umbilical cord by which he is tied to the womb of the world. Let men take but one step too many . . . and the cord snaps.

Did you experience the cold, the weight, the defeat with him? Such responses would be essential for effective reading of Exupéry's work.

Mark Twain is also well known for vivid description. Often he is wildly funny and his descriptive prose is effective because he exaggerates so graphically. The following excerpt from his book *Roughing It* needs no explanation; in it he describes an incident that occurred on his trip out west. It seems that the stage-coach broke down and the passengers joined a buffalo hunt while they were waiting for it to be repaired. It is typical of Mark Twain.

From

Roughing It

Mark Twain

Next morning just before dawn, when about five hundred and fifty miles from St. Joseph, our mud-wagon broke down. We were to be delayed five or six hours, and therefore we took horses, by invitation, and joined a party who were just starting on a buffalo hunt. It was noble sport galloping over the plain in the dewy freshness of the morning, but our part of the hunt ended in disaster and disgrace, for a wounded buffalo bull chased the passenger Bemis nearly two miles, and then he forsook his horse and took to a lone tree. He was very sullen about the matter for some twenty-four hours, but at last he began to soften little by little, and finally he said:

"Well, it was not funny, and there was no sense in those gawks making themselves so facetious over it. I tell you I was angry in earnest for awhile. I should have shot that long gangly lubber they called Hank, if I could have done it without crippling six or seven other people—but of course I couldn't, the old 'Allen's' [a revolver] so confounded comprehensive. I wish those loafers had been up in the tree; they wouldn't have wanted to laugh so. If I had had a horse worth a cent—but no, the minute he saw that buffalo bull wheel on him and give a bellow, he raised straight up in the air and stood on his heels. The saddle began to slip, and I took him round the neck and laid close to him, and began to pray. Then he came down and stood up on the other end awhile, and the bull actually stopped pawing sand and bellowing to contemplate the inhuman spectacle. Then the bull made a pass at him and uttered a bellow that sounded perfectly frightful, it was so close to me, and that seemed to literally prostrate my horse's reason, and make a raving distracted maniac of him, and I wish I may die if he didn't stand on his head for a quarter of a minute and shed tears. He was absolutely out of his mind—he was, as sure as truth itself, and he really didn't know what he was doing. Then the bull came charging at us, and my horse dropped down on all fours and took a fresh start—and then for the next ten minutes he would actually throw one handspring after another so fast that the bull began to get unsettled, too, and didn't know where to start in—and so he stood there sneezing, and shoveling dust over his back, and bellowing every now and then, and thinking he had got a fifteen-hundred dollar circus horse for breakfast, certain. Well, I was first out on his neck—the horse's, not the bull's—and then underneath, and next on his rump, and sometimes head up, and sometimes heels—but I tell you it seemed solemn and awful to be ripping and tearing and carrying on so in the presence of death, as you might say. Pretty soon the bull made a snatch for us and brought away some of my horse's tail (I suppose, but do not know, being pretty busy at the time), but *something* made him hungry for solitude and suggested to him to get up and hunt for it. And then you ought to have seen that spider-legged old skeleton go! and you ought to have seen the bull cut out after him, too—head down, tongue out, tail up, bellowing like everything, and actually mowing down the weeds, and tearing up the earth, and boosting up the sand like a whirlwind! By George, it was a hot race! I and the saddle were back on the rump, and I had the bridle in my teeth and holding on to the pommel with both hands. First we left the dogs behind; then we passed a jack rabbit; then we overtook a coyote, and were gaining on an antelope when the rotten girths let go and threw me about thirty yards off to the left, and as the saddle went down over the horse's rump he gave

The primary reason for cutting literature for interpretation is to make it conform to time limits imposed by the audience or the occasion. It isn't possible to read *most* prose selections in their entirety because there isn't enough time to do so; therefore, it is necessary to learn some principles of effective cutting.

Cutting Descriptive Prose

It would seem on the surface that descriptive prose is easy to cut because it is so wordy. It is true that description moves slowly; it must do so in order to give the reader a full visual appreciation of the picture the author is painting. But you must take care not to make deletions that will distort the picture.

A general rule for cutting descriptive prose is that you can cut down but not out. Decide first what descriptive elements are most important in giving the audience a clear and vivid picture; then look for those elements which are least important and cut them in length. Perhaps you will discover that some segments can be eliminated entirely. If so, take them out. But preserve fully those important elements of the description that give the audience the author's focus and style. The excerpt which follows has been cut from Mark Twain's *Life on the Mississippi* to sharpen the focus on the two men involved in the fracas, on the abruptness of the final outcome, and to preserve Mark Twain's literary style. Read it first as it has been cut; then go back over it again to see what has been eliminated.

From

Life on the Mississippi

Mark Twain

They was all about to make a break for him, but the biggest man there jumped up and says:

"Set whar you are, gentlemen. Leave him to me; he's my meat."

Then he jumped up in the air three times, and cracked his heels together every time. He flung off a buckskin coat that was all hung with fringes, and says, "You lay thar till

~~the chewin up's done," he flung his hat down, which was all over ribbons, and says, "You lay thar till his sufferin's over."~~

~~Then he jumped up in the air and cracked his heels together again, and shouted out:~~

"Whoo-oo-p. I'm the old original iron-jawed, brass-mounted, copper-bellied corpse-maker from the wilds of Arkansaw! Look at me! I'm the man they call Sudden Death and General Desolation! Sired by a hurricane, dam'd by an earthquake, half-brother to the cholera, nearly related to the smallpox on the mother's side! Look at me! I take nineteen alligators and a bar'l of whiskey for breakfast when I'm in robust health, and a bushel of rattlesnakes and a dead body when I'm ailing. ~~I split the everlasting rocks with my glance, and I squench the thunder when I speak! Whoo-oop!~~ Stand back and give me room, according to my strength! Blood's my natural drink, and the wails of the dying is music to my ear. Cast your eye on me, gentlemen! and lay low and hold your breath, for I'm 'bout to turn myself loose!"

All the time he was getting this off, he was shaking his head and looking fierce, and kind of swelling around in a little circle, tucking up his waistbands, and now and then straightening up and beating his breast with his fist, saying "Look at me, gentlemen!" When he got through, he jumped up and cracked his heels together three times, and let off a roaring "Whoo-oop! I'm the bloodiest son of a wildcat that lives!"

The man that had started the row tilted his old slouch hat down over his right eye; then he bent stooping forward, with his back sagged and his south end sticking out far, and his fists a-shoving out and drawing in in front of him, and so went around in a little circle about three times, swelling himself up and breathing hard. Then he straightened, and jumped up and cracked his heels together three times before he lit again (that made them cheer), and he began to shout like this:

"Whoo-oop! bow your neck and spread, for the kingdom of sorrow's a coming! Hold me down to the earth, for I feel my powers a-working! ~~Whoo-oop! I'm a child~~ of sin, ~~don't let me get a start!~~ Smoked glass, here, for all! Don't attempt to look at me with the naked eye, gentlemen! ~~When I'm play-~~

~~ful I use the meridians of longitude and parallels of latitude~~ ~~for a seine, and drag the Atlantic Ocean for whales!~~ I scratch my head with the lightning and purr myself to sleep with the thunder! When I'm cold, I bile the Gulf of Mexico and bathe in it; when I'm hot, I fan myself with an equinoctial storm; when I'm thirsty I reach up and suck a cloud dry like a sponge; when I range the earth hungry, famine follows in my tracks! Whoo-oop! ~~Bow your neck and spread!~~ I put my hand on the sun's face and make it night in the earth; I bite a piece out of the moon and hurry the seasons; I shake myself and crumble the mountains! ~~Contemplate me through leather—~~ ~~don't use the naked eye! I'm the man with a petrified heart~~ ~~and biler iron bowels!~~ The massacre of isolated communities is the pastime of my ideal moments, the destruction of nationalities the serious business of my life! The boundless vastness of the great American desert is my inclosed property, and I bury my dead on my own premises!" He jumped up and cracked his heels together three times before he lit (they cheered him again), and as he came down he shouted out: "Whoo-oop! bow your neck and spread, for the Pet Child of Calamity's a-coming!"

Then the other one went to swelling around and blowing again—the first one—the one they called Bob; next, the Child of Calamity chipped in again, bigger than ever; then they both got at it at the same time, swelling round and round each other and punching their fists most into each other's faces, and whooping and jawing like Injuns; then Bob called the Child names, and the Child called him names back again; Bob called him a heap of rougher names, and the Child come back at him with the very worst kind of language; next, Bob knocked the Child's hat off, and the Child picked it up and kicked Bob's ribbony hat about six foot; ~~Bob went and got it~~ ~~and said never mind, this warn't going to be the last of the~~ ~~thing, because he was a man that never forgot and never for-~~ ~~give, and so the Child better look out, for there was a time~~ ~~a-coming, just as sure as he was a living man, that he would~~ ~~have to answer to him with the best blood in his body. The~~ ~~Child said no man was willinger than he for that time to~~ ~~come and he would give Bob fair warning, now, never to~~ ~~cross his path again, for he could never rest till he had waded~~

~~in his blood, for such was his nature, though he was sparing him now~~ on ~~account of his family, if he had one.~~

Both of them was edging away in different directions, growling and shaking their heads and going on about what they was going to do; but a little black whiskered chap skipped up and says:

"Come back here, you couple of chicken-livered cowards, and I'll thrash the two of ye!"

And he done it too.

Undoubtedly you would have cut some of the segments that were left in, and you'd have left intact some of the lines that were cut. You must pick and choose the elements to be cut, keeping in mind that, for the most part, your audience will accept what you give them and if you've done your cutting well, they will be unaware that segments of the original are missing. Be careful that the segments— words, phrases, lines, paragraphs or pages—you delete do not distort the author's picture or his style and then be your own master. Cut to make a better oral performance.

EXPOSITORY PROSE

The term "expository" is often a confusing one to beginning interpreters. Your authors regard it as prose which concerns itself directly, by way of explanation or persuasion, with ideas or principles. This textbook is an example. It presents a succession of explanations and arguments, with a series of direct illustrations aimed at giving you an understanding of, an appreciation for, and skill in oral interpretation.

Essays, editorials, reports, diaries, journals, letters, speeches, and news stories are all examples of prose which seeks to inform the reader about something or persuade him to accept a particular point of view on matters important to the author of the material.

In the reading of expository prose, which is often material without a heavy emotional content, the responsibility of the reader is to understand fully and present clearly the primary arguments advanced by the writer. The entire essay or article must be read in order to determine what is the essential theme, the primary argument. After that, a study of the thoughts embodied in each paragraph—and each topic sentence—will tell you the author's main points. In the same way, you will discover illustrations and examples used by the author to add support or reading interest to the arguments advanced. President Kennedy's speech, "Toward A Strategy of Peace," needs little introduction here. Read it as an excellent example of contemporary expository prose. It was delivered at the commencement exercises for The American University in Washington, D. C. on June 10, 1963 during a tension-filled time when the President was trying to convince Russia to join in a ban on nuclear testing. Three days after this speech was given, Russia agreed to the ban. It is not a strongly emotional speech; it is low-key and subtle. But the underlying plea for understanding of ourselves and the Russians gives it a strong emotional foundation.

Toward a Strategy of Peace

John F. Kennedy

"There are few earthly things more beautiful than a University," wrote John Masefield, in his tribute to the English universities—and his words are equally true here. He did not refer to spires and towers, to campus greens and ivied walls. He admired the splendid beauty of the university, he said, because it was "a place where those who hate ignorance may strive to know, where those who perceive truth may strive to make others see."

I have, therefore, chosen this time and this place to discuss a topic on which ignorance too often abounds and the truth is too rarely perceived—yet it is the most important topic on earth: world peace.

What kind of peace do I mean? What kind of peace do we seek? Not a *Pax Americana* enforced on the world by American weapons of war. Not the peace of the grave or the security of the slave. I am talking about genuine peace, the kind of peace that makes life on earth worth living, the kind that enables men and nations to grow and to hope and to build a better life for their children—not merely peace for

Americans but peace for all men and women, not merely peace in our time but peace for all time.

I speak of peace because of the new face of war. Total war makes no sense in an age when great powers can maintain large and relatively invulnerable nuclear forces and refuse to surrender without resort to those forces. It makes no sense in an age when a single nuclear weapon contains almost 10 times the explosive force delivered by all of the Allied air forces in the Second World War. It makes no sense in an age when the deadly poisons produced by a nuclear exchange would be carried by the wind and water and soil and seed to the far corners of the globe and to generations yet unborn.

Today the expenditure of billions of dollars every year on weapons acquired for the purpose of making sure we never need to use them is essential to keeping the peace. But surely the acquisition of such idle stockpiles—which can only destroy and never create—is not the only, much less the most efficient, means of assuring peace.

I speak of peace, therefore, as the necessary rational end of rational men. I realize that the pursuit of peace is not as dramatic as the pursuit of war, and frequently the words of the pursuer fall on deaf ears. But we have no more urgent task.

Some say that it is useless to speak of world peace or world law or world disarmament—and that it will be useless until the leaders of the Soviet Union adopt a more enlightened attitude. I hope they do. I believe we can help them do it. But I also believe that we must reexamine our own attitude, as individuals and as a nation, for our attitude is as essential as theirs. And every graduate of this school, every thoughtful citizen who despairs of war and wishes to bring peace, should begin by looking inward—by examining his own attitude toward the possibilities of peace, toward the Soviet Union, toward the course of the cold war, and toward freedom and peace here at home.

First: Let us examine our attitude toward peace itself. Too many of us think it is impossible. Too many think it unreal. But that is a dangerous, defeatist belief. It leads to the conclusion that war is inevitable, that mankind is doomed, that we are gripped by forces we cannot control.

We need not accept that view. Our problems are manmade;

therefore they can be solved by man. And man can be as big as he wants. No problem of human destiny is beyond human beings. Man's reason and spirit have often solved the seemingly unsolvable, and we believe they can do it again.

I am not referring to the absolute, infinite concept of universal peace and good will of which some fantasies and fanatics dream. I do not deny the values of hopes and dreams, but we merely invite discouragement and incredulity by making that our only and immediate goal.

Let us focus instead on a more practical, more attainable peace, based not on a sudden revolution in human nature but on a gradual evolution in human institutions—on a series of concrete actions and effective agreements which are in the interest of all concerned. There is no single, simple key to this peace, no grand or magic formula to be adopted by one or two powers. Genuine peace must be the product of many nations, the sum of many acts. It must be dynamic, not static, changing to meet the challenge of each new generation. For peace is a process, a way of solving problems.

With such a peace there will still be quarrels and conflicting interests, as there are within families and nations. World peace, like community peace, does not require that each man love his neighbor; it requires only that they live together in mutual tolerance, submitting their disputes to a just and peaceful settlement. And history teaches us that enmities between nations, as between individuals, do not last forever. However fixed our likes and dislikes may seem, the tide of time and events will often bring surprising changes in the relations between nations and neighbors.

So let us persevere. Peace need not be impracticable, and war need not be inevitable. By defining our goal more clearly, by making it seem more manageable and less remote, we can help all peoples to see it, to draw hope from it, and to move irresistibly toward it.

Second: Let us reexamine our attitude toward the Soviet Union. It is discouraging to think that their leaders may actually believe what their propagandists write. It is discouraging to read a recent authoritative Soviet text on military strategy and find, on page after page, wholly baseless and incredible claims—such as the allegation that "American imperialist circles are preparing to unleash different types of wars . . . that there is a very real threat of a preventive war being unleashed by American imperialists against the Soviet Union . . . [and that] the political aims of the American imperialists are to enslave economically and politically the European and other capitalist countries . . . [and] to achieve world domination . . . by means of aggressive wars."

Truly as it was written long ago: "The wicked flee when no man pursueth." Yet it is sad to read these Soviet statements—to realize the extent of the gulf between us. But it is also a warning—a warning to the American people not to fall into the same trap as the Soviets, not to see only a distorted and desperate view of the other side, not to see conflict as inevitable, accommodation as impossible, and communication as nothing more than an exchange of threats.

No government or social system is so evil that its people must be considered as lacking in virtue. As Americans we find communism profoundly repugnant as a negation of personal freedom and dignity. But we can still hail the Russian people for their many achievements—in science and space, in economic and industrial growth, in culture and in acts of courage.

Among the many traits the peoples of our two countries have in common, none is stronger than our mutual abhorrence of war. Almost unique among the major world powers, we have never been at war with each other. And no nation in the history of battle ever suffered more than the Soviet Union suffered in the course of the Second World War. At least 20 million lost their lives. Countless millions of homes and farms were burned or sacked. A third of the nation's territory, including nearly two-thirds of its industrial base, was turned into a wasteland—a loss equivalent to the devastation of this country east of Chicago.

Today, should total war ever break out again—no matter how—our two countries would become the primary targets. It is an ironical but accurate fact that the two strongest powers are the two in the most danger of devastation. All we have built, all we have worked for, would be destroyed in the first 24 hours. And even in the cold war, which brings burdens and dangers to so many countries—including this nation's closest allies—our two countries bear the heaviest burdens. For we are both devoting massive sums of money to weapons that could be better devoted to combating ignorance, poverty, and disease. We are both caught up in a vicious and dangerous cycle in which suspicion on one side breeds suspicion on the other and new weapons beget counterweapons.

In short, both the United States and its allies, and the Soviet Union and its allies, have a mutually deep interest in a just and genuine peace and in halting the arms race. Agreements to this end are in the interests of the Soviet Union as well as ours, and even the most hostile nations can be relied upon to accept and keep those treaty obligations, and only those treaty obligations, which are in their own interest.

So let us not be blind to our differences, but let us also direct attention to our common interests and to the means by which those differences can be resolved. And if we cannot end now our differences, at least we can help make the world safe for diversity. For in the final analysis our most basic common link is that we all inhabit this planet. We all breathe the same air. We all cherish our children's future. And we are all mortal.

Third: Let us reexamine our attitude toward the cold war, remembering that we are not engaged in a debate, seeking to pile up debating points. We are not here distributing blame or pointing the finger of judgment. We must deal with the world as it is and not as it might have been had the history of the last 18 years been different.

We must, therefore, persevere in the search for peace in the hope that constructive changes within the Communist bloc might bring within reach solutions which now seem beyond us. We must conduct our affairs in such a way that it becomes in the Communists' interest to agree on a genuine peace. Above all, while defending our own vital interests, nuclear powers must avert those confrontations which bring an adversary to a choice of either a humiliating retreat or a nuclear war. To adopt that kind of course in the nuclear age would be evidence only of the bankruptcy of our policy—or of a collective death wish for the world.

To secure these ends, America's weapons are nonprovocative, carefully controlled, designed to deter, and capable of selective use. Our military forces are committed to peace and disciplined in self-restraint. Our diplomats are instructed to avoid unnecessary irritants and purely rhetorical hostility.

For we can seek a relaxation of tensions without relaxing our guard. And, for our part, we do not need to use threats to prove that we are resolute. We do not need to jam foreign broadcasts out of fear our faith will be eroded. We are unwilling to impose our system on any unwilling people, but we are willing and able to engage in peaceful competition with any people on earth.

Meanwhile we seek to strengthen the United Nations, to help solve its financial problems, to make it a more effective instrument of peace, to develop it into a genuine world security system—a system capable of resolving disputes on the basis of law, of insuring the security of the large and the small, and of creating conditions under which arms can finally be abolished.

At the same time we seek to keep peace inside the non-Communist world, where many nations, all of them our friends, are divided over issues which weaken Western unity, which invite Communist intervention, or which threaten to erupt into war. . . .

Speaking of other nations, I wish to make one point clear. We are bound to many nations by alliances. Those alliances exist because our concern and theirs substantially overlap. Our commitment to defend Western Europe and West Berlin, for example, stands undiminished because of the identity of our vital interests. The United States will make no deal with the Soviet Union at the expense of other nations and other peoples, not merely because they are our partners but also because their interests and ours converge.

Our interests converge, however, not only in defending the frontiers of freedom but in pursuing the paths of peace. It is our hope—and the purpose of Allied policies—to convince the Soviet Union that she, too, should let each nation choose its own future, so long as that choice does not interfere with the choices of others. The Communist drive to impose their political and economic system on others is the primary cause of world tension today. For there can be no doubt that, if all nations could refrain from interfering in the self-determination of others, the peace would be much more assured.

This will require a new effort to achieve world law, a new context for world discussions. It will require increased understanding between the Soviets and ourselves. And increased understanding will require increased contact and communication. One step in this direction is the proposed arrangement for a direct line between Moscow and Washington, to avoid on each side the dangerous delays, misunderstandings, and misreadings of the other's actions which might occur at a time of crisis.

We have also been talking in Geneva about other first-step measures of arms control, designed to limit the intensity of the arms race and to reduce the risks of accidental war. Our primary long-range interest in Geneva, however, is general and complete disarmament, designed to take place by stages, permitting parallel political developments to build the new institutions of peace which would take the place of arms. The pursuit of disarmament has been an effort of this Government since the 1920's. It has been urgently sought by the past three administrations. And however dim the prospects may be today, we intend to continue this effort—to continue it in order that all countries, including our own, can better grasp what the problems and possibilities of disarmament are.

The one major area of these negotiations where the end is in sight, yet where a fresh start is badly needed, is in a treaty to outlaw nuclear tests. The conclusion of such a treaty —so near and yet so far—would check the spiraling arms race in one of its most dangerous areas. It would place the nuclear powers in a position to deal more effectively with one of the greatest hazards which man faces in 1963, the further spread of nuclear arms. It would increase our security; it would decrease the prospects of war. Surely this goal is sufficiently important to require our steady pursuit, yielding neither to the temptation to give up the whole effort nor the temptation to give up our insistence on vital and responsible safeguards.

I am taking this opportunity, therefore, to announce two important decisions in this regard.

First: Chairman Khrushchev, Prime Minister Macmillan, and I have agreed that high-level discussions will shortly begin in Moscow looking toward early agreement on a comprehensive test ban treaty. Our hopes must be tempered with the caution of history, but with our hopes go the hopes of all mankind.

Second: To make clear our good faith and solemn convictions on the matter, I now declare that the United States does not propose to conduct nuclear tests in the atmosphere so long as other states do not do so. We will not be the first to resume. Such a declaration is no substitute for a formal binding treaty, but I hope it will help us achieve one. Nor would such a treaty be a substitute for disarmament, but I hope it will help us achieve it.

Finally, my fellow Americans, let us examine our attitude toward peace and freedom here at home. The quality and spirit of our own society must justify and support our efforts abroad. We must show it in the dedication of our own lives, as many of you who are graduating today will have a unique opportunity to do, by serving without pay in the Peace Corps abroad or in the proposed National Service Corps here at home.

But wherever we are, we must all, in our daily lives, live up to the age-old faith that peace and freedom walk together. In too many of our cities today the peace is not secure because freedom is incomplete. . . .

All this is not unrelated to world peace. "When a man's ways please the Lord," the Scriptures tell us, "he maketh even his enemies to be at peace with him." And is not peace, in the last analysis, basically a matter of human rights— the right to live out our lives without fear of devastation, the right to breathe air as nature provided it, the right of future generations to a healthy existence?

While we proceed to safeguard our national interests, let us also safeguard human interests. And the elimination of war and arms is clearly in the interest of both. No treaty, however much it may be to the advantage of all, however tightly it may be worded, can provide absolute security against the risks of deception and evasion. But it can, if it is sufficiently effective in its enforcement and if it is sufficiently in the interests of its signers, offer far more security and far fewer risks than an unabated, uncontrolled, unpredictable arms race.

The United States, as the world knows, will never start a war. We do not want a war. We do not now expect a war. This generation of Americans has already had enough—more than enough—of war and hate and oppression. We shall be prepared if others wish it. We shall be alert to try to stop it. But we shall also do our part to build a world of peace where the weak are safe and the strong are just. We are not helpless before that task or hopeless of its success. Confident and unafraid, we labor on—not toward a strategy of annihilation but toward a strategy of peace.

Letters involve the personal element in writing. Robert Browning did not write his letters to Elizabeth Barrett without having a great feeling for her. And she did not respond in an indifferent manner either. Consequently, the reader must incorporate the feeling of love these two had for each other in any reading of the letters that passed between them. And to read the letters of Michelangelo, you would have to know the background of them, why they were written, in order to understand what they reveal about him.

The letters of Michelangelo reveal much of the turmoil, the frustrations, the problems he met in his life as he tried to help his family. To understand Michelangelo's impatience, you must know about his life, his family obligations, the incessant demand on him for financial help as he tried to carve his career in Florence. Throughout the letters you can sense a feeling of irritation that he is called upon by his family for so many different things, of his own intense desire to make them understand the difficulty of his own financial problem.The letters clearly reveal the torment in Michelangelo as he deals with a family which is singularly unconcerned with his problems. You would not be able to read this letter with the proper irritation without knowing the background. Nor would you be able to read it well without knowing who some of the people mentioned are. For example, the reference to Buonarroto refers to his younger brother. Consiglio was a merchant. Piero de' Medici was the son of Lorenzo de' Medici, the ruling family in Florence. His reference to the image he is sculpturing for his own pleasure is to a Cupid on which he was working.

From

I, Michaelangelo, Sculptor

Irving Stone

Dearest father—I wish to tell you that last Friday Buonarroto arrived here. As soon as I found out, I went to call on him at the inn. He informed me about how you are getting along, and he told me that Consiglio, the mercer, vexes you a great deal, that he is unwilling to settle on any sort of agreement, and that he wants to have you arrested. I suggest that you try to come to an understanding with him, and give him a few ducats at once; then let me know what you agree that you should give him. I shall send it to you. Although, as I told you, I have little money, I shall try to borrow some to avoid taking it from the bank.

Do not be surprised if occasionally I write you in an angry tone; at times I am quite upset by things that befall one who is away from home.

I agreed to make a statue for Piero de' Medici, and I bought a piece of marble. I never began it, however, because he never kept his promise to me. For this reason I keep to myself, and I am sculpturing an image for my own pleasure. I bought a piece of marble for five ducats, but it wasn't any good. I just threw that money away. Later I bought another piece, also for five ducats. So that you must realize that I too spend money and have my own troubles. In spite of all this, I shall send you what you may ask me, even if I should have to sell myself as a slave.

Buonarroto has a room and he is comfortable, and as long as he will want to stay here he will never lack for anything. I do not have the facilities of keeping him with me, for I am living in someone else's home. The important thing is that I shall see to it that he never lacks what he needs.

(August 19, 1497)

In articles dealing with current problems, tone is important—what seems to concern the author. In the *mid-1960's* the emphasis was on civil rights and the conflict over Viet Nam. Many articles have been written about both. Some authors argue vehemently for civil rights, and to read such works the interpreter must share the author's indignation and fighting spirit. A great deal of emotion is involved. The same applies to Viet Nam. There are contrasting ideas about Viet Nam, but the reader must read the article in line with the author's own emotional viewpoint.

Since 1972 there have been many articles written concerning the Watergate affair. President Nixon's speeches in defense of himself are a good example of the type of emotionalism these years have produced. Many authors have written about the scandals in the White House, with varying degrees of emotion and concern. *The Imperial Presidency* by Arthur Schlesinger Jr. is an excellent example.

Since expository prose also concerns itself with biography and autobiography, these are significant matters for you to consider. In the reading of an autobiography, the essential requirement is to know the attitude, the feelings, the personality of the author telling his story. For example, in *Act One* by Moss Hart, you must consider that the playwright underwent many struggles and disillusionments before hitting the top—and that he was also influenced by a great many people. Suppose you were to read the section in which Moss and George Kaufman are working so strenuously on their first co-authored play. To read it with any semblance of feeling, you'd have to know what Moss Hart had gone through before this. In this instance, the selection is almost narrative even though it falls into the expository category. Autobiography is, by its essence, much more personal than biography since it is the author's own innermost feelings guiding the telling of the story.

As for biography, a second person is writing the story of someone else's life. To be sure, the author has had a close association with the person about whom he is writing. He seeks to know that individual's every thought, idea, concept, mood, temperament—before he starts to write. To be successful he must be an astute observer. You as the reader are then committed to a realistic and conscientious reproduction of both the author's concept and its relation to the subject itself. This is a case where further research into the life of a person being treated in a biography would be of help. Let us say, for example, you were to read *O'Neill* by Arthur and Barbara Gelb. It would be wise to combine the reading of this bibliography with a study of O'Neill's autobiographical plays, such as *Long Day's Journey Into Night*, plus biographies by other authors.

In the reading of humor, which is often a part of expository prose, Richard Armour's writings are excellent examples, as are those of Robert Benchley and James Thurber. Armour's treatment of the plots of Shakespeare's plays in *Twisted Tales From Shakespeare* is filled with biting satire and irony, so much so, in fact, that it is difficult to take the Shakespearean plot seriously after reading one of Armour's accounts. Yet, one must realize that the author is someone who has great love for Shakespeare. He is a professor and an authority on the Bard's writings, so his satire is even more potent. Here, the reader would have to share in Armour's enjoyment of the satire and give the reading a sense of exaggeration, always keeping in mind that the satire is gentle, not savage and biting.

In James Thurber's "University Days," Thurber pokes fun at himself and also at the academic system. In reading this selection, you, as the reader, must put yourself into Thurber's shoes, keeping in mind that in his later years he was almost totally blind and yet could still view his handicap as something humorous. You must be aware of the weakness of Thurber's eyes in order to convey the humor in the article with its true significance. And yet, you cannot empathize too deeply with Thurber's problem since he looked upon it lightly enough to write of it in humorous terms.

In all expository prose, it is vital to decide what is the central theme of the article, letter, or journal. Without knowing the theme, you cannot interpret meaningfully. Then you must associate the one isolated segment you choose to read with the total picture, keeping in mind the author's style of writing, his use of language, his sentence structure, his own background, and his own feelings about the subject he has chosen to discuss.

It is best to remember that much expository material is not suited to oral reading. A textbook on technical matters is an example. As was previously mentioned, Erich Fromm's philosophical treatises often do not lend themselves to oral reading because of the complexity of the theories advanced and because of the involved structure. Also, some expository material has limited audience appeal, so it should be approached with a good deal of care when being used for oral interpretation.

Cutting Expository Prose

Expository prose is the easiest of the three divisions of prose to cut. It is vital in cutting to read the entire selection and decide on the important points in the writing. Preserve the writer's central idea and his style; minor points or interesting side issues can be most easily cut. Of course you must be careful that what is left after you've finished cutting is more than an encyclopedic account; leave some meat on the bones of the ideas.

The following essay by Helen Keller, called "Three Days To See," lends itself well to oral interpretation because it makes its expository point in an interesting and vivid way. Read the selection as it has been cut first, omitting from your reading the words lined out. Then re-read the essay in its entirety and see if you agree with the cutting that has been done.

Three Days To See

Helen Keller

All of us have read thrilling stories in which the hero had only a limited and specified time to live. Sometimes it was as long as a year; sometimes as short as twenty-four hours. But always we were interested in discovering just how the doomed man chose to spend his last days or his last hours. I speak, of course, of free men who have a choice, not condemned criminals whose sphere of activities is strictly delimited.

Such stories set us thinking, wondering what we should do under similar circumstances. What events, what experiences, what associations should we crowd into those last hours as mortal beings? What happiness should we find in reviewing the past, what regrets?

Sometimes I have thought it would be an excellent rule to live each day as if we should die tomorrow. Such an attitude would emphasize sharply the values of life. We should live each day with a gentleness, a vigor, and a keenness of appreciation which are often lost when time stretches before us in the constant panorama of more days and months and years to come. There are those, of course, who would adopt the epicurean motto of "eat, drink, and be merry," but most people would be chastened by the certainty of impending death.

~~In stories, the doomed hero is usually saved at the last minute by some stroke~~ of fortune, ~~but almost always his sense of values is changed.~~ He becomes more appreciative ~~of the meaning of life~~ and its ~~permanent spiritual values. It has often been noted~~ that those ~~who live, or have lived, in the~~ shadow of death ~~bring a mellow sweetness~~ to ~~everything they do.~~

Most of us, however, take life for granted. We know that one day we must die, but usually we picture that day as far in the future. When we are in buoyant health, death is all but unimaginable. ~~We seldom think of it. The days stretch out in an endless vista. So we go about our petty tasks, hardly aware of our listless attitude toward life.~~

~~The same lethargy, I am afraid, characterizes the use of all our faculties and senses.~~ Only the deaf appreciate hearing, only the blind realize the manifold blessings that lie in sight. ~~Particularly does this observation apply to those who have lost sight and hearing in adult life. But those who have never suffered impairment of sight or hearing seldom~~ make the ~~fullest use of these blessed faculties. Their eyes and ears take in all sights and sounds hazily, without concentration, and with little appreciation. It is the same old story of not being grateful~~ for ~~what we have until we lose it, of not being conscious of health until we are ill.~~

I have often thought it would be a blessing if each human being were stricken blind and deaf for a few days at sometime during his early adult life. Darkness would make him more appreciative of sight; silence would teach him the joys of sound.

Now and then I have tested my seeing friends to discover what they see. Recently I was visited by a good friend who has just returned from a long walk in the woods, and I asked her what she had observed. "Nothing in particular," she replied. I might have been incredulous had I not been accustomed to such responses, for long ago I became convinced that the seeing see little.

How was it possible, I asked myself, to walk for an hour through the woods and see nothing worthy of note? I who cannot see find hundreds of things to interest me through mere touch. I feel the delicate symmetry of a leaf. I pass my hands lovingly about the smooth skin of a silver birch, or the rough shaggy bark of a pine. In spring I touch the branches of trees hopefully in search of a bud, the first sign of awakening Nature after her winter's sleep. I feel the delightful, velvety texture of a flower, and discover its remarkable convolutions; and something of the miracle of Nature is revealed to me. Occasionally, if I am very fortunate, I place my hand gently on a small tree and feel the happy quiver of a bird in full song. I am delighted to have the cool waters of a brook rush through my open fingers. To me a lush carpet of pine needles or spongy grass is more welcome than the most luxurious Persian rug. To me the pageant of seasons is a thrilling and unending drama, the action of which streams through my finger tips.

At times my heart cries out with longing to see all these things. If I can get so much pleasure from mere touch, how much more beauty must be revealed by sight. Yet, those who have eyes apparently see little. The panorama of color and action which fills the world is taken for granted. It is human, perhaps, to appreciate little that which we have and to long for that which we have not, but it is a great pity that in the world of light the gift of sight is used only as a mere convenience, rather than as a means of adding fullness to life.

If I were the president of a university I should establish a compulsory course in "How to Use Your Eyes." The professor would try to show his pupils how they could add joy to their lives by really seeing what passes unnoticed before them. He would try to awake their dormant and sluggish faculties.

Perhaps I can best illustrate by imagining what I should most like to see if I were given the use of my eyes, say, for just three days. And while I am imagining, suppose you, too, set your mind to work on the problem of how you would use your own eyes if you had only three more days to see. If with the oncoming darkness of the third night you knew that the sun would never rise for you again, how would you spend those precious intervening days? What would you most want to let your gaze rest upon?

I, naturally, should want most to see the things which have become dear to me through my years of darkness. You, too,

~~would want to let your~~ eyes ~~rest long on the things that have~~ ~~become dear~~ to ~~you so that you could~~ take the ~~memory of~~ ~~them with you into the night that loomed before~~ you.

If, by some miracle, I were granted three seeing days, to be followed by a relapse into darkness, I should divide the period into three parts.

On the first day, I should want to see the people whose kindness and gentleness and companionship have made my life worth living. First I should like to gaze long upon the face of my dear teacher, Mrs. Anne Sullivan Macy, who came to me when I was a child and opened the outer world to me. I should want not merely to see the outline of her face, ~~so that~~ ~~I could cherish~~ it in my ~~memory,~~ but to study that face and find in it the living evidence of the sympathetic tenderness and patience with which she accomplished the difficult task of my education. ~~I should like to see in her eyes that strength~~ ~~of character which has enabled her to stand firm in the face~~ ~~of difficulties, and that compassion for all humanity which~~ ~~she has revealed to me so often.~~

I do not know what it is to see into the heart of a friend through that "window of the soul," the eye. I can only "see" through my finger tips the outline of a face. I can detect laughter, sorrow, and many other obvious emotions. I know my friends from the feel of their faces. But I cannot really picture their personalities by touch. I know their personalities, of course, through other means, through the thoughts they express to me, through whatever of their actions are revealed to me. But I am denied that deeper understanding of them which I am sure would come through sight of them, through watching their reactions to various expressed thoughts and circumstances, through noting the immediate and fleeting reactions of their eyes and countenance.

~~Friends~~ who are ~~near to me I know well, because through~~ ~~the months and years they reveal themselves to me in all their~~ ~~phases; but of casual friends I have only~~ an ~~incomplete im-~~ ~~pression, an impression gained from a handclasp, from spoken~~ ~~words which I take from their lips with my finger tips, or~~ ~~which they tap into the palm of my hand.~~

~~How much easier, how much more satisfying it is for you~~ ~~who can see to grasp quickly the essential~~ qualities ~~of another~~

person by watching the subtleties of expression, the quiver
of a muscle, the flutter of a hand. But does it ever occur to
you to use your sight to see into the inner nature of a friend
or acquaintance? Do not most of you seeing people grasp
casually the outward features of a face and let it go at that?

For instance, can you describe accurately the faces of five
good friends? Some of you can, but many cannot. As an experiment, I have questioned husbands of long standing about
the color of their wives' eyes, and often they express embarrassed confusion and admit that they do not know. And,
incidentally, it is a chronic complaint of wives that their husbands do not notice new dresses, new hats, and changes in
household arrangements.

The eyes of seeing persons soon become accustomed to the
routine of their surroundings, and they actually see only the
startling and spectacular. But even in viewing the most spectacular sights the eyes are lazy. Court records reveal every
day how inaccurately "eyewitnesses" see. A given event will
be "seen" in several different ways by as many witnesses.
Some see more than others, but few see everything that is
within the range of their vision.

Oh, the things that I should see if I had the power of sight
for just three days!

The first day would be a busy one. I should call to me all
my dear friends and look long into their faces, imprinting
upon my mind the outward evidences of the beauty that is
within them. I should let my eyes rest, too, on the face of a
baby, so that I could catch a vision of the eager, innocent
beauty which precedes the individual's consciousness of the
conflicts which life develops.

And I should like to look into the loyal, trusting eyes of my
dogs—the grave, canny little Scottie, Darkie, and the stalwart
understanding great Dane, Helga, whose warm, tender, and
playful friendships are so comforting to me.

On that busy first day I should also view the small simple
things of my home. I want to see the warm colors in the rugs
under my feet, the pictures on the walls, the intimate trifles
that transform a house into home. My eyes would rest respectfully on the books in raised type which I have read, but

they would be more eagerly interested in the printed books which seeing people can read, for during the long night of my life the books I have read and those which have been read to me have built themselves into a great shining lighthouse, revealing to me the deepest channels of human life and the human spirit.

In the afternoon of that first seeing day, I should take a long walk in the woods and intoxicate my eyes on the beauties of the world of Nature, trying desperately to absorb in a few hours the vast splendor which is constantly unfolding itself to those who can see. On the way home from my woodland jaunt my path would lie near a farm so that I might see the patient horses plowing in the fields (perhaps I should see only a tractor!) and the serene content of men living close to the soil. And I should pray for the glory of a colorful sunset.

When dusk had fallen, I should experience the double delight of being able to see by artificial light, which the genius of man has created to extend the power of his sight when Nature decrees darkness.

In the night of that first day of sight, I should not be able to sleep, so full would be my mind of the memories of the day.

The next day—the second day of sight—I should arise with the dawn and see the thrilling miracle by which night is transformed into day. I should behold with awe the magnificent panorama of light with which the sun awakens the sleeping earth.

This day I should devote to a hasty glimpse of the world, past and present. I should want to see the pageant of man's progress, the kaleidoscope of the ages. How can so much be compressed into one day? Through the museums, of course. Often I have visited the New York Museum of Natural History to touch with my hands many of the objects there exhibited, but I have longed to see with my eyes the condensed history of the earth and its inhabitants displayed there—animals and the races of men pictured in their native environment; gigantic carcasses of dinosaurs and mastodons which roamed the earth long before man appeared, with his tiny stature and powerful brain, to conquer the animal kingdom; realistic presentations of the processes of evolution in animals,

~~in man, and in the implements which man has used to fashion for himself a secure home on this planet;~~ and a thousand and one other aspects of natural history.

~~I wonder how many readers of this article have viewed the panorama of the face of living things as pictured in that inspiring museum. Many, of course, have not had the opportunity, but I am sure that many who *have* had the opportunity have not made use of it. There, indeed, is a place to use your eyes. You who see can spend many fruitful days there, but I, with my imaginary three days of sight, could only take a hasty glimpse, and pass on.~~

My next stop would be the Metropolitan Museum of Art, for just as the Museum of Natural History reveals the material aspects of the world, so does the Metropolitan show the myriad facets of the human spirit. Throughout the history of humanity the urge to artistic expression has been almost as powerful as the urge for food, shelter, and procreation. And here, in the vast chambers of the Metropolitan Museum, is unfolded before me the spirit of Egypt, Greece, and Rome, as expressed in their art. ~~I know well through my hands the sculptured gods and goddesses of the ancient Nile land. I have felt copies of Parthenon friezes, and I have sensed the rhythmic beauty of charging Athenian warriors. Apollos and Venuses and the Winged Victory of Samothrace are friends of my finger tips. The gnarled, bearded features of Homer are dear to me, for he, too, knew blindness.~~

~~My hands have lingered upon the living marble of Roman sculpture as well as that of later generations. I have passed my hands over a plaster cast of Michelangelo's inspiring and heroic Moses; I have sensed the power of Rodin; I have been awed by the devoted spirit of Gothic wood carving. These arts which can be touched have meaning for me, but even they were meant to be seen rather than felt, and I can only guess at the beauty which remains hidden from me. I can admire the simple lines of a Greek vase, but its figured decorations are lost to me.~~

So on this, my second day of sight, I should try to probe into the soul of man through his art. ~~The things I knew through touch I should now see.~~ More splendid still, the whole magnificent world of painting would be opened to me, from the Italian Primitives, with their serene religious devotion, to the Moderns, with their feverish visions. I should look deep into the canvases of Raphael, Leonardo da Vinci, Titian, Rembrandt. I should want to feast my eyes upon the warm colors of Veronese, study the mysteries of El Greco, catch a new vision of Nature from Corot. Oh, there is so much rich meaning and beauty in the art of the ages for you who have eyes to see!

Upon my short visit to this temple of art I should not be able to review a fraction of that great world of art which is open to you. I should be able to get only a superficial impression. Artists tell me that for a deep and true appreciation of art one must educate the eye. One must learn through experience to weigh the merits of line, of composition, of form and color. If I had eyes, how happily would I embark upon so fascinating a study! Yet I am told that, to many of you who have eyes to see, the world of art is a dark night, unexplored and unilluminated.

It would be with extreme reluctance that I should leave the Metropolitan Museum, which contains the key to beauty—a beauty so neglected. Seeing persons, however, do not need a Metropolitan to find this key to beauty. The same key lies waiting in smaller museums, and in books on the shelves of even small libraries. But naturally, in my limited time of imaginary sight, I should choose the place where the key unlocks the greatest treasures in the shortest time.

The evening of my second day of sight I should spend at a theater or at the movies. Even now I often attend theatrical performances of all sorts, but the action of the play must be spelled into my hand by a companion. But how I should like to see with my own eyes the fascinating figure of Hamlet, or the gusty Falstaff amid colorful Elizabethan trappings! How I should like to follow each movement of the graceful Hamlet, each strut of the hearty Falstaff! And since I could see only one play, I should be confronted by a many-horned dilemma, for there are scores of plays I should want to see. You who have eyes can see any you like. How many of you, I wonder, when you gaze at a play, or any spectacle, realize and give thanks for the miracle of sight which enables you to enjoy its color, grace, and movement?

I cannot enjoy the beauty of rhythmic movement except in a sphere restricted to the touch of my hands. I can vision only dimly the grace of a Pavlova, although I know something of the delight of rhythm, for often I can sense the beat of music as it vibrates through the floor, I can well imagine that cadenced motion must be one of the most pleasing sights in the world. I have been able to gather something of this by tracing with my fingers the lines in sculptured marble; if this static grace can be so lovely, how much more acute must be the thrill of seeing grace in motion.

One of my dearest memories is of the time when Joseph Jefferson allowed me to touch his face and hands as he went through some of the gestures and speeches of his beloved Rip Van Winkle. I was able to catch thus a meager glimpse of the world of drama, and I shall never forget the delight of that moment. But, oh, how much I miss, and how much pleasure you seeing ones can derive from watching and hearing the interplay of speech and movement in the unfolding of a dramatic performance! If I could see only one play, I should know how to picture in my mind the action of a hundred plays which I have read or had transferred to me through the medium of the manual alphabet.

So, through the evening of my second imaginary day of sight, the great figures of dramatic literature would crowd sleep from my eyes.

The following morning, I should again greet the dawn, anxious to discover new delights, for I am sure that, for those who have eyes which really see, the dawn of each day must be a perpetually new revelation of beauty.

This, according to the terms of my imagined miracle, is to be my third and last day of light. I shall have no time to waste in regrets or longings; there is too much to see. The first day I devoted to my friends, animate and inanimate. The second revealed to me the history of man and Nature. Today I shall spend in the workaday world of the present, amid the haunts of men going about the business of life. And where can one find so many activities and conditions of men as in New York? So the city becomes my destination.

I start from my home in the quiet little suburb of Forest Hills, Long Island. Here, surrounded by green lawns, trees, and flowers, are neat little houses, happy with the voices and movements of wives and children, havens of peaceful rest for men who toil in the city. I drive across the lacy structure of steel which spans the East River, and I get a new and startling vision of the power and ingenuity of the mind of man. Busy boats chug and scurry about the river—racy speed boats, stolid, snorting tugs. If I had long days of sight ahead, I should spend many of them watching the delightful activity upon the river.

I look ahead, and before me rise the fantastic towers of New York, a city that seems to have stepped from the pages of a fairy story. What an awe-inspiring sight, these glittering spires, these vast banks of stone and steel—structures such as the gods might build for themselves! ~~This animated picture is a part of the lives of millions of people every day. How many, I wonder, give it so much as a second glance? Very few, I fear. Their eyes are blind to this magnificent sight because it is so familiar to them.~~

I hurry to the top of one of those gigantic structures, the Empire State Building, for there, a short time ago, I "saw" the city below through the eyes of my secretary. I am anxious to compare my fancy with reality. ~~I am sure I should not be disappointed in the panorama spread out before me, for to me it would be a vision of another world.~~

Now I begin my rounds of the city. First, I stand at a busy corner, merely looking at people, trying by sight of them to understand something of their lives. I see smiles and I am happy. I see serious determination, and I am proud. I see suffering, and I am compassionate.

I stroll down Fifth Avenue. I throw my eyes out of focus so that I see no particular object but only a seething kaleidoscope of color. I am certain that the colors of women's dresses moving in a throng must be a gorgeous spectacle of which I should never tire. ~~But perhaps if I had sight I should be like most other women—too interested in styles and the cut of individual dresses to give much attention to the splendor of the color in the mass.~~ And I am convinced, too, that I should become an inveterate window shopper, for it must be a delight to the eye to view the myriad articles of beauty on display.

From Fifth Avenue I make a tour of the city—to Park Avenue, to the slums, to factories, to parks where children play. I take a stay-at-home trip abroad by visiting the foreign quarters. Always my eyes are open wide to all the sights of both happiness and misery so that I may probe deep and add to my understanding of how people work and live. My heart is full of the images of people and things. My eye passes lightly over no single trifle; it strives to touch and hold closely each thing its gaze rests upon. Some sights are pleasant, filling the heart with happiness; but some are miserably pathetic. To these latter I do not shut my eyes, for they, too, are part of life. To close the eye on them is to close the heart and mind.

My third day of sight is drawing to an end. Perhaps there are many serious pursuits to which I should devote the few remaining hours, but I am afraid that on the evening of that last day I should again run away to the theater, to a hilariously funny play, so that I might appreciate the overtones of comedy in the human spirit.

At midnight my temporary respite from blindness would cease, and permanent night would close in on me again. Naturally in those three short days I should not have seen all I wanted to see. Only when darkness had again descended upon me should I realize how much I had left unseen. But my mind would be so crowded with glorious memories that I should have little time for regrets. Thereafter the touch of every object would bring a glowing memory of how that object looked.

Perhaps this short outline of how I should spend three days of sight does not agree with the program you would set for yourself if you knew that you were about to be stricken blind. I am, however, sure that if you actually faced that fate, your eyes would open to things you had never seen before, storing up memories for the long night ahead. You would use your eyes as never before. Everything you saw would become dear to you. Your eyes would touch and embrace every object that came within your range of vision. Then, at last, you would really see, and a new world of beauty would open itself before you.

I who am blind can give one hint to those who see—one admonition to those who would make full use of the gift of sight: Use your eyes as if tomorrow you would be stricken blind. And the same method can be applied to the other senses. Hear the music of voices, the song of a bird, the mighty strains of an orchestra, as if you would be stricken deaf tomorrow. Touch each object you want to touch as if tomorrow your tactile sense would fail. Smell the perfume of flowers, taste with relish each morsel, as if tomorrow you could never smell and taste again. Make the most of every sense; glory in all the facets of pleasure and beauty which the world reveals to you through the several means of contact which Nature provides. But of all the senses, I am sure that sight must be the most delightful.

You can see in this cutting that the concentration is on Helen's own delight in seeing. There is also another focus in the essay, however, centering around those who can see. Read the essay again and discover this other focus.

What would *you* cut if you were to prepare this essay for an oral performance? Be willing to experiment! Try different ways of getting her main idea across. Be willing to spend the time necessary for effective cutting.

NARRATIVE PROSE

Narrative prose tells a story. It has setting, plot, and characters, and moves through one or more climaxes. It is characterized by action. It can combine suspense, romance, excitement, tragedy, and comedy in one selection, or it can treat any one of them alone. Narrative prose usually takes the form of short stories and novels, but these terms refuse to be pinned down to any clear-cut definition. Where a short story ends (in length) and a novel begins is difficult to say. So we have short-short stories, short stories, short novels (some as short as a long short story) and novels. A short story, generally, picks up a situation as it moves toward its final climax and records events through that single climax to final resolution. A novel, on the other hand, generally (we can only talk in general terms) will pick up the action at the birth of the main character and record events all through his life, ending when his life ends. A look at a range of novels, however, would show a great deal of variation from this general identification. Sherwood Anderson's *Winesburg, Ohio,* for example, is the story of a town and recounts many situations in the lives of a variety of the townspeople.

You can see that narrative prose is a tremendously dynamic form; as quickly as someone tries to "fence it in," it breaks out in another direction. Narration seldom exists without description; the simple plot wouldn't hold interest without the author's finesse ir making the events and characters real, and this is accomplished by adding descriptive elements.

The chief purpose of narrative prose is to entertain; however, it may also be used to point up a problem that the author feels should be corrected or it may be used to instruct the reader in the author's point of view.

When you decide to read narrative prose to an audience, you must first read the selection in its entirety and establish the purpose the author had in writing this piece of literature. Take, for example, the suspenseful short story, "The Monkey's Paw" by W. W. Jacobs.[1] Is its purpose entertainment only? Or does the author want his readers to think about man's foolishness in wishing for things that he doesn't have? Read the story and think about the author's purpose.

Consider another example: Shirley Jackson's "The Lottery." Read it in its entirety, then ask yourself why she wrote it. Was it to record the action of the lottery? Did such a lottery as she describes really ever exist? Were people ever foolish enough to conduct themselves in the manner she describes?

After you've read it, think back over the story and you'll see that little details, such as the children picking up stones, take on great meaning when the end of the story is considered. The references the author makes to the decision made by other towns to do away with the lottery become more meaningful. The hints she gives that the lottery isn't one that people are anxious to win add to the suspense.

No, it was not written just to record the action of a real lottery held each June, but rather to highlight the fact that men have done things even more foolish and inhuman. Compare the fictional lottery with the real Salem witch trials. Which was most inhuman? Salem? Do we still, even today, carry on our own varieties of the lottery? Yes,

[1] This story may be found in *Anthology of Famous British Stories,* ed. by Bennett Cerf and Henry C. Moriarty. Modern Library.

we do. Perhaps we don't stone members of our communities literally but the influences are still with us.

If you were to read the story for an audience, you would have to be careful not to telegraph, too soon, the final overwhelming climax. Play down the gathering of the stones; don't labor the sections that talk of abandoning the lottery. Treat Mrs. Hutchinson's statement that her husband didn't have time to choose as an incident; play it down. In doing so you heighten the climax.

James Thurber conveys to his readers an understanding of very ordinary people in very ordinary circumstances. In his story "The Secret Life of Walter Mitty," we see Walter, a henpecked husband, retreat into his own world of daydreams where he is the hero. In a series of incidents, Thurber deftly transforms Mitty into a world renowned doctor, an aviator, a spy, an expert shot, and a hydroplane commander, and all the while he is on an errand in the city for his wife. The contrast between the real Mitty and the hero of his daydreams is most entertaining and probably serves also to remind us that we have our own daydreams.

Each of the examples of narrative discussed thus far in the chapter has contained dialogue. In this respect, narrative prose moves a step closer to drama because you, as the reader, must characterize the people in the stories you read aloud in order to make them *believable*. This means that you must visualize them clearly and fully and then work with voice and manner to breathe life into them. Naturally this brings us back to emotional response. The best way to get your audience to respond to the characters in your story is to establish and maintain images of them in the audience's mind. Work with vocal quality, rate, volume, and pitch to create the voice of each character (try to work with only two or three); then support the vocal representation with believable physical involvement. Your audience will have no difficulty telling who it is that says what. However, if you try to characterize too many people, you will confuse the audience. Choose two or three main characters and let the dialogue move through them. Other, less important people can be handled with your narrator's voice (your own) and your reading will be much more effective. Also, it's often possible to put comments that are actually made by additional characters into the mouths of the two or three that you decide to characterize.

Concentrate on becoming emotionally involved with your characters instead of trying to locate them physically in space. Such location is very difficult unless you have rehearsed thoroughly. And even with much rehearsal your audience may become confused or feel that they are watching a ping-pong game.

Cutting Narrative Prose

Several general rules for effective cutting of narrative prose should be considered.

1. Choose a selection that is suited to you, to your audience, and to the occasion, especially in terms of time. Then any cutting you have to do will be minimal.
2. If you choose a longer piece, make sure that it can stand alone without what comes before or after. Then make sure that your introduction fills in the gap.
3. Cut minor characters if they don't advance the plot or exercise some influence in the segment you are going to read.
4. Where possible, cut in large segments.
5. Paraphrase as necessary in order not to leave gaps in the meaning. Paraphrasing is often demanded when you cut large segments so that transition between the remaining elements is smooth.
6. Cut "he saids" wherever possible. Nothing is more disturbing to an audience than to hear a reader read as though he had no energy at all. For example: " 'We've got to get out and fight,' he shouted angrily." Cut the "he shouted angrily" and shout "We've got to get out and fight!"

   A reader is justified in retaining the speaker identification only when the speaker is first introduced. The "he said" is necessary there so that the audience can get acquainted with this new person. Thereafter, the "he said's" should be cut for that character and you should use your voice to identify him.
7. Be certain that neither the author's purpose nor his style is distorted or misdirected by your cutting.

Beyond the limits of these rules for cutting you are free to cut whatever you feel is necessary. Your guiding light should be: What essentials in the narrative should be retained when you are forced to read under a specific (and usually short) time limit?

Study the story that follows. Read it as it has been cut first, noting the flow of the action. Then reread it, adding those segments that have been lined out. Decide what you would do if you were to cut the story for an oral reading. This particular story is one of Stephen Crane's best. It contains all the qualities of a fine narrative. It is clearly drawn and has believable characters, action, and a well-developed plot. The climax may be a surprise.

The Bride Comes to Yellow Sky

Stephen Crane

I

The great pullman was whirling onward with such dignity of motion that a glance from the window seemed simply to prove that the plains of Texas were pouring eastward. Vast flats of green grass, dull-hued spaces of mesquit and cactus, little groups of frame houses, woods of light and tender trees, all were sweeping into the east, sweeping over the horizon, a precipice.

A newly married pair had boarded this coach at San Antonio. The man's face was reddened from many days in the wind and sun, and a direct result of his new black clothes was that his brick-colored hands were constantly performing in a most conscious fashion. From time to time he looked down respectfully at his attire. He sat with a hand on each knee, like a man waiting in a barber's shop. The glances he devoted to other passengers were furtive and shy.

The bride was not pretty, nor was she very young. She wore a dress of blue cashmere, with small reservations of velvet here and there, and with steel buttons abounding. She continually twisted her head to regard her puff sleeves, very stiff, straight, and high. They embarrassed her. It was quite apparent that she had cooked, and that she expected to cook, dutifully. The blushes caused by the careless scrutiny of some passengers as she had entered the car were strange to see upon this plain, under-class countenance, which was drawn in placid, almost emotionless lines.

They were evidently very happy. "Ever been in a parlor car before?" he asked, smiling with delight.

"No," she answered; "I never was. It's fine, ain't it?"

"Great! And then after a while we'll go forward to the diner, and get a big lay-out. Finest meal in the world. Charge a dollar."

"Oh, do they?" cried the bride. "Charge a dollar? Why, that's too much—for us—ain't it, Jack?"

"Not this trip, anyhow," he answered bravely. "We're going to go the whole thing."

Later he explained to her about the trains. "You see, it's a thousand miles from one end of Texas to the other; and this train runs right across it, and never stops but four times." He had the pride of an owner. He pointed out to her the dazzling fittings of the coach; and in truth her eyes opened wider as she contemplated the sea-green figured velvet, the shining brass, silver, and glass, the wood that gleamed as darkly brilliant as the surface of a pool of oil. At one end a bronze figure sturdily held a support for a separated chamber, and at convenient places on the ceiling were frescoes in olive and silver.

To the minds of the pair, their surroundings reflected the glory of their marriage that morning in San Antonio; this was the environment of their new estate; and the man's face in particular beamed with an elation that made him appear ridiculous to the Negro porter. This individual at times surveyed them from afar with an amused and superior grin. On other occasions he bullied them with skill in ways that did not make it exactly plain to them that they were being bullied. He subtly used all the manners of the most unconquerable kind of snobbery. He oppressed them; but of this oppression they had small knowledge, and they speedily forgot that infrequently a number of travelers covered them with stares of derisive enjoyment. Historically there was supposed to be something infinitely humorous in their situation.

"We are due in Yellow Sky at 3:42," he said, looking tenderly into her eyes.

"Oh, are we?" she said, as if she had not been aware of it. To evince surprise at her husband's statement was part of her wifely amiability. She took from a pocket a little silver watch; and as she held it before her, and stared at it with a frown of attention, the new husband's face shone.

"I bought it in San Anton' from a friend of mine," he told her gleefully.

"It's seventeen minutes past twelve," she said, looking up at him with a kind of shy and clumsy coquetry. A passenger, noting this play, grew excessively sardonic, and winked at himself in one of the numerous mirrors.

At last they went to the dining car. ~~Two rows of Negro waiters, in glowing white suits, surveyed their entrance with the interest, and also the equanimity, of men who had been forewarned. The pair fell to the lot of a waiter who happened to feel pleasure in steering them through their meal. He viewed them with the manner of a fatherly pilot, his countenance radiant with benevolence. The patronage, entwined with the ordinary deference, was not plain to them. And yet, as they returned to their coach, they showed in their faces a sense of escape.~~

To the left, miles down a long purple slope, was a little ribbon of mist where moved the keening Rio Grande. The train was approaching it at an angle, and the apex was Yellow Sky. Presently it was apparent that, as the distance from Yellow Sky grew shorter, the husband became commensurately restless. His brick-red hands were more insistent in their prominence. ~~Occasionally he was even rather absent-minded and faraway when the bride leaned forward and addressed him.~~

As a matter of truth, Jack Potter was beginning to find the shadow of a deed weigh upon him like a leaden slab. He, the town marshal of Yellow Sky, a man known, liked, and feared in his corner, a prominent person, had gone to San Antonio to meet a girl he believed he loved, and there, after the usual prayers, had actually induced her to marry him, without consulting Yellow Sky for any part of the transaction. He was now bringing his bride before an innocent and unsuspecting community.

~~Of course people in Yellow Sky married as it pleased them, in accordance with a general custom; but such was Potter's thought of his duty to his friends, or of their idea of his duty, or of an unspoken form which does not control men in these matters, that he felt he was heinous. He had committed an extraordinary crime. Face to face with this girl in San Antonio, and spurred by his sharp impulse, he had gone headlong over all the social hedges. At San Antonio he was like a man hidden in the dark. A knife to sever any friendly duty, any form, was easy to his hand in that remote city. But the hour of Yellow Sky—the hour of daylight—was approaching.~~

He knew full well that his marriage was an important thing

to his town. It could only be exceeded by the burning of the new hotel. His friends could not forgive him. Frequently he had reflected on the advisability of telling them by telegraph, but a new cowardice had been upon him. He feared to do it. And now the train was hurrying him toward a scene of amazement, glee, and reproach. He glanced out of the window at the line of haze swinging slowly in toward the train.

~~Yellow Sky had a kind of brass band, which played painfully, to the delight of the populace. He laughed without heart as he thought of it. If the citizens could dream of his prospective arrival with his bride, they would parade the band at the station and escort them, amid cheers and laughing congratulations, to his adobe home.~~

He resolved that he would use all the devices of speed and plainscraft in making the journey from the station to his house. Once within that safe citadel, he could issue some sort of vocal bulletin, and then not go among the citizens until they had time to wear off a little of their enthusiasm.

The bride looked anxiously at him. "What's worrying you, Jack?"

He laughed again. "I'm not worrying, girl; I'm only thinking of Yellow Sky."

She flushed in comprehension.

A sense of mutual guilt invaded their minds and developed a finer tenderness. They looked at each other with eyes softly aglow. But Potter often laughed the same nervous laugh; the flush upon the bride's face seemed quite permanent.

The traitor to the feelings of Yellow Sky narrowly watched the speeding landscape. "We're nearly there," ~~he said.~~

Presently the porter came and announced the proximity of Potter's home. ~~He held a brush in his hand, and, with all his airy superiority gone, he brushed Potter's new clothes as the latter slowly turned this way and that way. Potter fumbled out a coin and gave it to the porter, as he had seen others do. It was a heavy and muscle-bound business, as that of a man shoeing his first horse.~~

The porter took their bag, and as the train began to slow they moved forward to the hooded platform of the car. Presently the two engines and their long string of coaches rushed into the station of Yellow Sky.

"They have to take water here," said Potter, from a constricted throat and in mournful cadence, as one announcing death. Before the train stopped his eye had swept the length of the platform, and he was glad and astonished to see there was none upon it but the station agent, who, with a slightly hurried and anxious air, was walking toward the water tanks. When the train had halted, the porter alighted first, and placed in position a little temporary step.

"Come on, girl," said Potter, hoarsely. As he helped her down they each laughed on a false note. He took the bag from the Negro, and bade his wife cling to his arm. As they slunk rapidly away, his hangdog glance perceived that they were unloading the two trunks, and also that the station agent, far ahead near the baggage car, had turned and was running toward him, making gestures. He laughed, and groaned as he laughed, when he noted the first effect of his marital bliss upon Yellow Sky. He gripped his wife's arm firmly to his side, and they fled. Behind them the porter stood, chuckling fatuously.

II

The California express on the Southern Railway was due at Yellow Sky in twenty-one minutes. There were six men at the bar of the Weary Gentleman saloon. One was a drummer who talked a great deal and rapidly; three were Texans who did not care to talk at that time; and two were Mexican sheep-herders, who did not talk as a general practice in the Weary Gentleman saloon. The barkeeper's dog lay on the boardwalk that crossed in front of the door. His head was on his paws, and he glanced drowsily here and there with the constant vigilance of a dog that is kicked on occasion. Across the sandy street were some vivid green grass-plots, so wonderful in appearance, amid the sands that burned near them in a blazing sun, that they caused a doubt in the mind. They exactly resembled the grass-mats used to represent lawns on the stage. At the cooler end of the railway station, a man without a coat sat in a tilted chair and smoked his pipe. The fresh-cut bank of the Rio Grande circled near the town, and there could be seen beyond it a great plum-colored plain of mesquit.

Save for the busy drummer and his companions in the saloon, Yellow Sky was dozing. ~~The newcomer leaned gracefully upon the bar, and recited many tales with the confidence of a bard who has come upon a new field.~~

"~~—and at the moment that the old man fell downstairs with the bureau in his arms, the old woman was coming up with two scuttles of coal, and of course—~~"

The drummer's tale was interrupted by a young man who suddenly appeared in the open door. He cried: "Scratchy Wilson's drunk, and has turned loose with both hands." The two Mexicans at once set down their glasses and faded out of the rear entrance of the saloon.

~~The drummer, innocent and jocular, answered: "All right, old man. S'pose he has? Come in and have a drink, anyhow."~~

~~But the information had made such an obvious cleft in every skull in the room that the drummer was obliged to see its importance. All had become instantly solemn. "Say," said he, mystified, "what is this?" His three companions made the introductory gesture of eloquent speech; but the young man at the door forestalled them.~~

"~~It means, my friend,~~" ~~he answered, as he came into the saloon, "that for the next two hours this town won't be a health resort."~~

The barkeeper went to the door, and locked and barred it; reaching out of the window, he pulled in heavy wooden shutters, and barred them. Immediately a solemn, chapel-like gloom was upon the place. The drummer was looking from one to another.

"But say," he cried, "what is this, anyhow? You don't mean there is going to be a gun fight?"

"Don't know whether there'll be a fight or not" answered one man, grimly, "but there'll be some shootin'—some good shootin'."

The young man who had warned them waved his hand. "Oh, there'll be a fight fast enough, if any one wants it. Anybody can get a fight out there in the street. There's a fight just waiting."

The drummer seemed to be swayed between the interest of a foreigner and a perception of personal danger.

"What did you say his name was?" ~~he asked.~~

"Scratchy Wilson," they answered in chorus.

"And will he kill anybody? What are you going to do? Does this happen often? Does he rampage around like this once a week or so? Can he break in that door?"

"No; he can't break down that door," replied the barkeeper. "He's tried it three times. But when he comes you'd better lay down on the floor, stranger. He's dead sure to shoot at it, and a bullet may come through."

Thereafter the drummer kept a strict eye upon the door. The time had not yet been called for him to hug the floor, but, as a minor precaution, he sidled near to the wall. "Will he kill anybody?" he said again.

The men laughed low and scornfully at the question.

"He's out to shoot, and he's out for trouble. Don't see any good in experimentin' with him."

"But what do you do in a case like this? What do you do?"

A man responded: "Why, he and Jack Potter—"

"But," in chorus the other men interrupted, "Jack Potter's in San Anton'."

"Well, who is he? What's he got to do with it?"

"Oh, he's the town marshal. He goes out and fights Scratchy when he gets on one of these tears."

"Wow!" said the drummer, mopping his brow. "Nice job he's got."

The voices had toned down to mere whisperings. The drummer wished to ask further questions, which were born of an increasing anxiety and bewilderment; but when he attempted them, the men merely looked at him in irritation and motioned him to remain silent. A tense waiting hush was upon them. In the deep shadows of the room their eyes shone as they listened for sounds from the street. One man made three gestures at the barkeeper, and the latter, moving like a ghost, handed him a glass and a bottle. The man poured a full glass of whisky, and set down the bottle noiselessly. He gulped the whiskey in a swallow, and turned again toward the door in immovable silence. The drummer saw that the barkeeper, without a sound, had taken a Winchester from beneath the bar. Later he saw this individual beckoning to him, so he tiptoed across the room.

"You better come with me back of the bar."

~~"No thanks," said the drummer, perspiring; "I'd rather be where I can make a break for the back door."~~

~~Whereupon the man of bottles made a kindly but peremptory gesture. The drummer obeyed it, and, finding himself seated on a box with his head below the level of the bar, balm was laid upon his soul at sight of various zinc and copper fittings that bore a resemblance to armor plate. The barkeeper took a seat comfortably upon an adjacent box.~~

~~"You see," he whispered, "this here Scratchy Wilson is a wonder with a gun—a perfect wonder; and when he goes on the war-trail, we hunt our holes—naturally. He's about the last one of the old gang that used to hang out along the river here. He's a terror when he's drunk. When he's sober he's all right—kind of simple—wouldn't hurt a fly—nicest fellow in town. But when he's drunk—whoo!"~~

There were periods of stillness. "I wish Jack Potter was back from San Anton'," said the barkeeper. "He shot Wilson up once—in the leg—and he would sail in and pull out the kinks in this thing."

Presently they heard from a distance the sound of a shot, followed by three wild yowls. It instantly removed a bond from the men in the darkened saloon. There was a shuffling of feet. They looked at each other. "Here he comes," they said.

III

A man in a maroon-colored flannel shirt, which had been purchased for purposes of decoration, ~~and made principally by some Jewish women on the East Side of New York,~~ rounded a corner and walked into the middle of the main street of Yellow Sky. In either hand the man held a long, heavy, blue-black revolver. Often he yelled, and these cries rang through a semblance of a deserted village, shrilly flying over the roofs in a volume that seemed to have no relation to the ordinary vocal strength of a man. It was as if the surrounding stillness formed the arch of a tomb over him. These cries of ferocious challenge rang against walls of silence. And his boots had red tops with gilded imprints, of the kind beloved in winter by little sledding boys on the hillsides of New England.

The man's face flamed in a rage begot of whisky. His eyes, rolling, and yet keen for ambush, hunted the still doorways and windows. He walked with the creeping movement of the midnight cat. As it occurred to him, he roared menacing information. The long revolvers in his hands were as easy as straws; they were moved with an electric swiftness. The little fingers of each hand played sometimes in a musician's way. Plain from the low collar of the shirt, the cords of his neck straightened and sank, straightened and sank, as passion moved him. The only sounds were his terrible invitations. The calm adobes preserved their demeanor at the passing of this small thing in the middle of the street.

There was no offer of fight—no offer of fight. The man called to the sky. There were no attractions. He bellowed and fumed and swayed his revolvers here and everywhere.

The dog of the barkeeper of the Weary Gentleman saloon had not appreciated the advance of events. He yet lay dozing in front of his master's door. At sight of the dog, the man paused and raised his revolver humorously. At sight of the man, the dog sprang up and walked diagonally away, with a sullen head, and growling. The man yelled, and the dog broke into a gallop. As it was about to enter an alley, there was a loud noise, a whistling, and something spat the ground directly before it. The dog screamed, and, wheeling in terror, galloped headlong in a new direction. Again there was a noise, a whistling, and sand was kicked viciously before it. Fear-stricken, the dog turned and flurried like an animal in a pen. The man stood laughing, his weapons at his hips.

Ultimately the man was attracted by the closed door of the Weary Gentleman saloon. He went to it and, hammering with a revolver, demanded drink.

The door remaining imperturbable, he picked a bit of paper from the walk, and nailed it to the framework with a knife. He then turned his back contemptuously upon this popular resort and, walking to the opposite side of the street and spinning there on his heel quickly and lithely, fired at the bit of paper. He missed it by a half-inch. He swore at himself, and went away. Later he comfortably fusilladed the windows of his most intimate friend. The man was playing with this town; it was a toy for him.

But still there was no offer of fight. The name of Jack Potter, his ancient antagonist, entered his mind, and he concluded that it would be a glad thing if he should go to Potter's house, and by bombardment induce him to come out and fight. He moved in the direction of his desire, chanting Apache scalp-music.

When he arrived at it, Potter's house presented the same still front as had the other adobes. Taking up a strategic position, the man howled a challenge. But this house regarded him as might a great stone god. It gave no sign. After a decent wait, the man howled further challenges, mingling with them wonderful epithets.

Presently there came the spectacle of a man churning himself into deepest rage over the immobility of a house. He fumed at it as the winter wind attacks a prairie cabin in the North. To the distance there should have gone the sound of a tumult like the fighting of two hundred Mexicans. As necessity bade him, he paused for breath or to reload his revolvers.

IV

Potter and his bride walked sheepishly and with speed. Sometimes they laughed together shamefacedly and low.

"Next corner, dear," he said finally.

They put forth the efforts of a pair walking bowed against a strong wind. Potter was about to raise a finger to point the first appearance of the new home when, as they circled the corner, they came face to face with a man in a maroon-colored shirt, who was feverishly pushing cartridges into a large revolver. Upon the instant the man dropped his revolver to the ground and, like lightning, whipped another from its holster. The second weapon was aimed at the bridegroom's chest.

There was a silence. Potter's mouth seemed to be merely a grave for his tongue. He exhibited an instinct to at once loosen his arm from the woman's grip, and he dropped the bag to the sand. As for the bride, her face had gone as yellow as old cloth. She was a slave to hideous rites, gazing at the apparitional snake.

The two men faced each other at a distance of three paces. He of the revolver smiled with a new and quiet ferocity.

"Tried to sneak up on me," he said. "Tried to sneak up on me!" His eyes grew more baleful. As Potter made a slight movement, the man thrust his revolver venomously forward. "No; don't you do it, Jack Potter. Don't you move a finger toward a gun just yet. Don't you move an eyelash. The time has come for me to settle with you, and I'm goin' to do it my own way, and loaf along with no interferin'. So if you don't want a gun bent on you, just mind what I tell you."

Potter looked at his enemy. "I ain't got a gun on me, Scratchy," he said. "Honest, I ain't." He was stiffening and steadying, but yet somewhere at the back of his mind a vision of the Pullman floated: the sea-green figured velvet, the shining brass, silver, and glass, the wood that gleamed as darkly brilliant as the surface of a pool of oil—all the glory of the marriage, the environment of the new estate. "You know I fight when it comes to fighting, Scratchy Wilson; but I ain't got a gun on me. You'll have to do all the shootin' yourself."

His enemy's face went livid. He stepped forward, and lashed his weapon to and fro before Potter's chest. "Don't you tell me you ain't got no gun on you, you whelp. Don't tell me no lie like that. There ain't a man in Texas ever seen you without no gun. Don't take me for no kid." His eyes blazed with light, and his throat worked like a pump.

"I ain't takin' you for no kid," answered Potter. His heels had not moved an inch backward. "I'm takin' you for a damn fool. I tell you I ain't got a gun, and I ain't. If you're goin' to shoot me up, you better begin now; you'll never get a chance like this again."

So much enforced reasoning had told on Wilson's rage; he was calmer. "If you ain't got a gun, why ain't you got a gun?" he sneered. "Been to Sunday school?"

"I ain't got a gun because I've just come from San Anton' with my wife. I'm married," said Potter. "And if I'd thought there was going to be any galoots like you prowling around when I brought my wife home, I'd had a gun, and don't you forget it."

"Married!" said Scratchy, not at all comprehending.

"Yes, married. I'm married," said Potter, distinctly.

"Married?" ~~said Scratchy.~~ Seemingly for the first time, he saw the drooping, drowning woman at the other man's side. "No," ~~he said.~~ He was like a creature allowed a glimpse of another world. He moved a pace backward, and his arm, with the revolver, dropped to his side. "Is this the lady?" ~~he asked.~~

"Yes; this is the lady," ~~answered Potter.~~

There was another period of silence.

"Well," ~~said Wilson at last, slowly,~~ "I s'pose it's all off now."

"It's all off if you say so, Scratchy. You know. I didn't make the trouble." Potter lifted his valise.

"Well, I 'low it's off, Jack," ~~said Wilson.~~ He was looking at the ground. "Married!" ~~He was not a student of chivalry; it was merely that in the presence of this foreign condition he was a simple child of the earlier plains.~~ He picked up his starboard revolver, and placing both weapons in their holsters, he went away. His feet made funnel-shaped tracks in the heavy sand.

One additional problem in the reading of narrative is that there is a tendency to bring vitality and life to the dialogue sections and then a temptation to drop vitality, interest, and color in the reading of the descriptive, narrative, and expository sections. The mood the author intended to create in his story, the explanations he felt necessary for the total effect are vitally important. They are the framework around which the plot revolves and they are the setting in which the characters move. Much of the suspense is built in the expository and narrative sections.

For example, Ernest Hemingway's The Old Man and the Sea has very little dialogue. Yet, the battle of the old man to catch the fish and then to get it back to land is vital, exciting, emotionally moving —the core of the book. The reader cannot go over any of these sections lightly. He must use a faster pace in the exciting sections dealing with the catch itself; he must show the relief when he lands the fish; he must indicate the panic the old man feels as the sharks attack the fish.

Another short story is included here for your study. No cutting has been done. Read the story and decide what must be done to highlight the fact that the heroine does not realize she has been offered a wedding trip around the world by an honest-to-goodness millionaire.

A Lickpenny Lover

O. Henry

There were 3,000 girls in the Biggest Store. Masie was one of them. She was eighteen and a saleslady in the gents' gloves. Here she became versed in two varieties of human beings— the kind of gents who buy their gloves in department stores and the kind of women who buy gloves for unfortunate gents. Besides this wide knowledge of the human species, Masie had acquired other information. She had listened to the promulgated wisdom of the 2,999 other girls and had stored it in a brain that was as secretive and wary as that of a Maltese cat. Perhaps nature, foreseeing that she would lack wise counsellors, had mingled the saving ingredient of shrewdness along with her beauty, as she has endowed the silver fox of the priceless fur above the other animals with cunning.

For Masie was beautiful. She was a deep-tinted blonde, with the calm poise of a lady who cooks butter cakes in a window. She stood behind her counter in the Biggest Store; and as you closed your hand over the tape-line for your glove measure you thought of Hebe; and as you looked again you wondered how she had come by Minerva's eyes.

When the floorwalker was not looking Masie chewed tutti fruiti; when he was looking she gazed up as if at the clouds and smiled wistfully.

That is the shopgirl smile, and I enjoin you to shun it unless you are well fortified with callosity of the heart, caramels and a congeniality for the capers of Cupid. This smile belonged to Masie's recreation hours and not to the store; but the floorwalker must have his own. He is the Shylock of the stores. When he comes nosing around the bridge of his nose is a toll-bridge. It is goo-goo eyes or "git" when he looks toward a pretty girl. Of course not all floorwalkers are thus. Only a few days ago the papers printed news of one over eighty years of age.

One day Irving Carter, painter, millionaire, traveller, poet, automobilist, happened to enter the Biggest Store. It is due to him to add that his visit was not voluntary. Filial duty took him by the collar and dragged him inside, while his mother philandered among the bronze and terra-cotta statuettes.

Carter strolled across to the glove counter in order to shoot a few minutes on the wing. His need for gloves was genuine; he had forgotten to bring a pair with him. But his action hardly calls for apology, because he had never heard of glove-counter flirtations.

As he neared the vicinity of his fate he hesitated, suddenly conscious of this unknown phase of Cupid's less worthy profession.

Three or four cheap fellows, sonorously garbed, were leaning over the counters, wrestling with the mediatorial hand-coverings, while giggling girls played vivacious seconds to their lead upon the strident string of coquetry. Carter would have retreated, but he had gone too far. Masie confronted him behind her counter with a questioning look in eyes as coldly, beautifully, warmly blue as the glint of summer sunshine on an iceberg drifting in Southern seas.

And then Irving Carter, painter, millionaire, etc., felt a warm flush rise to his aristocratically pale face. But not from diffidence. The blush was intellectual in origin. He knew in a moment that he stood in the ranks of the ready-made youths who wooed the giggling girls at other counters. Himself leaned against the oaken trysting place of a cockney Cupid with a desire in his heart for the favour of a glove salesgirl. He was no more than Bill and Jack and Mickey. And then he felt a sudden tolerance for them, and an elating, courageous contempt for the conventions upon which he had fed, and an unhesitating determination to have this perfect creature for his own.

When the gloves were paid for and wrapped Carter lingered for a moment. The dimples at the corners of Masie's damask mouth deepened. All gentlemen who bought gloves lingered in just that way. She curved an arm, showing like Psyche's through her shirt-waist sleeve, and rested an elbow upon the show-case edge.

Carter had never before encountered a situation of which he had not been perfect master. But now he stood far more awkward than Bill or Jack or Mickey. He had no chance of meeting this beautiful girl socially. His mind struggled to recall the nature and habits of shopgirls as he had read or heard of them. Somehow he had received the idea that they sometimes did not insist too strictly upon the regular channels of introduction. His heart beat loudly at the thought of proposing an unconventional meeting with this lovely and virginal being. But the tumult in his heart gave him courage.

After a few friendly and well-received remarks on general subjects, he laid his card by her hand on the counter.

"Will you please pardon me," he said, "if I seem too bold; but I earnestly hope you will allow me the pleasure of seeing you again. There is my name; I assure you that it is with the greatest respect that I ask the favour of becoming one of your fr——— acquaintances. May I not hope for the privilege?"

Masie knew men—especially men who buy gloves. Without hesitation she looked him frankly and smilingly in the eyes, and said:

"Sure. I guess you're all right. I don't usually go out with strange gentlemen, though. It ain't quite ladylike. When should you want to see me again?"

"As soon as I may," said Carter. "If you would allow me to call at your home, I———."

Masie laughed musically. "Oh, gee, no!" she said, emphatically. "If you could see our flat once! There's five of us in three rooms. I'd just like to see ma's face if I was to bring a gentleman friend there!"

"Anywhere, then," said the enamored Carter, "that will be convenient to you."

"Say," suggested Masie, with a bright-idea look in her peach-blow face; "I guess Thursday night will about suit me. Suppose you come to the corner of Eighth Avenue and Forty-eighth Street at 7:30. I live right near the corner. But I've got to be back home by eleven. Ma never lets me stay out after eleven."

Carter promised gratefully to keep the tryst, and then hastened to his mother, who was looking about for him to ratify her purchase of a bronze Diana.

A salesgirl with small eyes and an obtuse nose strolled near Masie, with a friendly leer.

"Did you make a hit with his nobs, Masie?" she asked familiarly.

"The gentleman asked permission to call," answered Masie, with the grand air, as she slipped Carter's card into the bosom of her waist.

"Permission to call!" echoed small eyes, with a snigger. "Did he say anything about dinner in the Waldorf and a spin in his auto afterward?"

"Oh, cheese it!" said Masie wearily. "You've been used to swell things, I don't think. You've had a swelled head ever since that hose-cart driver took you out to a chop suey joint. No, he never mentioned the Waldorf; but there's a Fifth Avenue address on his card, and if he buys the supper you can bet your life there won't be no pigtail on the waiter that takes the order."

As Carter glided away from the Biggest Store with his mother in his electric runabout, he bit his lip with a dull pain at his heart. He knew that love had come to him for the first time in all the twenty-nine years of his life. And that the object of it should make so readily an appointment with him at a street corner, though it was a step toward his desires, tortured him with misgivings.

Carter did not know the shopgirl. He did not know that her home is often either a scarcely habitable tiny room or a domicile filled to overflowing with kith and kin. The street corner is her parlour, the park is her drawing room; the avenue is her garden walk; yet for the most part she is as inviolate mistress of herself in them as is my lady inside her tapestried chamber.

One evening at dusk, two weeks after their first meeting, Carter and Masie strolled arm-in-arm into a little, dimly lit park. They found a bench, tree-shadowed and secluded, and sat there.

For the first time his arm stole gently around her. Her golden-bronze head slid restfully against his shoulder.

"Gee!" sighed Masie thankfully. "Why didn't you ever think of that before?"

"Masie," said Carter earnestly, "you surely know that I love you. I ask you sincerely to marry me. You know me well enough by this time to have no doubts of me. I want you, and

I must have you. I care nothing for the difference in our stations."

"What is the difference?" asked Masie curiously.

"Well, there isn't any," said Carter quickly, "except in the minds of foolish people. It is in my power to give you a life of luxury. My social position is beyond dispute, and my means are ample."

"They all say that," remarked Masie. "It's the kid they all give you. I suppose you really work in a delicatessen or follow the races. I ain't as green as I look."

"I can furnish you all the proofs you want," said Carter gently. "And I want you, Masie. I loved you the first day I saw you."

"They all do," said Masie, with an amused laugh, "to hear 'em talk. If I could meet a man that got stuck on me the third time he'd seen me I think I'd get mashed on him."

"Please don't say such things," pleaded Carter. "Listen to me, dear. Ever since I first looked into your eyes you have been the only woman in the world for me."

"Oh, ain't you the kidder!" smiled Masie. "How many other girls did you ever tell that?"

But Carter persisted. And at length he reached the flimsy, fluttering little soul of the shopgirl that existed somewhere deep down in her lovely bosom. His words penetrated the heart whose very lightness was its safest armour. She looked up at him with eyes that saw. And a warm glow visited her cool cheeks. Tremblingly, awfully, her moth wings closed, and she seemed about to settle upon the flower of love. Some faint glimmer of life and its possibilities on the other side of her glove counter dawned upon her. Carter felt the change and crowded the opportunity.

"Marry me, Masie," he whispered softly, "and we will go away from this ugly city to beautiful ones. We will forget work and business, and life will be one long holiday. I know where I should take you—I have been there often. Just think of a shore where summer is eternal, where the waves are always rippling on the lovely beach and the people are happy and free as children. We will sail to those shores and remain there as long as you please. In one of those far-away cities there are grand and lovely palaces and towers full of beautiful pictures and statues. The streets of the city are water, and one travels about in————"

"I know," said Masie, sitting up suddenly. "Gondolas."

"Yes," smiled Carter.

"I thought so," said Masie.

"And then," continued Carter, "we will travel on and see whatever we wish in the world. After the European cities we will visit India and the ancient cities there, and ride on elephants and see the wonderful temples of the Hindoos and Brahmins and the Japanese gardens and the camel trains and chariot races in Persia, and all the queer sights of foreign countries. Don't you think you would like it, Masie?"

Masie rose to her feet.

"I think we had better be going home," she said coolly. "It's getting late."

Carter humoured her. He had come to know her varying, thistle-down moods, and that it was useless to combat them. But he felt a certain happy triumph. He had held for a moment, though but by a silken thread, the soul of his wild Psyche, and hope was stronger within him. Once she had folded her wings and her cool hand had closed about his own.

At the Biggest Store the next day Masie's chum, Lulu, waylaid her in an angle of the counter.

"How are you and your swell friend making it?" she asked.

"Oh, him?" said Masie, patting her side curls. "He ain't in it any more. Say, Lu, what do you think that fellow wanted me to do?"

"Go on the stage?" guessed Lulu breathlessly.

"Nit; he's too cheap a guy for that. He wanted me to marry him and go down to Coney Island for a wedding tour!"

SUMMARY

Prose is generally categorized as fiction or nonfiction. Nonfiction concerns itself primarily with explanation and persuasion, takes the form of essays, editorials, diaries, histories, and letters. Fiction consists of short stories, novels, fables, and tales.

Prose may also be looked at in another way. It may be descriptive, expository, or narrative. Descriptive prose relies on imagery. When cutting descriptive prose, follow the general rule to cut down but not out. Retain the most vivid elements of descriptive writing.

Expository prose is writing which concerns itself directly, by way of explanation or persuasion, with ideas or principles.

Narrative prose tells a story. It has setting, plot, and characters, and has one or more climaxes. It is characterized by action. It combines suspense, romance, excitement, tragedy, and comedy in one selection or it can treat any one of them alone.

Several general rules for effective cutting of narrative prose should be considered:

1. Choose a selection that generally fits time requirements. Then the cutting will be minimal.
2. Cut minor characters.
3. Where possible cut in large segments rather than in small bits.
4. Paraphrase in order not to leave large gaps in meaning.
5. Cut "he said's" wherever possible.
6. Be certain that neither the author's purpose nor his style has been distorted by your cutting.

chapter eleven

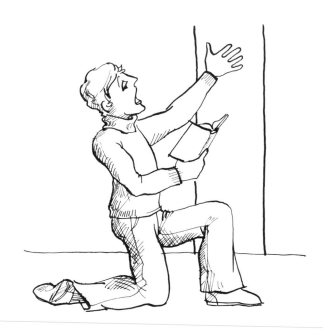

How do I read drama?

Drama is a mirror of life. It comments on social problems, on matters of national and international importance, on the weaknesses, strengths, and foibles of human nature—on life itself. It is often born of narrative prose, but it brings silent pages alive.

A HISTORY OF DRAMA

The conflict between drama and oral interpretation was mentioned earlier, but in actuality, they are closely allied in their respective histories. Drama was the original form—it is older than religion. Theatre began with the first primitive man who thought that by imitating animals he could insure good hunting. Eventually, man began to express himself in dance and rituals, perpetuating the dramatic form.

The classical period in Greece brought the first real form to theatre. Greek theatre consisted of three types of plays: *tragedies,* based on noble themes and heroic legends of the gods; *satires,* burlesques of the legends; and *comedies,* which dealt with the farcical aspects of life. The Greek drama grew out of the dithyramb, a choral hymn of praise to the god Dionysus, god of wine and fertility.

Thespis became the first actor when he stepped out of the chorus and took on the role of narrator—and later a specific character. These developments led to the establishment of drama as a vital part of the cultural life of the Greeks.

Plays were performed in open-air amphitheatres, and for the most part, the themes were noble and tragic, although such writers as Aristophanes chose to satirize life. Sophocles, Aeschylus, Euripides, and Aristophanes were some of the most prominent Greek playwrights. Their actors often wore masks for the purpose of character differentiation, rather than relying on vocal and bodily interpretation.

When cultural life in Greece declined, both drama and oral interpretation also declined, and these forms did not reappear until the

Middle Ages. Drama was reborn within the church as part of the masses celebrating special holidays, but eventually the rituals and the priests began to be satirized. As a result the church banned the plays from the services. This marked the beginning of involvement of laymen in theatre, and the development of theatre guilds—and travelling dramatic troups. The subject matter of the plays at this time was almost completely Biblical—very elaborate stagings of the Creation, Heaven and Hell, and the passing of Angels between Heaven and Earth.

The Renaissance brought with it a renewed interest in drama and oral reading. Initially, the performances were given for aristocratic audiences and the plays were written by poets of the courts. But the form which gained the greatest amount of popularity with the general public was the *commedia dell'arte.* The actors wore masks and costumes. The commedia was based on improvisation and its primary feature was the uninhibited actions of the actors.

Although the *commedia dell'arte* developed in Italy, the theatre was also growing in other European countries. Spanish writers such as Lope de Rueda, Lope de Vega, Cervantes, and Calderón advanced playwriting as an art. And there was also a rebirth of drama in England, with the works of Christopher Marlowe, Thomas Kyd, Ben Jonson, and William Shakespeare.

In France, the first professional playwright was Alexandre Hardy, but Corneille, Racine, and Molière also made classic contributions to the theatre. Molière's satirical comedies such as *Tartuffe, Le Malade Imaginaire, The School for Wives, Le Bourgeois Gentilhomme,* and *The Doctor in Spite of Himself,* were popular in the seventeenth century, as they are today. Any of these works would be excellent material for oral interpretation.

In England, with Cromwell and the upsurge of the Puritan theology, the theatre died down, but it was later given new life in the Restoration period. Plays by Sir George Etherege, William Congreve, and William Wycherley became very popular, with their themes of heartless seduction and sophisticated evil. Up to this time, young boys had played the roles of women, but Restoration drama brought the first women to the stage.

The eighteenth century produced the comedies of Oliver Goldsmith and Richard Brinsley Sheridan. Goldsmith's *She Stoops to Conquer* and Sheridan's *The Rivals* and *School for Scandal* are still popular, and they offer appropriate material for interpretative reading. John Gay also achieved fame with his *The Beggar's Opera,* from which *The Threepenny Opera* was taken.

The theatre in Germany was also advancing, with the works of

Johann Friedrich Schiller and Goethe. Goethe's *Faust* is one of the world's best known dramas. All over Europe the theatre became a medium for social protest. Romanticism and melodrama were popular. Henrik Ibsen was one of the most vocal playwrights with such plays as *Hedda Gabbler, Ghosts,* and *The Master Builder.* In France, Emile Zola and Andre Antoine started the movement called "naturalism"—to bring drama to the utter reality and naturalness of life, to escape from some of the artifices and excesses that had become a part of the theatre.

However, Russia produced a man who exerted the greatest influence on drama and on acting. Constantine Stanislavsky, working with the Moscow Art Theatre, protested against the old ideas of acting. His was an attempt to bring a more realistic approach to characterization.

The twentieth century has produced such playwrights as Eugene O'Neill, who adapted techniques from the past. In *Great God Brown* he borrowed from the Greeks the use of masks, and *Mourning Becomes Electra* was based on the Greek trilogy. *Long Day's Journey Into Night* is an expression of nineteenth-century naturalism.

Arthur Miller's plays, *Death of a Salesman, After the Fall,* and *Incident at Vichy,* carried on the tragic themes. And Tennessee Williams probed the weaknesses of mankind in his *Streetcar Named Desire, Suddenly Last Summer,* and *The Glass Menagerie.*

It was in the latter part of the nineteenth century and the first part of the twentieth century that George Bernard Shaw wrote his great plays—*Major Barbara, Mrs. Warren's Profession, Pygmalion, Arms and the Man, Caesar and Cleopatra,* and *St. Joan.*

The modern theatre has taken on many different forms—it has been called avant-garde, "theatre of the absurd,"—and the plays are studies in surrealism and existentialism. Eugene Ionesco's *The Chairs* and *The Bald Soprano,* Jean-Paul Sartre's *No Exit,* Jean Genet's *The Balcony,* and Samuel Beckett's *Waiting for Godot* are all examples of plays which project reality beyond logic and literal observation.

Just as drama has changed in theory and in style over hundreds of years, so has the art of oral interpretation—and the two continue to change and to grow.

STRUCTURE OF THE PLAY

A play is a story—or at times an idea—told in dialogue form.

Usually it contains two or three acts, although in the beginning there was no specific act separation. Plays went to five acts during Shakespeare's time, then to four and finally three. There are, of course, exceptions. Structurally, the form can vary. John Osborne's *Inadmissible Evidence* has two acts; Peter Weiss' *The Investigation* is not divided into acts. Eugene O'Neill's *Long Day's Journey Into Night* has four acts but his *Mourning Becomes Electra* is comprised of three plays, the first having four acts, the second five, and third four. O'Neill also separated his *Strange Interlude* into two parts with the first having five acts and the second four. He has been noted for the marathon length of his works—as well as for his versatility and characterization. It was not unusual, in such plays as *Electra* and *Strange Interlude,* for the play to begin at 7:30 P.M. and end at midnight.

Some have considered that a play must have a theme, thesis, root idea, central idea, goal, aim, driving force, subject, purpose, plan, plot. But according to Lajos Egri in his noted book on playwriting, *The Art of Dramatic Writing,* ". . . we choose the word 'premise' because it contains all the elements the other words try to express and because it is less subject to misinterpretation."[1] It is his feeling that no idea or situation is strong enough to provide a basis for a play. It must have a premise. It must head down a certain road. It must be about something.

Whatever theory is used, there is one common requirement— plays must have conflict. Certainly Mr. Egri's theory provides that essential. And certainly the reader must know the premise if he is to interpret the play meaningfully.

Stylistically speaking, plays have employed all forms or writing techniques. They have gone from the poetic form of the Greek drama to the blank verse of Shakespeare, a form also used by such modern playwrights as Maxwell Anderson in his *Winterset, Elizabeth the Queen,* and *Mary of Scotland.* Plays have also been written in documentary style, as in the days of German expressionism and the "Living Newspaper" during the Depression in America. A similar technique was recently used in *The Investigation* by Peter Weiss. O'Neill used a different style in *Strange Interlude,* adopting the form of spoken thoughts similar to the "asides" in earlier melodramas, although his was a far more extensive use of the device whereby an actor speaks to the audience about what is happening on stage—with the other actors on stage supposedly not able to hear the comments. Generally

[1] Lajos Egri, The *Art of Dramatic Writing,* (New York, 1960) p. 2.

speaking, though, the dialogue and style of most plays are in realistic conversational form, and the three act division is the most frequently used.

The general structure of a play is as follows: The playwright introduces the primary problem, the conflict, and the most important characters in the first act. In the second act the conflict is extended, new characters may be introduced, but definite steps are taken toward the resolution of the conflict. The crisis, the height of the conflict, the moment of decision where the characters turn one way or the other occurs at the end of the second act. The third act provides the resolution of the problem—or the submission to it—and completes the roles the characters play in the conflict.

Let us take for an example Eugene O'Neill's autobiographical play, *Long Day's Journey Into Night*. In the first act we meet Tyrone, his sons Jamie and Edmund, and his wife, Mary. We learn of the family's concern over Mary's addiction to dope and we also learn what brought it about. We see their hope that she may be able to defeat the addiction, but by the end of the first act we know she is not going to win her battle. We also learn of Edmund's illness and Jamie's furtive enjoyment of his irresponsible life and his hatred for his father. In Act Two we discover that Mary is back on dope and we feel the deep disappointment her sons experience because of her weakness. They confront her with their awareness of her relapse, as does Tyrone, but she refuses to admit she has taken dope. The separation of the members of the family increases. In the third act Mary is even further under the influence. Her mind wanders continually back to her past. We learn more of what makes Mary what she is. She completely rejects Tyrone's condemnation for taking the dope. In the fourth act the family has given up hope. Edmund resents his father for the penny-pinching actions that have led Mary to drugs and have resulted in his, Edmund's, being sent to a state hospital to be treated for consumption. Jamie has left the house in anger to spend the night in town drinking and whoring. Tyrone tries to explain why he has been so careful with money by telling Edmund of his own unhappy, poverty-ridden childhood. Then Edmund tells his father what matters to him in life. Jamie returns after Tyrone has left and gives Edmund an account of his night—and then in a drunken and bitter moment of revelation he tells of his jealousy and hatred for Edmund because the latter has been given most of his parents' attention. Jamie brokenly confesses at the same time his love for his brother but lets us feel the depth of his loneliness. Tyrone joins his sons, condemns

Jamie again for a wasted life, and at this moment Mary enters the room, now totally under the influence of dope—completely unaware of her family in the room. The final tragedy is complete. Hope has been utterly destroyed. There is no illusion.

The play extends, time-wise, from dawn to late night, and in that brief period we see the cross-currents, the complexities, the tragedies of the lives of four people.

Division into acts can also call for further division. Many times an act will be divided into scenes. Such a form is often necessary for a change in scenery within the act or for purposes of climactic structure. Each scene has its own minor climax building to the major climax and final resolution.

In spite of such division, however, the play must have continuity —it must move smoothly from one new development to another. Of course, this is not true of the structure of such plays as *The Chairs* by Ionesco or *Mother Courage* by Brecht or *Endgame* by Beckett, as these purposely employ sudden and jarring changes of thought and idea because they were written as an existentialist revolt against the rigid structuring of writing. But the average play moves with smooth transitions.

Richard Brinsley Sheridan's *The School for Scandal* is carefully plotted. Each scene moves into the next smoothly, but the scenes are complete within themselves. An excellent example is the famous closet scene.

From

The School for Scandal

Richard Brinsley Sheridan

A Library in Joseph Surface's House. Joseph Surface and Servant.

JOSEPH SURFACE: No letter from Lady Teazle?
SERVANT: No, sir.
JOSEPH SURFACE: (*aside*) I am surprised she has not sent, if she is prevented from coming. Sir Peter certainly does not suspect me. Yet I wish I may not lose the heiress

through the scrape I have drawn myself into with the wife. However, Charles's imprudence and bad character are great points in my favor.

(*Knocking*)

SERVANT: Sir, I believe that must be Lady Teazle.

JOSEPH SURFACE: Hold! See whether it is or not before you go to the door. I have a particular message for you if it should be my brother.

SERVANT: 'Tis her ladyship, sir; she always leaves the chair at the milliner's in the next street.

JOSEPH SURFACE: Stay, stay! Draw that screen before the window—that will do. My opposite neighbor is a maiden lady of so curious a temper.

(*Servant draws the screen, and exits*)

I have a difficult hand to play in this affair. Lady Teazle has lately suspected my views on Maria; but she must by no means be let into that secret—at least, till I have her more in my power.

(*Enter Lady Teazle*)

LADY TEAZLE: What, sentiment in soliloquy now? Have you been very impatient? O lud! don't pretend to look grave. I vow I couldn't come before.

JOSEPH SURFACE: O madam, punctuality is a species of constancy very unfashionable in a lady of quality.

LADY TEAZLE: Upon my word, you ought to pity me. Do you know Sir Peter is grown so ill-natured to me of late, and so jealous of Charles too—that's the best of the story, isn't it?

JOSEPH SURFACE: (*aside*) I am glad my scandalous friends keep that up.

LADY TEAZLE: I am sure I wish he would let Maria marry him, and then perhaps he would be convinced; don't you, Mr. Surface?

JOSEPH SURFACE: (*aside*) Indeed I do not—(*aloud*) Oh, certainly I do! for then my dear Lady Teazle would also be convinced how wrong her suspicions were of my having any design on the silly girl.

LADY TEAZLE: Well, well, I'm inclined to believe you. But isn't it provoking to have the most ill-natured things said of one? And there's my friend Lady Sneerwell has circulated I don't know how many scandalous tales of me, and all without any foundation, too; that's what vexes me.

JOSEPH SURFACE: Ay, madam, to be sure, that is the provoking circumstance—without foundation. Yes, yes, there's the mortification, indeed; for, when a scandalous story is believed against one, there certainly is no comfort like the consciousness of having deserved it.

LADY TEAZLE: No, to be sure, then I'd forgive their malice; but to attack me, who am really so innocent, and who never say an ill-natured thing of anybody—that is, of any friend; and then Sir Peter, too, to have him so peevish, and so suspicious, when I know the integrity of my own heart—indeed 'tis monstrous!

JOSEPH SURFACE: But, my dear Lady Teable, 'tis your own fault if you suffer it. When a husband entertains a groundless suspicion of his wife, and withdraws his confidence from her, the original compact is broken, and she owes it to the honor of her sex to endeavor to outwit him.

LADY TEAZLE: Indeed! So that, if he suspects me without cause, it follows, that the best way of curing his jealousy is to give reason for't?

JOSEPH SURFACE: Undoubtedly—for your husband should never be deceived in you: and in that case it becomes you to be frail in compliment to his discernment.

LADY TEAZLE: To be sure, what you say is very reasonable, and when the consciousness of my innocence—

JOSEPH SURFACE: Ah, my dear madam, there is the great mistake; 'tis this very conscious innocence that is of the greatest prejudice to you. What is it makes you negligent of forms and careless of the world's opinion? why, the consciousness of your own innocence. What makes you thoughtless in your conduct and apt to run into a thousand little imprudences? why, the consciousness of your own innocence. What makes you impatient of Sir Peter's temper, and outrageous at his suspicions? why, the consciousness of your innocence.

LADY TEAZLE: 'Tis very true!

JOSEPH SURFACE: Now, my dear Lady Teazle, if you would but once make a trifling faux pas, you can't conceive how cautious you would grow, and how ready to humor and agree with your husband.

LADY TEAZLE: Do you think so?

JOSEPH SURFACE: Oh, I'm sure on't! and then you would find all scandal would cease at once, for—in short, your character at present is like a person in a plethora, absolutely dying from too much health.

LADY TEAZLE: So, so; then I perceive your prescription is that I must sin in my own defence, and part with my virtue to preserve my reputation?

JOSEPH SURFACE: Exactly so, upon my credit, ma'am.

LADY TEAZLE: Well, certainly this is the oddest doctrine, and the newest receipt for avoiding calumny.

JOSEPH SURFACE: An infallible one, believe me. Prudence, like experience, must be paid for.

LADY TEAZLE: Why, if my understanding were once convinced—

JOSEPH SURFACE: Oh, certainly, madam, your understanding should be convinced. Yes, yes—Heaven forbid I should persuade you to do anything you thought wrong. No, no, I have too much honor to desire it.

LADY TEAZLE: Don't you think we may as well leave honor out of the argument? (*rises*)

JOSEPH SURFACE: Ah, the ill effects of your country education, I see, still remain with you.

LADY TEAZLE: I doubt they do, indeed; and I will fairly own to you, that if I could be persuaded to do wrong, it would be by Sir Peter's ill usage sooner than your honorable logic, after all.

JOSEPH SURFACE: Then, by this hand, which he is unworthy of—(*taking her hand*)
(*Enter Servant*)
'Sdeath, you blockhead—what do you want?

SERVANT: I beg your pardon, sir, but I thought you would not choose Sir Peter to come up without announcing him.

JOSEPH SURFACE: Sir Peter!—Oons—the devil!

LADY TEAZLE: Sir Peter! O lud! I'm ruined! I'm ruined!

SERVANT: Sir, 'twasn't I let him in.

LADY TEAZLE: Oh! I'm quite undone! What will become of me now, Mr. Logic?—Oh! mercy, he's on the stairs—I'll

get behind here—and if ever I'm so imprudent again—
(*Goes behind the screen*)

(*At this point, Sir Peter Teazle arrives and tells Sir Joseph he fears his wife, Lady Teazle, is being untrue to him. The man in question he believes to be Joseph's brother, Charles. Sir Peter also says he has left the bulk of his fortune to his wife, a fact that does not escape Lady Teazle as she hides behind the screen. Sir Peter then discusses his views about Joseph's alleged attention to a milliner. Their conversation is interrupted with the announcement that Charles demands admittance. Sir Peter is about to hide when he spies a skirt behind the screen, but Sir Joseph assures him it is only the milliner who has been plaguing him. Sir Peter goes into a closet. Charles enters and he and Joseph discuss Sir Peter's feelings about Charles's attentions to Lady Teazle, and Charles says he always thought it was Joseph who was being attentive to her and receiving the attentions. Joseph, not wishing Sir Peter to hear more, says Sir Peter is hiding in the closet, so Charles says he is only playing a joke on Joseph. Then Sir Peter comes out and says he knew of Joseph's interest in the milliner and she was hiding behind the screen. Charles pulls down the screen. Now continue the scene.*)

(*Joseph Surface enters just as Charles throws down the screen*)

CHARLES SURFACE: Lady Teazle, by all that's wonderful!

SIR PETER: Lady Teazle, by all that's damnable!

CHARLES SURFACE: Sir Peter, that is one of the smartest French milliners I ever saw. Egad, you seem all to have been diverting yourselves here at hide and seek, and I don't see who is out of the secret. Shall I beg your ladyship to inform me? Now a word!—Brother, will you be pleased to explain this matter? What! is Morality dumb too?—Sir Peter, though I found you in the dark, perhaps you are not so now! All mute! Well—though I can make nothing of the affair, I suppose you perfectly understand one another; so I'll leave you to yourselves. (*going*) Brother, I'm sorry to find you have given that worthy man grounds for so much uneasiness—Sir Peter! there's nothing in the world so noble as a man of sentiment!

(*Exit Charles Surface. They stand for some time looking at each other.*)

JOSEPH SURFACE: Sir Peter—notwithstanding—I confess—that appearances are against me—if you will afford me your patience—I make no doubt—but I shall explain everything to your satisfaction.

SIR PETER: If you please, sir.

JOSEPH SURFACE: The fact is, sir, that Lady Teazle, knowing my pretensions to your ward Maria—I say, sir, Lady Teazle, being apprehensive of the jealousy of your temper — and knowing my friendship to the family—she, sir, I say —called here—in order that—I might explain these pretensions—but on your coming—being apprehensive—as I said—of your jealousy—she withdrew—and this, you may depend on it, is the whole truth of the matter.

SIR PETER: A very clear account, upon my word; and I dare swear the lady will vouch for every article of it.

LADY TEAZLE: For not one word of it, Sir Peter!

SIR PETER: How! don't you think it worth while to agree in the lie?

LADY TEAZLE: There is not one syllable of truth in what that gentleman has told you.

SIR PETER: I believe you, upon my soul, ma'am!

JOSEPH SURFACE: (*aside to Lady Teazle*). 'Sdeath, madam, will you betray me?

LADY TEAZLE: Good Mr. Hypocrite, by your leave, I'll speak for myself.

SIR PETER: Ay, let her alone, sir: you'll find she'll make a better story than you, without prompting.

LADY TEAZLE: Hear me, Sir Peter! I came here on no matter relating to your ward, and even ignorant of this gentleman's pretensions to her. But I came, seduced by his insidious arguments, at least to listen to his pretended passion, if not to sacrifice your honor to his baseness.

SIR PETER: Now, I believe, the truth is coming, indeed!

JOSEPH SURFACE: The woman's mad!

LADY TEAZLE: No, sir; she has recovered her senses, and your own arts have furnished her with the means. Sir

Peter, I do not expect you to credit me—but the tenderness you express for me, when I am sure you could not think I was a witness to it, has penetrated so to my heart, that had I left the place without the shame of this discovery, my future life should have spoken the sincerity of my gratitude. As for that smooth-tongued hypocrite, who would have seduced the wife of his too credulous friend, while he affected honorable addresses to his ward—I behold him now in a light so truly despicable that I shall never again respect myself for having listened to him.
(*Exit Lady Teazle*)

JOSEPH SURFACE: Notwithstanding all this, Sir Peter, Heaven knows—

SIR PETER: That you are a villain! and so I leave you to your conscience.

JOSEPH SURFACE: You are too rash, Sir Peter; you shall hear me. The man who shuts out conviction by refusing to—
(*Exeunt, Joseph Surface talking*)

PHYSICAL DESCRIPTION

The playwright, in addition to structuring his work so that it clearly presents the story, must describe in detail what is in the set—where the doors are, what furniture is present, what kind of light is in the room. He must also describe the characters. O'Neill goes into great detail in the description of the main characters while some other playwrights deal quite superficially with character description. In *Long Day's Journey Into Night,* O'Neill lets the reader know all about the house, the people, the atmosphere.

From

Long Day's Journey Into Night

Eugene O'Neill

(*Scene: Living room of James Tyrone's summer home on a morning in August, 1912.*)

At rear are two double doorways with portieres. The one at right leads into a front parlor with the formally arranged, set appearance of a room rarely occupied. The other opens on a dark, windowless back parlor, never used except as a passage from living room to dining room. Against the wall between the doorways is a small bookcase, with a picture of Shakespeare above it, containing novels by Balzac, Zola, Stendhal, philosophical and sociological works by Schopenhauer, Nietzsche, Marx, Engels, Kropotkin, Max Sterner, plays by Ibsen, Shaw, Strindberg, poetry by Swinburne, Rossetti, Wilde, Ernest Dowson, Kipling, etc. In the right wall, rear, is a screen door leading out on the porch which extends halfway around the house. Farther forward, a series of three windows looks over the front lawn to the harbor and the avenue that runs along the water front. A small wicker table and an ordinary oak desk are against the wall, flanking the windows. In the left wall, a similar series of windows looks out on the grounds in back of the house. Beneath them is a wicker couch with cushions, its head toward rear. Farther back is a large glassed-in bookcase with sets of Dumas, Victor Hugo, Charles Lever, three sets of Shakespeare, the *World's Best Literature* in fifty large volumes, Hume's *History of England*, Thiers' *History of the Consulate and Empire*, Smollett's *History of England*, Gibbon's *Roman Empire* and miscellaneous volumes of old plays, poetry, and several histories of Ireland. The astonishing thing about these sets is that all the volumes have the look of having been read and reread.

The hardwood floor is nearly covered by a rug, inoffensive in design and color. At center is a round table with a green shaded reading lamp, the cord plugged in one of the four sockets in the chandelier above. Around the table within reading-light range are four chairs, three of them wicker arm-chairs, the fourth (at right front of table) a varnished oak rocker with leather bottom. It is around 8:30. Sunshine comes through the windows at right. And as the curtain rises, the family have just finished breakfast. Mary Tyrone and her husband enter together from the back parlor, coming from the dining room.

Mary is fifty-four, about medium height. She still has a young, graceful figure, a trifle plump, but showing little evidence of middle-aged waist and hips, although she is not tightly corseted. Her face is distinctly Irish in type. It must once have been extremely pretty, and is still striking. It does not match her healthy figure but is thin and pale with the bone structure prominent. Her nose is long and straight, her mouth wide with full, sensitive lips. She uses no rouge or any sort of makeup. Her high forehead is framed by thick, pure white hair. Accentuated by her pallor and white hair, her dark brown eyes appear black. They are unusually large and beautiful, with black brows and long curling lashes.

What strikes one immediately is her extreme nervousness. Her hands are never still. They were once beautiful hands, with long, tapering fingers, but rheumatism has knotted the joints and warped the fingers, so that now they have an ugly crippled look. One avoids looking at them, the more so because one is conscious she is sensitive about their appearance and humiliated by her inability to control the nervousness which draws attention to them. She is dressed simply but with a sure sense of what becomes her. Her hair is arranged with fastidious care. Her voice is soft and attractive. When she is merry, there is a touch of Irish lilt in it.

Her most appealing quality is the simple, unaffected charm of a shy convent-girl youthfulness she has never lost—an innate unworldly innocence.

While O'Neill describes setting and characters in detail, no such care was exercised by classical playwrights such as Shakespeare. He merely named the locale of the scene and devoted no space at all to a description of the characters. Such detail he left to the actor. And, as such, he provided the actor—or the reader—with a very real challenge.

CLIMAX IN DRAMA

The playwright must be concerned with the structural climaxes to a scene. He must think, too, of the effect of such technical devices as a curtain's falling on a peak moment, of lights being used to heighten a scene. For instance, in Arthur Miller's *All My Sons,* the confrontation scene between the father and the son at the end of the second act is carefully motivated. The climax is the high point of the play. It is the moment toward which all events previously have been building, and it is the moment calling for the final resolution in the third act. The effect of the falling curtain and the dimming lights adds greatly to the emotional impact of the scene.

The playwright, however, is often at the mercy of other people involved in the production. A director may interpret the play in a different manner from that intended by the author. And the director can further add to this conception by directing the actors to play their roles in a manner consistent with his interpretation. In some cases, it is true that the playwright demands and is given a voice in the direction of his play. Then he can insist that his intentions and premises be retained. But, often, particularly if he is not a playwright of recognized stature, he is powerless to prevent misinterpretations of his work.

Sometimes, however, such misinterpretations can work to the benefit of the playwright. When *Arsenic and Old Lace* was presented for production, the author saw it as a serious play. The director decided it would be great comedy and staged it as a comedy. The play became a smash hit.

THE READING OF DRAMA

Perhaps in no other form of literature is involvement with characters more important than in drama. In the reading of drama you must present in a realistic manner the stories of people, their conflicts, their dreams, their hopes. And you must breathe life into them through their dialogue. Consequently, it is imperative in choosing a play, that you read it in its entirety. Do not make the mistake of reading only a scene because that scene can very often not present a clear picture of either the plot or the people involved, and meaning will be distorted.

Characterization

The principal concern in the oral reading of a play is to know the characters. You must know *all* about them— and then use vocal and physical details for differentiation.

If you are reading a scene with two or three characters—it is never wise to try to do more than three—their differences should be brought about through your characterization. In *Becket,* the King is inclined to be temperamental, impulsive, excitable, and very sensitive. These characteristics would guide you in your reading of the part. Becket, on the other hand, particularly in the last half of the play, has a quiet inner strength, a confidence, a peace. There *is* a difference between these two men as there is between any two people. The King would probably speak in a higher voice, especially under stress, and at a somewhat faster rate. Becket would be read with a calmer, slower pace, though earlier in the play, when they are friends living the full life, Becket is more outwardly vigorous, more expansive, less reserved.

An equally dramatic contrast exists in the fourth act of *Long Day's Journey Into Night,* where Tyrone and Edmund are both drunk. But—Tyrone is the father, an older person with more maturity and strength. Edmund, on the other hand, is not well. He is frail, younger, highly sensitive, a dreamer.

A reader, in his introduction, must always inform his audience of the events that have taken place prior to the beginning of the scene to be read. It need not be a long, detailed summary. Only the most essential facts should be given so that the audience may have a clear concept of the people and the situation. The reader is not obligated to tell what happens after the scene is over.

To help the reader in presenting clear-cut and firm characterizations in the reading of drama, the playwright often provides excellent clues as to the type of emotion demanded in a scene. After the name of the character, the author will insert in parenthesis such words as "angrily," "slowly," "spirited," and so forth. And at other times, he may interrupt the dialogue in a scene to indicate the pause for a character's reflection or a sudden change in attitude or mood, such as, "he pauses, glares at Mary, and then slowly and with anger, he turns on her."

All such clues add to the reader's understanding of the people in the play, but they should not be read aloud by the interpreter. They are his clues to interpretation.

The playwright also reveals much of the characters' feelings in their dialogue. For example, note how Hamlet tells his innermost thoughts and emotions in such soliloquies as "To be or not to be" and "Oh, that this too too solid flesh would melt." Both of these speeches give the reader clues as to the type of person Hamlet is. In addition, other characters in the play tell much about other personalities, all of which are significant clues to the interpreter. In Jean Anouilh's *Becket,* the King in the opening scene not only tells the kind of person Becket was, but he also reveals much of their past association.

Becket

Jean Anouilh

Act One

(The King enters from the back. He is wearing his crown, and is naked under a big cloak. The King hesitates a moment before the tomb; then removes his cloak with a swift movement and the Page takes it away. He falls to his knees on the stone floor and prays, alone, naked, in the middle of the stage. Behind the pillars, in the shadows, one senses the disquieting presence of unseen lookers-on.)

KING: Well, Thomas Becket, are you satisfied? I am naked at your tomb and your monks are coming to flog me. What an end to our story! You, rotting in this tomb, larded with my barons' dagger thrusts, and I, naked, shivering in the draughts, and waiting like an idiot for those brutes to come and thrash me. Don't you think we'd have done better to understand each other?
Becket in his Archbishop's robes, just as he was on the day of his death, has appeared on the side of the stage, from behind a pillar. He says softly:
BECKET: Understand each other? It wasn't possible.
KING: I said, "In all save the honor of the realm." It was you who taught me that slogan, after all.
BECKET: I answered you. "In all save the honor of God." We were like two deaf men talking.
KING: How cold it was on that bare plain at La Ferté-Bernard, the last time we two met! It's funny, it's always been cold, in our story. Save at the beginning, when we were friends. We had a few fine summer evenings together, with the girls. . . .
He says suddenly:
Did you love Gwendolen, Archbishop? Did you hate me, that night when I said, "I am the King," and took her from you? Perhaps that's what you never could forgive me for?

BECKET: (*Quietly*)   I've forgotten.

KING: Yet we were like two brothers, weren't we—you and I? That night it was a childish prank— a lusty lad shouting "I am the King!" . . . I was so young. . . . And every thought in my head came from you, you know that.

BECKET: (*Gently, as if to a little boy*)   Pray, Henry, and don't talk so much.

KING: (*Irritably*)   If you think I'm in the mood for praying at the moment . . .

Becket quietly withdraws into the darkness and disappears during the King's next speech.

I can see them through my fingers, spying on me from the aisles. Say what you like, they're an oafish lot, those Saxons of yours! To give oneself over naked to those ruffians! With my delicate skin. . . . Even you'd be afraid. Besides, I'm ashamed. Ashamed of this whole masquerade. I need them though, that's the trouble. I have to rally them to my cause, against my son, who'll gobble up my kingdom if I let him. So I've come to make my peace with their saint. You must admit it's funny. You've become a saint and here am I, the King, desperately in need of that great amorphous mass which could do nothing, up till now, save lie inert beneath its own enormous weight, cowering under blows, and which is all-powerful now. .What use are conquests, when you stop to think? They are England now, because of their vast numbers, and the rate at which they breed—like rabbits, to make good the massacres. But one must always pay the price—that's another thing you taught me, Thomas Becket, when you were still advising me. . . . You taught me everything. . . . (*Dreamily*) Ah, those were happy times. . . . At the peep of dawn—well, our dawn that is, around noon, because we always went to bed very late— you'd come into my room, as I was emerging from the bathhouse, rested, smiling, debonair, as fresh as if we'd never spent the entire night drinking and whoring through the town.

He says a little sourly:

That's another thing you were better at than me. . . .

Becket also shows the change within himself in his confession scene.

Act Three

BECKET: Yet it would be simple enough. Too simple perhaps. Saintliness is a temptation too. Oh, how difficult it is to get an answer from You, Lord! I was slow in praying to You, but I cannot believe that others, worthier than I, who have spent years asking You questions, have been better than myself at deciphering Your real intentions. I am only a beginner and I must make mistake after mistake, as I did in my Latin translations as a boy, when my riotous imagination made the old priest roar with laughter. But I cannot believe that one learns Your language as one learns any human tongue, by hard studying, with a dictionary, a grammar and a set of idioms. I am sure that to the hardened sinner, who drops to his knees for the first time and murmurs Your name, marveling, You tell him all Your secrets, straightaway, and that he understands. I have served You like a dilettante, surprised that I could still find my pleasure in Your service. And for a long time I was on my guard because of it. I could not believe this pleasure would bring me one step nearer You. I could not believe that the road could be a happy one. Their hair shirts, their fasting, their bells in the small hours summoning one to meet You, on the icy paving stones, in the sick misery of the poor ill-treated human animal—I cannot believe that all these are anything but safeguards for the weak. In power and in luxury, and even in the pleasures of the flesh, I shall not cease to speak to You, I feel this now. You are the God of the rich man and the happy man too, Lord, and therein lies Your profound justice. You do not turn away Your eyes from the man who was given everything from birth. You have not abandoned him, alone in his ensnaring facility. And he may be Your true lost sheep. For Your scheme of things, which we mistakenly call Justice, is secret and profound and You plumb the hidden depths of poor men's puny frames as carefully as those of kings. And

beneath those outward differences, which blind us, but which to You are barely noticeable; beneath the diadem or the grime, You discern the same pride, the same vanity, the same petty, complacent preoccupation with oneself. Lord, I am certain now that You meant to tempt me with this hair shirt, object of so much vapid self-congratulation! this bare cell, this solitude, this absurdly endured winter cold—and the conveniences of prayer. It would be too easy to buy You like this, at so low a price. I shall leave this convent, where so many precautions hem You round. I shall take up the miter and the golden cope again, and the great silver cross, and I shall go back and fight in the place and with the weapons it has pleased You to give me. It has pleased You to make me Archbishop and to set me, like a solitary pawn, face to face with the King, upon the chessboard. I shall go back to my place, humbly, and let the world accuse me of pride, so that I may do what I believe is my life's work. For the rest, Your will be done.
He crosses himself.

The mechanical idea of placing one character to your left, another to your right, and one in the middle for differentiation and location, has been suggested by a number of authorities, but we have found that great care must be used with this method, for there is often the danger of confusing character location, and a mix-up in placement causes confusion and a loss of attention on the part of the audience. This method can also lead the audience to feel that they are watching a tennis match. The mechanics of locating characters can get in the way of the material.

Others have suggested a higher voice for one part and a lower voice for the other. The mere matter of raising or lowering a voice does not, however, assure a meaningful characterization.

A man's reading of a woman's part might be handled with a higher tone but it should not be so high that it sounds more like a squeak. In the same way, a girl trying to lower her voice just to portray a man can often distort the character of the man completely and make her look understandably ridiculous. If you have the characters clearly in mind, if you know what kinds of people they are, how they feel and react in a scene, how these emotions and feelings change with the progress of the scene, and how they relate to other characters, you will make the distinctions without any artifices.

To help the reader in another way to interpret characters, other clues are provided in the dialogue. A person who speaks in a coarse, ungrammatical manner is generally an uneducated person, or he is perhaps speaking in a style peculiar to a certain locale. For instance, those from the deep South have their own style of speaking, and playwrights usually convey that style in the writing of the dialogue. On the other hand, a person using a wide vocabulary and speaking with an understanding of the niceties of language is ordinarily educated, refined, from a higher level of society. Such dialogue is in itself a valuable clue to the interpreter. An excellent example is a comparison of the dialogue of Professor Higgins with that of Liza in the earlier scenes of the play *Pygmalion*. (See page 120.)

In the reading of dialogue, it is necessary to remember that you cannot build a scene toward a climax by pausing after each character's speech. To do so stops the movement completely, and in drama a scene must move. If you find yourself reading a scene with two people who talk in very short segments of dialogue, your problems will be evident. If the scene calls for a glib, conversational quality, such as is found in Noel Coward's *Private Lives* or *Blithe Spirit*, pauses between speeches would utterly destroy Coward's intent. Learn to change from one character to another quickly and with consistency. However, when pauses are called for (and often the author indicates these pauses), you should take advantage of them, for they heighten a change in emotion or idea. They are there for a purpose. It is not always wise to read a scene where the dialogue is too short because changing character rapidly imposes too much of a problem for the reader.

There are some types of plays which require a rather rapid pace. Farce is an example. It usually deals with ordinary people who are caught up in extraordinary circumstances. In farce, the ridiculous becomes the accepted; the characters are in a state of confusion, they are involved in frantic activities. As for the characters themselves, they are usually mixtures of innocence and roguery, and they are the embodiment of an attitude or a concept. One of the favorite themes of farce is marriage. The following scenes from *Let's Get a Divorce* by Victorien Sardou and Emile de Najac (English version by Angela and Robert Goldsby), is typical of the farcical treatment of marriage and divorce. The characters are sophisticated and worldly; their attitudes are superficial, and their manner is glib and casual. The primary difficulty in reading this scene orally, is to identify the distinct difference between the two men. A word of caution: in the reading of

farce, you must remember that the characters take themselves seriously. They should not be read as though they think what they say
or do is funny.

From

Let's Get A Divorce

Victorien Sardou and Émile de Najac

Exit BASTIEN. *Enter* CLAVIGNAC.

DES PRUNELLES: Well! So you're back in Reims.

CLAVIGNAC: [*cheerfully*] That's right. I'm back in Reims.

DES PRUNELLES: [*shaking hands*] Everyone thinks you're
dead. Where the devil have you been?

CLAVIGNAC: In Spain.

DES PRUNELLES: In Spain?

CLAVIGNAC: A pleasure trip.

DES PRUNELLES: Lucky man! You're free—free as a bachelor.

CLAVIGNAC: [*taking the chair from under the table and sitting*] Only separated.

DES PRUNELLES: [*sitting on pouf*] It's the same thing———

CLAVIGNAC: Oh, not at all. My wife still dreams up ways to
madden me. By the way, I trust your wife is well?

DES PRUNELLES: My God, yes. But how does Madame
Clavignac drive you mad?

CLAVIGNAC: As you know, I'm giving her alimony. That in
itself is unfair. The situation I surprised her in made it apparent that she could handle her own affairs. But that was
the verdict, so I said nothing, and I paid, and I'm still paying. But my wife finds this allowance too niggardly, and so,
to increase it, she has devised an abominable trick. The moment I settle down, no matter where, riverside, seaside, or
mountainside, she arrives flaunting some idiotic male or
other, and a flood of scandal follows, a torrent. People smile
at me knowingly; the local newspapers ring with her
prowess; the lawsuit is once again revived. This drives me

mad. I beg her to leave me alone. "Oh, I'd be only too happy," she replies, "but who will pay my transportation, my hotel, my dressmaker, etc." Then the bill—ten, twelve thousand francs. . . . I pay up. She flies off . . . and the game has been played.

DES PRUNELLES: You mean she followed you to Spain?

CLAVIGNAC: Ah, no. This time the game was mine. I let it be known I was going to spend the winter in Algeria. And at this moment she is descending upon Africa. . . . That's my revenge.

DES PRUNELLES: Then you'll stay here?

CLAVIGNAC: Twenty-four hours.

DES PRUNELLES: No longer?

CLAVIGNAC: Just time enough to collect my rents and take some papers to my lawyer.

DES PRUNELLES: Another lawsuit?

CLAVIGNAC: No. But the divorce law will be voted in, and I intend to waste no time in deepening the abyss between Madame and me. Once divorced, she can play whatever game she likes. If she wants, I'll play with her.

DES PRUNELLES: Then you think divorce will be voted in?

CLAVIGNAC: I certainly hope so.

DES PRUNELLES: Ah, if we only knew! . . . You'll dine with me?

CLAVIGNAC: No, it's you who'll dine with me.

DES PRUNELLES: Indeed?

CLAVIGNAC: This morning at the Club, we got together a party for dinner tonight—a bachelor party like the good old days. It's all on me. We plan to have some lovely ladies. That thought doesn't fill you with terror, does it?

DES PRUNELLES: Oh dear! Lovely ladies . . . at a time like this?

CLAVIGNAC: Bah! They'll make you young again. Seven-thirty tonight at Dagneau's. Agreed?

DES PRUNELLES: No, I really can't.

CLAVIGNAC: Come, now.

DES PRUNELLES: Word of honor.

CLAVIGNAC: You're not going to try and make me swallow that nonsense, are you?

DES PRUNELLES: But I just can't do it, really!

CLAVIGNAC: Don't go too far, you know, or I'll send you my seconds.

DES PRUNELLES: That's fine. Exactly what I want.

CLAVIGNAC: What? A duel?

DES PRUNELLES: I'm reaching that point.

CLAVIGNAC: You?

DES PRUNELLES: Me!

CLAVIGNAC: [*lowering his voice*] And for your——?

DES PRUNELLES: Naturally!

CLAVIGNAC: Oh, ho! In that case, let's be serious, and tell me all. There's certainly no one better qualified to understand such a problem than I.

DES PRUNELLES: [*putting his hands on* CLAVIGNAC's *shoulders and seating him on the pouf*] Ah, my good old friend, in our marrying the two of us have done——

CLAVIGNAC: A remarkably silly thing. I agree.

DES PRUNELLES: [*sitting*] But you, you deserved your fate.

CLAVIGNAC: Thank you.

DES PRUNELLES: You married a flirt, who was continually bombarded by billets-doux sent by slingshot over the convent wall, and who returned their fire.

CLAVIGNAC: And you never warned me before I married?

DES PRUNELLES: Play fair. You never asked.

CLAVIGNAC: That's true.

DES PRUNELLES: Whereas I, I married a modest young thing, well brought up . . . You should know; you've been a guest in their house. A little lively, perhaps——

CLAVIGNAC: I'll say! She used to box the ears of all her servants.

DES PRUNELLES: You never told me that.

CLAVIGNAC: Play fair. You never asked.

DES PRUNELLES: In any case, everything promised happiness, and after a rather tempestuous youth I felt I had earned my tranquillity.

CLAVIGNAC: And instead of a haven?

DES PRUNELLES: Ah, my good friend, it's the open sea in a raging storm!

CLAVIGNAC: Stirred up by?

DES PRUNELLES: Does one ever know? It's just the incompatibility of wills. Madame wants to go out; monsieur wants to stay in. One is stifling where the other freezes. One gets up when the other goes to bed. In brief, they agree on only one thing the need to avoid each other. My marriage is like Florian's fable of the Rabbit and the Duck. Imagine *them* married! It's idiotic, but what can you do?

CLAVIGNAC: My case exactly.

DES PRUNELLES: The comedy is heightened by the entrance of a fop, bedecked with the most tantalizing cravats, and gifted by nature with that fine aroma of silliness which women so drunkenly inhale. "Ah! How beautiful he is! How empty-headed he is! He shall be everything to me and I shall be everything to him." And, to top it off, this insipid beauty is my cousin.

CLAVIGNAC: Adhémar?

DES PRUNELLES: [*rising*] The glorious Adhémar—government bird-watcher supreme! He arrives on the scene booted up to here, jangling his spurs, snapping his whip . . . What chance have I against a musketeer?

CLAVIGNAC: The fable changes: "Leda and the Swan."

DES PRUNELLES: Oh, no. Not yet.

CLAVIGNAC: [*rising*] Hmmmmm . . .

DES PRUNELLES: No. There are still two reassuring signs.

CLAVIGNAC: Namely?

DES PRUNELLES: First, Madame des Prunelles always acts like a sulky bulldog in my presence. The first day she smiles at me, my fate is sealed.

CLAVIGNAC: I see.

DES PRUNELLES: And secondly, she's very preoccupied with divorce! Proof that she's still struggling. When she stops struggling, she *won't* be bothered with divorce.

CLAVIGNAC: She's talked to you about it?

DES PRUNELLES: No, but this literature! Look. Lawbooks. [*He points to the books and picks one of them up.*] Volume VI, "On Divorce"—all of them: divorce, divorce, and divorce. Footnoted, annotated, underlined, and every page dogeared.

CLAVIGNAC: My poor man, defend yourself!

DES PRUNELLES: To the last bullet. . . . Only I'm sick—oh, I'm so sick, my poor friend. Catastrophe is all around me.

I feel it, I smell it. . . . One moment of forgetfulness and I'm lost.

CLAVIGNAC: If that's the way it is, you'd better go slow.

DES PRUNELLES: I plan to strike an unexpected and brilliant blow—today.

CLAVIGNAC: Today?

DES PRUNELLES: Within the hour. I have declared that the visits of this creature were odious to me, and that I would only tolerate him, like any other relative, on official "at home" days: otherwise I would throw him out the window. This lead to that familiar scene with all its wifely clichés, "That's all that was needed, monsieur, for you to insult your wife . . ."

CLAVIGNAC: ". . . with your slanderous suspicions . . ."

DES PRUNELLES: ". . . it would serve you right . . ."

TOGETHER: ". . . if I justified them."

DES PRUNELLES: I held firm! Now I only see Adhémar on visiting days. But the minute my back is turned, he rushes in through the garden. You see, the scoundrel has rented a room right opposite my house. [*He crosses to window, and points off right.*]

CLAVIGNAC: [*following him*]   And so?

DES PRUNELLES: And so, thanks to my mechanical talents, all last night I worked on a little trap in which he will be caught this afternoon. He will get angry. I will tweak his ears. He will provoke me. We shall fight a duel.

CLAVIGNAC: And he will kill you.

DES PRUNELLES: Then I shall find peace.

CLAVIGNAC: How does this mousetrap work?

DES PRUNELLES: Oh, it's childish. Imagine, a little piece of coiled spring——Ssshhh! Here she is.

CLAVIGNAC: Your wife?

Cyprienne appears in the vestibule, followed by Josépha, to whom she gives an order. She is evidently in a sour mood.

DES PRUNELLES: Oh, my God!

CLAVIGNAC: What?

DES PRUNELLES: Isn't she smiling?

CLAVIGNAC: I should say not.

DES PRUNELLES: No?

CLAVIGNAC: Damn it, no!

DES PRUNELLES: [*brightening*]   Ah, my friend, thank God! You reassure me.

One of the crucial lessons in the reading of drama is to learn when the characters' ideas or moods change. These must be clearly brought out to convey the full meaning of the scene or the dialogue. If the reader does not know the emotion inherent in a scene and how and why that emotion changes, he is unable to read with full meaning.

In *Becket,* one of the most dramatic moments comes in the scene on the beach where Becket and the King meet after having been separated. Here are two proud men, yet both want, deep within themselves, to reach out to the other, to tear down the reserves, to recapture the closeness they once felt. They are unable to do so because of conflicting ideals. The King cannot let himself give in to Becket, and Becket cannot deny his faith to accede to the King's wishes. The reader must show this conflict, the invisible wall that separates the men, and he must reveal the inner conflicts as the scene progresses.

The moods change in this manner. On the first meeting there is a quietness, an uneasiness, an appraisal of each other, an indulgence in idle remarks to keep from facing the central conflict. The emotion suddenly changes when Becket makes his first reference to God and the King says, "If we start straightway, we're sure to quarrel! Let's talk about trivial things." There has been a momentary flare-up and then a mechanical return to matters of insignificance. The King is petulant, fighting within himself as he talks about horses, hawks, his son. Then the mood changes to one of pleasurable reminiscence as the King speaks of the old days. Yet, mingled with this reminiscence is evidence of the King's annoyance at Becket's dedication to the faith. Finally, unable to contain his feelings he bursts out with "Becket, I'm bored!" And immediately he cries out for Becket's help.

Shortly after, both Becket and the King make clear what their obligations are. The King asks Becket if he will make a concession but Becket refuses to change his principles, and the King then offers him a chance to return to England. Suddenly, they both express the physical coldness they feel—but it is the coldness of two men who cannot return to what they once were.

Unable to keep inside any longer his vital concern over the loss of friendship, the King blurts out, "You never loved me, did you, Becket?" Becket reaffirms his love for the King but more for his God. Then the King, in another switch of emotion, cries, "I never should have seen you again. It hurts too much." We are now at the point where the King expresses what he really feels. When Becket tries to comfort him, the King's pride again returns and he insists he wants no pity. And so the two men part—never to see one another again.

In Elmer Rice's *The Adding Machine,* both Mrs. Zero and Mr. Zero have long soliloquies. Mrs. Zero is a gossip in one part of the dialogue, a nagging wife in another, a jealous woman in still another, while Mr. Zero goes from being proud of his reliability in his work to sensual interest in another woman, to self-defense and rationalization about killing a man, to his prejudices about Negroes and Jews. His lack of culture and background is evident in the type of dialogue and in the principles and bias expressed.

The reader must remember that no character remains the same within a given framework of time. He moves from one mood to another, often with startling rapidity. The Old Man in Ionesco's *The Chairs* moves back and forth from one mood to another abruptly and sharply. In one scene in the beginning of the play, he is reminiscent about the past. He is dreamy, very old. Then suddenly he changes into a spasm of crying for his dead mother. He goes back to his earlier days as he weeps convulsively. From that mood he as quickly turns to the "reality" (if it can be called that) of the present moment.

To realize fully such changes, pacing is very important. In the beginning of *The Chairs,* the pace is slow, dreamy; there is a sense of pervading unreality. Then there is a change to a faster pace as the Old Man becomes annoyed with the Old Woman. The little argument ends almost as soon as it begins, and then to please the Old Woman, the Old Man starts to tell the age-old story. The pace is slow at first as they speak of the city they once knew; then it quickens as they start the hysterical laughter. Gradually exhausted by the laughing, they return to the slow, languid pace for just a moment, and then a faster, more explosive kind of pacing follows as the Old Man begins his crying again for his mother. And so the play switches from one pacing to another, from the hectic rapidity of the arrival of the guests, to the reminiscence with guests about the past and a quieter, slower pace. And so on.

The reader, as can be seen, has a tremendous task in the reading of drama. That is one reason why his involvement must be deep enough to handle such demands. Drama requires more subjectivity than objectivity if it is to reflect life. It requires ease in dealing with emotion and in perception of changes in the structure. Some students may fear this assignment more than others in the beginning, but perhaps because drama enables them to break down their reserve in many cases, the assignment usually becomes most enjoyable.

CHOOSING THE SCENE

Choosing the scene to be read is difficult. As was mentioned previously, you must read the entire play, or at least a good condensation of it. You cannot summarily select a scene without knowing how it relates to the rest of the play. For example, if you read the second scene between the Public and the Private Gar in *Philadelphia, Here I Come*, you would have no understanding of the relationship between the two. You might assume they were two separate people instead of one being the other's alter ego. Or if you were to choose only the beach scene from *Becket* you would have no awareness of the basis for that scene.

It is also important to select a scene that fits your sex and maturity. For instance, it would not be advisable for a girl to attempt the scene between the Captain and Mr. Roberts in *Mister Roberts*. She would not be able to give a very true or honest interpretation of these two men. As far as maturity is concerned, any one who has not experienced life in its more complex aspects, who has never known a marriage that has degenerated, for example, would not be able to give any depth to the reading of a play like *Who's Afraid of Virginia Woolf*.

Another consideration in the selection of a scene is that it must be able to stand alone. The reader might decide to do the scene in the first act of C. S. Forester's *Payment Deferred* where Marble meets his nephew for the first time and plots his murder. Or he might do the scene where father and son face each other realistically in *The Subject Was Roses*.

The scene chosen should begin at a definite point and build to a climax. The following scene from *Taming of the Shrew* is an excellent example of such a scene.

Taming of the Shrew

William Shakespeare

Petruchio, a man of the world, has decided to wed Katharina the shrew, a woman whom no man has been able to tame. Petruchio is as much enamoured of her dowry as he is of Katharina. He begins his unusual courting in this scene.

PETRUCHIO: Good morrow, Kate; for that's your name, I hear.
KATHARINA: Well have you heard, but something hard of hearing:
They call me Katharine that do talk of me.
PETRUCHIO: You lie, in faith, for you are called plain Kate.
And bonny Kate, and sometimes Kate the Curst;
But Kate, the prettiest Kate in Christendom,
Kate of Kate-Hall, my superdainty Kate,
For dainties are all Kates— and therefore, Kate,
Take this of me, Kate of my consolation:
Hearing thy mildness praised in every town,
Thy virtues spoke of, and thy beauty sounded,
Yet not so deeply as to thee belongs,
Myself am moved to woo thee for my wife.
KATHARINA: Moved! in good time. Let him that moved you hither
Remove you hence. I knew you at the first
You were a movable.
PETRUCHIO: Why, what's a movable?
KATHARINA: A joined stool.
PETRUCHIO: Thou hast hit it. Come, sit on me.
KATHARINA: Asses are made to bear, and so are you.
PETRUCHIO: Women are made to bear, and so are you.
KATHARINA: No such jade as you, if me you mean.
PETRUCHIO: Alas, good Kate, I will not burden thee!
For knowing thee to be but young and light—
KATHARINA: Too light for such a swain as you to catch,
And yet as heavy as my weight should be.
PETRUCHIO: Should be! should—buzz!
KATHARINA: Well ta'en, and like a buzzard.
PETRUCHIO: O slow-winged turtle! shall a buzzard take thee?
KATHARINA: Ay, for a turtle, as he takes a buzzard.
PETRUCHIO: Come, come, you wasp. I' faith, you are too angry.
KATHARINA: If I be waspish, best beware my sting.
PETRUCHIO: My remedy is then to pluck it out.
KATHARINA: Aye, if the fool could find it where it lies.
PETRUCHIO: Who knows not where a wasp does wear his sting?
In his tail.

KATHARINA: In his tongue.

PETRUCHIO: Whose tongue?

KATHARINA: Yours, if you talk of tails; and so farewell.

PETRUCHIO: What, with my tongue in your tail? nay, come again,

Good Kate, I am a gentleman.

KATHARINA: That I'll try.

(*She strikes him*)

PETRUCHIO: I swear I'll cuff you if you strike again.

KATHARINA: So may you lose your arms.

If you strike me, you are no gentleman.

And if no gentleman, why then no arms.

PETRUCHIO: A herald, Kate? O, put me in thy books!

KATHARINA: What is your crest? a coxcomb?

PETRUCHIO: A combless cock, so Kate will be my hen.

KATHARINA: No cock of mine. You crow too like a craven.

PETRUCHIO: Nay, come, Kate, come. You must not look so sour.

KATHARINA: It is my fashion when I see a crab.

PETRUCHIO: Why, here's no crab, and therefore look not sour.

KATHARINA: There is, there is.

PETRUCHIO: Then show it me.

KATHARINA: Had I a glass, I would.

PETRUCHIO: What, you mean my face?

KATHARINA: Well aimed of such a young one.

PETRUCHIO: Now, by Saint George, I am too young for you.

KATHARINA: Yet you are withered.

PETRUCHIO: 'Tis with cares.

KATHARINA: I care not.

PETRUCHIO: Nay, hear you, Kate. In sooth you scape not so.

KATHARINA: I chafe you, if I tarry. Let me go.

PETRUCHIO: No, not a whit. I find you passing gentle.

'Twas told me you were rough and coy and sullen,

And now I find report a very liar;

For thou are pleasant, gamesome, passing courteous,

But slow in speech, yet sweet as springtime flowers.

Thou canst not frown, thou canst not look askance,

Nor bite the lip, as angry wenches will,

Nor hast thou pleasure to be cross in talk,

But thou with mildness entertain'st thy wooers,
With gentle conference, soft and affable.
Why does the world report that Kate doth limp?
O slanderous world! Kate like the hazel twig
Is straight and slender, and so brown in hue
As hazel nuts, and sweeter than the kernels.
O, let me see thee walk. Thou dost not halt.

KATHRINA: Go, fool, and whom thou keep'st command.

PETRUCHIO: Did ever Dian so become a grove
As Kate this chamber with her princely gait?
O, be thou Dian, and let her be Kate
And then let Kate be chaste and Dian sportful!

KATHARINA: Where did you study all this goodly speech?

PETRUCHIO: It is extempore, from my mother wit.

KATHARINA: A witty mother! Witless else her son.

PETRUCHIO: Am I not wise?

KATHARINA: Yes. Keep you warm.

PETRUCHIO: Marry, so I mean, sweet Katharine, in thy bed.
And therefore, setting all this chat aside,
Thus in plain terms: Your father hath consented
That you shall be my wife, your dowry 'greed on,
And, will you, nill you, I will marry you.
Now Kate, I am a husband for your turn.
For, by this light whereby I see thy beauty.
Thy beauty, that doth make me like thee well,
Thou must be married to no man but me;
For I am he am born to tame you Kate,
And bring you from a wild Kate to a Kate
Conformable as other household Kates.
Here comes your father. Never make denial.
I must and will have Katharine to my wife.

It is unwise to select any scene which relies heavily on props and which demands a great deal of action. It is equally bad to choose one that has too many characters. Because props are unnecessary for the clarity of the scenes and because the plot involves only two characters, William Gibson's *Two for the Seesaw* is a good choice. The confrontation scene between Pizarro and Atahualpa in the last act of *Royal Hunt of the Sun* would be another good choice since it does not depend on any technical effects for its impact. Likewise, the first scene in Oliver Goldsmith's *She Stoops to Conquer* between Mr. and Mrs. Hardcastle would make an effective reading. The King's great speech about love in the end of the first act of *Camelot* would be excellent too; It deals only with the King and is complete within itself.

It is also wise not to choose a scene that has several character entrances and exits as these are difficult to convey. Wherever possible, such exits and entrances should be cut, but if this is not possible, the reader should insert a line or a word to indicate the person has exited. If a character enters, the reader could turn his head to the left or to the right, give a sign of recognition, and perhaps mention the person's name. Often, of course, the person leaving has a line such as "I have to go now" or "see you later" which makes it clear he is exiting. No added information is then needed, and the reader does not say "he exits" or "he enters." Nor does he read such stage directions as "he moved about the room restlessly, then sat down on the sofa, and put his head in his hands . . ." And obviously the reader doesn't read any directions about the mood the character is experiencing, such as "angrily." It is up to the voice, the characterization, to convey this mood.

Is it possible to do more than one scene from a play? This is a question often asked by students. Yes, if proper narrative comment is provided to give a bridge between scenes. While the authors prefer to avoid the need for narrative abridgement, at times it can be used effectively. For example, one could do a reading of *Becket* with narrative continuity. The sequence would be this: the King's speech in the beginning at Becket's tomb; the King's appointment of Becket as Archbishop; Becket's confession in the church; the first conflict between the King and Becket; and finally, the scene at the beach.

However, it is better to select a complete scene or a long speech for oral reading. The narrative technique is more often used for a professional reading of an entire play with necessary cuts.

THE CUTTING OF A PLAY

It is always wise to cut minor characters that do not contribute materially or meaningfully to the scene. But make sure these characters do not, in total aspect, play significant parts in the scene. Omit repetition of thought or idea in scenes. If one character makes the point with his dialogue, there is no need for another to repeat the same thought. Select a scene that does not have too many exits and entrances. Cut out exits and entrances whenever possible. At times, one scene can be telescoped into another for a more cohesive whole and for complete development of some conflict. Cut out intervening dialogue that does not advance the progress of the scene.

Elements of the scene which are designed more for playing on the stage and not for clear interpretation by a reader should be cut. In short, some scenes depend largely on lighting and sound effects for a complete response. Such scenes should be omitted. Remember, you are obligated to read the scene and make it meaningful, to give the desired response; the only equipment you have is your voice and your body through your emotional response to the material.

If a scene is interrupted by comments from other characters, outside of the central figures you are dealing with, omit these characters. For instance, in the play within the play scene in *A Midsummer Night's Dream,* your concentration is on Bottom, Quince, and other townsfolk. As a result the comments of Theseus, Demetrius, and the others, while amusing, are not essential for effective reading.

Naturally, you should omit all stage directions. These are not to be read—except on rare occasions when some comment or direction is necessary for clarity. To drop into the role of narrator or expositor would cause you to lose too much contact with the essential part of your material—the dialogue.

These are a few points to consider. To explain further, let us look at this scene from *A Midsummer Night's Dream* and note the cuts. Because of the number of characters, this scene is a real challenge to the oral reader.

From

A Midsummer Night's Dream

William Shakespeare

Re-enter Philostrate.

PHILOSTRATE: So please your grace, the Prologue is ad-dress'd.
THESEUS: Let him approach. (*Flourish of trumpets*) *Enter Quince for the Prologue.*

PROLOGUE: If we offend, it is without good will
That you should think we come not to offend,
But with good will. To show our simple skill,
That is the true beginning of our end.
Consider then, we come but in despite.
We do not come, as minding to content you,
Our true intent is. All for your delight,
We are not here. That you should here repent you,
The actors are at hand; and, by their show,
You shall know all, that you are like to know.
THESEUS: This fellow doth not stand upon points.
LYSANDER: He hath rid his prologue like a rough colt; he
knows not the stop. A good moral, my lord; it is not enough
to speak, but to speak true.
HIPPOLYTA: Indeed he hath played on his prologue like a
child on a recorder; a sound, but not in government.
THESEUS: His speech was like a tangled chain; nothing im-
paired, but all disordered. Who is next?
Enter Pyramus and Thisby, Wall, Moonshine, and Lion.
PROLOGUE: Gentles, perchance you wonder at this show;
But wonder on, till truth makes all things plain.
This man is Pyramus, if you would know;
This beauteous lady Thisby is certain.
This man, with lime and rough-cast, doth present
Wall, that vile Wall which did these lovers sunder;
And through Wall's chink, poor souls, they are content
To whisper. At the which let no man wonder.
This man, with lanthorn, dog, and bush of thorn,
Presenteth Moonshine; for, if you will know,
By moonshine did these lovers think no scorn
To meet at Ninus' tomb, there, there to woo.
This grisly beast, which Lion hight by name,
The trusty Thisby, coming first by night,
Did scare away, or rather did affright;
And, as she fled, her mantle she did fall,
Which Lion vile with bloody mouth did stain.
Anon comes Pyramus, sweet youth and tall,
And finds his trusty Thisby's mantle slain:
Whereat, with blade, with bloody blameful blade,
He bravely broach'd his boiling bloody breast:
And Thisby, tarrying in mulberry shade,

His dagger drew, and died. For all the rest,
Let Lion, Moonshine, Wall and lovers twain
At large discourse, while here they do remain.
Exeunt Prologue, Pyramus, Thisby, Lion, and Moonshine.

THESEUS: I wonder if the lion be to speak.

DEMETRIUS: No wonder, my lord: one lion may, when many
asses do.

WALL.   In this same interlude it doth befall
That I, one Snout by name, present a wall;
And such a wall, as I would have you think,
That had in it a crannied hole or chink,
Through which the lovers, Pyramus and Thisby,
Did whisper often very secretly.
This loam, this rough-case, and this stone, doth show
That I am the same wall; the truth is so:
And this the cranny is, right and sinister,
Through which the fearful lovers are to whisper.

~~THESEUS: Would you desire lime and hair to speak better?~~

~~DEMETRIUS: It is the wittiest partition that ever I heard
discourse, my lord.~~

THESEUS: Pyramus draws near the wall: silence!

Re-enter Pyramus.

PYRAMUS: O grim-look'd night! O night with hue so black!
O night, which ever art when day is not!
O night, O night! alack, alack, alack,
I fear my Thisby's promise is forgot!
And thou, O wall, O sweet, O lovely wall,
That stand'st between her father's ground and mine!
Show me thy chink, to blink through with mine eyne!
(*Wall holds up his fingers*)
Thanks, courteous wall; Jove shield thee well for this!
But what see I? No Thisby do I see.
O wicked wall, through whom I see no bliss!
Cursed be thy stones for thus deceiving me!

THESEUS: The wall, me thinks, being sensible, should curse
again.

PYRAMUS: No, in truth, sir, he should not. "Deceiving me" is
Thisby's cue: she is to enter now, and I am to spy her
through the wall. You shall see, it will fall pat as I told you.
Yonder she comes.

Re-enter Thisby.

THISBY: O wall, full often hast thou heard my moans,
For parting my fair Pyramus and me!
My cherry lips have often kiss'd thy stones,
Thy stones with lime and hair knit up in thee.

PYRAMUS: I see a voice: now will I to the chink,
To spy an I can hear my Thisby's face.
Thisby!

THISBY: My love thou art, my love I think.

PYRAMUS: Think what thou wilt, I am thy lover's grace;
And, like Limander, am I trusty still.

THISBY: And I like Helen, till the Fates me kill.

PYRAMUS: Not Shafalus to Procrus was so true.

THISBY: As Shafalus to Procrus, I to you.

PYRAMUS: Will thou at Ninny's tomb meet me straightway?

THISBY: 'Tide life, 'tide death, I come without delay.

Exeunt Pyramus and Thisby.

WALL: Thus have I, wall, my part discharged so;
And being done, thus wall away doth go.

THESEUS: Now is the mural down between the two neighbors.

DEMETRIUS: No remedy, my lord, when walls are so willful to hear without warning.

HIPPOLYTA: This is the silliest stuff that ever I heard.

THESEUS: The best in this kind are but shadows; and the worst are no worse, if imagination amend them.

HIPPOLYTA: It must be your imagination then, and not theirs.

THESEUS: If we imagine no worse of them than they of themselves, they may pass for excellent men. Here come two noble beasts in, a man and a lion.

Re-enter Lion and Moonshine.

LION: You, ladies, you, whose gentle hearts do fear
The smallest monstrous mouse that creeps on floor,
May now perchance both quake and tremble here,
When lion rough in wildest rage doth roar,
Then know that I, one Snug the joiner, am
A lion-fell, nor else no lion's dam;
For, if I should as lion come in strife
Into this place, 'twere pity on my life.

THESEUS: A very gentle beast, and of good conscience.

DEMETRIUS: The very best at a beast, my lord, that e'er I saw.

LYSANDER: This lion is a very fox for his valor.

THESEUS: True; and a goose for his discretion.

DEMETRIUS: Not so, my lord; for his valor cannot carry his discretion; and the fox carries the goose.

THESEUS: His discretion, I am sure, cannot carry his valor; for the goose carries not the fox. It is well; leave it to his discretion, and let us listen to the moon.

MOONSHINE: This lanthorn doth the horned moon present—

DEMETRIUS: He should have worn the horns on his head.

THESEUS: He is no crescent, and his horns are invisible within the circumference.

MOONSHINE: This lanthorn doth the horned moon present; Myself, the man-i'-th'-moon do seem to be.

THESEUS: This is the greatest error of all the rest; the man should be put into the lantern. How is it else the man-i'-th'-moon?

DEMETRIUS: He dares not come there for the candle; for, you see, it is already in snuff.

HIPPOLYTA: I am aweary of this moon: would he would change!

THESEUS: It appears, by his small light of discretion, that he is in the wane; but yet, in courtesy, in all reason, we must stay the time.

LYSANDER: Proceed, Moon.

MOONSHINE: All that I have to say, is, to tell you that the lanthorn is the moon; I, the man-i'-th'-moon; this thorn-bush, my thorn-bush; and this dog, my dog.

DEMETRIUS: Why, all these should be in the lantern; for all these are in the moon. But, silence! here comes Thisby.

(*Re-enter Thisby*)

THISBY: This is old Ninny's tomb. Where is my love?

LION: (*Roaring*) Oh——

DEMETRIUS: Well roared, Lion.

THESEUS: Well run, Thisby.

HIPPOLYTA.   Well shone, Moon. Truly, the moon shines with good grace.

(*The Lion shakes Thisby's mantle, and exits*)

THESEUS: Well moused, Lion.

DEMETRIUS: And then came Pyramus.

LYSANDER: And so the lion vanished.

(*Re-enter Pyramus*)

PYRAMUS: Sweet Moon, I thank thee for thy sunny beams;
  I thank thee, Moon, for shining now so bright;
  For, by thy gracious, golden, glittering gleams,
  I trust to take of truest Thisby sight.
  But stay, O spite!
  But mark, poor knight,
  What dreadful dole is here!
  Eyes, do you see?
  How can it be?
  O dainty duck! O dear!
  Thy mantle good,
  What, stain'd with blood!
  Approach, ye Furies fell!
  O Fates, come, come,
  Cut thread and thrum;
  Quail, crush, conclude, and quell!
THESEUS: This passion, and the death of a dear friend,
  would go near to make a man look sad.
HIPPOLYTA: Beshrew my heart, but I pity the man.
PYRAMUS: O wherefore, Nature, didst thou lions frame?
  Since Lion vile hath here deflower'd my dear;
  Which is—no, no—which was the fairest dame
  That lives, that loved, that liked, that look'd with cheer.
  Come, tears, confound;
  Out, sword, and wound
  The pap of Pyramus;
  Ay, that left pap,
  Where heart doth hop: (*Stabs himself*)
  Thus die I, thus, thus, thus.
  Now I am dead,
  Now am I fled;
  My soul is in the sky:
  Tongue, lose thy light;
  Moon, take thy flight: (*Exit Moonshine*)
  Now die, die, die, die, die. (*Dies*)

The following are scenes from two plays for further study. The first play, Ibsen's *The Wild Duck*, translated by Otto Reinert, is an example of the author's naturalism and his esthetic use of words that give his works a poetic quality. While reading the scene, keep the following questions in mind:

1. What type of person is Hjalmar? Upon what clues do you base your description?
2. Describe Gina as she appears to you, physically and emotionally.
3. What purpose does Hedvig serve in the scene?
4. What prompts the emotional tension in the scene and what tensions are apparent?
5. Are there any lines of dialogue that can be cut?
6. In the reading of the scene, the tendency might be to emphasize Hjalmar and give less attention to Gina. Would doing so be justified or correct?
7. What clues do you see to the pace of the scene? Where would the pace vary?
8. Where are the major changes in direction in the scene?
9. To what extent would you use physical action to support the emotional tensions of the scene?

From

The Wild Duck—Act V

Henrik Ibsen

HEDVIG *waits a moment, glances towards the living room door, stands on tiptoe, takes the double-barreled pistol down from the shelf, looks at it.* GINA, *with broom and dust cloth, enters from the living room.* HEDVIG *quickly puts the pistol back, without* GINA's *noticing.*

GINA: Don't fool with father's things, Hedvig.

HEDVIG: (*leaving the shelf*)   I just wanted to straighten up some.

GINA: Why don't you go into the kitchen and see if the coffee is keeping hot? I am taking a tray with me when I go down.

(HEDVIG *goes into the kitchen.* GINA *starts putting the studio in order. After a short while, the door to the outside is hesitantly opened and* HJALMAR *looks in. He is wearing a coat but no hat. He looks unkempt and unwashed. His eyes are dull and lusterless.*)

GINA: (*stands staring at him, still with the broom in her hand*) Bless you, Ekdal—so you did come back, after all!

HJALMAR: (*enters, answers in a dull voice*) I return only to leave.

GINA: Yes, yes, I suppose. But good Lord! how you look!

HJALMAR: Look?

GINA: And your nice winter coat? I'd say that's done for.

HEDVIG: (*in the kitchen door*) Mother, don't you want me to—(*Sees* HJALMAR, *gives a shout of joy and runs towards him.*) Father! Father!

HJALMAR: (*turning away, with a gesture*) Go away! Go away! (*To* GINA) Get her away from me, I say!

GINA: (*in a low voice*) Go into the living room, Hedvig. (HEDVIG *leaves silently.*)

HJALMAR: (*busy pulling out the table drawer*) I need my books with me. Where are my books?

GINA: Which books?

HJALMAR: My scientific works, of course—the technical journals I need for my invention.

GINA: (*looking on the shelf*) Do you mean these over here, with no covers on them?

HJALMAR: Yes, yes, of course.

GINA: (*puts a pile of journals down on the table*) Don't you want me to get Hedvig to cut them open for you?

HJALMAR: No. Nobody needs to cut any pages for me. (*Brief silence.*)

GINA: So you *are* going to leave us, Ekdal?

HJALMAR: (*rummaging among the books*) That goes without saying, I should think.

GINA: All right.

HJALMAR: (*violently*) For you can hardly expect me to want to stay where my heart is pierced every single hour of the day!

GINA: God forgive you for thinking so bad of me!

HJALMAR: Proof—!

GINA: Seems to me, you're the one who should bring proof.

HJALMAR: After a past like yours? There are certain claims —I might call them the claims of the ideal—

GINA: What about Grandpa? What is *he* going to do, poor old man?

HJALMAR: I know my duty. The helpless one goes with me. I'll go out and make arrangements—H'm (*Hesitantly.*) Has anybody found my hat on the stairs?

GINA: No. Have you lost your hat?

HJALMAR: I most certainly had it on when I came home last night; there isn't the slightest doubt about that. But now I can't find it.

GINA: Good Lord! Where did you go with those two drunks?

HJALMAR: Oh, don't ask about inessentials. Do you think I'm in a mood for remembering details?

GINA: I only hope you haven't got a cold, Ekdal (*Goes into the kitchen.*)

HJALMAR: (*speaking to himself, in a low voice, angrily, as he empties the drawer*) You're a scoundrel, Relling!—A villain is what you are!—Miserable traitor!—I'd gladly see you assassinated—!

(*He puts aside some old letters, discovers the torn gift letter from the day before, picks it up and looks at the two pieces, puts them down quickly as* GINA *enters.*)

GINA: (*putting a tray with food down on the table*) Here's a drop of coffee, if you want it. And some salt meat sandwiches.

HJALMAR: (*glancing at the tray*) Salt meat? Never under this roof! True it is, I haven't taken solid nourishment for almost twenty-four hours, but that can't be helped.—My notes! My incipient memoirs! Where is my diary—all my important papers! (*Opens the door to the living room, but steps back.*) If she isn't there, too!

GINA: Heavens, Ekdal. She's got to be somewhere.

HJALMAR: Leave! (*He makes room,* HEDVIG, *scared, enters the studio. With his hand on the door knob; to* GINA.) During the last moments I spend in my former home I wish to be spared the sight of intruders—(*Enters the living room.*)

HEDVIG: (*starts, asks her mother in a low and trembling voice*) Does that mean me?

GINA: Stay in the kitchen, Hedvig, or no—go to your own

room. (*To* HJALMAR, *as she enters the living room.*) Wait a minute, Ekdal. Don't make such a mess in the dresser. I know where everything is.

HEDVIG: (*remains motionless for a moment, in helpless fright, presses her lips together not to cry, clenches her hands, whispers*) The wild duck!

(*She tiptoes over to the shelf and takes the pistol down, opens the doors to the inner attic, goes inside, closes behind her.* HJALMAR *and* GINA *are heard talking in the living room.*)

HJALMAR: (*appears with some notebooks and a pile of old papers, which he puts down on the table*) The bag obviously won't be big enough. There are thousands of things I need to take with me!

GINA: (*entering with the bag*) Can't you leave most of it behind for now and just pick up a clean shirt and some underwear?

HJALMAR: Phew—! These exhausting preparations—! (*Takes off his overcoat and throws it on the sofa.*)

GINA: And there's the coffee getting cold too.

HJALMAR: H'm. (*Without thinking, he takes a sip, and then another one.*)

GINA: (*dusting off the back of chairs*) How are you ever going to find a large enough attic for the rabbits?

HJALMAR: You mean I have to drag all those rabbits along, too?

GINA: Grandpa can't do without his rabbits—you know that as well as I do.

HJALMAR: He'll have to get used to that. I shall have to give up higher values in life than a bunch of rabbits.

GINA: (*dusting off the shelf*) Shall I put the flute in for you?

HJALMAR: No. No flute for me. But give me my pistol.

GINA: You want that old pistol?

HJALMAR: Yes. My loaded pistol.

GINA: (*looking for it*) It's gone. He must have taken it inside with him.

HJALMAR: Is he in the attic?

GINA: Sure, he's in the attic.

HJALMAR: H'm. The lonely grayhead—(*He eats a sandwich, empties his cup of coffee.*)

GINA: If only we hadn't rented that room, you could have moved in there.

HJALMAR: And stay under the same roof as—! Never! Never again!

GINA: But couldn't you stay in the living room for a day or two? There you'd have everything to yourself.

HJALMAR: Not within these walls!

GINA: How about down at Relling's and Molvik's, then?

HJALMAR: Don't mention their names to me! I get sick just thinking about them. Oh no—it's out into the wind and the snowdrifts for me—to walk from house to house seeking shelter for father and myself.

GINA: But you have no hat, Ekdal! You've lost your hat, remember?

HJALMAR: Oh, those two abominations! Rich in nothing but every vice! A hat must be procured. (*Takes another sandwich.*) Arrangements must be made. After all, I don't intend to catch my death. (*Looks for something on the tray.*)

GINA: What are you looking for?

HJALMAR: Butter.

GINA: Just a moment. (*Goes out into the kitchen.*)

HJALMAR: (*shouting after her*) Oh never mind. Dry bread is good enough for me.

GINA: (*bringing a plate with butter*) Here. This is supposed to be freshly churned.

(*She pours him another cup of coffee. He sits down on the sofa, puts more butter on his bread, eats and drinks in silence.*)

HJALMAR: (*after a pause*) Could I, without being disturbed by anyone—and I mean *anyone*—stay in the living room for a day or two?

GINA: You certainly can, if you want to.

HJALMAR: You see, I don't know how to get all of father's things moved out on such short notice.

GINA: And there is this, too, that first you'd have to tell him that you don't want to live together with the rest of us any more.

HJALMAR: (*pushing his cup away*) Yes, yes, yes. I shall have to go into all those intricate relationships once again, to explain—I must think, I must have air to breathe, I can't bear all the burdens in one single day.

GINA: Of course not. And in such awful weather too—

HJALMAR: (*moving* WERLE's *letter*) I notice this piece of paper still lying around.

GINA: Well, *I* haven't touched it.

HJALMAR: Not that it concerns *me*—

GINA: I'm sure *I* don't expect to make use of it—

HJALMAR: Nevertheless, I suppose we shouldn't let it get completely lost. In all the fuss of moving, something might easily—

GINA: I'll take care of it, Ekdal.

HJALMAR: For the gift letter belongs to father, first of all. It's his affair whether he wants to make use of it or not.

GINA: (*with a sigh*) Yes, poor old Grandpa—

HJALMAR: Just to make sure—Is there any glue?

GINA: (*walks over to the shelf*) Here's a bottle.

HJALMAR: And a brush?

GINA: Here. (*Brings him both.*)

HJALMAR: (*picks up a pair of scissors*) Just a strip of paper on the back—(*Cuts and glues.*) Far be it from me to lay hand on somebody else's property—least of all the property of a poverty-stricken old man.—Well—not on—that other one's, either.—There, now! Leave it to dry for a while. And when it's dry, remove it. I don't want to lay eyes on that document again—ever!

The second play, *The Garbage Hustler,* is an original, unproduced play by Dr. George Savage and George Savage Jr.[2] Dr. Savage was the former head of the playwriting department at the University of California, at Los Angeles. This play is a comedy about a middle aged man who has done his share of philandering. Daisy, one of his former

[2] Copies of the complete play may be obtained by writing to Dr George Savage, 1818 Overland Avenue, Los Angeles, California 90024.

loves, lives next door to M. C. and his wife, Beth. Again, here are some questions to keep in mind as you read the scene:

1. What elements of plot are revealed in the dialogue?
2. How would you describe both characters, their attitudes, their personalities as they are revealed in the scene?
3. What educational background would you say each had?
4. Are there deep emotions in this scene or are the attitudes calm and matter of fact?
5. What influence does the wine have on Daisy? How does it affect the pacing of her lines?
6. Would you consider these people moral or immoral?
7. What effect does the repetition of Daisy's "don't you know" line have on her character?
8. How would you best convey the sense of middle age in both of these characters?

The Garbage Hustler

George Savage and George Savage Jr.

Act I, Scene 2.

M.C.: Well, Daisy.

DAISY: You'd better have some of this wine.

M.C.: No thanks, Daisy.

DAISY: I bought two but there's only one left, don't you know.

M.C.: What bad thing happened that you should bring me wine?

DAISY: April's gonna have Danny's baby.

M.C.: Yeah, Danny told me. What's wrong with that?

DAISY: I ain't sure, M.C. But I think Danny is your son, don't you know . . . I believe you *are* the father of my boy Danny.

(*M.C. stares at Daisy. Suddenly M.C. grabs the bottle*).

M.C.: Why did you keep it to yourself?

DAISY: At the time Danny was more useful as someone else's son . . . You got married to Beth. You was sent overseas. And had all that trouble with the war, don't you know.

(*M.C. crosses C*)

Whenever I felt like tellin', you wasn't there to talk to. I kept puttin' it off, thinkin' maybe it wouldn't matter. I've sort of expected Danny to be drafted.

M.C.: If I was you, I'd be ashamed of myself.

DAISY: I am. I am. I drank a whole bottle of wine already.

M.C. So have I, almost. It's good wine . . . but it don't change things. You're a hell of a mother. Beth would never do anything like that.

(*Daisy takes the bottle from M.C.*)

DAISY: I guess I'm the rotten apple that spoiled the barrel. I'm the rotten old apple, don't you know. (*Daisy takes a drink*)

M.C.: The real start of all this trouble was when a circus came to my mother's town in the 1920's. My father was a Roustabout. A handsome rascal. The circus he was in went bankrupt. My mother could never find him again. Time sure took a turn for the worse after I was born. On account of me, my mother lost her job as a dancer. When I was eight years old, the stock market crashed. One day I decided to strike out on my own. I joined the Army and, the first thing I knew, the world was at war. (*M.C. takes the bottle from Daisy*)

DAISY: You can't blame yourself for the Depression and World-War II.

M.C.: I did ruin my mother's dancing career and Beth's marriage. I shouldn't ever leave the dump except to drive Big Thunder through the alleys.

DAISY: I'm the one who should live in the garbage dump. Bein' around all the fires would be good preparation for my life in the here-ever-after.

M.C.: Havin' so much of my blood in him, that poor little baby of April's would sure be off to a bad start.

DAISY: Tell April I'll make all the arrangements for her across the border.

M.C.: We're all goin' to die. Those that die sooner, suffer less.

(*Daisy puts her arm around M.C. to comfort him*)

DAISY: There! There!

M.C.: Oh, what's the use, Daisy?

DAISY: Don't feel so bad, M.C.

M.C.:   My whole life has been a burden on everyone.

(*Daisy draws away*)

DAISY: You've made a lot of lonely women happy. (*Daisy takes the bottle*)

M.C.:   That's somethin' I guess.

DAISY: It really is.

M.C.:   Don't ever let anything like this happen again.

(*Daisy takes a drink*)

DAISY: I'll try not to.

M.C.:   Good luck, Daisy.

DAISY: You're not mad at me anymore?

M.C.:   No. Just go away, Daisy. I'll take care of everything.

(*M.C. takes the bottle from Daisy*)

DAISY: It's too bad they're brother and sister. They would've made such a nice couple . . . Goodbye, M.C.

M.C.:   Goodbye, Daisy. I hope you'll find more happiness in life than I've found. (*M.C. helps an unsteady Daisy over the fence*)

DAISY: You made a lot of lonely women happy, M.C. You made a lot of lonely women happy. (*Daisy exits unsteadily down the alley L. Daisy's voice gradually fades away*) You've made a lot of lonely women happy. You've made a lot of women happy.

RECORDINGS OF PLAYS

Of particular interest and value to readers of drama are the many recordings of dramatic interpretations by noted actors. While it is true that most of these recordings have a cast of players rather than a single performer, and though these cast albums are more Readers Theatre than individual interpretation, the mere fact that recording companies have gone to the expense of creating such records indicates a wide public interest in the art.

Certainly any serious student of oral interpretation should acquaint himself with these recordings, for he can learn much about the art by listening to the "experts." It is not that the student should set out to imitate the readings, but he can gain valuable aids in content analysis, in the use of pauses and pacing, and in characterization. Two records of note are Jason Robards' *Readings from the Works of Eugene O'Neill* on Columbia Records, and Ingrid Bergman's *The Human Voice,* a one-woman drama. Robards' album contains scenes from *Long Day's Journey Into Night, A Moon for the Misbegotten, The Hairy Ape,* and *The Iceman Cometh.* The actor is noted for his interpretations of O'Neill. He also is featured with Jack Dodson on a recording of *Hughie,* also by O'Neill.

Miss Bergman's *The Human Voice* for Caedmon is a drama by Jean Cocteau, told entirely by a woman on the telephone. While it may be considered by some as acting more than interpretation, it must be remembered that Miss Bergman creates the illusion solely by the use of her voice with no technical help of any kind, so in that sense, it is an expert example of interpretation.

There are, of course, countless other recordings. Columbia has recorded Shaw's *Don Juan in Hell,* with Charles Boyer, Sir Cedric Hardwicke, Charles Laughton, and Agnes Moorehead, as well as *John Brown's Body* by Stephen Vincent Benét with Tyrone Power, Judith Anderson, and Raymond Massey. They have also given us two remarkable recordings of Sir John Gielgud's production, *Ages of Man,* featuring excerpts from Shakespeare. The company's other Shakespearean albums include *Homage to Shakespeare* with Dame Edith Evans, Sir John Gielgud, and Margaret Leighton and *Soul of An Age* with Sir Michael Redgrave and Sir Ralph Richardson.

In addition, full versions of such Shakespearean plays as *Othello, Hamlet, Macbeth, King Lear,* and *Julius Caesar* have been recorded.

One of the more popular ventures has been the recording of complete plays with original casts. These are actors playing definite roles. But again you must keep in mind that the medium is the record —not the stage—and that, therefore, the performer must depend more on interpretation than on acting. He uses the voice alone—and the emotional response to the material.

A select list of recordings is given on the following pages:

Brecht on Brecht—featuring Dane Clark, Anne Jackson, Lotta Lenya in excerpts from the writings of Bertolt Brecht.

Dylan— by Sidney Michaels. The dramatic version of the life of Dylan Thomas, with Alec Guinness.

Everyman—the old morality play with Burgess Meredith.

Moss Hart—reading some of his own works, including *Lady in the Dark* and *Man Who Came to Dinner,* as well as excerpts from his autobiography *Act One.*

Hostage—by Brendan Behan with Geoff Garland, Julie Harris, Diane Webster, Moultrie Patten.

Krapp's Last Tape—by Samuel Beckett with Donald Davis.

Luv—by Murray Schisgall with Alan Arkin, Eli Wallach, Anne Jackson.

A Man's A Man— by Bertolt Brecht.

Arthur Miller—reading from his plays *The Crucible* and *Death of a Salesman.*

Sir Michael Redgrave—reading from Chekhov.

John Millington Synge—*Riders to the Sea.*

Strange Interlude—Eugene O'Neill's marathon play with Betty Field, Jane Fonda.

The Subject Was Roses—Pulitzer Prize play by Frank Gilroy, with Jack Albertson, Irene Dailey, Martin Sheen.

Under Milk Wood—another example of Readers Theatre. A reading of the work by Dylan Thomas.

Waiting for Godot—by Samuel Beckett with Bert Lahr, E. G. Marshall, Kurt Kasznar.

Who's Afraid of Virginia Woolf—Edward Albee's play with the original Broadway cast: Arthur Hill, Uta Hagen, George Grizzard, and Melinda Dillon.

The Zoo Story—by Edward Albee with Mark Richardson and William Daniels.

Caedmon Records offers many selections, including the following:

The Balcony—by Jean Genet.

The Glass Menagerie—by Tennessee Williams with Montgomery Clift, Julie Harris, Jessica Tandy, and David Wayne.

St. Joan—by George Bernard Shaw, with Siobhan McKenna.

Marat/Sade—by Peter Weiss with the original London and New York cast.

Uncle Vanya—by Anton Chekhov with Sir Laurence Olivier.

The Shakespeare Recording Society, in association with Caedmon, offers the following records of Shakespearean works:

Measure for Measure with John Gielgud and Margaret Leighton.

The Taming of the Shrew with Trevor Howard and Margaret Leighton.

Twelfth Night with Siobhan McKenna.

The Winter's Tale with Sir John Gielgud.

Richard II with Sir John Gielgud.

Romeo and Juliet with Claire Bloom and Albert Finney.

Macbeth with Anthony Quayle, Ffrangcan Davies.

As You Like It with Vanessa Redgrave.

Coriolanus with Richard Burton and Jessica Tandy.

Cymbeline with Claire Bloom and Pamela Brown.

RCA Victor also produces some Shakespearean records, including scenes from the sound track of the film of *Taming of the Shrew* with Elizabeth Taylor and Richard Burton; Sir Laurence Olivier's *Othello* and his *Henry V. A Man For All Seasons* by Robert Bolt is another of their productions.

The Theatre Recording Society has made available many theatrical productions:

Cyrano de Bergerac with Sir Ralph Richardson and Anna Massey.

Death of a Salesman with Lee J. Cobb and Mildred Dunnock.

Lysistrata with Hermione Gingold and Stanley Holloway.

Five One-Act Plays by William Butler Yeats with Siobhan McKenna, Patrick Magee, Cyril Cusack and Joyce Redman.

The Master Builder by Henrik Ibsen with Sir Michael Redgrave.

The Family Reunion by T. S. Eliot with Flora Robson, Paul Scofield, and Sybil Thorndike.

She Stoops to Conquer by Oliver Goldsmith with Alastair Sim and Claire Bloom.

The School for Scandal by Richard Brinsley Sheridan with Sir Ralph Richardson, Sir John Gielgud.

And, of course, there are many, many others.

SUMMARY

Drama is a mirror of life, a commentary on the people who live it. As such, its history dates back to the first man who imitated animals and who indulged in rituals as a form of expression. Drama, however, began to achieve a basic form in Greece with festivals to Dionysus. Greek plays as such, were of three types: tragedies, satires, and burlesques.

Among the more noted playwrights in Greece were Sophocles, Aeschylus, Euripides, and Aristophanes.

A highlight of the rebirth of drama occurred in England with the advent of such noted playwrights as Ben Jonson, Marlowe, Kyd, and, of course, Shakespeare.

The Restoration period in England was a glorious time for drama. With sophisticated plays of seduction and evil, and with the works of such playwrights as Richard Brinsley Sheridan and Oliver Goldsmith, theatre was indeed lively.

The nineteenth century saw drama moving into the realm of naturalism and at times it was an instrument of social protest. The twentieth century continued this trend with the works of Eugene O'Neill and Arthur Miller.

A new development of the twentieth century was the emergence of the avant-garde theatre, the "theatre of the absurd," an expression of the existentialists who revolted against the rigid principles of play construction.

A play is usually divided into three acts, and often sub-divided with scenes, but the structural form can vary from one act to two and three acts. Shakespeare used a five-act structure; O'Neill employed a four-act division, and he also used the trilogy.

In most cases, the divisions are made as follows: The first act introduces the main characters, sets the scene, and reveals the primary conflicts. The second act develops the characters and builds to the moment of decision—the dénouement, the crisis. The third act brings about the resolution. This technique can, of course, change according to playwrights' own theories. Generally avant-garde theatre observes no structural devices.

The playwright often has little to say about how his work is interpreted in the theatre. The director or producer may have a different concept of the play than does the author, and the cast may be guided along the roads of that interpretation. At times, the playwright can have a voice in the direction his play is to take, but this usually occurs after he has become a success.

Students would do well to listen to the recordings made by prominent actors and actresses. Actual reproductions of many famous contemporary and classical plays are available, and they provide excellent clues for interpretation. They will be of particular value in studying characterization, a primary problem in the reading of drama.

Although some teachers of oral interpretation have been concerned about the use of acting techniques, the trend seems to be toward a much closer interrelationship between the two. However, interpretation and acting remain separate entities because of their distinctive characteristics.

chapter twelve

How do I read
for readers theatre?

In recent years there has been a most interesting new development in the interpretative field—Readers Theatre. It has its origins in the long historical development of oral interpretation, and it is coming more and more into focus as a specific literary medium with its own merit. It can be defined as an oral reading of various types of literature by a group of two or more people. Music or other amplification may be used to enhance the dramatic values of the presentation. It often embodies movement; the literature being read may be memorized or read from scripts. It is, in short, a close union of the techniques of interpretation and theatre, as it borrows from each for total effect. However, Readers Theatre, by design, is dramatic without being theatrical.

While a definitive exploration of Readers Theatre cannot be made in this brief space, there are certain essentials to consider. The first is the selection of material. Readers Theatre draws from many types of material. Programs have been devised using headlines from newspapers, related pieces from the works of one author, produced and unproduced plays, letters from one person to another, writings on critical world issues, musical theatre productions, such as *You're a Good Man, Charlie Brown*. In short, almost any literature can be worked into this dramatic form. A program is limited only by the imagination of those producing it.

One college built an entire program around the writings of Lawrence Ferlinghetti. His poem, "I Am Waiting," was used as the focal point, the theme, and from that the production went into more of his works. Another college presented a Readers Theatre version of the musical, *You're a Good Man, Charlie Brown*.

Some years ago Charles Laughton gave a series of readings across the country. From this experience he formed a company consisting of Sir Cedric Hardwicke, Agnes Moorehead, and Charles Boyer. They took the third act from George Bernard Shaw's *Man and Superman* and put it into a Readers Theatre program under the title of *Don Juan in Hell*. It was an instant success and has recently been revived with Paul Henreid, Ricardo Montalban, Edward Mulhare, and

Miss Moorehead. Their production embodied many of the traditional aspects of Readers Theatre in that the actors appeared in evening clothes, carried scripts on stage which were placed on music stands, and sat in chairs at the back of the stage out of the playing area. When they made their entrances, they moved down stage and sat on stools or stood for the major scenes.

This brings us to the second consideration—the type of *staging* to be used.

Some productions use chairs or platforms, some use a bare stage, some use impressionistic sets.[1]

Settings are varied, just as the amount and kind of movement are varied. In the case of *Don Juan in Hell,* little movement was used. The actors came on stage in a line, moved up stage and sat on four chairs. Each actor would rise while speaking, and only slight movements were used for emphasis.

Rigidly specified movement is more typical of Readers Theatre. In *Dear Liar,* based on the letters between Bernard Shaw and Mrs. Patrick Campbell, the two performers stood at opposite ends of the stage and read the letters. The same was true in the production of *Dear Love,* the letters of Robert and Elizabeth Barrett Browning. However, in a production of *Spoon River Anthology* there was more movement, particularly to highlight transitions from one sequence to another. In one production of Dylan Thomas' *Under Milk Wood,* there was a great deal of movement, with concentration on visually dramatic patterns.

Exits and entrances demand considerable attention on the part of the director of a Readers Theatre program. There are several techniques which may be used. The reader may merely return to his stool or chair and turn his back to the audience to indicate an exit. An entrance may be shown by turning around and facing the audience, or by physically walking on stage from the "wings." In a showing of Kenneth Grahame's *The Reluctant Dragon,* all of the characters were on stage with their backs to the audience when the play began, with the Dragon up center. As the narrator opened the play, she made comments about each character. As each was introduced, he or she turned around and faced the audience. During the Dragon's scene, for emphasis, the characters of Sir George and the Boy moved up stage and sat on either side of the Dragon. When the focus moved away from the Dragon, the two moved back to their original chairs.

Focus and *involvement* are the third and fourth essential considerations and both are related to movement.

---

[1] For a description of a set used in a professional production, see *The World of Carl Sandburg,* published by Samuel French.

By focus we mean the direction of audience contact. *On stage focus* means that the readers relate directly to each other much as is done by actors in a play. There is a close association between the performers as they react to and interact with each other. The audience is recognized as being present but there is no emphasis on direct contact with them. *Off stage focus* means that the attention is directed to the audience. There is a definite attempt to relate to them and not to the other performers on stage. There is no interaction between readers. It is objective in approach in contrast to the subjectivity of on stage focus. There are also combinations of these two types of focus, but whatever type of focus is used, the most important consideration remains the effective communication of the material.

To present a Readers Theatre production effectively brings up the question of the depth of *involvement*—the degree of characterization.

The "readers" in the professional production of *Don Juan in Hell* were decidedly involved in their roles and went beyond the objectivity usually associated with interpretation. They moved into the subjective role of the actor. It is true that in the small amount of movement and in the use of stands and stools, they were following the traditional precepts of Readers Theatre, but in the delineation of their characters they were showing a very real depth of characterization and involvement. It could be said they were actors rather than interpreters.

In the case of *Spoon River Anthology,* however, there was a difference. The performers in *Don Juan in Hell* were playing only one role and therefore, it was easier to be subjective. In the Edgar Lee Masters' work, each reader read several different characters. It is not possible, under those conditions, to make the audience believe that a reader is actually each of the townspeople he presents. It is true that in the first television production of this "play," the readers were most believable in their impressions of the various characters. However, since they had to move from one role to another so frequently, audience believability was necessarily altered from a subjective association with the character to an objective appreciation of the reader. The same is true of productions that have been done of *Under Milk Wood,* but there have been some presentations where the performers were trying intently to become each and every person they portrayed.

Generally speaking, performers playing more than one role in Readers Theatre may become deeply involved in characterization, in order to bring the material into focus, to give it meaning, and to provide the necessary emotional atmosphere for the audience. In the final analysis each producer of a Readers Theatre program must decide for himself the direction in which he wishes to move. Variety of material and emotional commitment are, however, necessary. As Agnes Moorehead once remarked, "You cannot spend an entire evening reading just the poems of Elizabeth Barrett Browning. Your program must contain variety and dramatic interest."

To help in the creation of mood in a production, *music* is often used, and this is the fifth consideration.

Music helps to heighten a mood, to give emphasis to a dramatic moment, to serve as background to a scene, to be used directly as a part of the production itself. It is, of course, the integral part of any reading derived from a musical production, such as *You're A Good Man, Charlie Brown.* In other cases entire productions can be built around the music of a country as has been done in the case of Chicano music. In such an instance the songs serve to emphasize the beliefs and ideals of a people.

Music also serves technical purposes, such as indicating the end of one sequence and the beginning of another. The use of music, like the use of lighting, is an amplification of a program. It adds dramatic emphasis and mood.

There are two other considerations that should be given attention—*costuming* and the use of *narrator.*

In many cases, costumes are not used, although their use has recently become more and more popular. Naturally, in a production in which each actor plays many roles, a symbolic costume representing the general type of the various characters has been used. Where the performers play only one role, more freedom can be used with costumes. There are, of course, productions, such as *Don Juan in Hell,* where the readers appear in evening clothes, with no attempt at costuming.

The narrator is in most cases a very important consideration. He is used most often to introduce a program, to help define transitions, to set a scene, to describe physical action that cannot be shown in the reading. Other productions do not employ a narrator at all, or they use the various readers to form a chorus to serve as narrator.

The use of narrator and of music, then, is dependent solely on the material and the producer or director of the program. Both are frequently used in Readers Theatre.

The points made in this discussion may serve as guides for any original production. The following script, *Elijah,* was written for Readers Theatre.[2] It is adapted from *The Bible,* and serves as an ex-

---

[2] Copies of this script may be obtained from Dr. Jerry Pickering, California State University, Fullerton, California. Note: This script may be presented without payment of a royalty fee.

cellent vehicle for the use of imaginative techniques. How would you stage a production of *Elijah*? Would you use music? Would you assign different readers each role or would you combine roles in one specific interpreter? Would you use lighting? Would you stage it without costumes? Read it and decide how you would handle your own production.

Elijah

Dr. Jerry Pickering

This script is a contemporary Readers Theatre adaptation of the Old Testament materials concerning the Prophet Elijah. It is obviously, in some cases, designed to be humorous, but essentially it is a serious treatment of a heroic man who dared the might of nations in the service of his god. It is the intention of the script to provide Elijah with the humanity that he must have had by avoiding, at least in part, the cliché interpretation of the fire breathing Prophet from out of the desert.

The setting for the play is quite simple, requiring only three playing levels connected by some sort of stairway—an abstract version of a double-decked pageant wagon and platea. Furnishings and stage decoration should be kept to a minimum. Lighting effects, on the other hand, should be rather complex, with area lighting for each of the three playing areas and a spot for the upper levels. In one case an effect of distant lightning should be used, though it may be replaced by the sound of thunder.

Sound requirements are not difficult. The voice of Deus may be amplified, depending on the reader doing the role. For preshow music, a Georgian chant may be used. It is obviously of much later origin than the materials of the script, but it is congenial with the semi-medieval style of the production. For Jezebel's dance (optional) any appropriate music may be used. A sound effect of distant but powerful thunder may be substituted for the lightning called for in the lighting requirements, or may be used in conjunction with the lightning.

The script may also be produced in a more stationary style, with stools and reading stands. In such cases there should be three reading levels, with Deus and Bonus Angelus on the upper level, Elijah on level two, and the rest of the characters arranged on level three.

Cast of Characters

Bonus Angelus, Deus, Elijah, Ahab, Widow, Obadiah, Jezebel

Preshow music should come up full as the house-lights dim, and then fade out as a tight spot on the upper level reveals Bonus Angelus

BONUS ANGELUS: (*The first part of his speech is delivered as a formal chant*)   The Lord is gracious and great; God without beginning and without end. He is maker unmade and all might is in him. The Lord is life and the pathway thereto, and all is as he commands. *Benedicamus Domino.* (*Dropping the formal manner he becomes the backfence gossip*) It was in the thirty-eighth year of Asa, who was then King of Judah, that the evil Ahab, son of Omri, began his reign over Israel. For twenty-two years Ahab reigned out of Samaria, doing more evil in the sight of the Lord than any of the kings before him. Oh, our Lord was most sorely vexed. It was the least of Ahab's crimes that he lived in the sins of Jeroboam—and *everybody* knows what *he* did. And then Ahab actually married Jezebel, who was the daughter of Ethbaal, King of the Phoenicians— and *everybody* knows what *she* was like.

And then Ahab turned from the worship of the Eternal Lord God and began to serve and worship Baal. What he did was terrible, and the Lord waxed wroth. Ahab erected a temple to Baal in Samaria, and in the temple he placed Baal's altar. To please Jezebel he also caused to be erected a graven image of Astarte.

Oh, Ahab did more to irritate the Lord God of Israel than all those kings who had preceded him. So, the Lord in his

wrath determined to punish Ahab, and to carry God's word
to the Israelites he selected Elijah the Tishbite. . . .

(*The spot illuminating Bonus Angelus fades and lights come
up on the lower level, where Ahab and Jezebel are seated
drinking and feasting, and on the second level where Elijah
crouches. Jezebel may dance if desired. All freeze except
Elijah*)

DEUS: (*From the darkness of the upper level*) Elijah!
Elijah!

(*Elijah looks about in bewilderment. A tight spot comes
up on the upper level, revealing God*)

Do you know who I am, Elijah?
ELIJAH: (*Frightened*) No!
DEUS: I am the Lord God of Israel. (*Pause*) *Your* God,
Elijah.

(*Elijah nods in mute though uncertain assent*)

I have selected you as my prophet, and I have a message
which you are to deliver to Ahab in the name of the Lord
God. Do you understand?
ELIJAH: Not exactly, God.
DEUS: You are to tell Ahab that if he persists in his sin—if he
does not repent and turn from his evil ways into the path
of righteousness—I shall bring a great drought upon the
land.
ELIJAH: Yes, God. I understand. But why do you not appear
to Ahab yourself? He would listen to you, but I . . . I don't
think he'll listen to me.
DEUS: Perhaps, in my own good time. I work in mysterious
ways. But for now you must deliver my message. . . . Are
you afraid, Elijah?
ELIJAH: Yes, God. Sorely.
DEUS: Deliver the message, and be not afraid, for you are
in the service of the Lord God.

(*Light fades upon Deus*)

ELIJAH: (*Croaks*) Ahab! (*A bit louder*) Ahab! (*Summoning up all his courage*) (*Loudly*) Ahab! Hear me!

(*Ahab and Jezebel begin to move again*)

AHAB: Who is this ragged old man?

(*Jezebel shakes her head in bewilderment*)

You should know, old man, that I am Ahab the great, king of kings, ruler of all Israel. My word is law, and to displease me is painful death. Now, knowing this, do you still call upon me?

ELIJAH: (*Literally shaking with fear*) I have a message that must be delivered, Oh mighty king.

AHAB: Speak then. Deliver it, but on the pain of death take care that it does not displease me.

(*Jezebel may rise and circle teasingly about Ahab while Elijah, shaken, delivers God's message*)

ELIJAH: (*Haltingly*) As . . . as the . . . as the Lord God of Israel lives. . . . He whom I serve. . . . There shall be neither dew nor rain these years, except as I give orders, and a drought will fall upon the land.

(*The light fades on the lower level, and Elijah looks wildly about him*)

I did as you said, God. Help me!

(*Spot on the upper level comes up, revealing God*)

DEUS: You did well, Elijah. You are my prophet.

ELIJAH: (*With courage born of fear*) But he'll kill me! Ahab will have me flayed alive, and the dogs will gnaw at my bones.

DEUS: I will save you, Elijah, for you are my prophet, and only I may command your death.

ELIJAH: Thank you, God. (*Shudders*) It is truly comforting to know that it will be you who orders my death instead of Ahab.

DEUS: But you must do as I tell you, absolutely and without question. Is that understood, Elijah?

ELIJAH: Of course it is. I'm no fool. I understand perfectly. Unquestioning obedience.

DEUS: Then do as I tell you and depart from here. Go into the desert and hide yourself at the brook called Kerith, which flows east of the Jordan.

ELIJAH: Into the desert, God? But I don't like the desert. I don't. . . . It's hot and full of sand and serpents. Must I go into the desert?

DEUS: Without question, Elijah. Without *any* questions. You will drink water from the brook, and I have ordered the ravens to feed you.

ELIJAH: Ugh! I have to eat ravens? I don't think I'll like that either.

DEUS.   You are not to eat the ravens. They will bring you food. Farewell, Elijah.

(*Lights fade on the upper and second levels. Lights come up on the lower level, which now contains a stunted looking bush and some rocks. Elijah walks out of the darkness of the levels and seats himself on one of the rocks. He is grumbling to himself*)

ELIJAH: I don't like the desert. No, I don't like it at all. I *despise* the desert. During the day I burn, and at night I freeze. In the morning the niggardly ravens bring me a crust of bread, in the evening a tiny gobbet of goat meat. (*Looks up*) I'm very glad you're with me, God. (*In a lower voice*) But couldn't the ravens come thrice a day, bearing heavy burdens of good, warm food? (*He pauses, then makes a gesture of dismissal*) Aah! Even the brook is drying up. I shall wither and blow away with the endless sand.

DEUS: (*Voice only*) You shall live, Elijah, for you must still do the Lord's work.

ELIJAH: (*Looking about for the source of the voice*)   May I leave the desert now, God? I don't like it here at all.

DEUS: You may leave. From here you must go to Zarephath, which belongs to Sidon, and stay there until I summon you. I have ordered a widow there to provide for you.

ELIJAH: (*A happy and somewhat lustful smile*)   A widow, God? After three years in the desert I am to dwell with a widow?

DEUS: (*Meaningfully*)   A most *good* and *modest* widow, Elijah.

ELIJAH: (*Face falling dejectedly*)   As you say, God. I shall go to Zarephath, there to dwell with the *good, modest* widow.

(*Lights on the lower level fade and come up on the second level, which has now been set with a minimum amount of simple furniture, appropriate to the house of a poor widow. The widow is in the house, holding a small bundle of sticks*)

ELIJAH: Please....

(*The widow starts at the sound of his voice*)

1 expire of thirst. Give me a little water to drink.

(*The widow nods*)

And as you believe that the Lord God of Israel lives, please give me a bite of food to eat.

WIDOW: I have no food, man from out of the desert, except for a bit of meal in a jar, and a few drops of oil in a flask. (*She indicates the small bundle of sticks under her arm*) I was just gathering wood that I might cook all that is left for myself and my son. I would like us to eat this once before we die.

ELIJAH: (*For the first time beginning to sound like the prophet*)   Do not be afraid, woman. Go and do as you have just said; but first make a small cake for me, and then make something for yourself and your son. For this is the promise of the Lord God of Israel, that the jar of meal shall not be used up, nor the flask of oil diminished, before that day when God sends rain, and the drought is off the land.

(*The lights fade. The spot comes up on the upper level, revealing Deus*)

DEUS: Here you will remain, Elijah, for three years at my command, until it is time to remove the drought and bring rain upon the land.

(*Spot fades and the lights come up on the second level, revealing Elijah seated on the level and the widow standing on the stairs*)

WIDOW: He is worse than he was yesterday. There is no breath left in him. My son is dying and the Lord has forsaken us.

(*She sits and covers her face with her hands*)

ELIJAH: The Eternal God does not forsake those who serve him truly, and who do not turn from him. (*Worriedly, in a soft voice*) Do you, God?

WIDOW: Servant of the Lord—you who have come from out of the desert—what have you to do with my life? Have you come here to call God's attention to some hidden, unknown sin of mine? Are you here to have my son killed?

ELIJAH: I will intercede for your son. God will hear me.

(*The lights on the upper level come up slowly as he climbs the stairs and kneels beside the small pad where a child rests, hidden by a blanket*)

Oh, Eternal my God, have you brought evil onto this widow with whom I am staying by killing her son? (*He bends his head to touch the child and then raises his face to the heavens*) Oh, Eternal Lord God of Israel, let the child's life return to him.

(*The child moves under the blanket, and Elijah gently places
a hand on him, as if in benediction*)

Rest, child, for the Lord is with you. (*To the heavens*)
Thank you, God. (*Calling to the widow*) Your son lives. He
will soon be well.

WIDOW: Now I know truly that you are a man of God, and
that He speaks through your lips.

(*Widow freezes*)

DEUS: (*Voice only*)   Elijah, it is now the third year of the
drought. Go, you, and show yourself to Ahab. When you
have done this I will send rain upon the land.

ELIJAH: Show myself to Ahab? But he'll kill me. He will have
me served up in tiny pieces.

DEUS: I am the Eternal Lord God of Israel! Go, Elijah.

ELIJAH: (*Defeated*)   Yes, God.

(*Lights fade to dark on all levels, and come up on the lower
level, revealing Ahab and Obadiah*)

AHAB: This drought goes on and on, Obadiah. Famine and
pestilence rage in Samaria, and Baal and Astarte do nothing
. . . nothing. Therefore, we must divide up and search the
land for a spring or brook. Perhaps we can find grass to
keep at least the horses and mules alive, so that the beasts
will not be lost to us.

OBADIAH: I will search closely, mighty king, as you command.

(*As Ahab exits, Obadiah pretends to search about with exaggerated eagerness. As soon as Ahab is gone, Obadiah drops
his pretense of searching*)

OBADIAH: Woe is me! Sometimes I think that kings are even
greater fools than common men.

(*Elijah enters upon the platea and Obadiah, immediately
recognizing him, bows low*)

Is that you, my Lord?

ELIJAH: I . . . I think so. Who do *you* think I am?

OBADIAH: Are you truly the prophet Elijah?

ELIJAH: (*A bit taken aback by this reception*) Yes, It's me. I have come to show myself to Ahab. Go and tell your lord, the king, that Elijah is here.

OBADIAH: Tell me, great prophet, what sin I have committed that you would send me into Ahab's power and make me lose my life under the most painful of circumstances? As surely as the Lord God of Israel lives, there is not a nation or realm where Ahab has not sent in search of you. When you were not found he made the ruler of each nation take formal oath that they had not discovered you—that they were not hiding you. And now you bid me to go and tell him that "Elijah is here"?

Have you not heard that, when Jezebel was slaughtering the prophets of the Eternal Lord God, I hid a hundred of them in a cave, feeding them on bread and water? I saved them. . . . Well, at least I saved them for a little while. And now you bid me to go to my Lord Ahab and tell him that "Elijah is here"! He will put me to death for my pains, and eventually he will destroy you as well.

ELIJAH: (*Questioningly*) God? Lord God, where are you? Must I show myself to Ahab, only to end a small drought? (*He waits, but there is no answer. To Obadiah*) I'm afraid that there is no choice. I must confront Ahab immediatetly.

OBADIAH: On your head be it. (*Exits*)

ELIJAH: (*Looks reproachfully toward Heaven*) Being your prophet is not an easy job, you know. . . . And it's dangerous, too. It isn't every man who would consent to be a prophet. (*Short pause*) I could have been a farmer. . . .

(*Spot comes up on the upper level revealing God*)

DEUS: Your sacrifice is noted, Elijah.

ELIJAH: (*A bit mollified*) Well, that's something, at least. Now if only Ahab would suddenly drop dead.

DEUS: He will not die, until struck by an Aramaean arrow, and the dogs will lick up his blood.

(*The light fades on the upper level as Elijah shudders. Ahab climbs to the second level*)

AHAB: Elijah! You! You who are the ruin of all Israel!

ELIJAH: I'm not the one who has ruined Israel. It is you and yours who have forsaken the Lord God to follow and worship Baal. Again I am here to deliver a message to you. . . . (*He bows his head for a moment, as if asking and receiving guidance*)

DEUS: (*While Elijah is standing with bowed head. Voice only*) Send you now to the ends of the land and gather all Israel at Mount Karmel. Bring your four-hundred and fifty prophets of Baal, and the four-hundred prophets of Astarte who are maintained by Jezebel.

ELIJAH: (*Raises his head. Beginning to sound like the wild-eyed prophet from out of the desert*)   This I command in the name of the Eternal, who is the Lord God of Israel!

(*Ahab shrinks from the presence of Elijah. The lights fade on the second level and come up slowly on the upper level as Elijah mounts the stairs. Elijah faces the audience and addresses them as if they represented all of Israel*)

People of Israel, how long will you hobble along in this faith and that? If the Eternal Lord is truly God, then follow him. If Baal is the true God, then worship him. But at least you should know certainly which is which.

I—I alone—am left as prophet of the Eternal Lord God of Israel, while Baal has four-hundred and fifty prophets and Astarte has four-hundred. Their numbers are too great for me to contest with them individually, so I propose a contest. Bring two bullocks and place them out on the plain, laying them on wood but putting no fire beneath them. You call upon your god, and I will call upon the Eternal Lord God of Israel. The god who answers by fire, he is the true god.

(*There are cries of assent from those characters who are offstage*)

Choose one bullock for yourselves and dress it first—for there are many of you—but put no fire underneath. Then call upon your god to kindle the flames and roast the bullock, and we will have a feast in his honor, for he will have demonstrated that he is the true god and deserving of reverence.

(*A call from offstage: "The bullock is ready"*)

Call upon Baal, who is your god! If he is truly god, then let him answer.

(*From offstage voices call, variously, "Baal," "Great Baal," and "Baal, answer us"*)

Shout, for he is a god! Perhaps he is musing, or away on business, or asleep. He must be awakened. Shout! Call to him!

(*The offstage voices of the Israelites continue to call upon Baal: "Great Baal, answer your servants"; "Baal, hear our plea"; "Baal, fire the sticks beneath your bullock"*)

Close, now! Attend me and hear what I say.

(*The Israelites give off their prayers*)

While you were praying to Baal, I sent those I can trust to prepare the bullock of the Lord God. It is ready, and his altar, which you allowed to crumble, has been repaired. Water has been poured on the bullock, and on the altar, and water has been placed in a trench about the area of sacrifice. All is in readiness.

(*The offstage Israelites, who have been ad-libbing to each other* sotto voce *during this announcement fall silent on the last sentence. Elijah throws open his arms to the heavens*)

Oh, Eternal God of Abraham and Isaac! Lord God of Israel! This day be it known that Thou art God in Israel, and that I am Thy servant, and that all this have I done at Thy bidding. Hear me, Lord God, hear me and let these, your people, know that Thou art truly God, and make their minds turn to Thee once more! (*Falls to his knees*) Oh, my God!

(*Lightning flashes behind Elijah, and thunder rolls. The off-stage Israelites cry out: "The Eternal Lord God lives"; "He is the true God of Israel!"; "He is the one and only true God!"*)

Seize the prophets of the false Baal. Let none of them escape!

(*The offstage Israelites cry out: "Seize the false prophets!"; "Let none escape!" Obadiah climbs up to join Elijah on the upper level*)

ELIJAH: Go. Look out at the sea.
OBADIAH: (*Looks out toward audience*)   There is nothing.
ELIJAH: Look again.
OBADIAH: (*Looks, shading his eyes*)   A cloud is rising up out of the sea, small as a man's fist.
ELIJAH: The drought is ended, as God promised. Go and tell Ahab to hasten, lest this rain stop him before he reaches Jezebel.

(*Obadiah exits*)

End me, God. Strike me down into the dust, for I can stand no more of this. Oh, Lord God, I am mortal, as was my father and his father before him. The concerns of God weigh heavily on me.
DEUS: (*Voice only*)   Your time is not yet, Elijah. There is still work for you to do.
ELIJAH: I have been given news of Jezebel.
DEUS: I know.
ELIJAH: She has heard of the deaths of the prophets of Baal and Astarte, and she has announced that as surely as I am Elijah and she Jezebel, she will face death at the hands of the gods if by tomorrow at this time she does not end my life, as I did theirs.
DEUS: Fear not, Elijah. Jezebel will not harm you. Now, eat and drink, lest the journey prove too much for you.

ELIJAH: Journey? What journey?
DEUS: Eat and drink.

(*Elijah mimes eating a small cake and drinking from a flask of water*)

ELIJAH: That was very good cake, Lord, and very good water, too—though on the whole water is water and there is very little difference between one sip and another. Still, it was good and I am strong again.
DEUS: Husband that strength, Elijah. You will need it for your journey.
ELIJAH: (*Apprehensive*) I will need such strength, God?
DEUS: You must go to Horeb, which is my mountain, and there take shelter in a cave on the mountainside.
ELIJAH: Horeb? That is a long journey, Lord.
DEUS: Indeed it is. It will take you forty days and forty nights, during which time you will neither eat nor drink.
ELIJAH: (*Protesting*) But . . . but God . . . (*There is no answer, and so he rises painfully and begins the journey*)

(*The light fades on the upper level and comes up on the second level as Elijah walks down the stairs. He speaks mournfully*)

A cave. A bitter cold cave on the side of a mountain. Why couldn't I just once be ordered to wait in a palace? Oh, it's cold, and the wind cuts like a knife.

(*Spot comes up on the upper level, revealing God*)

DEUS: What are you doing here, Elijah?
ELIJAH. (*Confused*) What am I doing here? But. . . . But you. . . . Oh! (*The last in a drawn-out exclamation of real pain*) I have been zealous for you, Eternal God of Hosts. The Israelites have forsaken you, breaking down your altars and killing your prophets. I am the only one left, and they seek me to take my life.
DEUS: Go outside, Elijah, and stand before me on the mountain.

(*Elijah steps forward to the front of the level*)

ELIJAH: I feel a great wind, God, but you are not in it. (*Pause*) I feel the earth tremble, but you are not in its trembling. (*Pause*) I see fire, but again you are not there in its heat and light. (*Pause*) I hear a gentle whisper and. . . . (*Falls on his knees and covers his face*)

DEUS: What are you doing here, Elijah?

ELIJAH: I have been zealous for the Eternal God of Hosts. The Israelites have forsaken you, breaking down your altars and killing your prophets. I am the only one left, and they seek me to take my life. Now I am here to do your will.

DEUS: Go back. Take the desert road to Damascus. When you arrive you shall appoint Hazael to be King of Aram; Jehu, the grandson of Nimshi, to be King of Israel; and Elisha, the son of Shaphat, to succeed you as prophet. Whoever escapes the sword of Hazael shall Jehu slay, and whoever escapes the sword of Jehu shall Elisha slay. I will spare seven thousand men in Israel; all who have never bowed down to Baal. That is my will, Elijah.

ELIJAH: (*Patient resignation*) Yes, God.

(*Lights fade on second level and come up on the lower level, revealing Ahab and Jezebel. Ahab is angry and sullen*)

JEZEBEL: Why are you so depressed, my lord and husband? You didn't even touch your supper, and it was delicious.

AHAB: I asked Naboth of Jesreel to let me buy his vineyard— I even offered him another vineyard to replace it—and he said he wouldn't sell it to me.

JEZEBEL: Aren't you even in command of your own kingdom? Get up and eat your supper. I'll get you the vineyard of Naboth.

AHAB: How? He said that in the name of God he would never give me his property, which was the property of his father.

JEZEBEL: You asked him to sell to you, and he refused. I shall command . . . command his death. I will write a letter in your name to the governors of Jesreel. I will tell them to proclaim a fast and a gathering. At the gathering they will have two men confront Naboth and charge him with breaking the fast and cursing God and the king. Then they will take him outside the town and stone him to death. After that you will take possession of Naboth's vineyard, which he refused to let you buy, for he will be dead.

AHAB: Oh, that is a marvelous plan. Truly you are a queen of queens.

(*Lights on the lower level fade. Light comes up on the second level, revealing Elijah*)

DEUS: (*Voice only*)   Elijah! Elijah, my prophet!

ELIJAH: (*Looks up desperately*)   Yes, God.

DEUS: You must leave.

ELIJAH: Again? Must I?

DEUS: You must go to confront Ahab. He is in the vineyard of my servant Naboth, of which he has taken possession. Give him this message from the Lord God of Israel. Say to him, "You have killed, and you have taken possession, have you?" Say to him, "Where dogs licked up the blood of Naboth, there shall dogs lick up your blood."

ELIJAH: (*Weary resignation*)   Yes, God.

DEUS: Then go now, Elijah.

(*Lights on the second level fade as Elijah walks down the stairs. Lights come up on the lower level, revealing Ahab. Elijah confronts him*)

ELIJAH: (*Doggedly repeating the message*)   You have killed and taken possession, have you? Where the dogs licked up the blood of Naboth, there shall dogs lick up your blood.

AHAB: So you know what was done to Naboth. . . .

ELIJAH: (*He does not know, and is a bit uncertain*)   I . . . I know what was done, and because you have sold yourself to no purpose, doing what is evil in the sight of God, I will bring evil on you. I will cleanse the world of you.

(*Ahab freezes*)

DEUS: (*Voice only*)   You exceed my message, Elijah, but because you are my prophet I will make your words come to pass.

ELIJAH: Thank you, God.

(*Ahab begins to move again*)

I will strip Ahab of every male child, and of free and fettered alike in all Israel. Your house will fare like the house of Jeroboam, the son of Nebat, and like the house of Baasha, the son of Abijah, for the provocations that have made Israel sin. Anyone belonging to Ahab, who dies in the city, the dogs shall devour him. Anyone who dies out in the country, wild birds will eat him. Finally, the dogs will eat Jezebel in the territory of Jesreel.

AHAB: (*Cries out in real terror*)   Bring me sackcloth and ashes, that I may repent of my sins before the Eternal Lord God of Israel! (*Freezes*)

(*Spot on upper level comes up, revealing God*)

DEUS: Elijah, do you see how Ahab humbles himself before me?

ELIJAH: Yes, God.

DEUS: As he humbles himself before me, I will not bring evil in his reign. I will bring evil on his house during his son's reign. (*Pause*) It is over, Elijah, my prophet. Ahab is humbled and Shaphat will now succeed you to carry my word to the people of Israel.

ELIJAH: Did I do well?

DEUS: You did well, Elijah, in my sight.

ELIJAH: (*Kneels*)   Thank you, God.

(*Music comes up lightly. Lights fade slowly to black*)

RADIO AND TELEVISION

The art of interpretation is not limited to the stage, the recital hall, or the classroom. It is also suited, in different ways, to both radio and television.

Colleges which are fortunate enough to have both a broadcasting studio and a closed circuit television can find exciting new learning experiences in the adaptation of oral interpretation or Readers Theatre programs to radio or television. However, the demands for each of these media are quite different and must be given due consideration.

In radio, the emphasis is on the hearing. Visual pictures, intricate staging, and costuming are not important. In this medium, too, the reader as the individual is important. There may be other readers on the program, but it is the one person speaking at the time on whom the listening audience centers its attention.

The reader's voice quality must attract and sustain the listener's attention. Vocal variety is also significant because it is the voice, coupled with the emotional response of the reader to his material, that maintains interest. Consequently, the technique of speaking over a microphone must be mastered for effective radio performance.

In radio, too, there is no need for movement on the part of the performers. The customary procedure is to stand at a microphone and read the script. Any indications of movement, such as a performer leaving or entering, are usually handled by the reader's moving slowly away from the microphone to convey an exit, or drawing closer to the microphone for an entrance.

It has been some time since oral interpretation as such has been heard on radio. Radio programing today is generally made up of news and music, but for many years radio was also a medium for dramatic performance. Some of the finest plays were adapted or written specifically for radio. Lucille Fletcher's *Sorry, Wrong Number* was an outstanding suspense drama, written for radio. Here is an excerpt from that play. The various techniques that were used for radio are indicated in the script.

From

Sorry, Wrong Number

Lucille Fletcher

OPERATOR: Your call, please?

MRS. STEVENSON: Operator—for Heaven's sake—will you ring that Murray Hill 4-0098 number again? I can't think what's keeping him so long.

OPERATOR: Ringing Murray Hill 4-0098. (*Rings. Busy signal.*) The line is busy. Shall I ——

MRS. STEVENSON: (*Nastily*) I can hear it. You don't have to tell me. I know it's busy. (*Slams down receiver.*) [SCENE: *Spotlight fades off on* 2ND OPERATOR.] [SCENE: MRS. STEVENSON *sinks back against pillows again, whimpering to herself fretfully. She glances at clock, then turning, punches her pillows up, trying to make herself comfortable. But she isn't. Whimpers to herself as she squirms restlessly in bed.*] If I could only get out of this bed for a little while. If I could get a breath of fresh air—or just lean out the window —and see the street. . . . [SCENE: *She sighs, reaches for pill bottle, shakes out a pill. As she does so:*] (*The phone rings. She darts for it instantly.*) Hello, Elbert? Hello. Hello. Hello. Oh—what's the *matter* with this phone? HELLO? HELLO? (*Slams down receiver.*) [SCENE: *She stares at it, tensely.*] (*The phone rings again. Once. She picks it up.*) Hello? Hello. . . . Oh—for Heaven's sake—who *is* this? Hello. Hello. HELLO. (*Slams down receiver. Dials operator.*) [SCENE: *Spotlight comes on* L., *showing* 3RD OPERATOR, *at spot vacated by* DUFFY.]

3RD OPERATOR: Your call, please?

MRS. STEVENSON: (*Very annoyed and imperious.*) Hello. Operator. I don't know what's the matter with this telephone tonight, but it's positively driving me crazy. I've never seen such inefficient, miserable service. Now, look. I'm an invalid, and I'm very nervous, and I'm *not* supposed to be annoyed. But if this keeps on much longer . . .

3RD OPERATOR: (*A young sweet type*) What seems to be the trouble, madam?

MRS. STEVENSON: Well—everything's wrong. The whole world could be murdered, for all you people care. And now —my phone keeps ringing. . . .

OPERATOR: Yes, madam?

MRS. STEVENSON: Ringing and ringing and ringing every five seconds or so, and when I pick it up, there's no one there.

OPERATOR: I am sorry, madam. If you will hang up, I will test it for you.

MRS. STEVENSON: I don't want you to test it for me. I want you to put through that call—whatever it is—at once.

OPERATOR: (*Gently*) I am afraid that is not possible, madam.

MRS. STEVENSON: (*Storming*) Not possible? And why— may I ask?

OPERATOR: The system is automatic, madam. If someone is trying to dial your number, there is no way to check whether the call is coming through the system or not—unless the person who is trying to reach you complains to his particular operator ——

MRS. STEVENSON: Well, of all the stupid, complicated . . . ! And meanwhile *I've* got to sit here in my bed, *suffering* every time that phone rings—imagining everything. . . .

OPERATOR: I will try to check it for you, madam.

MRS. STEVENSON: Check it! Check it! That's all anybody can do. Of all the stupid, idiotic . . . ! (*She hangs up.*) Oh— what's the use . . . [SCENE: 3RD OPERATOR *fades out of spotlight, as*] (*Instantly* MRS. STEVENSON's *phone rings again. She picks up receiver. Wildly.*) Hello. HELLO. Stop ringing, do you hear me? Answer me? What do you want? Do you realize you're driving me crazy? [SCENE: *Spotlight goes on* R. *We see a* MAN *in eye-shade and shirt-sleeves, at desk with phone and telegrams.*] Stark, staring . . .

MAN: (*Dull flat voice.*) Hello. Is this Plaza 4-2295?

MRS. STEVENSON: (*Catching her breath*) Yes. Yes. This is Plaza 4-2295.

WESTERN UNION: This is Western Union. I have a telegram here for Mrs. Elbert Stevenson. Is there anyone there to receive the message?

MRS. STEVENSON: (*Trying to calm herself*) I am Mrs. Stevenson.

WESTERN UNION: (*Reading flatly*) The telegram is as follows: "Mrs. Elbert Stevenson. 53 North Sutton Place, New York, New York. Darling. Terribly sorry. Tried to get you for last hour, but line busy. Leaving for Boston eleven p. m. tonight on urgent business. Back tomorrow afternoon. Keep happy. Love. Signed. Elbert."

MRS. STEVENSON: (*Breathlessly, aghast, to herself.*) Oh . . no . . .

WESTERN UNION: That is all, madam. Do you wish us to deliver a copy of the message?

MRS. STEVENSON: No—no, thank you.

WESTERN UNION: Thank you, madam. Good night. (*He hangs up phone.*) [SCENE: *Spotlight on* WESTERN UNION *immediately out.*]

MRS. STEVENSON: (*Mechanically, to phone*)   Good night. (*She hangs up slowly. Suddenly bursting into.*) No—no—it isn't true! He couldn't do it! Not when he knows I'll be all alone. It's some trick—some fiendish . . . [SCENE: *We hear sound of train roaring by outside. She half rises in bed, in panic, glaring toward curtains. Her movements are frenzied. She beats with her knuckles on bed, then suddenly stops, and reaches for phone.*] (*She dials operator.*) [SCENE: *Spotlight picks up* 4TH OPERATOR, *seated* L.]

OPERATOR: (*Coolly*)   Your call, please?

MRS. STEVENSON: Operator—try that Murray Hill 4-0098 number for me just once more, please.

OPERATOR: Ringing Murray Hill 4-0098. (*Call goes through. We hear ringing at other end. Ring after ring.*) [SCENE: *If telephone noises are not used visually, have* OPERATOR *say after a brief pause: "They do not answer."*]

MRS. STEVENSON: He's gone. Oh—Elbert, how could you? How could you . . . ? (*She hangs up phone, sobbing pityingly to herself, turning restlessly.*) [SCENE: *Spotlight goes out on* 4TH OPERATOR.] But I can't be alone tonight. I can't. If I'm alone one more second . . . [SCENE: *She runs hands wildly through hair.*] I don't care what he says—or what the expense is—I'm a sick woman—I'm entitled . . . [SCENE: *With trembling fingers she picks up receiver again.*] (*She dials* INFORMATION.) [SCENE: *The spotlight picks up* INFORMATION OPERATOR, *seated* R.]

INFORMATION: This is Information.

MRS. STEVENSON: I want the telephone number of Henchley Hospital.

INFORMATION: Henchley Hospital? Do you have the address, madam?

MRS. STEVENSON: No. It's somewhere in the 70's, though. It's a very small, private and exclusive hospital where I had my appendix out two years ago. Henchley. H-E-N-C——

INFORMATION: One moment, please.

MRS. STEVENSON: Please—hurry. And please—what *is* the time?

INFORMATION: I do not know, madam. You may find out the time by dialing Meridian 7-1212.

MRS. STEVENSON: (*Irritated*)   Oh—for Heaven's sake! Couldn't you ——?

INFORMATION: The number of Henchley Hospital is Butterfield 7-0105, madam.

MRS. STEVENSON: Butterfield 7-0105. (*She hangs up before she finishes speaking, and immediately dials number as she repeats it.*) [SCENE: *Spotlight goes out on* INFORMATION.] (*Phone rings.*) [SCENE: *Spotlight picks up a* WOMAN *in nurse's uniform, seated at desk,* L.]

WOMAN: (*Middle-aged, solid, firm, practical.*) Henchley Hospital, good evening

MRS. STEVENSON.   Nurses' Registry.

WOMAN: Who was it you wished to speak to, please?

MRS. STEVENSON: (*High-handed*)   I want the Nurses' Registry at once. I want a trained nurse. I want to hire her immediately. For the night.

WOMAN: I see. And what is the nature of the case, madam?

MRS. STEVENSON: Nerves. I'm very nervous. I need soothing—and companionship. My husband is away—and I'm ——

WOMAN: Have you been recommended to us by any doctor in particular, madam?

MRS. STEVENSON: No. But I really don't see why all this catechizing is necessary. I want a trained nurse. I was a patient in your hospital two years ago. And after all, I *do* expect to *pay* this person——

WOMAN: We quite understand that, madam. But registered nurses are very scarce just now—and our superintendent has asked us to send people out only on cases where the physician in charge feels it is absolutely necessary.

MRS. STEVENSON: (*Growing hysterical*)   Well—it *is* absolutely necessary. I'm a sick woman. I—I'm very upset. Very. I'm alone in this house—and I'm an invalid—and tonight I overheard a telephone conversation that upset me dreadfully. About a murder—a poor woman who was going to be murdered at eleven-fifteen tonight—in fact, if someone doesn't come at once—I'm afraid I'll go out of my mind. . . .(*Almost off handle by now.*)

WOMAN: (*Calmly*) I see. Well—I'll speak to Miss Phillips as soon as she comes in. And what is your name, madam?

MRS. STEVENSON: Miss Phillips. And when do you expect her in?

WOMAN: I really don't know, madam. She went out to supper at eleven o'clock.

MRS. STEVENSON: Eleven o'clock. But it's not eleven yet. (*She cries out.*) Oh, my clock *has* stopped. I thought it was running down. What time is it? [SCENE: WOMAN *glances at wristwatch.*]

WOMAN: Just fourteen minutes past eleven. . . .(*Sound of phone receiver being lifted on same line as* MRS. STEVENSON's. *A click.*)

MRS. STEVENSON: (*Crying out*) What's *that?*

WOMAN: What was what, madam?

MRS. STEVENSON: That—that click just now—in my own telephone? As though someone had lifted the receiver off the hook of the extension phone downstairs. . . .

WOMAN: I didn't hear it, madam. Now—about this . . .

MRS. STEVENSON: (*Scared*) But I *did*. There's someone in this house. Someone downstairs in the kitchen. And they're listening to me now. They're . . . [SCENE: *She puts hand over her mouth.*] (*Hangs up phone.*) [SCENE: *She sits there, in terror, frozen, listening.*] (*In a suffocated voice.*) I won't pick it up. I won't let them hear me. I'll be quiet —and they'll think . . . (*With growing terror.*) But if I don't call someone now—while they're still down there— there'll be no time. . . . (*She picks up receiver. Bland buzzing signal. She dials operator. Ring twice.*) [SCENE: *On second ring, spotlight goes on* R. *We see* 5TH OPERATOR.]

OPERATOR: (*Fat and lethargic*) Your call, please?

MRS. STEVENSON: (*A desperate whisper*) Operator—I—I'm in desperate trouble . . .I ——

OPERATOR: I cannot hear you, madam. Please speak louder.

MRS. STEVENSON: (*Still whispering*) I don't dare. I—there's someone listening. Can you hear me now?

OPERATOR: Your call, please? What number are you calling, madam?

MRS. STEVENSON: (*Desperately*) You've got to hear me. Oh

—please. You've got to help me. There's someone in this house. Someone who's going to murder me. And you've got to get in touch with the   . (*Click of receiver being put down in* MRS. STEVENSON's *line. Bursting out wildly.*) Oh—there it is . . . he's put it down . . . he's put down the extension . . . he's coming . . .(*She screams.*) he's coming up the stairs. . . . [SCENE: *She thrashes in bed, phone cord catching in lamp wire, lamp topples, goes out. Darkness.*] (*Hoarsely.*) Give me the Police Department. . . . [SCENE: *We see on the dark* C. *stage, the shadow of door opening.*] (*Screaming.*) The police! . . . [SCENE: *On stage, swift rush of a shadow, advancing to bed—sound of her voice is choked out, as*]

OPERATOR: Ringing the Police Department. (*Phone is rung. We hear sound of a train beginning to fade in. On second ring,* MRS. STEVENSON *screams again, but roaring of train drowns out her voice. For a few seconds we hear nothing but roaring of train, then dying away, phone at police headquarters ringing.*) [SCENE: *Spotlight goes on* DUFFY, L. *stage.*]

DUFFY: Police Department. Precinct 43. Duffy speaking. (*Pause.*) [SCENE: *Nothing visible but darkness on* C. *stage.*] Police Department. Duffy speaking. [SCENE: *A flashlight goes on, illuminating open phone to one side of* MRS. STEVENSON's *bed. Nearby, hanging down, is her lifeless hand. We see the second man,* GEORGE, *in black gloves, reach down and pick up phone. He is breathing hard.*]

GEORGE. Sorry. Wrong number. (*Hangs up.*) [SCENE: *He replaces receiver on hook quietly, exits, as* DUFFY *hangs up with a shrug, and CURTAIN FALLS.*]

Another memorable program was Orson Welles' Mercury Theatre presentation of *War of the Worlds,* a show based on an invasion of the country by men from Mars. So realistic was this one that it created panic in the United States. Then there were such stalwarts as *First Nighter,* a series of original dramas for radio, and *Suspense,* featuring the theatre of suspense.

Radio is probably not as good a medium for interpretation as is television, since it has no visual elements. Listeners today are used to doing other things while listening to radio programs, but television is a different matter. Since it is visual, concentration on the part of the listener is more essential.

The differences between television and radio are obvious; the performers are usually in costume. Each performer is a personality by himself, but the audience's attention is drawn to the group as a whole. The performers memorize the script, much as an actor does; there are no limitations as to subject matter or sets. Since the visual aspects are so important, action and movement are vital. Unlike radio, which leaves so much to the imagination of the listener, television brings reality to the listener.

Readers Theatre—and oral interpretation—have been produced effectively on television. *Spoon River Anthology,* as revised by Charles Aidman, was originally done on television. Agnes Moorehead's *That Fabulous Redhead* is another. Hal Holbrook's one-man show, *Mark Twain Tonight,* was a notable television success. Equally well-received was Sir John Gielgud's *Ages of Man* which was such a standout on its first appearance that a second program was arranged. This, like the Holbrook show, was a one-man effort. In both cases, there was not a real set, and the performers used very little movement. They proved that television can hold the attention of the audience without a good deal of visual effect. The notable distinction, however, is that the performer must be sufficiently impressive to sustain concentrated attention for a period of time.

Television is moving more and more into importance as a medium for the field of interpretation. Its possibilities are limitless. Its results can be outstanding—and artistically exciting. Some colleges are already experimenting with television, even to the extent of doing full productions directed and performed by students. Others have their own special television stations.

Equally important is the growing use of video tape in classrooms as a learning device. Students are videotaped as they do a reading. They later see themselves on the television monitor. It is a decidedly effective way to see strong points and correct weak ones. So the art of interpretation moves into new focus in the classroom, into the demanding world of television. It is no longer just a medium for the stage from which it has, so far, received its greatest emphasis.

SUMMARY

Readers Theatre is taking its place as a specific literary medium with its own merit. It can be defined as an oral reading of various types of literature by a group of two or more people.

There are certain essentials to consider:

1. Selection of material, with emphasis on variety
2. Staging
3. Focus
4. Involvement
5. Mood

Music is an integral part of any Readers Theatre program that is derived from a musical production, but it can be used to serve technical purposes as well. You may wish to use music and lighting for the amplification of a program—to add dramatic emphasis and heighten a desired mood. Costuming and the use of a narrator are two additional considerations.

Radio and television have done much to advance oral interpretation. Each has made its unique contribution; with radio the emphasis is on hearing; with television, it is on the visual. In its heyday radio was a medium for dramatic performances. Today television is used more and more frequently for oral interpretation; its possibilities are limitless.

chapter thirteen

How do I read poetry?

How or when poetry began as a form of expression no literary historian would venture to guess. However, it can be said that poetic expression was used together with music, dance, pagan rituals, and other rhythmic forms in early tribal ceremonials. Poetry is inherently emotional. While poetry is not the largest body of literature, it has certainly been used by man to express his views about virtually every emotion and every experience imaginable.

It is difficult to define poetry because it is such a dynamic form of expression. Because poetic forms are constantly changing, no attempt to define poetry has been successful in controlling its growth or containing its shape. Even so, a look at some "definitions" by a few great poets and thinkers is in order.

William Wordsworth referred to poetry as "the imaginative expression of strong feeling, usually rhythmical . . ."

Samuel Taylor Coleridge distinguished between prose and poetry when he wrote, "Prose: words in their best order; poetry: the best words in the best order."

Archibald MacLeish said, "A poem should not *mean* but *be*."

Thomas Macaulay wrote: "By poetry we mean the art of employing words in such a manner as to produce an illusion of the imagination, the art of doing by means of words what the painter does by means of colors."

Archibald MacLeish suggests that poetry should *be* an experience, not *tell* of one. So poetry depends a great deal on emotion and imagination in presenting its meaning. There are no bounds on the kinds of ideas about which poetry has been written. Man, nature, the joys and problems of living, and dying—all these have been given full treatment by the world's poets. Where we came from, why we are here, what happens to us at death—all these have been explored through centuries of poetry. Poetry has been written to record events, to preserve ideas and moods, to protest "wrongs" and herald "rights." It has been written in deepest sorrow and in lightest humor. No experience of man has escaped the poet's pen.

THE CONTENTS OF POETRY

What do we mean when we say poetry is emotional and imaginative? The definition by Coleridge is the first clue. "The best words in the best order," he said. His idea of the "best words" leads us into a discussion of poetic imagery. The poet relies heavily on imagery to put across his meaning. Read the following lines of poetry by John Donne and you'll quickly see the imaginative use of words. The lines are taken from his poem "The Indifferent."

> I can love both fair and brown:
> Her whom abundance melts, and her whom want betrays;
> Her who loves loneness best, and her who masks and plays;
> Her whom the country formed, and whom the town;
> Her who believes, and her who tries;
> Her who still weeps with spongy eyes,
> And her who is dry cork and never cries.
> I can love her, and her, and you, and you;
> I can love any, so she be not true. . . .

In the first line the poet highlights his idea. He says that he can love a variety of women. In the lines that follow he extends the idea into details of this variety. He can love plump and lean, quiet and flirtatious, country bred and city bred, saintly and worldly, weepy-eyed and hard; and then to make the idea final, he finishes on an impersonal note—with the idea that he can love any woman, so long as she does not love only him—so long as she doesn't tie him down. The poem is really an identification of the case for those against constancy, against loving one person forever.

Now compare Donne's way of saying it with the prose treatment of the idea given in the above paragraph. Is there any question about which is more imaginative? emotional?

The poem by Donne and, in fact, poetry in general, derives its emotion and imagination from the use of *imagery*—or what are most often called *figures of speech*. There are many such devices, but three which are most important for you to learn to recognize are *simile, metaphor,* and *allegory*. A *simile* is a figure of speech which makes a comparison between two things, using the word "like" or other connecting words. For example, if a poet wrote "My love is like a red, red rose," he would have written a simile.

A *metaphor* is also a comparison, but it omits the connecting word or words. So if the same poet wrote "My love is a red, red rose," he would have a metaphor. The implication in such a comparison is that the poet's lover has all the qualities of the red, red rose. The poem by Donne in this chapter is loaded with metaphors. The comparisons he implies are identified in the paragraph that follows the poem.

An *allegory* is an extended comparison. In short, a poem (or prose selection) which tells a story on more than one level of meaning is an allegory. Walt Whitman's poem "O Captain! My Captain!" is an example of allegory. The poem on the surface speaks of a sea captain and a sea voyage; yet, the captain is Lincoln, the ship is the ship of state, and the voyage, the Civil War. Read the poem with allegory in mind.

O Captain! My Captain!

Walt Whitman

O Captain! my Captain! our fearful trip is done!
The Ship has weather'd every rack, the prize we sought is
    won,
The port is near, the bells I hear, the people all exulting,
While follow eyes the steady keel, the vessel grim and
    daring;
    But O heart! heart! heart!
    O the bleeding drops of red,
    Where on the deck my Captain lies,
    Fallen cold and dead.

O Captain! my Captain! rise up and hear the bells;
Rise up—for you the flag is flung—for you the bugle trills,
For you bouquets and ribbon'd wreaths—for you the shores
    a-crowding,
For you they call, the swaying mass, their eager faces
    turning;

Here Captain; dear father!
This arm beneath your head!
It is some dream that on the deck,
You've fallen cold and dead.

My Captain does not answer, his lips are pale and still,
My father does not feel my arms, he has no pulse nor will,
The ship is anchor'd safe and sound, its voyage closed and
     done,
From fearful trip the victor ship comes in with object won;
     Exult O Shores, and ring O bells!
     But I with mournful tread,
     Walk the deck my Captain lies,
     Fallen cold and dead.

Allegory is not only found in poetry; fables, parables, many
nursery rhymes, and other types of literature can be read on more
than one level and thus, as extended metaphors, are allegorical.

Other figures of speech that you might wish to recognize and
work with are these:

Personification is a device often used in which an object or an
idea is given human qualities. Thus a poet might write of "opportunity
knocking," "pines whispering," or of an animal "singing" to its mate.
In his poem "The Express," Stephen Spender uses personification of
the express train when he writes,

Without bowing and with restrained unconcern
She passes the houses . . .

Apostrophe is similar to personification in that the poet ad-
dresses an object or an idea as he would a person. Percy Bysshe
Shelley speaks directly to the wind throughout his poem "Ode to the
West Wind." At one point he pleads,

Make me thy lyre, even as the forest is . . .

Hyperbole is exaggeration used to make a point or heighten the
effect of the poem. This figure of speech is used most often in humor-

ous poetry, as in the case of Oliver Wendell Holmes' "The Deacon's Masterpiece," which is also known as "The Wonderful One-Hoss Shay." Only the first two stanzas are included here.

The Deacon's Masterpiece

or

The Wonderful One-Hoss Shay

Oliver Wendell Holmes

Have you heard of the wonderful one-hoss shay,
That was built in such a logical way
It ran a hundred years to a day,
And then, of a sudden, it——ah, but stay,
I'll tell you what happened without delay,
Scaring the parson into fits,
Frightening people out of their wits,—
Have you ever heard of that, I say?

Seventeen hundred and fifty-five.
Georgius Secundus was then alive,—
Snuffy old drone from the German hive.
That was the year when Lisbon-town,
And Braddock's army was done so brown,
Left without a scalp to its crown.
It was on the terrible Earthquake-day
That the Deacon finished the one-hoss shay. . . .

This poem, too, is an allegory. Look it up and see if you can detect the institution the poem satirizes.

Synecdoche is a figure of speech through which the poet attempts to identify the whole of something by naming one of its parts. Perhaps the easiest way to identify this figure of speech is to show how we commonly use the same device when we speak of seeing so many "heads" of cattle or we count "noses" or we leave town on "wheels."

Metonymy is akin to synecdoche in that the poet uses one word to suggest another. With metonymy, however, the poet may be working with a problem and its solution, a cause and its effect (or the reverse of these), or a symbol to stand for what it symbolizes. Thus a poet might use "the Crown" to refer to the royal family of England or to the ruling body of the country. He might use "The Eagle" as a reference to the United States, "The Lion" as a reference to England, and "The Bear" as a reference to Russia.

The implication in all of this for you as an interpreter of such literature is that you must be careful to reveal the use of figures of speech in the works you choose to read. This does not mean that you should be able to name them as you confront them in literature, but you should understand why they were used and what they are intended to convey to your audience.

In addition to figures of speech, the content of poetry is marked by beauty and vividness of language. "The best words in the best order." The order of the words in poetry will be discussed later in the chapter, but more should be said about the best words.

Students often shun poetry because they feel it is phony, too artificial, too formal. In reality, poetry is the most vivid, colorful, imaginative type of literature. Many times it would take a page of prose to say what is included in a few words of poetry. Read the following sonnet by Shakespeare and note all the implications it contains. After you have thought about it for a few minutes, ask yourself how many paragraphs of prose it would take to say the same thing with the same implications.

Sonnet 18

William Shakespeare

Shall I compare thee to a summer's day?
Thou art more lovely and more temperate;
Rough winds do shake the darling buds of May,
And summer's lease hath all too short a date;
Sometime too hot the eye of heaven shines,
And often is his gold complexion dimmed;
And every fair from fair sometime declines,
By chance, or nature's changing course untrimmed.

But thy eternal summer shall not fade,
Nor lose possession of that fair thou owest,
Nor shall death brag thou wander'st in his shade
When in eternal lines to time thou growest:
So long as men can breathe, or eyes can see,
So long lives this, and this gives life to thee.

Another example should convince you that beauty, vividness, and concentration of idea into a few words are the chief distinguishing characteristics of the contents of poetry. This second sonnet is an excellent illustration of those characteristics.

Sonnet 73

William Shakespeare

That time of year thou mayst in me behold,
When yellow leaves, or none, or few, do hang
Upon those boughs which shake against the cold,
Bare ruin'd choirs, where late the sweet birds sang.
In me thou see'st the twilight of such day,
As after sunset fadeth in the west,
Which by and by black night dost take away,
Death's second self, that seals up all in rest.
In me thou see'st the glowing of such fire,
That on the ashes of his youth does lie,
As the death-bed whereon it must expire,
Consum'd with that which it was nourish'd by.
    This thou perceiv'st, which makes thy love more strong,
    To love that well, which thou must leave ere long.

THE SHAPE OF POETRY

That poetry exists in many shapes has already been stated. This section of the chapter will identify some of the characteristics of the shape of poetry that are important for the interpreter of literature. There are three general classes into which poetry may be put: narrative, dramatic, and lyric.

Long narrative poems (with a story line) are called epics. *The Iliad, The Odyssey, Beowulf, The Song of Roland,* and *The Aeneid* are all examples of epic poetry. No doubt other examples come to your mind. Alfred Noyes' *The Drake* is an epic poem of our modern time. But a poem needn't be an epic in order to be classed as a narrative poem. Poetry abounds in the narrative form. Robert Frost's "Out, Out," John Keats' "Eve of St. Agnes," Alfred Noyes' "The Highwayman" are all examples; the list could go on and on.

Dramatic poetry is any poetry which utilizes techniques of drama in order to achieve its effects. Much of the drama that Shakespeare wrote is called poetic drama—dialogue written in poetic form. Robert Browning's *Pippa Passes* is an example of a more modern play written in this form. Dramatic poetry is usually marked by dialogue between speakers (perhaps just one speaker and another person who listens), a dramatic situation, and an unfolding of one or more qualities of the speaker or speakers. Robert Frost's "The Death of the Hired Man" is an excellent example of this class of poetry. Walt Whitman's "Come Up From the Fields, Father," is an example of a dramatic ballad.

The third class is called lyric poetry. Its mode is best identified by the fact that it reveals the personal feelings of the poet. It is usually short and always emotional. It, more than any other class of poetry, reveals the mood, the personality, the soul of its author. It is easier to cite authors of lyric poetry here than it is to identify particular poems because there are so many such "thoughts" revealed by poets like Emily Dickinson, Sara Teasdale, Conrad Aiken, A. E. Housman, Percy Bysshe Shelley, John Keats, and Walter de la Mare. Several lyric poems are included to illustrate the mode.

I'm Nobody! Who Are You?

Emily Dickinson

I'm nobody! Who are you?
Are you nobody, too?
Then there's a pair of us—don't tell!
They'd banish us, you know.

How dreary to be somebody!
How public, like a frog
To tell your name the livelong June
To an admiring bog!

My Heart Leaps Up

William Wordsworth

My heart leaps up when I behold
A rainbow in the sky:
So was it when my life began;
So it is now I am a man;
So be it when I shall grow old,
Or let me die!
The Child is father of the Man;
And I could wish my days to be
Bound each to each by natural piety.

To His Coy Mistress

Andrew Marvell

Had we but World enough, and time,
This coyness, Lady, were no crime.
We would sit down, and think which way
To walk, and pass our long Love's Day.
Thou by the Indian Ganges side
Should'st Rubies find: I by the Tide
Of Humber would complain. I would
Love you ten years before the Flood:
And you should if you please refuse
Till the Conversion of the Jews.
My vegetable Love should grow
Vaster than Empires, and more slow.

An hundred years should go to praise
Thine Eyes, and on thy Forehead Gaze.
Two hundred to adore each Breast:
But thirty thousand to the rest.
An Age at least to every part,
And the last Age should show your Heart.
For Lady, you deserve this State,
Nor would I love at lower rate.
  But at my back I always hear
Time's winged Chariot hurrying near:
And yonder all before us lie
Deserts of vast Eternity.
Thy Beauty shall no more be found,
Nor, in thy marble Vault, shall sound
My echoing Song. Then Worms shall try
That long preserv'd Virginity,
And your quaint Honour turn to dust,
And into ashes all my Lust.
The Grave's a fine and private place,
But none, I think, do there embrace.
  Now therefore, while the youthful hue
Sits on thy skin like morning dew,
And while thy willing Soul transpires
At every pore with instant Fires,
Now let us sport us while we may;
And now, like am'rous birds of prey,
Rather at once our Time devour,
Than languish in his slow-chapt pow'r.
Let us roll all our Strength, and all
Our sweetness, up into one Ball,
And tear our Pleasures with rough strife
Through the Iron gates of Life.
Thus, though we cannot make our Sun
Stand still, yet we will make him run.

So much for the classification of poetry. Now for a further look at its shape. Some poets write in verse. Verse is that highly structured form which sets arbitrary limits on line length (meter) and it uses rhyme. Often the rhyming pattern and the metrical system used present problems for the beginning reader. The temptation is to read the poem the way it is written, without considering meaning. The sad result under these conditions is that the meaning is distorted or obscured, and the only element the listener hears is the rhythm. In a sense this situation presents a paradox for the reader of poetry. The only possible answer to the problem is to read poetry with concentration on the meaning; subordinate rhyme and meter to meaning in your reading, and that amount of rhythm that should be apparent, will be. If you read poetry in such a way that the rhyme and meter dominate, meaning is often lost.

A separate look at the two will help. A poem may be written in rhyme. Consider these lines from William Wordsworth's "Daffodils."

> I wandered lonely as a cloud
> That floats on high o'er vales and hills
> When all at once I saw a crowd,
> A host, of golden daffodils.

Did you notice that the final words in the first and third lines rhyme? And that the same is true of the second and fourth lines? The rhyme scheme for the poem is *a b a b*. Here is another example. Note that these lines from Andrew Marvell's "To His Coy Mistress" (the complete poem is included earlier in this chapter) rhyme is an *aa bb* pattern.

> Had we but World enough, and time,
> This coyness, Lady, were no crime.
> We would sit down, and think which way
> To walk, and pass our long Love's Day.

Another kind of rhythm is achieved through three poetic devices called alliteration, assonance, and onomatopoeia. Alliteration is the repetition of the initial letter or sound of words or syllables in a line or in successive lines of poetry. Notice the repetitious use of the "s" sound in these lines by Wordsworth.

A Slumber Did My Spirit Seal

A slumber did my spirit seal;
I had no human fears:
She seemed a thing that could not feel
The touch of earthly years.
No motion has she now, no force;
She neither hears nor sees;
Rolled round in earth's diurnal course,
With rocks, and stones, and trees.

Assonance is a similar device except that it is a repetition of vowel sounds instead of consonants. Such repetition adds to the rhythm inside the lines of poetry. The following sets of words illustrate assonance. The fact that they also rhyme is incidental; rhyme is not a necessary characteristic of assonance.

first sweet sleep of night
vile and violence will suffice
the freedom of sleep
the tolling of the bell rang over the knoll.

The third device which heightens rhythm is *onomatopoeia.* Anytime a poet uses a word which suggests the sound it represents, he is working with onomatopoeia. Thus we read of the

buzz of bees
whirr of wind
drone of flies
hiss of snakes

and so on.
All three of these devices add to the rhythm and beauty of poetry and all three add to the problems of the beginning reader as he tries to concentrate on meaning.

Meter is another element of structure that tends to handicap the beginning reader. Simply, meter is the system (and there are several varieties) of choosing words in lines of poetry which follow a prescribed pattern of stressed and unstressed syllables. A poem will illustrate one such system and point up the inherent problem that meter brings to oral interpretation. The poem tells of an encounter with death—not a happy, light, carefree subject. But the meter, if allowed to dominate the reading of the poem, will make it *seem* light and carefree. A mark like this (◡) indicates that the syllable it appears above is not stressed, while this mark (/) indicates that the syllable is to be stressed.

The Chariot

Emily Dickinson

Because I could not stop for Death—
He kindly stopped for me—
The carriage held but just Ourselves—
And Immortality.

We slowly drove—He knew no haste
And I had put away
My labor and my leisure too,
For His Civility—

We passed the School, where Children strove
At Recess—in the Ring—
We passed the Fields of Gazing Grain—
We passed the Setting Sun—

Or rather—He passed Us—

The Dews drew quivering and chill—

For only Gossamer, my Gown—

My Tippet—only Tulle—

We paused before a House that seemed

A Swelling of the Ground—

The Roof was scarcely visible—

The Cornice—in the Ground—

Since then—'tis Centuries—and yet

Feels shorter than the Day

I first surmised the Horses' Heads

Were toward Eternity—

In this particular poem each unaccented syllable is followed by one which received stress or accent. This pattern of meter (◡ /) is called *iambic;* the reverse (/ ◡), as in the word under, is called *trochaic.* Two other metric patterns deserve mention. The word incorrect illustrates the pattern called *anapestic.* In this pattern two unstressed syllables are followed by one which is stressed (◡◡ /). The reverse of anapestic meter is called *dactylic,* which requires that each stressed syllable be followed by two which are unstressed; the word yesterday illustrates dactylic meter (/◡◡).

Metrical feet, whether they are iambic, trochaic, anapestic, or dactylic, are then combined into lines which are named according to the number of feet they contain. For example, the Dickinson poem is said to be written in *iambic quatrimeter.* This means that there are four iambic feet in each line or in most of the lines of the poem. Actually each line of iambic quatrimeter in the poem is followed by a line of iambic trimeter. But since the first line of the poem contains four iambic-feet and the pattern is repeated in each of the six stanzas of the poem, the poem would be identified as having been written in iambic quatrimeter. It is enough, then, to recognize that one metrical foot per line is called *monometer*, two feet per line of poetry *bimeter*, three feet *trimeter*, four feet *quatrimeter*, five feet *pentameter*, six feet *hexameter*, and so on.

You couldn't help but notice the strong rhythm and meter even when you accented the words (not syllables) that carry meaning in the poem. Another way to concentrate on meaning in reading poetry with such a strong rhyme and meter is to write it out in sentences. Here is the Dickinson poem again written in sentences.

The Chariot

Because I could not stop for Death—He kindly stopped for me—The carriage held but just Ourselves—And Immortality.

We slowly drove—He knew no haste and I had put away my labor and my leisure too, For His Civility—

We passed the School, where Children strove At Recess—in the Ring—We passed the Fields of Gazing Grain—We passed the Setting Sun—Or rather—He passed Us—

The Dews drew quivering and chill—For only Gossamer, my Gown—My Tippet—only Tulle—

We paused before a House that seemed A Swelling of the Ground—The Roof was scarcely visible—The Cornice—in the Ground—

Since then—'tis Centuries—and yet Feels shorter than the Day I first surmised the Horses' Heads Were toward Eternity.—

Reading the poem in this way should have made it easier to concentrate on meaning. You must have noticed that rhythm was still present in your reading. The difference is that the rhyme and meter were not allowed to *dominate* your reading.

Look again at the poem "The Chariot" as Emily Dickinson wrote it. Notice that each group of four lines is set off from the other groups. These are the stanzas of the poem; a stanza might be likened to a paragraph of prose. A definite distinction must be made between the two terms, however. A paragraph (in prose) is generally regarded as a unit of thought. A stanza is a more arbitrary division of lines of poetry into whatever units the poet deems advisable or desirable, usually dictated by rhyme or rhythm.

The smallest stanza is, of course, the *couplet*—two lines of poetry which rhyme, separated from at least two other lines which also rhyme but on a different sound than the first two. The lines that follow were taken from Alexander Pope's "An Essay on Criticism." Note that each set of two lines rhyme. Had he chosen to do so Pope could have set each couplet apart from the others in separate stanzas. Rather, he chose to use stanzas of varying lengths according to the ideas they contain.

From

An Essay on Criticism

Alexander Pope

'Tis hard to say, if greater want of skill
Appear in writing or in judging ill;
But, of the two, less dangerous is the offense
To tire our patience, than mislead our sense.
Some few in that, but numbers err in this,
Ten censure wrong for one who writes amiss;
A fool might once himself alone expose,
Now one in verse makes many more in prose.

Stanzas three lines long are called *tercets;* those four lines long *quatrains.* And so on.

There is a great deal of material concerning the structure of poetry that has been left unsaid in this chapter. There are many books written on the subject and there are courses in college devoted to building the skill of understanding and appreciating poetry. It is the feeling of your authors, however, that the information presented here is essential to the effective oral reading of poetry. More information on the structure of poetry would add confusion rather than clarity.

Students often ask whether or not they can read their own material. Our answer is *Yes, by all means!* But use care in selecting poems from the material you have written. Be certain that they fit your audience. If you have your instructor's permission and you have chosen the poetry with your particular audience in mind, go ahead and try it on them. The final test of poetry and verse is whether or not it communicates with those who read and listen to it. Your audience will tell you quickly how successful you are both as poet and reader.

The chief problem in reading your own material is that you will, perhaps, get carried away with your writing skill and not concentrate on reading skill. Some of our greatest poets fail when they read their own materials for this very reason.

The poems that follow are excellent for oral interpretation. Their imagery is clear and vivid; their meaning is heightened through oral reading. They were written when Ester Lee was a college student. She has read them on many occasions before varied audiences, and they have always met with enthusiastic approval.

Oh of Little Worth to Dream

Ester Lee

Oh of little worth to dream!
To muse in muted, vignetted projection;
Linger in obtrusive reality.
Remain only on the brink,
Hesitating to step for fear it is
But a cloud upon which you creep.

You merely play where fairies play,
Bend and sway with the breezes,
Sing and Laugh with the sunbeams,
Dance and cry with the raindrops,
And just stand by as life teases.
Oh of little worth to dream!

Wake Me Each Morning

Ester Lee

Wake me
    each morning
With your
    smiling face
All
    sadness
      and sorrow
    of yesterday erased.
Let life and joy
Through my veins
Run with rapture
As I gaze upon you
And my journey renew.
Walk with me hand in hand
Through
      the
        day
And though we're parted
Let me feel your hand clasping mine
    Pulling
        when I slacken
    Tightening
        when I weaken
Caressing when I obey.
Carry me
    into the night;
Tuck me in
    in sweet surrender,
Knowing no fear
Of
  the
    night
Because of your light;
Blanket me with your arms

And then
  gladly
    I bid the day
 DEPART!

SUMMARY

Poetry is characterized by content which is concentrated and imaginative; it is nearly always emotional.

There are three general classifications of poetry: narrative, dramatic, and lyric. Poetry is condensed through the employment of figures of speech, which include metaphor and simile. An extended metaphor is an allegory, a poem which may be read on two or more levels of meaning. Other important figures of speech are *personification, metonymy,* and *synecdoche.*

The shape of poetry is determined at times by the poet's use of rhyme and meter. The four major metrical patterns are *iambic, trochaic, anapestic,* and *dactylic.* Metrical feet are combined into lines named according to the number of feet they contain. *Assonance, alliteration,* and *onomatopoeia* are devices of internal rhythm in poetry.

Rhyme and meter are characteristics of much poetry which present a special problem to the beginning reader, but it is a problem which can be overcome by concentrating on the meaning of the poem.

Don't be afraid to read your own poetry to your audiences so long as it meets the criteria of effective oral interpretation.

ADDITIONAL POETRY FOR PRACTICE AND STUDY

Jazz Fantasia

Carl Sandburg

Drum on your drums, batter on your banjos, sob on the long, cool winding saxophones. Go to it, O jazzmen.

Sling your knuckles on the bottoms of the happy tin pans, let your trombones ooze, and go husha-husha-hush with the slippery sand-paper.

Moan like an autumn wind high in the lonesome treetops, moan soft like you wanted somebody terrible, cry like a racing car slipping away from a motorcycle cop, bang-bang! you jazzmen, bang altogether drums, traps, banjoes, horns, tin cans—make two people fight on the top of a stairway and scratch each other's eyes in a clinch tumbling down the stairs.

Can the rough stuff . . . now a Mississippi steamboat pushes up the night river with a hoo-hoo-hoo-oo . . . and the green lanterns calling to the high soft stars . . . a red moon rides on the humps of the low river hills . . . go to it, O jazzmen.

My Sabbath

Emily Dickinson

Some keep the Sabbath going to church—
I keep it staying at home—
With a bobolink for a chorister—
And an orchard, for a dome—

Some keep the Sabbath in surplice—
I just wear my wings—
And instead of tolling the bell, for church,
Our little sexton—sings.

God preaches, a noted clergyman—
And the sermon is never long,
So instead of going to Heaven at last—
I'm going, all along.

The Passionate Shepherd to His Love

Christopher Marlowe

Come live with me, and be my love,
And we will all the pleasures prove
That valleys, groves, hills and fields,
Woods, or steepy mountain yields.

And we will sit upon the rocks,
Seeing the shepherds feed their flocks,
By shallow rivers, to whose falls
Melodious birds sing madrigals.

And I will make thee beds of roses,
And a thousand fragrant posies,
A cap of flowers, and a kirtle,
Embroider'd all with leaves of myrtle;
A gown made of the finest wool,
Which from our pretty lambs we pull,
Fair-lined slippers for the cold,
With buckles of the purest gold;

A belt of straw, and ivy-buds,
With coral clasps and amber studs;
And if these pleasures may thee move,
Come live with me, and be my love.

The shepherd-swains shall dance and sing
For thy delight each May morning;
If these delights thy mind may move,
Then live with me and be my love.

Freedom

Langston Hughes

Freedom will not come
Today, this year
  Nor ever

Through compromise and fear.

I have as much right
As the other fellow has
   To stand
On my two feet
And own the land.

I tire so of hearing people say,
Let things take their course.
Tomorrow is another day.
I do not need my freedom when I'm dead.
I cannot live on tomorrow's bread.
   Freedom
   Is a strong seed
   Planted
   In a great need.
   I live here, too.
   I want freedom
   Just as you.

Sonnet 29

William Shakespeare

When in disgrace with fortune and men's eyes,
I all alone beweep my outcast state,
And trouble deaf heaven with my bootless cries,
And look upon myself and curse my fate,
Wishing me like to one more rich in hope,
Featur'd like him, like him with friends possess'd,
Desiring this man's art, and that man's scope,
With what I most enjoy contented least,
Yet in these thoughts myself almost despising,
Haply I think on thee, and then my state,
Like to the lark at break of day arising,
From sullen earth sings hymns at heaven's gate,
For thy sweet love rememb'red such wealth brings,
That then I scorn to change my state with kings.

A Coney Island of the Mind

Lawrence Ferlinghetti

15

Constantly risking absurdity
                    and death
          whenever he performs
                    above the heads
                              of his audience

the poet like an acrobat
                    climbs on rime
                              to a high wire of his own making
and balancing on eyebeams
                    above a sea of faces
          paces his way
                    to the other side of day
     performing entrechats
                    and sleight-of-foot tricks
and other high theatrics
                    and all without mistaking
          anything
                    for what it may not be
     For he's the super realist
                    who must perforce perceive
          taut truth
                    before the taking of each stance or step
in his supposed advance
                    toward that still higher perch
where Beauty stands and waits
                    with gravity
                              to start her death-defying leap

And he
          a little charleychaplin man
                    who may or may not catch
          her fair eternal form
                    spreadeagled in the empty air
          of existence

Song

John Donne

Go and catch a falling star,
Get with child a mandrake root,
Tell me where all past years are,
Or who cleft the Devil's foot,
Teach me to hear mermaids singing,
Or to keep off envy's stinging,
    And find
    What wind
Serves to advance an honest mind.

If thou be'st born to strange sights,
Things invisible to see,
Ride ten thousand days and nights,
Till age snow white hairs on thee,
Thou, when thou return'st wilt tell me
All strange wonders that befell thee,
    And swear
    No where
Lives a woman true, and fair.

If thou find'st one, let me know,
Such a pilgrimage were sweet;
Ye do not, I would not go,
Though at next door we might meet;
Though she were true, when you met her,
And last till you write your letter,
    Yet she
    Will be
False, ere I come, to two, or three.

The Collar

George Herbert

I struck the board, and cried, "No more.
    I will abroad.
What? shall I ever sigh and pine?

My lines and life are free, free as the road,
Loose as the wind, as large as store.
Shall I be still in suit?
Have I no harvest but a thorn
To let me blood, and not restore
What I have lost with cordial fruit?
Sure there was wine
Before my sighs did dry it: there was corn
Before my tears did drown it.
Is the year only lost to me?
Have I no bays to crown it?
No flowers, no garlands gay? all blasted?
   All wasted?
Not so, my heart; but there is fruit,
And thou hast hands
Recover all thy sigh-blown age
On double pleasures; leavy thy cold dispute
Of what is fit and not. Forsake thy cage,
Thy rope of sands,
Which petty thoughts have made, and made to thee
Good cable, to enforce and draw,
And be thy law,
While thou didst wink and wouldst not see.
Away; take heed:
I will abroad.
Call in thy death's-head there, tie up thy fears.
He that forbears
To suit and serve his need,
   Deserves his load."
But as I rav'd and grew more fierce and wild
At every word,
Methought I heard one calling, Child!
And I replied, My Lord.

Loneliness

Loyal Shegonee

The deafening tic-tic-tic of the clock,
The thunder of my own thoughts rumble 'round

The dark room crowding its silence in upon me.
Where are my friends? What is there to do?
The slow steady pounding of my lonesome heart,
The never-ending thump-thump-thump of my pulse
Against a wet pillow, the only living sounds to listen to!
Visions drift slowly past my eyes . . .
Visions of scarred, contorted trees standing in barren,
    desolate fields . . .
Visions of solitary children standing in deserted alleys
With tears washing clean rivulets down their dirty faces . . .
Visions of old men, old women, dying with hopelessness
And agony twisted into their aged masks of death . . .
Visions of neglected tombstones crumbling by
Abandoned churches . . . Oh God!
Where are my friends?
Someone, please come and talk to me!

Man's Pride

F. Ricardo Gomez

Long days of loneliness, and plight
Stinking brown sweat filtering through a mass of
uncut hair:
Entering sheepishly into the corners of my red,
sun-swollen eyes

Enduring the burning, itching sensations so as not
to break my rhythm nor my stride
Unable to break the hypnotic spell
Developed to black-out the boiling sun, and forget
the years of stooping—
Like a loyal hound, instinctively my rough,
calloused hands,
search for #1's amidst a field of ripened pumpkins.
I hear growers convincing each other as I near the
tractor

These people want no other kind of work
They were born to wander, to live and die happily

wrestling fruits from stems and vines—
Reacting invisibly to the outsiders in camp—
Wondering why and what they offered in exchange
to photograph our lives—
Others talk of escaping our chains of coolie wages—
Through a strike—
Listening at first, because I know I wear trousers
that once belonged to one of them—
I see my son in winter clothes in July—
I try to understand their talk of opportunities
Although none had ever come—
Except to some—   Crew leaders—
My fear is soon replaced by rage;
As I see others like myself long denied the right to
live
Like other human beings—
So often are trapped by accepting
superficial contracts
And grower advice—
I join in a Huelga—

I am still stooping and sweating in the sun
But now I have pride
I am now paid as a man
Gone are the days of the timid, trained hound
My child will not understand

Face of Poverty

Lucy Smith

No one can communicate to you
The substance of poverty—
Can tell you either the shape,
        or the depth,
                or the breadth
Of poverty—
Until you have lived with her intimately.

No one can guide your fingers
Over the rims of her eye sockets,
Over her hollow cheeks—
Until perhaps one day
In your wife's once pretty face
You see the lines of poverty;
Until you feel
In her now skinny body,
The protruding bones,
The barely covered ribs,
The shrunken breasts of poverty,

Poverty can be a stranger
In a far-off land:
An alien face
Briefly glimpsed in a newsreel,
An empty rice bowl
In a skinny brown hand,
Until one bleak day
You look out the window—
And poverty is the squatter
In your own backyard.

Poverty wails in the night for milk,
Not knowing the price of a quart.
It is desperation in your teen-ager's face,
Wanting a new evening gown for the junior prom,
After going through school in rummage store clothes.
It is a glass of forgetfulness sold over the bar.
And poverty's voice is a jeer in the night—
    "You may bring another child
    Into the rat race that is your life;
    You may cut down on food
    To buy contraceptives;
    You may see your wife walk alone
    Down some back alley route
    To a reluctant appointment
    With an unsterile knife—
    Or you may sleep alone."

And one morning shaving
You look in the mirror—
And never again will poverty be alien,
For the face of poverty is not over your shoulder,
The face of poverty is your own.
And hearing the break in your wife's voice
At the end of a bedtime story,
You realize that somewhere along the way
The stock ending in your own story went wrong.
And now you no longer ask
That you and your wife
Will live happily ever after—
But simply that you
And your wife
And your children
Will live.

Where is the romantic life?

Le Roi Jones

There's cold slush in the streets, two letters
from simple minded white "theatregoers," on the desk,
Little Anthony on his plastic side, waiting for his play,
Miles of work, and music stumbling beside me. I want any-
    thing
you got, having nothing, myself, I want what I want, what I
    think
I want
I want
what you have, having nothing, myself,
I want
what you are, being nothing, myself,
I want always to be
where I am, and feel
good about it. Some
nerve.

Harlem

Langston Hughes

Here on the edge of hell
Stands Harlem—
Remembering the old lies,
The old kicks in the back,
The old "Be patient"
They told us before.

Sure, we remember.
Now when the man at the corner store
Says sugar's gone up another two cents,
And bread one,
And there's a new tax on cigarettes—
We remember the job we never had,
Never could get,
And can't have now
Because we're colored.

So we stand here
On the edge of hell
In Harlem
And look out on the world
And wonder
What we're gonna do
In the face of what
We remember.

Freedom's Plow

Langston Hughes

When a man starts out with nothing,
When a man starts out with his hands
Empty, but clean,

When a man starts out to build a world,
He starts first with himself
And the faith that is in his heart—
The strength there,
The will there to build.

First in the heart is the dream.
Then the mind starts seeking a way.
His eyes look out on the world,
On the great wooded world,
On the rich soil of the world,
On the rivers of the world.

The eyes see there materials for building,
See the difficulties, too, and the obstacles.
The hand seeks tools to cut the wood,
To till the soil, and harness the power of the waters.
Then the hand seeks other hands to help,
A community of hands to help—
Thus the dream becomes not one man's dream alone,
But a community dream.
Not my dream alone, but *our* dream.
Not my world alone,
But *your world and my world,*
Belonging to all the hands who build.

A long time ago, but not too long ago,
Ships came from across the sea
Bringing Pilgrims and prayer-makers,
Adventurers and booty seekers,
Free men and indentured servants,
Slave men and slave masters, all new—
To a new world, America!

With billowing sails the galleons came
Bringing men and dreams, women and dreams.
In little bands together,
Heart reaching out to heart,
Hand reaching out to hand,
They began to build our land.
Some were free hands
Seeking a greater freedom,

Some were indentured hands
Hoping to find their freedom,
Some were slave hands
Guarding in their hearts the seed of freedom.
But the word was there always:
      FREEDOM.

Down into the earth went the plow
In the free hands and the slave hands,
In indentured hands and adventurous hands,
Turning the rich soil went the plow in many hands
That planted and harvested the food that fed
And the cotton that clothed America.
Clang against the trees went the ax in many hands
That hewed and shaped the rooftops of America.
Splash into the rivers and seas went the boat-hulls
That moved and transported America.
Crack went the whips that drove the horses
Across the plains of America.
Free hands and slave hands,
Indentured hands, adventurous hands,
White hands and black hands
Held the plow handles,
Ax handles, hammer handles,
Launched the boats and whipped the horses
That fed and housed and moved America.
Thus together through labor,
All these hands made America.
Labor! Out of labor came the villages
And the towns that grew to cities.
Labor! Out of labor came the rowboats
And the sailboats and the steamboats,
Came the wagons, stage coaches,
Out of labor came the factories,
Came the foundries, came the railroads,
Came the marts and markets, shops and stores,
Came the mighty products moulded, manufactured,
Sold in shops, piled in warehouses,
Shipped the wide world over;
Out of labor—white hands and black hands—

Came the dream, the strength, the will,
And the way to build America.
Now it is Me here, and You there.
Now it's Manhattan, Chicago,
Seattle, New Orleans,
Boston and El Paso—
Now it is the U.S.A.

A long time ago, but not too long ago, a man said:

ALL MEN ARE CREATED EQUAL . . .
ENDOWED BY THEIR CREATOR
WITH CERTAIN INALIENABLE
    RIGHTS . . .
AMONG THESE LIFE, LIBERTY
AND THE PURSUIT OF HAPPINESS.

His name was Jefferson. There were slaves then ,
But in their hearts the slaves believed him, too,
And silently took for granted
That what he said was also meant for them.
It was a long time ago,
But not so long ago at that, Lincoln said:

NO MAN IS GOOD ENOUGH
TO GOVERN ANOTHER MAN
WITHOUT THAT OTHER'S CONSENT.

There were slaves then, too,
But in their hearts the slaves knew
What he said must be meant for every human being—
Else it had no meaning for anyone.
Then a man said:

BETTER TO DIE FREE,
THAN TO LIVE SLAVES.

He was a colored man who had been a slave
But had run away to freedom.
And the slaves knew
What Frederick Douglass said was true.
With John Brown at Harpers Ferry, Negroes died .
John Brown was hung.

Before the Civil War, days were dark,
And nobody knew for sure
When freedom would triumph.
"Or if it would," thought some.
But others knew it had to triumph.
In those dark days of slavery,
Guarding in their hearts the seed of freedom,
The slaves made up a song:

KEEP YOUR HAND ON THE PLOW!
HOLD ON!

That song meant just what it said: *Hold on!*
Freedom will come!

KEEP YOUR HAND ON THE PLOW!
HOLD ON!

Out of war, it came, bloody and terrible!
But it came!
Some there were, as always,
Who doubted that the war would end right,
That the slaves would be free,
Or that the union would stand.
But now we know how it all came out.
Out of the darkest days for a people and a nation,
We know now how it came out.
There was light when the battle clouds rolled away.
There was a great wooded land,
And men united as a nation.

America is a dream.
The poet says it was promises.
The people say it *is* promises—that will come true.
The people do not always say things out loud,
Nor write them down on paper.
The people often hold
Great thoughts in their deepest hearts
And sometimes only blunderingly express them,
Haltingly and stumbling say them,
And faultily put them into practice.
The people do not always understand each other.

But there is, somewhere there,
Always the *trying* to understand,
And the *trying* to say,
"You are a man. Together we are building our land."

America!
Land created in common,
Dream nourished in common,
Keep your hand on the plow! Hold on!
If the house is not yet finished,
Don't be discouraged, builder!
If the fight is not yet won,
Don't be weary, soldier!
The plan and the pattern is here,
Woven from the beginning
Into the warp and woof of America:

ALL MEN ARE CREATED EQUAL.

NO MAN IS GOOD ENOUGH
TO GOVERN ANOTHER MAN WITHOUT
THAT OTHER'S CONSENT.

BETTER DIE FREE,
THAN LIVE SLAVES.

Who said those things? Americans!
Who owns those words? America!
Who is America? You, me!
We are America!
To the enemy who would conquer us from without,
We say, NO!
To the enemy who would divide
and conquer us from within,
We say, NO!

FREEDOM!
BROTHERHOOD!
DEMOCRACY!

To all the enemies of these great words:
We say, NO!

A long time ago,
An enslaved people heading toward freedom
Made up a song:
    Keep Your Hand On The Plow! Hold On!
That plow plowed a new furrow
Across the field of history.
Into that furrow the freedom seed was dropped.
From that seed a tree grew, is growing, will ever grow.
That tree is for everybody,
For all America, for all the world.
May its branches spread and its shelter grow
Until all races and all peoples know its shade.

    KEEP YOUR HAND ON THE PLOW!
    HOLD ON!

chapter fourteen

How do I read
children's literature

The limitless possibilities for the interpreter in the area of children's literature are often overlooked—or relegated to a secondary position. In reality, the interpreter would do well to begin his study of oral interpretation by reading the fables, legends, fairy tales, nursery rhymes, adventure stories, animal stories, plays, or biographies that make up this vast literature.

Perhaps in no other branch of literature does the material involve such "getting out of oneself" as does children's literature. Many teachers have found that beginning a course in oral interpretation with the reading of a selection such as "Billy Goats Gruff" can do much to teach bodily and emotional involvement. In fact, the authors have used that story as an initial tension-reliever and as a first lesson in expressing emotion. Since the students realize that such a story, designed for children, calls for exaggerated characterization to make the goats and the troll vivid and real, it is comparatively easy for them to forget themselves and have fun with the characters. The results of such a practice session are an immediate recognition of the need for emotional involvement in interpretation and an easing of tensions as students realize that they can make literature live through oral reading.

Reading for children requires consideration of both the sensory appeals and the qualities in the literature designed to reach that appeal. Children like repetition of sounds; they like rhymes and it makes no difference whether or not the rhymes make sense; they like animals with human traits; they like suspense and humor and stories filled with dialogue; they like enthusiasm in the reader and bodily movement and facial expressions, plus noticeable varieties in volume and pacing.

You must be careful to observe all the above aspects of reading children's literature and to make each one impressive. If you are going to read to an audience of children, you will read at a somewhat slower pace to make certain they catch every new development, every new thought. And you will work to read any moments of suspense in the story with a good deal of dramatic involvement. In short, you will exaggerate the literary qualities to achieve the necessary response from a child. But at the same time, you must not produce an aura of superiority and talk down to your audience. Your focus is on them and the material.

If you were to read the same literature to an adult, however, you would not indulge in such exaggeration. The material would probably be read in a more sophisticated manner with only a suggestion of the characterization and suspense; it would be approached with the attitudes of the adult rather than with the heart and mind of the child. For an audience comprised of adults and children, on the other hand, you would do well to center your attention on the children's likes and interests. In doing so you might even succeed in transporting the adults back to their childhood days.

NURSERY RHYMES

The nursery rhymes are a good example. Many of the nursery rhymes are favorites of the children. It doesn't matter at all that they do not make sense in a modern setting. Let us look at "Sing a Song of Sixpence." To a child, the fact that there is no relationship between pie and rye does not matter. And he does not question how blackbirds baked in a pie can be alive and singing when the pie is opened. All that counts is his fondness for the rhyme pattern and his own visualization of the theme. Read the selection to children with that in mind—with an emphasis on the rhyme. However, if you were to read it to an adult audience, you would have to consider the historical setting for the writing of this rhyme. "Sing A Song Of Sixpence" was a political satire of the time. The king referred to is King Henry VIII of England. The queen is his wife, Catherine of Spain. The maid is Anne Boleyn, handmaiden of Catherine and mistress of Henry. The blackbirds are the dark whispers about the indiscretions of the king. Specifically, the rhyme refers to the moves Henry made to divorce his wife so he could marry Anne Boleyn. The rhyme takes on an entirely different meaning in this context, but it is a context that would have no meaning to a child.

The same is true of "Georgie Porgie, pudding and pie—." This rhyme makes little or no sense if it is analyzed for what it says, but children do not care. They love to hear the rhyme pattern. To an adult, however, it takes on meaning when one considers that this too was a satire. Georgie Porgie was King George I of England. He was a lazy, indolent man who was lowly even in his sensual pleasures. The nursery rhyme is a biting satire on his inadequacies as a King and as a person.

Children also like a repetition in names given to animals in stories. A good example of this is Henny-Penny. The repetition of the sounds in the first syllables of the name are important to the children in your audience. This device is carried out further in the story with Cocky-Locky, Goosey-Loosey, Turkey-Lurkey, Foxy-Loxy.

Repetition is also a feature in the rhymes "The Crooked Man" and "The Five Little Pigs."

> There was a crooked man,
> Who walked a crooked mile;
> He found a crooked sixpence
> Against a crooked stile;
> He bought a crooked cat,
> Which caught a crooked mouse,
> And they all lived together
> In a little crooked house.

> This little pig went to market
> This little pig stayed home,
> This little pig had roast beef,
> This little pig had none
> This little pig cried "Wee, wee, wee"
> All the way home.

The love of repetition of sound or idea is carried out further in "The Little Red Hen." The little hen asks, in each sequence, the dog, the cat, the pig, and the turkey to help her plant the wheat, cut it, thresh it, grind it, and bake the flour. In each case, the animals answer "I won't."

> "I won't," said the dog.
> "I won't," said the cat.
> "I won't," said the pig.
> "I won't," said the turkey.

And in each case, the hen answers, "I will, then," and adds, "Cluck, cluck." Then when it is time to eat the bread, the hen asks them who will eat the bread. Each says, "I will," but this time the hen says, "No, I will . . . Cluck, cluck."

The Fable

The repetition in dialogue in this story serves to emphasize the ambition of hen and the laziness of the others. The fable also teaches a lesson, illustrates a moral value.

Perhaps in no other form of children's literature is the moral element so heavily involved as in Aesop's *Fables*.

"Belling the Cat" is a good example.

One day the mice held a general council to consider what they might do to protect themselves against their common enemy, the Cat. Some said one thing and some said another, but at last a young mouse stood up and announced that he had a plan which he thought would solve the problem.

"You will all agree," said he, "that our chief danger lies in the unexpected and sly manner in which our enemy comes upon us. Now, if we could receive some warning of her approach, we could easily hide from her. I propose, therefore, that a small bell be obtained and attached by a ribbon to the neck of the Cat. In this way we could always know when she was coming and be able to make our escape."

This proposal was met with great applause, until an old mouse arose and said, "This is all very fine, but who among us is so brave? Who will bell the Cat?" The mice looked at one another in silence and nobody volunteered. Moral: It is easier to suggest a plan than to carry it out.

In the reading of such fables, the interpreter must make the problem very clear to the children; he must characterize the "young" and the "old" mouse in particular.

James Thurber satirizes many of the fables and stories in children's literature, thereby using these tales for the more sophisticated tastes of the adult. The incorporation of Thurber's versions will be good in a program for an audience composed of children and adults. His version of "Little Red Riding Hood," called "The Little Girl and the Wolf," is an example, as is "Unicorn in the Garden." He pokes great fun at the stories and then at the end makes his central point with a satirical version of the moral lesson. In "The Little Girl and the Wolf," his moral is: "It's not as easy to fool little girls nowadays as it used to be," and in "Unicorn in the Garden," it is: "Don't count your boobies until they're hatched."

One of the more effective moral lessons—although it is not heavily labored but is rather subtly implied—is found in A. A. Milne's story of Pooh Bear's visit to Rabbit from *Winnie the Pooh*. Gluttony is the theme. Yet, while Milne has a moral, he is actually far more concerned with the characterization of Pooh and of Rabbit and with the story itself than with preaching a lesson. In fact, all of the stories from *Winnie the Pooh* emphasize the characters. With Milne, of course, dialogue is a key element, as is humor. We can see this in a section from the story:

. . . Well, he was humming this hum to himself, and walking along gaily, wondering what everybody else was doing, and what it felt like, being somebody else, when suddenly he came to a sandy bank, and in the bank was a large hole.

"Aha!" said Pooh. (*Rum-tum-tiddle-um-tum.*) "If I know anything about anything, that hole means Rabbit," he said, "and Rabbit means Company," he said, "and Company means Food and Listening-to-Me-Humming and such like. *Rum-tum-tum-tiddle-um.*"

So he bent down, put his head into the hole, and called out:

"Is anybody at home?"

There was a sudden scuffling noise from inside the hole, and then silence.

"What I said was, 'Is anybody at home?'" called out Pooh very loudly.

"No!" said a voice; and then added, "You needn't shout so loud. I heard you quite well the first time."

"Bother!" said Pooh. "Isn't there anybody here at all?"

"Nobody."

Winnie-the-Pooh took his head out of the hole, and thought for a little, and he thought to himself, "There must be somebody there, because somebody must have said 'Nobody!' "

Rabbit and Pooh become quite unique characters, and when an interpreter reads this story, "Pooh Goes Visiting," he must make certain that both Pooh and Rabbit are carefully characterized and that, unlike many children's stories, the dialogue is not merely a device but an integral part of the characterization.

The interpreter must also remember that these stories, like the poems from *When We Were Very Young,* were written by Milne for his son, Christopher Robin, who is the main character in all the Pooh books. These were told over and over to Christopher when he was a young boy. Few authors have been able so successfully to enter into the child's world of fantasy as Milne in his poems, "Corner of the Street," "Lines and Squares," and "Halfway Down."

Milne used rhyme patterns in his poetry to heighten the child's involvement and to make the poems memorable. So conscious was he of rhyme in his poem "The Three Foxes" that he made up words purely for the sake of rhyming, and we get "sockses" to rhyme with foxes.

The interpreter must emphasize those words made up for rhyme purposes, but he must also make the experiences of the three foxes seem very delightful.

One of the most effective of all of Milne's works for the interpreter is "Vespers," the lovely prayer of Christopher Robin. This poem could be read for an adult and a child in just about the same way because what it says has meaning for both.

REPETITION AS LEARNING

The Dr. Seuss books have been extremely popular in the realm of children's literature because, through the use of repetition and vivid illustrations, children are taught, among other things, how to distinguish colors and read the alphabet while they are being entertained.

The unique role here for the interpreter is to make the characters very definitive.

In *The Cat in the Hat Comes Back*, Seuss helps a child to learn the alphabet with the characters of Little Cats, A, B, C, D, E, F, G, etc. Each cat has a purpose in the story. To further emphasize the alphabet, Seuss often uses it backwards as "Take your Little Cats, G, F, E, D, C, B, A." Reading the story aloud would emphasize the use of the alphabet which is the real reason for the story.

Seuss' books have also been popular because of his unusual characters. The Cat in the Hat is by himself unique, as are the little cats. Equally distinctive are such machines as the car with all kinds of arms to clean up the house. These symbols intrigue a child who loves to be a part of the world of fantasy. The unreal is very real to him and a reader must keep that in mind.

GOOD AND EVIL

Children's literature, particularly fairy tales, is also concerned with good and evil, with the very good and the very bad. Children love to be scared by such things as witches and bad animals like the fox and the wolf. The fox, for instance, appears in the fable of Henny-Penny and is the big badman of the Uncle Remus stories, which are excellent choices for the interpreter of children's literature because of the challenging characterizations they offer; Uncle Remus, the little boy, the rabbit, the fox, and the others. To read these stories effectively you must emphasize the suspenseful moments when Br'er Rabbit seems to be in great danger at the hands of Br'er Fox and then at the last minute manages to escape. The climax occurs when Br'er Fox is foiled—again. Br'er Rabbit is sly and clever, and Br'er Fox is first the villainous schemer and then frustrated and angry when he is defeated once more. You must present Uncle Remus as the kindly, enthusiastic old man, and read the dialogue as the author intended and wrote—in dialect.

Witches and giants are also popular villains. The witch in "Hansel and Grethel" and in *Wizard of Oz* are graphic examples of the kind of evil that pervades most children's stories. The witches must be made very vivid and very real for children if they are to share in the suspense. In the same way, characters like Dorothy and Hansel and Grethel must be read with sensitivity. Both these stories contain a good deal of suspense, and the interpreter should read them so that the heroes and heroines appear to be in very real danger.

Read "Hansel and Grethel" and give all the vividness you can to your interpretation. Bring each of the characters to life. You might wish to "cut" the story for practice before you read it orally.

Hansel And Grethel

The Brothers Grimm

Near a great forest there lived a poor woodcutter and his wife, and his two children; the boy's name was Hansel and the girl's Grethel. They had very little to bite or to sup, and once, when there was great dearth in the land, the man could not even gain the daily bread. As he lay in bed one night thinking of this, and turning and tossing, he sighed heavily, and said to his wife,

"What will become of us? We cannot even feed our children; there is nothing left for ourselves."

"I will tell you what, husband," answered the wife; "we will take the children early in the morning into the forest, where it is thickest; we will make them a fire, and we will give each of them a piece of bread, then we will go to our work and leave them alone; they will never find the way home again, and we shall be quit of them."

"No, wife," said the man, "I cannot do that; I cannot find in my heart to take my children into the forest and to leave them there alone; the wild animals would soon come and devour them."

"O you fool," said she, "then we will all four starve; you had better get the coffins ready,"—and she left him no peace until he consented.

"But I really pity the poor children," said the man.

The two children had not been able to sleep for hunger, and had heard what their step-mother had said to their father. Grethel wept bitterly, and said to Hansel, "It is all over with us."

"Do be quiet, Grethel," said Hansel, "and do not fret; I will manage something." And when the parents had gone to sleep he got up, put on his little coat, opened the backdoor, and slipped out. The moon was shining brightly, and the white flints that lay in front of the house glistened like pieces of silver. Hansel stooped and filled the little pocket of his coat as full as it would hold. Then he went back again, and said to Grethel,

"Be easy, dear little sister, and go to sleep quietly; God will not forsake us," and laid himself down again in his bed.

When the day was breaking, and before the sun had risen, the wife came and awakened the two children, saying,

"Get up, you lazy bones; we are going into the forest to cut wood."

Then she gave each of them a piece of bread, and said,

"That is for dinner, and you must not eat it before then, for you will get no more."

Grethel carried the bread under her apron, for Hansel had his pocket full of the flints. Then they set off all together on their way to the forest. When they had gone a little way Hansel stood still and looked back towards the house, and this he did again and again, till his father said to him,

"Hansel, what are you looking at? take care not to forget your legs."

"O father," said Hansel, "I am looking at my little white kitten, who is sitting up on the roof to bid me good-bye."

"You young fool," said the woman, "that is not your kitten, but the sunshine on the chimney pot."

Of course Hansel had not been looking at his kitten, but had been taking every now and then a flint from his pocket and dropping it on the road.

When they reached the middle of the forest the father told the children to collect wood to make a fire to keep them warm; and Hansel and Grethel gathered brushwood enough for a little mountain; and it was set on fire, and when the flame was burning quite high the wife said,

"Now lie down by the fire and rest yourselves, you children, and we will go and cut wood; and when we are ready we will come and fetch you."

So Hansel and Grethel sat by the fire, and at noon they each ate their pieces of bread. They thought their father was in the wood all the time, as they seemed to hear the strokes of the axe; but really it was only a dry branch hanging to a withered tree that the wind moved to and fro. So when they had stayed there a long time their eyelids closed with weariness, and they fell fast asleep. When at last they awoke it was night, and Grethel began to cry, and said.

"How shall we ever get out of this wood?" But Hansel comforted her, saying,

"Wait a little while longer, until the moon rises, and then we can easily find the way home."

And when the full moon got up Hansel took his little sister by the hand, and followed the way where the flint stones shone like silver, and showed them the road. They walked on the whole night through, and at the break of day they came to their father's house. They knocked at the door, and when the wife opened it and saw that it was Hansel and Grethel she said,

"You naughty children, why did you sleep so long in the wood? We thought you were never coming home again!"

But the father was glad, for it had gone to his heart to leave them both in the woods alone.

Not very long after that there was again great scarcity in those parts, and the children heard their mother say at night in bed to their father,

"Everything is finished up; we have only half a loaf, and after that the tale comes to an end. The children must be off; we will take them farther into the wood this time, so that they shall not be able to find the way back again; there is no other way to manage."

The man felt sad at heart, and he thought,

"It would be better to share one's last morsel with one's children."

But the wife would listen to nothing that he said, but scolded and reproached him. He who says A must say B too, and when a man has given in once he has to do it a second time.

But the children were not asleep, and had heard all the talk. When the parents had gone to sleep Hansel got up to go out and get more flint stones, as he did before, but the wife had locked the door, and Hansel could not get out; but he comforted his little sister, and said,

"Don't cry, Grethel, and go to sleep quietly, and God will help us."

Early the next morning the wife came and pulled the children out of bed. She gave them each a little piece of bread—less than before; and on the way to the wood Hansel crumbled the bread in his pocket, and often stopped to throw a crumb on the ground.

"Hansel, what are you stopping behind and staring for?" said the father.

"I am looking at my little pigeon sitting on the roof, to say good-bye to me," answered Hansel.

"You fool," said the wife, "that is no pigeon, but the morning sun shining on the chimney pots."

Hansel went on as before, and strewed bread crumbs all along the road.

The woman led the children far into the wood, where they had never been before in all their lives. And again there was a large fire made, and the mother said,

"Sit still there, you children, and when you are tired you can go to sleep; we are going into the forest to cut wood, and in the evening, when we are ready to go home we will come and fetch you."

So when noon came Grethel shared her bread with Hansel, who had strewed his along the road. Then they went to sleep, and the evening passed, and no one came for the poor children. When they awoke it was dark night, and Hansel comforted his little sister, and said,

"Wait a little Grethel, until the moon gets up, then we shall be able to see our way home by the crumbs of bread that I have scattered along it."

So when the moon rose they got up, but they could find no crumbs of bread, for the birds of the woods and of the fields had come and picked them up. Hansel thought they might find the way all the same, but they could not. They went on all that night, and the next day from the morning until the evening, but they could not find the way out of the wood, and they were very hungry, for they had nothing to eat but the few berries they could pick up. And when they were so tired that they could no longer drag themselves along, they lay down under a tree and fell asleep.

It was now the third morning since they had left their father's house. They were always trying to get back to it, but instead of that they only found themselves farther in the wood, and if help had not soon come they would have been starved. About noon they saw a pretty snow-white bird sitting on a bough, and singing so sweetly that they stopped to listen. And when he had finished the bird spread his wings and flew before them, and they followed after him until they came to a little house, and the bird perched on the roof, and when they came nearer they saw that the house was built of bread, and roofed with cakes; and the window was of transparent sugar.

"We will have some of this," said Hansel, "and make a fine meal. I will eat a piece of the roof, Grethel, and you can have some of the window—that will taste sweet."

So Hansel reached up and broke off a bit of the roof, just to see how it tasted, and Grethel stood by the window and gnawed at it. Then they heard a thin voice call out from inside,

"Nibble, nibble, like a mouse,
Who is nibbling at my house?"

And the children answered,

"Never mind,
It is the wind."

And they went on eating, never disturbing themselves. Hansel, who found that the roof tasted very nice, took down a great piece of it, and Grethel pulled out a large round windowpane, and sat her down and began upon it. Then the door opened, and an aged woman came out, leaning upon a crutch. Hansel and Grethel felt very frightened, and let fall what they had in their hands. The old woman, however, nodded her head, and said,

"Ah, my dear children, how come you here? you must come indoors and stay with me, you will be no trouble."

So she took them each by the hand, and led them into her little house. And there they found a good meal laid out, of milk and pancakes, with sugar, apples, and nuts. After that she showed them two little white beds, and Hansel and Grethel laid themselves down on them, and thought they were in heaven.

The old woman, although her behaviour was so kind, was a wicked witch, who lay in wait for children, and had built the little house on purpose to entice them. When they were once inside she used to kill them, cook them, and eat them, and then it was a feast-day with her. The witch's eyes were red, and she could not see very far, but she had a keen scent, like the beasts, and knew very well when human creatures were near. When she knew that Hansel and Grethel were coming, she gave a spiteful laugh, and said triumphantly,

"I have them, and they shall not escape me!"

Early in the morning, before the children were awake, she got up to look at them, and as they lay sleeping so peacefully with round rosy cheeks, she said to herself,

"What a fine feast I shall have!"

Then she grasped Hansel with her withered hand, and led him into a little stable, and shut him up behind a grating; and call and scream as he might, it was no good. Then she went back to Grethel and shook her, crying,

"Get up, lazy bones; fetch water, and cook something nice for your brother; he is outside in the stable, and must be fattened up. And when he is fat enough I will eat him."

Grethel began to weep bitterly, but it was of no use, she had to do what the wicked witch bade her.

And so the best kind of victuals was cooked for poor Hansel, while Grethel got nothing but crab-shells. Each morning the old woman visited the little stable, and cried,

"Hansel, stretch out your finger, that I may tell if you will soon be fat enough."

Hansel, however, used to hold out a little bone, and the old woman, who had weak eyes, could not see what it was, and supposing it to be Hansel's finger, wondered very much that it was not getting fatter. When four weeks had passed and Hansel seemed to remain so thin, she lost patience and could wait no longer.

"Now then, Grethel," cried she to the little girl; "be quick and draw water; be Hansel fat or be he lean, tomorrow I must kill and cook him."

Oh what a grief for the poor little sister to have to fetch water, and how the tears flowed down over her cheeks!

"Dear God, pray help us!" cried she; "if we had been devoured by wild beasts in the wood, at least we should have died together."

"Spare me your lamentations," said the old woman; "they are of no avail."

Early next morning Grethel had to get up, make the fire, and fill the kettle.

"First we will do the baking," said the old woman; "I have heated the oven already, and kneaded the dough."

She pushed poor Grethel towards the oven, out of which the flames were already shining.

"Creep in," said the witch, "and see if it is properly hot so that the bread may be baked."

And Grethel once in, she meant to shut the door upon her and let her be baked, and then she would have eaten her. But Grethel perceived her intention, and said,

"I don't know how to do it: how shall I get in?"

"Stupid goose," said the old woman, "the opening is big enough, do you see? I could get in myself!" and she stooped down and put her head in the oven's mouth. Then Grethel gave her a push, so that she went in farther, and she shut the iron door upon her, and put up the bar. Oh how frightfully she howled! but Grethel ran away, and left the wicked witch to burn miserably. Grethel opened the stable door and cried,

"Hansel, we are free! the old witch is dead!"

Then out flew Hansel like a bird from its cage as soon as the door was opened. How rejoiced they both were! how they fell each on the other's neck! and danced about, and kissed each other! And as they had nothing more to fear they went over all the old witch's house, and in every corner there stood chests of pearls and precious stones.

"This is something better than flint stones," said Hansel, as he filled his pocket, and Grethel, thinking she also would like to carry something home with her, filled her apron full.

"Now, away we go," said Hansel;—"if we only can get out of the witch's wood."

When they had journeyed a few hours they came to a great piece of water.

"We can never get across this," said Hansel, "I see no stepping-stones and no bridge."

"And there is no boat either," said Grethel; "but here comes a white duck; if I ask her she will help us over." Se she cried,

> "Duck, duck, here we stand,
> Hansel and Grethel, on the land,
> Stepping-stones and bridges we lack,
> Carry us over on your nice white back."

And the duck came accordingly, and Hansel got upon her and told his sister to come.

"No," answered Grethel, "that would be too hard upon the duck; we can go separately, one after the other."

And that was how it was managed, and after that they went on happily, until they came to the wood, and the way grew more and more familiar, till at last they saw in the distance their father's house. Then they ran till they came up to it, rushed in at the door, and fell on their father's neck. The man had not had a quiet hour since he left his children in the wood; but his wife was dead. And when Grethel opened her apron the pearls and precious stones were scattered all over the room, and Hansel took one handful after another out of his pocket. Then was all care at an end, and they lived in great joy together.

In the Oz books by Frank Baum, the uniqueness of the characters offers wonderful challenges for the interpreter. The Cowardly Lion, for instance, is a very definite person. He is humorous and yet pathetic in his cowardice, and the interpreter must demonstrate both qualities. The Tin Woodman is certainly an unreal character, but not to children. They can believe he exists. He, too, must have sympathetic understanding on the part of the reader, as must the Scarecrow. The interpreter, then, in the reading of such stories must not allow himself to disbelieve in such unreal people—he must put himself into the world of the child and make fantasy seem to be reality if he is to move his audience to respond. He can never be totally objective in the reading of children's literature.

The Giant in "Jack and the Beanstalk" is a much different Giant from the one in "The Selfish Giant." The former is huge, menacing, gruff, belligerent, and dangerous. The interpreter would characterize him with a full voice, and a slower, more ponderous pace. The latter Giant, however, demands a different treatment. He begins as a gruff, selfish person, but then becomes kindly, a friend of the children; so there is far more contrast in his character. The interpreter would want to make him loved by his audience, to give him more sensitive qualities.

One could go on and on with a discussion of children's literature. There are adventure stories such as *King Arthur and His Knights of the Round Table;* the colorful Thornton W. Burgess animal stories, including *The Adventures of Buster Bear; Bambi,* a delightful challenge to the sensitivity of a reader; *Peter Pan; Tom Sawyer; Huckleberry Finn;* Walter Farley's *The Black Stallion; My Friend Flicka; Thunderhead;* many stories of history, and the wonderful tales of Hans Christian Andersen and the Brothers Grimm.

There is also "Snow White and the Seven Dwarfs," with the interpreter's need for precise characterization of the seven dwarfs to make each one different; there is "Cinderella" with the need to make the two daughters and their mother real (as witches) and to give reality to the other non-human characters who fill this age-old legend. And certainly one cannot forget *Mary Poppins* and her appeal to children of all ages.

You will discover when you wish to find children's material to read that there is an endless supply. You have very likely read many of the stories yourself as a child and can easily decide which to choose. If you want to find something different or unusual, such magazines as *The Saturday Review of Literature* often list new books for children, and several times a year there is a general survey of books worthy of note. In addition, browsing through a book store can provide many choices. At least in children's literature, the problem of selecting material is much simpler than it is for other forms of literature.

It is significant that as interpreters you are called upon to show emotion and feeling, to make characters believable. The world of fantasy, the world of the child, offers the best place for a basic study of both these essential characteristics.

SUMMARY

Children's literature makes a good beginning point for the interpreter, for in characterizing the people involved you can learn the essential qualities of characterization, bodily movement, and contrast in tone and pace. In reading the role of a goat or a fox, for instance, you need not worry about appearing ridiculous because you think more of appealing to a child than to an adult. You forget yourself; and consequently, the pressure is lessened.

Reading for children requires a specialized style. Pay careful attention to rhyme in such literature as nursery rhymes because children love repetition of sound. Emphasize dialogue since it is easy for them to follow and read at a slower pace than you would for other forms of literature to make certain each incident and sequence is clear. Over-exaggerate in most cases and over-dramatize action and suspense sequences. But do not "talk down" to an audience by emphasizing yourself more than the material. Concern yourself with the material and its demands. The child does not see you as a reader—he sees you as a storyteller bringing to life real beings.

Reading children's literature for an adult audience requires more subtlety, less exaggeration, and a consideration of the reasons for the writing of such literature as nursery rhymes. More concern is given to the political satire that is implicit in such rhymes.

Characterization is essential in the reading of children's literature because children regard animals as humans and they feel a real identity with both the non-human and human characters. A. A. Milne's Pooh stories as well as the Dr. Seuss books offer excellent opportunities for the interpreter to devise unique characterizations to delight the children in his audience.

Moral lessons are taught in children's literature, especially in fables; and good and evil are personified in many works, including fairy tales, Uncle Remus stories, and Oz books, "Hansel and Grethel," and "Snow White and the Seven Dwarfs."

Among the types of children's literature available to the interpreter are legends, fairy tales, fables, nursery rhymes, biographies, and histories.

EXERCISES

1. Read the story of "The Three Little Pigs." Imagine yourself as each of the three pigs. Devise your own characterization and then read this story aloud. Also decide whether the wolf is to be a sophisticated wolf, a not-so-bright wolf, an educated wolf, or what.
2. Try "Billy Goats Gruff." Change your voice level for each little goat. Decide how each is different from the others. Then feel a surge of energy and of expansion within the body as you read the troll. How do you pace him—slowly, ponderously? Then instill aggressiveness and authority in the last Billy Goat. Read the "Trip, trap, trip, trap" with contrasts in pace and tone to convey the heaviness or lightness of each goat.
3. Read "Snow White and the Seven Dwarfs." Carefully decide how you want to read each dwarf, what kind of voice you want to use, what kind of pacing. Is one to be nervous and excitable? Is one to be shy and reserved? Then read the parts. Call in your little brother or sister or any of the children in the neighborhood and read the story to them. See how they react—and what they say to you about it. Ask them if they liked the reading. They'll tell you.
4. Read the *Wizard of Oz*. First, read the scene of the tornado. See if you can successfully create, by use of faster pace and excitement, the fury of the tornado. Have you ever been in a big windstorm? If so, try to remember it. Now—read the witch as she threatens to take Dorothy's dog. What level are you going to use? Usually, she is read with a high, screechy voice and with a slight nasal quality, but how do you see her? Characterize the Tin Woodman, the Scarecrow, and the Cowardly Lion.
5. Read "Custard the Dragon" by Ogden Nash and put into your interpretation all that you've learned from this chapter. The Nash poem is excellent for practice because it illustrates nearly all of the points about the uniqueness of children's literature.

The Tale of Custard the Dragon

Ogden Nash

Belinda lived in a little white house,
With a little black kitten and a little gray mouse,
And a little yellow dog and a little red wagon,
And a realio, trulio, little pet dragon.

Now the name of the little black kitten was Ink,
And the little gray mouse, she called her Blink,
And the little yellow dog was sharp as Mustard,
But the dragon was a coward, and she called him Custard.

Custard the dragon had big sharp teeth,
And spikes on top of him and scales underneath,
Mouth like a fireplace, chimney for a nose,
And realio, trulio daggers on his toes.

Belinda was as brave as a barrel full of bears,
And Ink and Blink chased lions down the stairs,
Mustard was as brave as a tiger in a rage,
But Custard cried for a nice safe cage.

Belinda tickled him, she tickled him unmerciful,
Ink, Blink and Mustard, they rudely called him Percival,
They all sat laughing in the little red wagon
At the realio, trulio, cowardly dragon.

Belinda giggled till she shook the house,
And Blink said Weeck! which is giggling for a mouse,
Ink and Mustard rudely asked his age,
When Custard cried for a nice safe cage.

Suddenly, suddenly they heard a nasty sound,
And Mustard growled, and they all looked around.
Meowch! cried Ink, and Ooh! cried Belinda,
For there was a pirate, climbing in the winda.

Pistol in his left hand, pistol in his right,
And he held in his teeth a cutlass bright,
His beard was black, one leg was wood;
It was clear that the pirate meant no good.

Belinda paled, and she cried Help! Help!
But Mustard fled with a terrified yelp,
Ink trickled down to the bottom of the houschold,
And little mouse Blink strategically mouseholed.

But up jumped Custard, snorting like an engine,
Clashed his tail like irons in a dungeon,
With a clatter and a clank and a jangling squirm
He went at the pirate like a robin at a worm.

The pirate gaped at Belinda's dragon,
And gulped some grog from his pocket flagon,
He fired two bullets, but they didn't hit,
And Custard gobbled him, every bit.

Belinda embraced him, Mustard licked him,
No one mourned for his pirate victim.
Ink and Blink in glee did gyrate
Around the dragon that ate the pyrate.

But presently up spoke little dog Mustard,
I'd have been twice as brave if I hadn't been flustered.
And up spoke Ink and up spoke Blink,
We'd have been three times as brave, we think,
And Custard said, I quite agree
That everybody is braver than me.

Belinda still lives in her little white house,
With her little black kitten and her little gray mouse,
And her little yellow dog and her little red wagon,
And her realio, trulio, little pet dragon.

Belinda is as brave as a barrel full of bears,
And Ink and Blink chase lions down the stairs,
Mustard is as brave as a tiger in a rage,
But Custard keeps crying for a nice safe cage.

Part Four

THE FUTURE

chapter fifteen

Where do I go from here?

So now we come to the end of our discourse on the art of oral interpretation. But—we have also reached the beginning.

It would be unfortunate to assume that oral interpretation is something only to be involved in when you are taking the course. It can be a lasting experience. Think for a moment of what has happened to you during this course. Are you not better able to express yourself emotionally? Have you not gained a wider appreciation of literature? Do you not know more of the emotional values in literature —and the freedom that you feel as you express those values?

You can add to this experience and make yourself grow even more if you look at the opportunities offered to continue your participation in oral interpretation. For one thing, you should take advantage of every chance to hear artists in the interpretative field. Check your newspapers to see what colleges, professional organizations, and civic groups are offering experiments in Readers Theatre, concert readings of new plays, readings of poetry or prose or drama. And note, too, what television is offering. There are many examples of the art of interpretation that have been presented on television, as for instance, Hal Holbrook's *Mark Twain I onight*. In addition, each month brings new recordings and performances by the greatest artists of the day. Caedmon Records, for instance, has a wide repertoire of interpretative readings by artists such as Julie Harris, Lotte Lenya, and Cyril Ritchard. Some feel that the Shakespearean albums of these societies are more theatre than interpretation. But remember that the artists, in the recording session, assemble in a room and read the roles without any use of physical action, lights, costumes, or props. Their voices and their voices alone must do the job for them, must bring to life their characters and the play. So, in reality, the recordings are an even greater challenge to the artists than would be the case if they gave concert performances of the plays; by appearing in person the actors would have the extra benefit of facial and bodily expressions to help convey the richness of the works.

Often students approach interpretative recordings with a "Do I have to listen to that?" attitude. Yet, just as often, once they have heard the recordings, they find them exciting and worthwhile. So make certain you at least give yourself the chance to hear these renowned artists in performance.

Now, what can *you* do to continue your work? At the local or civic level, you could arrange programs of interpretative reading. Let it be known that you are willing to be part of an entertainment program in your community. Encourage others, who have ability, to do the same. And to extend this kind of participation even further, you could initiate a Readers Theatre program. You could also hold an evening of reading from noted plays— or from works of recognized poets and authors. The recordings of *Brecht on Brecht,* of Edgar Lee Masters' *Spoon River Anthology* are two examples of the types of program that can be arranged on the writings of one author.

The important thing is that you start to do something. And it is equally necessary to be inventive in the types of programs you plan. Perhaps you'd like to add music as background for readings. It has been done—and is becoming accepted even more. An example of the intermingling of music and reading would be Rod McKuen's *The Sea,* with orchestral background. Music can do much to help set a mood, although of course it is the reader who basically must create the moods. There was a time when it was thought that the interpreter must do nothing but read and interpret and that any other effects took him out of the realm of true interpretation. There are sufficient indications now to prove that such theories are becoming outdated.

Interpretation can also be a good medium for the entertainment of children. A program, geared to the children in your community, could be made up of excerpts from nursery rhymes, fairy tales, and other forms of children's literature.

In a like manner, a concert reading could be done in your church with various people reading excerpts from the Bible. You could build a reading around the Beatitudes, or deal with the challenging statements of the prophets in the Old Testament. Or you could create a program from the seven last words of Christ. For an even more ambitious project, a concert reading of some of the exciting religious plays might be presented. One such play is *Christ in the Concrete City* by P. W. Turner, available through Baker's Plays in Boston, Massachusetts. This lends itself particularly well to a Readers' Theatre presentation.

The field is limitless—and so are the possibilities. The important thing is to do something, to start a program. Don't let what you have learned go to waste.

THE PROFESSIONAL VIEWPOINT

Much has been written in this text about the art of interpretation, but too often textbooks ignore the views and ideas and techniques of the prominent artists engaged in this field. We have written to six of the best known interpreters, and they have offered here their personal opinions. They are also, we must add, among the finest actors in the world today.

Sir John Gielgud

Sir John Gielgud has done much to give impetus to Interpretation with his world-wide tours of *Ages of Man,* a program of Shakespearean readings. The show has also been recorded. No finer example of the art of the interpreter exists than this particular recording. When he first conceived *Ages of Man,* he was not certain how to handle it, but then, after much experiment and selective effort, he said: "I devised *Ages of Man* to combine a certain amount of improvised relation directly with the audiences in a very slight and unacademic manner, making links between the excerpts.

"I chose speeches mostly with some veins of consecutive narrative interests as well as with poetic contrast in mood, rhythm, and content, and only acted 'full out' in two or three of the most obviously dramatic and powerful excerpts. The intense concentration, keeping of gesture and physical movement to a minimum, the difficulty of attacking each excerpt with full confidence of the character to be implied and the fact of remaining on stage alone for so long a time were the main problems to be solved. The conclusion, necessary to each speech, was also difficult to determine. One needs great experience in the playing of the whole scene and in interpreting the different styles of writing in the various plays chosen.

"In my own case, I took as great care in presenting the young characters, to indicate vocally the age and vigour of the personages, as I would in directing a young actor. Thus I feel the attempt to *imply* rather than *impersonate* is far more likely to be successful, besides being an effective contrast to the older, more dramatic characters. I was also careful to place the sonnet and poems in places where rests were needed both for actor and audience and not to have too many love or death scenes together. The idea of doing Romeo's death and following with that of Lear seems extremely successful, for instance, though at first it seemed hard to reconcile that Romeo speech with the section depicting age."

Sir John Gielgud's comments are of particular value to a young person who is attempting to arrange a program. In addition, his views on characterization of age are significant, with special emphasis on his views of implication and impersonation. It is also well to listen to the wide tonal range of his voice for a lesson in the beauty of the voice and its importance in interpretation.

Cyril Ritchard

Cyril Ritchard has made several recordings in the interpretative field, and one of his most successful has been *Alice in Wonderland,* which he did for Caedmon.

Mr. Ritchard believes firmly in the close relationship between actor and interpreter. As he says, "I think an actor *is* an interpreter. But for recording purposes, a good interpreter, or reader, need not be a good actor except vocally.

"In the reading of poetry, prose, or drama, the main thing is to study the inner meaning of the literature and then to rehearse it aloud until it eventually becomes your own. However, it is important not to be carried away by the music of your own voice. It is necessary that an interpreter be caught up emotionally with the emotions of the text, to be involved."

As to his views on the primary obligation of the interpreter, Mr. Ritchard says firmly, "The greatest challenge the reader faces is to interpret—in the complete sense and with the complete dedication to the poetry, drama, or prose."

One notices immediately Mr. Ritchard's dedication to his material in the many recordings he has made. In addition to his views of interpretation, his superb diction is a model to follow.

Julie Harris

Julie Harris, one of the finest actresses on the stage today, has made an impressive recording of *The Poems and Letters of Emily Dickinson* for Caedmon Records. When undertaking this assignment she may have found the material and her role different, but she merely remarked, "They seem the same to me."

When she prepares a reading, she uses much the same technique that she does when she is preparing for a role in a play or a film.

"Whether I'm reading poetry or prose or drama, I try to digest the material thoroughly by reading it over and over to myself every day.

Naturally, such rehearsal is always oral. I feel my involvement in my material must be total, at least for the time of study or of performance."

It is also her view that it is rather forbidding for a person who has not been used to displaying emotion to be confronted with the need for such outpouring of feeling as is required in interpretation.

For those students who find the reading of poetry awesome, a conscientious listening to Miss Harris' Emily Dickinson album would be advisable.

Lotte Lenya

Lotte Lenya, the prominent German actress, is an authority on the interpretation of the works of Bertolt Brecht in particular, although her talents are extensive enough to enable her to handle any dramatic demands. It is simply that her association with Brecht has been given considerable emphasis.

One of her records has been *Brecht on Brecht* which was a form of Readers Theatre presenting the works of Brecht. She has also done other recordings, such as *The Stories of Kafka.*

"In order to play a role, I must become the character," Miss Lenya states. "I feel the same about interpretation. My interpretation comes through my conceptions of the character as a human being under any circumstances, whether presented in the play or not. In other forms of literature, such as poetry and prose, to understand completely the meaning and intent of the author is necessary. The reading follows without further preparation or technique.

"Whatever I am doing, whether it is as an actress in a play or an interpreter of poetry or prose, I must become totally involved to interpret to others my conception of material."

Her background in German theatre has made her feel even more intensely the importance of involvement since European artists are inclined to work on the theory of *becoming* rather than *implying.*

"What can I say to the beginning interpreter? I can only say how I feel about the work. Well, to me the challenge is to give to listeners the meanings which I have derived from intensive study. They may differ, but if they have been stimulated, I have met my greatest challenge."

Agnes Moorehead

Agnes Moorehead, who appeared on the stage, in motion pictures, and on television, was also a renowned interpreter. Her death was indeed a loss to the field of interpretation and to the theatre. Her one-woman show played to capacity audiences all over the country, and she appeared on several albums in the Readers Theatre form.

Miss Moorehead's views differed to a degree from those expressed above since she was very much inclined to make a specific distinction between interpretation and acting.

"The interpreter acts with his mind—the actor uses movement. This does not mean that the actor does not interpret also, but he can use movement. The interpreter must use primarily his voice—and creative imagination—as the main instruments.

"My strongest advice to the beginning student, then, is to work with the voice and use imaginative creativity in the voice. Study it and characterization as much as would the actor. Know what effects you can use, such as music or sound effects. *Know your material cold.* But, above all, the voice must be used with depth."

As to the question of involvement, Miss Moorehead said, "The interpreter should not involve himself—he cannot get involved since he must go from dialogue to the narrative form. He is also called upon to read several characters. He must *represent,* therefore, the character rather than *be* it."

Miss Moorehead had ample opportunity to test her theories in her one-woman show. She learned from it that the interpreter cannot merely stand and read.

"He must have movement. When an interpreter presents a show, such as Sir John Gielgud's *Ages of Man,* or my own show, he is not really doing oral interpretation. He is presenting theatre. I do not feel an audience will sit still for two hours of readings of Elizabeth Barrett Browning's poetry. But an audience will be attentive for an hour of this if it is interpreted with good voice and movement. The big advantage for a person like Sir John Gielgud is that the public sees him in an acting form. And he is wise in that he picks material that is dramatically compelling and that those who see it can identify with.

"To me, there is no one form of material that is more difficult to do than another. All that counts is: Is it an exciting piece? Does it move an audience? Can it sustain you for two hours? So— it's all very well and good to believe you must remain true to the material, but you cannot forget that the audience is out front and it is they you must please. So choosing your type of material is vital necessity."

Miss Moorehead's comment is similar to Miss Lenya's:

"If they have been stimulated, I have met my greatest challenge." That should be the emphasis for every student of oral interpretation—

to be stimulated first of all yourself, and then to stimulate others by making the literature speak through you. Make the words you read leap out of the pages and become alive!

And so we come to the beginning—there is no end unless you close the book.

INDEX